Critical Consciousness
in Curricular Research

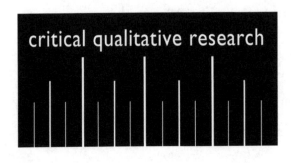

critical qualitative research

Shirley R. Steinberg and Gaile S. Cannella
Series Editors

Vol. 9

The Critical Qualitative Research series
is part of the Peter Lang Education list.
Every volume is peer reviewed and meets
the highest quality standards for content and production.

PETER LANG
New York • Washington, D.C./Baltimore • Bern
Frankfurt • Berlin • Brussels • Vienna • Oxford

Critical Consciousness in Curricular Research

Evidence from the Field

Edited by Lisa William-White, Dana Muccular,
Gary Muccular, and Ayanna F. Brown

PETER LANG
New York • Washington, D.C./Baltimore • Bern
Frankfurt • Berlin • Brussels • Vienna • Oxford

Library of Congress Cataloging-in-Publication Data

Critical consciousness in curricular research: evidence from the field/
edited by Lisa William-White, Dana Muccular,
Gary Muccular, Ayanna F. Brown.
pages cm. — (Critical qualitative research; vol. 9)
Includes bibliographical references and index.
1. Curriculum change—United States. 2. Home and school—United States.
3. Critical pedagogy—United States. 4. Education—Research—United States.
I. William-White, Lisa Yvette, editor of compilation.
LB1570.H62   375'.001—dc23   2012039917
ISBN 978-1-4331-2015-2 (hardcover)
ISBN 978-1-4331-2014-5 (paperback)
ISBN 978-1-4539-0958-4 (e-book)
ISSN 1947-5993

Bibliographic information published by **Die Deutsche Nationalbibliothek.**
Die Deutsche Nationalbibliothek lists this publication in the "Deutsche
Nationalbibliografie"; detailed bibliographic data is available
on the Internet at http://dnb.d-nb.de/.

The paper in this book meets the guidelines for permanence and durability
of the Committee on Production Guidelines for Book Longevity
of the Council of Library Resources.

© 2013 Peter Lang Publishing, Inc., New York
29 Broadway, 18th floor, New York, NY 10006
www.peterlang.com

Printed in the United States of America

If a man does not keep pace with his companions, perhaps it is because he hears a different drummer. Let him step to the music which he hears, however measured or however far away.
—Henry David Thoreau, Walden, 1854

This book is dedicated to all those educational-equity-seeking, progressive, radical, and free-thinking individuals who are committed to teaching and conducting research against the grain.

Contents

Acknowledgments

This book would not be possible without the influences of many—my students who have shaped my thinking about teaching and learning; my colleagues whose insights help me to envision new possibilities for transformative pedagogy; and numerous scholars whose work continuously challenges me to think in new ways about critical consciousness and curriculum transformation. Particularly, I am thankful to have discovered the work of William Pinar and his methodology (currere), which has provided me with language to contextualize my journey, my teaching, and the path that lies ahead as I *run the course*.

In conceiving this book, there were many influences: familial, historic, political, collegial, and philosophical. Yet, noteworthy here is the influence of curriculum theorist William Pinar at the University of British Columbia, whose methods, vision, and scholarly insight motivates this work. This collection also embraces emancipatory critical qualitative research traditions and alternative research methods that continue to be spearheaded by scholars such as Norman Denzin at the University of Illinois, Urbana-Champaign, and Arthur Bochner and Carolyn Ellis at the University of South Florida, to name a few. From them, we draw much inspiration for this volume and the alternative ways of writing qualitative research. Furthermore, I also would like to thank Dr. Joanne Larson, from the University of Rochester, and Dr. Jana Noel, California State University Sacramento, for their support of this curricular endeavor.

In addition, it is with sincere appreciation and gratitude that I thank Dr. Shirley Steinberg for her continued vision and legacy in supporting social justice advocacy and for her belief in this project. And finally and not insignificantly, is my appreciation for the support of Chris Myers, Stephen Mazur, and Sophie Appel, who guided me through the process of bringing this project to fruition.

This book is dedicated to my fore parents; my grandparents (Anderson, Harris, House), my parents (Eddie and Dorothy William); my siblings (Lorraine and Ayanna); and Roland, all of whom continue to support and encourage my ideas and pursuits.

Most importantly, I dedicate this book to my three daughters—Jazmin, Natalia, and Devanie. Of all the lessons learned through my educational journey to date, my daughters continually teach me that knowledge comes with the recognition that I still have much to learn; skills develop as I continually reflect on my life's purpose in envisioning the future; and disposition is further cultivated when I pursue deeds guided by moral purpose and undertaken for the benefit of others.

— *Lisa William-White*
Elk Grove, California (2012)

This book and the collaborative effort put forth is dedicated to: my family ("the tribe") that has raised me (my aunts, uncles, and elder cousins); my late grandparents (James "Deacon" and Mary Jones; Curtis and Louise Christine Roberts); and my parents (Walter and Linda Jones) for teaching me about prayer, purposeful living, power, life, love, strength, optimism, and unity. I have been blessed with a family that has taught me the foundations of my identity through their lived experiences; have encouraged me to advocate for myself in the field of education; and to never cease in pursuing the tangible and intangible things that I most desire out of life.

Additionally and endearingly, I dedicate this book to my supportive husband (Gary Muccular Jr.), who continues to show me respect, patience, and love on a daily basis and through every trial and triumph. What I have obtained and continue to learn from him in this journey is that I must always actively pray, reflect, and think critically about any circumstance. Ultimately, this active prayer and reflection of my journey has allowed for me to be a better woman for not only the people who surround me; this active reflection has also allowed me to heal from life's wounds, and to be a better woman for myself.

— *Dana Muccular*
Sacramento, California (2012)

First, I would like to give honor and praise to my lord and savior, Jesus Christ. I *am* because you are, for all things remain possible through him. The wisdom obtained through my personal and educational journey is not my own, but gained to share with family, friends, and peers. I pray that I do well to continuously represent you in my work.

This book is dedicated to my great-grandmother (Marie Bigbee), mother (Michelle Mack), and my father (Gary Muccular Sr.). Thank you for giving me the drive to go further in my education, while instilling in me the purpose and power of manhood and family. To my siblings, Nekisha Smith, Gregory Mack Sr., Carlin Muccular, and Michelle Mack; I love you all. God has blessed you all with tremendous talents and gifts. Continue to share them with the world.

Affectionately, I dedicate this book to my intelligent and lovely wife, Dana Muccular, who has been the best blessing that I have received in life. I look forward to our future together professionally, spiritually, and in life. Thank you for cultivating my ideas and strengthening my academic voice.

    — *Gary Muccular Jr.*
    Sacramento, California (2012)

Grateful that I can be.
Thankful that I can be.
Blessed that I have been able to be.
Hopeful that I will be able to continue and be better.

Not everyone has the opportunity to share in laughter, play, critical thinking, writing, and more laughter with their siblings. Thank you, Lisa, for your leadership and vision. Most importantly, thank you for your laughter and play. And to Lorraine, who offers endless support and encouragement, I am thankful for your consistency.

To Zawadi and Ezra, kisses and hugs are never enough. I can spend all my days being held by you and watching the light in your eyes.

To Samuel, thirteen down, forever to go. I wouldn't have it any other way.

Elizabeth House (Sam House), Lucianne Harris, Mattie Carter (David Carter), Willie Mae (Willie James), and Dorothy Jean Anderson William (Eddie L. Williams). Thank God spice runs in the blood!

    — *Ayanna F. Brown*
    Forest Park, IL (2012)

Preface

LISA WILLIAM-WHITE

The Virulent Winds That Blow

Curricular decision making is philosophical
And pedagogical
It's shaped by the virulent winds that blow
It's political
Many times, acultural...
And a powerful,
symbolic artifact
...Revealing views
on cultural capital!

It's embroiled in federal discourses
Policies
And *mandates!*
It's shackled to federal bureaucracy
And ideologies
Dictated by the feds
And the State
....
All of this, in the historic moment, reflects and shapes
The teaching landscape!

Lisa William-White (2013)

We reside in the age of one-size-fits-all public education, where teacher-proof curriculum and prepackaged assessments dictate student learning and educator practice. With little regard for students' diverse intelligences, levels of English proficiency, or learning preferences; and with little concern for their levels of cognitive aptitude or socio-emotional functioning, bureaucrats establish and direct learning goals. And as they undertake these efforts, little consideration is given to sociopolitical and affective issues that also shape learning. Given this, students' dispositions toward subject-matter content are rendered insignificant; their resistance to or disengagement from regimented and disembodied schooling rituals engenders little sympathy; and in places like Tucson, Arizona, their outright refusal to be regulated through miseducation and censorship is met with cynicism about the types of messages students are exposed to by their teachers, and within classroom materials. At the same time, teachers, just like their students, are treated as automatons in their own profession, disembodied from their own intellectual knowledge, history, and craft.

Educators are conditioned, instead, to accept the current curriculum landscape—one that negates students' backgrounds, experiences, and unique learning needs. Ladson-Billings (1998) told us that we are teaching in "dangerous times"— when curriculum choice and teachers' rights to autonomous decision making is implicated. We can see this regulation when we listen carefully to the dominant narrative of this era, which tells us that teachers are ill-prepared to teach in the nation's public schools, that teacher education programs are ineffective, and that teacher "effectiveness" should be measured by students' achievement on standardized tests, allowing them to receive merit pay if they raised test scores.

Therefore, on the road towards achieving adequate yearly progress to meet standards constructed and produced by politicians, business leaders, and the testing industry, we are told that all students can achieve if we use the right "scientifically" approved teaching methods and curriculum. And if students do not achieve, as evidenced by their test scores, then the teachers and administrators are to blame. And they are getting plenty of it. Principals' effectiveness is evaluated by the school's ability to meet the state's criterion for adequate yearly progress for all student subgroups. Administrators, as a consequence, try to rally their staff in establishing benchmarks, interventions, and gimmicks focused on raising the scores of those children who are in the quartile just below "proficiency" to avoid further scrutiny and sanctions from the state. And in some districts, those children who score far below competency on test scores are outright ignored in the effort to meet state mandates for "progress."

Furthermore, we reside in an era that gives little regard to the economic conditions that shape families and communities. Oblivious to the effects of diminished employment opportunities available to families, or the reduced quality of life for an increasingly eroding middle class; or even with blinders on related to the lack of health-care access or inadequate nutrition for children of poor families, we march along with our pacing guides to meet the standards. With a fierce sense of preparation-for-testing-urgency, some schools go to great lengths to feed children breakfast and healthy snacks the week of testing, and engage in school-wide rallies to speak with children about the importance of getting rest and doing their best on upcoming exams. We call for more accountability through better and more efficient testing, and we listen intently as the curricular landscape is further shaped by the nation's mayors' advocacy for common core standards and more teacher accountability. Notwithstanding the fact that there is nothing common about people within a heterogeneous, multilingual, and multicultural America, we assume that all people must embody a common knowledge base with little attention paid to diverse world views, values, experiences, and epistemologies that make up the cultural milieu. At the same time, we recognize the inherent problems that stem from complete teacher autonomy whereby those who are employed in the poorest schools exalt reductionist learning activities and goals.

Consequently, in classrooms we are told to construct objectives and student learning outcomes that begin with: BTEOTL SWBAT ("By the end of the lesson, students will be able to…"). And we form these ends-means objectives with an expectation of quantifiable formative or summative assessments in mind. Thus, written on black boards throughout K–12 public schools and within all syllabi in higher education, our learning objectives are posted to inform students, and any spectators, that we embrace positivist forms of knowing. And anyone who drops by to observe the day's lesson or any organizational body that prepares a program review or audit for school or teacher education accreditation will know what the instructional focus, scope, or sequence intends, including how those intentions align with criterion set forth by political bodies (district, state, and nation). And, all of this takes place without any examination as to whether or not those terminal learning objectives—the curriculum-as-planned—is meaningful and comprehensible to the students served, or to their families; or whether the imposed learning values align with the values, needs, and interests of our learners. This is made more problematic by the leadership within educational institutions—those leaders who themselves do not know how to lead or do not know how to hold teachers accountable for their best teaching—culturally responsive teaching.

The truth of the matter is that much of the public discourse today about education reform, pedagogy, and curriculum has become conflated with economic realities, which have completely submerged the roots of systemic and persistent societal and educational inequity. Instead, we focus our efforts on the elusive and ambiguous notion of "rigor," so that we can ensure that American students are the most competitive in the world—to invert our diminished placement in the global education rankings. And in the process, we've bought into a manufactured educational crisis that has produced many casualties.

Since the launching of Sputnik by the Soviets in 1957, we have been engaged in varied global competitions that have had educational implications—the space race, the arms race, and now we are "racing to the top" in our pursuit of global dominance; and our failure to win this manufactured race to be the "best" is laid at the feet of the public educational system.

The philosophical and moral discourses on why we are in competition is not taken up here; rather those discourses can be examined in the works of Henry Giroux, Peter McLaren, and William Pinar. Yet, Pinar's views (2012) are worth mentioning here. He contends that the failure to achieve world supremacy is not viewed as the responsibility of politicians or of business and industry; neither is it viewed as the responsibility of spiritual or moral leaders, or chief financial officers of the nation's institutions. Rather, failure is manufactured and improperly placed on the back of public education. Consequently, the object of bureaucrats' discontent then becomes student achievement outcomes and those educators who prepare students in our public institutions.

The implications are that students and educators are caught in a war on varied fronts, and there are causalities; students are the first ones. They are not the subject of learning; they are objectified—merely bodies under surveillance, measured and regulated by the state and the nation. Administrators are pawns in the system—shackled to structures and strictures that dictate their professional lives by an assessment of worth. This is made more problematic however by faculty and educational leaders who themselves do not know how to lead, and those who do not come from an intellectual tradition of understanding curriculum as a complicated conversation. Then there are the educators at the chalk face (those at the front of the classroom). Those most intimately involved in the teaching act are silenced and marginalized, increasingly removed from curriculum choice and instructional decision making. This, too, proves difficult. We recognize the inherent problems that stem from complete teacher autonomy, whereby those who are employed in the poorest schools rely upon teaching to tests, or they utilize scripted and/or antiquated lesson plans, worksheets, and activities based on reductionist learning activities and goals. Moreover, there are those who do not know how to teach, inspire, or build on students' talents, experiences, and knowledges.

In sum, to be a highly qualified educator in the 21st century demands that educators (broadly defined), at all levels, understand these aforementioned concerns and the current political climate in which we are positioned; this includes intensive deep examination of how pedagogy and curriculum is situated within a sociopolitical field with competing ideologies, discourses, and above all else, motivations. Is it plausible to believe that emergent educators along with practicing teachers and community educators can engage in deep study and reflection on their personal and professional lives to reclaim their voice and power to effect change in our nation's schools if given time and opportunity to do so? Teachers "need to do more than simply implement others' policies and visions" (Transforming Teaching, 2011, p. ii). Rather, suited up with deep historic and sociopolitical understandings to support sound praxis, we must navigate this tumultuous terrain to form coalitions where a unity of purpose toward liberatory teaching and learning can be actualized.

This vision is where this book begins. There is a fundamental difference between curriculum-as-planned, and curriculum-as-lived (Aoki cited in Pinar & Irvin, 2005). To be explicit, curriculum theory is a journey through curriculum experience, a notion that harkens to Dewey's concept of experiential education (1938), threading the subjective experience through academic knowledge, as Pinar (2012) states. From this standpoint "[c]urriculum ceases to be a thing, and it is more than a process. It becomes a verb, an action, a social practice, a private meaning, and a public hope. Curriculum is not just the site of our labor, it becomes the product of our labor, changing as we are changed by it (Pinar, Reynolds, Slattery, & Taubman, 1995, p. 848).

This book contributes to the discourses on curriculum—the complicated conversation and the efforts to transform the system. This book conveys curricular practice wherein the autobiographies—the currere of progressive and critical pedagogues—are illuminated, those who advocate for equity and revolution in K–12 curriculum reform, in higher education, in teacher preparation, and in communities. Brought together in this volume are diverse curricular journeys, forged by lived experiences and critical consciousness—all explicated to reveal the political, philosophical, and pedagogical discourses and policies that shape the current curricular landscape. The vision for this book reflects my knowledge of each of these educator's commitments to equity, and our shared curricular conversations, including how we are *all* produced and constructed by the virulent winds that blow.

Structure of the Book

Chapters in this volume provide snapshots that embrace the intersectionality between homes, classrooms, and alternative spaces in an effort to showcase the dialectic between educators, their curricular approaches, and forces that seek to undermine agentry for democratic learning opportunities. The depth and breadth of the challenges are chronicled in this volume through narrative, descriptive, interpretive, ethnographic, autoethnographic, autobiographic, case study, essay, visual, and poetic work, including the multitude of ways that educators strive and fight for more socially, culturally, linguistically, and politically responsive curriculum.

This timely volume heralds a call for revolution and renewed hope in the field of curriculum studies; it's a call to illuminate the forces that seek to undermine transformative praxis and curricular innovation; it resists positivist forms of knowing, constructing and studying curriculum. And, it trumpets a call to reveal hegemonic power relations within classrooms, institutions, community spaces; and between institutions and the communities they purport to serve.

Part One presents home, family and community knowledges that are rendered invisible or are silenced in K–12 schools and higher education; or those that are reified as sites devoid of meaningful information to shape the learning context. Authors within this section describe the cultural capital and funds of knowledge that shape their educational journeys, while provoking thought about the many facets of students' and teachers' lives that remain untapped well-springs for knowledge construction and learning.

Contributions in Part Two reveal the forces that undermine radical and progressive curriculum development in school spaces. Here, we see how educators articulate how their lived experiences shape their personal philosophies about education, which in turn aids their efficacy to work against the grain.

Part Three provides portraits of curricular engagement, activity, and agency within the third space: community and alternative projects and dissident ways of knowing; efforts that emerge in spite of the climate and forces that thwart emancipatory efforts at liberatory teaching and learning. This research showcases the intersectional, interdisciplinary, experiential and experimental curricular efforts that engage teachers and learners. In sum, I have immense respect for each of these educators and am honored to have their work represented in this anthology.

References

Transforming teaching: Connecting professional responsibility with student learning. (2011). *Commission on Effective Teachers and Teaching.* Retrieved March 30, 2012, from http://www.nea.org/assets/docs/Transforming_Teaching%282%29.pdf

Dewey, (1938). *Experience and Education.* New York: Kappa Delta Pi.

Ladson-Billings, G. (1998). Teaching in dangerous times: Culturally relevant approaches to teacher assessment. *Journal of Negro Education,67*(3), 255–267.

Pinar, W. F., & Irvin, R. L. (Eds.). (2005). *Curriculum in a new key: The collected works of Ted Aoki.* Mahwah, NJ: Lawrence Erlbaum Associates.

Pinar, W. (2012). *What Is Curriculum Theory?* (2nd ed.). New York: Routledge.

Pinar, W., Reynolds, W. M., Slattery, P., & Taubman, P. M. (1995). *Understanding Curriculum.* New York: Peter Lang.

William-White, L. (2013). Becoming a Teacher in an Era of Curricular Standardization and Reductionist Learning Outcomes: A Poetic Interpretation. In P.L. Thomas (Ed.) *Becoming and Being a Teacher: Confronting Traditional Norms to Create New Democratic Realities.* (43-62). New York: Peter Lang.

Foreword

Education Under Seige

JOANNE LARSON

Education and education research are under siege by neoliberal non-educators who think that because they went to school they know how schools should be run. This situation has brought schools to the brink of collapse and challenges critical educators to step forward. This book takes that step. Readers will be pleased to engage work that takes seriously the interpretative genre of research and the work of counter hegemony in curriculum studies. Authors in this volume authentically reflect bell hooks' (1994) work on engaged pedagogy through narrative risk taking and by deep connection between theory and practice.

The book is an explicit call to unify praxis around liberatory teaching and learning as an outright revolutionary stance in these dangerous times of oppressive mandates. The work represents a much-needed contribution to the contemporary field of curriculum studies told by a new generation of teachers and researchers. Through autoethnography, poetry, and other textual moves, authors reconstruct monologic discourses "about" a wide variety of people from non-dominant groups to dialogically inclusive spaces for teaching and learning and for conducting research.

What are the consequences of "doing school" for progressive, liberatory teachers in the contemporary context of reductionist curricula? This is one of the key questions these authors engage and a question they ask critical educators to answer ourselves. This book paves a clear path to where we need to go in order to personally and professionally make the changes needed to address the worsening inequities that are perpetuated by contemporary schooling.

I have been increasingly frustrated with how "we" do education in this country these days. As this book deftly addresses, the "we" of curriculum implementation have excluded teachers and students for much too long. Curriculum packages aligned with federal legislation are making a tidy profit at the expense of authentic, critical teaching and learning while perpetuating the absence of huge numbers of people. The authors in this volume represent these voices in curriculum.

Part of the problem of reductionist curriculum is the entrenchment of power elites in crucial decision-making positions and their desire to keep things the way they are—they are the primary beneficiaries of reductionist curriculum and accountability systems, especially since "they" tend to be the ones who own the companies that produce the textbooks and testing materials and who stand to make a tidy profit from mandating these packages in federal legislation (Larson, forthcoming, 2007).

Who are these power elites? Tyack and Cuban (1995) describe what they call policy elites as those people who manage the economy, have privileged access to the media and to politicians, educational leaders, and people who control foundations. I would call these same people power elites and would agree with Tyack and Cuban that they are the same groups of people today as they have been since the beginning of U.S. public education. I would add textbook publishers to the mix and politicians themselves, not just those who have privileged access to them. One example of the way these power elites work to maintain control and earn a profit is Reading First legislation. Research has now shown clearly that Reading First was a failure and its entrenchment in U.S. literacy policy was a result of the relationship between the McGraws of McGraw-Hill publishing and the Bush family and was not based on adequate research (Coles, 2003; USDOE, 2006). The "good old boys" network was at play and McGraw-Hill made substantial profit from being named as *the* way to meet NCLB reading markers in early childhood (Coles 2003; Osborn, 2007).

Alliances between textbook publishers and various levels of government through implementation of educational mandates and increasing reliance on high-stakes standardized tests has resulted in narrow, selective, and minimalist goals that facilitate control over educational content and processes, and have silenced discussion about other possible goals for education (Larson, Allen, & Osborn, 2010, p. 372). Particular views, those of the power elite, are thus reified in education through these strategic partnerships between "old family friends" who are now in high-ranking political positions and CEOs of major corporations and publishing houses (Osborn, 2007). "Like the normalizing gaze of the examination, the disciplinary power of curriculum is exercised through its invisibility; invisibility achieved through a focus on sameness, and supposed neutrality, which legitimates and may even disguise the exercise of power" (Larson, Allen, & Osborn, 2010, p. 372). The disguise must be revealed and dismantled so that "we the people" can take back our schools. This volume is a clear step in that direction.

References

Coles, G. (2003). *Reading the Naked Truth: Literacy, Legislation and Lies*. Portsmouth, NH: Heinemann.

hooks, b. (1994). *Teaching to Transgress: Education as the Practice of Freedom*. New York: Routledge.

Larson, J. (forthcoming). *Radical Equality and Education: Starting Over in American Schooling*. New York: Routledge.

Larson, J. (2007) *Literacy as Snake Oil: Beyond the Quick Fix* (2nd ed.). New York: Peter Lang.

Larson, J., Allen, A.-R., & Osborn, D. (2010). Curriculum and the publishing industry. In B. McGraw, E. Baker, & P. Peterson (Eds.), *International Encyclopedia of Education* (3rd ed., pp. 368–373). Philadelphia: Elsevier.

Osborn, D. (2007). Digging up the family tree: America's forced choice. In J. Larson (ed.), *Literacy as Snake Oil: Beyond the Quick Fix* (2nd ed., pp. 171–188). New York: Peter Lang.

Tyack, D., & Cuban, L. (1995). *Tinkering Toward Utopia: A Century of Public School Reform*. Cambridge, MA: Harvard University Press.

U.S. Department of Education Office of Inspector General (2006). *The Reading First Program's Grant Application Process Final Inspection Report*. http://www.ed.gov/about/offices/list/oig/aireports/i13f0017.pdf

Introduction

The Current Historic Moment

LISA WILLIAM-WHITE

In the United States today, there is an ever-encroaching knowledge regime that dominates discussion of curriculum content, that dictates teaching methods and strategies for curriculum implementation (U.S. Dept. of Education, 2004), and that prescribes the types of assessments that should be utilized for teaching and learning in K–12 schools (Emery & Ohanian, 2004; Reynolds, 2003). For example, with the increased march towards national standards through the Common Core State Standard Initiatives, in tandem with Arne Duncan's endorsement of this mayor-driven plan, combined with the corporate takeover of school curriculum by textbook publishers (Jobrack, 2012), pre-service and practicing educators are shackled to de facto curricular mandates; they are expected to contextualize their teaching within prescriptive goals—antithetical to the lived experiences of culturally and linguistically diverse (CLD) learners.

Though President Barack Obama seeks to redefine the federal role in American education, championing innovation to improve learning, we must examine the ideology embedded in Race to the Top (RTTP). First, he calls for a "world-class" education as a "moral imperative" in America. This sounds promising for the millions of poor and minority children who experience inequity and an opportunity-to-learn gap in public education (National Opportunity to Learn Campaign, 2009). Further, he insists that raising learning expectations is our "national priority." This, too, sounds promising for the many CLD students who languish in classrooms where their unique talents and abilities remain untapped well-springs for contextualized learning and creativity. Finally, President Obama even states that the "teacher standing in front of the classroom" is the "most important factor" shaping student success (U.S. Department of Education, 2010, p. 1).

Yet, while President Obama has urged Congress to embrace his blueprint in the reauthorization of the Elementary and Secondary Education Act (ESEA), the cornerstone of his plan for reform shapes the curricular dialogue in ways that should give us pause. This is due to his emphasis on the utilization of a *new* generation of assessments, the usage of college- and career-ready standards, and the utilization of evidenced-based instructional models for curriculum implementation (U.S. Department of Education, 2010). In sum, these plans do not speak to the power of the teacher to transform learning by making content comprehensible for students by relating learning to their lives. Rather, like that of George Bush's No Child Left Behind, Obama promises more of the same—a focus on standardization and accountability.

From here, school reform, continues to be "deformed" as the nation's leaders further extol standards-based learning to compete with other industrialized nations that currently outperform us. We have been on the outcomes-based educational path ever since the Soviet's launched Sputnik in 1957. That historic moment, fueled by Cold War tensions, signaled to many that the U.S. no longer proved to be superior to the Soviets with respect to national security and technological superiority. Were our scientists subpar; was our military bush-league? Questions such as these would fuel the discourses related to the space race, and would be tied to ideas about public education's effectiveness in preparing educated children (Pinar, 2012). Subsequently, the success of the Soviets would prove to be an event that could be exploited by political interests.

With each president of the United States from John F. Kennedy onward, increased federal money and intensified discourse and ideology focused on American competitiveness. Today, in our quest to be the best, politicians and leaders from business and industry continue to focus on the notion of competition by speaking about vouchers for education and greater choice for parents. President Obama's RTTP program exalts competition, encouraging schools to compete for federal funding to aid instructional innovation. Clearly, as Pinar (2012) suggests, we are in a race to nowhere in American education in our efforts to leave no child behind (p. 15). Yet, we are leaving behind an education focused on self-development through academic study; and, we ignore the fact that democratic education in public schools is directly tied to our historic strivings for social, civic, and equitable education, not merely the "economic strength" of the nation (National Opportunity to Learn Campaign, 2009, p. 26). Furthermore, we divest from supporting the professional development of teachers in meaningful ways, diminishing their roles and expertise within their profession and within the very act of teaching.

The discourse related to curriculum is not confined to the K–12 system. We also witness intensified discourses related to standards, curriculum articulation, and the need for cohesive assessment initiatives between K–12 and higher education, all of which is taking place with such stakeholders at the table as American College Testing Program (ACT), the College Board, and the National Association of State Boards of Education (Common Core State Standards Initiative, n.d.). This focus on standards, testing, and by implication, curriculum is due in large part to the significant percentage of students who graduate from U.S. high schools without the requisite knowledge and preparation to matriculate into baccalaureate-level courses, all of which are indicators (to political and business stakeholders) that the educational system needs reform. And nowhere is this belief system more evident and politically clear than at the 2008 Harvard Business School Summit focused on, of all things, the crisis in American education. There, entrepreneurial educators such as Kevin Johnson, Michelle Rhee, Steven Barr, and Wendy Kopp engaged in dialogue about the need to reform the system by focusing on learning outcomes and disrupting barriers to student achievement vis-à-vis "unaccountable teachers, dysfunctional schools and systemic barriers" (Harvard Business School, 2008). "Student learning outcomes" proves to be the common catchphrase that shapes assessment-driven dialogues related to K–12 education, but also between this system and higher education.

The conversation surrounding student learning outcomes, pedagogy, and curriculum is further complicated when framed by discussion of the economic impact of curriculum remediation in higher education. According to the National Center for Education Statistics, 28 percent of entering freshmen enrolled in at least one remedial reading, writing, or mathematics course in the fall of 2000 (National Center for Education Statistics, n.d.). In addition, national data from the U.S. Department of Education found that 34 percent of all new entering college students required at least one remedial education class; and 43 percent of those enrolled in a community college required some remedial education (Vandal, 2010). Moreover, an analysis done by the Bill and Melinda Gates Foundation's *Strong American Schools* estimated that remedial education costs states and students up to $2.3 billion annually (Vandal, 2010, p. 4). In turn, many financially strapped states are cutting the costs of remedial education in higher education, focusing instead on initiatives that promote rigorous high school graduation standards.

Thus, the rhetoric surrounding curriculum and its intended goals is a "complicated conversation" (Pinar, 2012, p. 1). And yet, those who are new to the field of education, and those who desire to teach within the K–16 system, are often ill prepared to engage in these discussions. It is not their fault, entirely. Some argue that there is a lack of uniformity in strong academic preparation for emergent teachers with respect to varied curriculum models and practices (Commission on Effective Teachers and Teaching, 2011, p. 10–11). Others argue that opportunities to develop curriculum are shrinking, while state education departments exercise more control in developing curriculum (Reynolds, 2003). Moreover, the schooling climate moves further toward curriculum narrowing while failing to cultivate curricula that draw upon diverse epistemologies. The outcomes of curriculum reductionism, in turn, "leave[s] too many of America's 50 million elementary and secondary school students unprepared for civic engagement, higher education, careers, and family life" (Commission on Effective Teachers and Teaching, 2011). At the same time, removing curriculum from the hands of classroom teachers reinforces anti-intellectualism and further de-professionalizes the career path.

Furthermore, a curriculum conceived of as a product continues to be a powerful artifact reflecting cultural values formed by those who hold the power to determine what *is* while denigrating the knowledges and experiences of other social groups. Notwithstanding the dictum of a common curriculum raises serious concern for critical multicultural educators who understand how subjectivity is central to the learning process. Early on, Kincheloe and Steinberg (1997) argued against this curriculum monoculturalism, suggesting that a common culture "has never existed in the West" (p. 4). This is due to the historic and pervasive social, political, and economic inequities that exist for CLD populations in the United States. Thus, student identity is critical in the teaching context, and homogenizing learning, or ignoring how diverse communities—including teachers—approach the social and cultural process of learning, is problematic.

Hence, for educators whose practices embody a reconstructionist educational agenda, these discourses are disconcerting, as they fail to consider what happens in classrooms, how students make sense of what they are presented, and how knowledge is mediated between teachers and students (Giroux, 1997). Inevitably, affirming the subjectivity of learners and embracing an embodied pedagogy is fundamental to providing space to interrogate the forces that shape CLD learners' lives within a democracy (See Appendix).

Moreover, curriculum conceptualization and implementation is constituted (in part) in three fundamental ways. First, curriculum is product, process, and praxis—shaped by cultural, social, and political forces. As a product, curriculum is framed by and within ideologies and values that may not align with the worldviews and values of teachers or their learners, notions that must be unveiled and made transparent within schooling. The very notion of what is knowledge is inscribed through educators' curricular choices and is made manifest through the artifacts created and produced within learning settings.

Second, as process, curriculum is constructivist, and must allow for deep inquiry, exploration, meaning-making, and innovation (Kincheloe & Steinberg, 1993). Teachers must give "creative wings to their imaginations" to engage learners in meaningful systems of practice (Freire, 1970/2000, p. 51), where learners' intelligences and knowledge are unshackled from corporate models of schooling

(Pinar, 2004, p. 31). Yet, processes of inquiry too often are subject to regimentation and bureaucratic policies shaping curriculum.

Third, praxis (action guided by theory and reflection) is embodied practice; the teacher, and her teaching processes enable the teacher and the learner to engage in dialogic and transformative learning experiences for personal, community, and societal impact. Yet, the dialogic nature of inquiry for personal growth, self-knowledge, and community engagement is co-opted by national goals that ingrain and reinforce social efficiency ideologies over learner-centered and social reconstructionist goals. Nowhere are these tensions more evident than in Tucson, Arizona, where the School Board recently banned ethnic studies and censored the works of varied authors, among them Freire's (1970) *Pedagogy of the Oppressed*. Thus, events like these beg the questions: what should be taught in schools and how should it be taught? Moreover, it is unmistakable that curriculum innovation, transformative teaching, and learning for multicultural and multilingual populations hang in the balance. In sum, the robust discussions surrounding curriculum politics demand that pre-service teachers and practicing teachers, including nontraditional educators, understand curriculum studies in deep and profound ways.

Ideology and Theoretical Underpinnings of This Book

A systematic understanding of curriculum—the *currere*—as school knowledge, life history, and intellectual development for self-transformation is the theoretical foundation that unites the work in this volume (Pinar, 1974, 1975, 1988, 1991, 1995, 2012; Pinar & Grumet, 1976; Castenell & Pinar, 1993; Kincheloe & Steinberg, 1993; Pinar, Reynolds, Slattery, & Taubman,1995). The currere, introduced by Pinar (1974), articulates an autobiographical theory of curriculum that is "reflexive" (Grumet, 1976), and that enables one to examine and reveal self and society. *Currere* is the Latin infinitive of curriculum, which refers to a strategy devised to disclose experience. Understanding the currere as an autobiographical and biographical text is our aim, whereby the educator, the curriculum, and political theory are unified and revealed (Pinar et al., 1995). Thus, the "personal practical knowledge" of educators (and learners) is privileged through their life histories and praxis (Pinar et al., 1995, p. 517).

The psychoanalytic method of currere (regression, progression, analysis, and synthetical) is an embodied process where one retells the story of one's educational experiences; imagines future possibilities for self-understanding and educational practice; and analyzes the relationships between past, present, and future life, history, and practice to develop new ways of thinking about education. The life *lived* and the life *sought* materializes as one examines the complexity and subtlety of the present. Murrell's (2002) notion of a living curriculum embodied by self and cultural understanding in real-world contexts supports the currere—reflection on one's past in relation to one's present; analysis of how these shape the future.

With viewing teachers' life experiences can come deepened understanding of the forces that shape their agency (Pinar & Grumet, 1976, p. vii). In sum, what educators tell students through curriculum represents both "who we want them to think we are and who they might become (Castenell & Pinar, 1993, p. 5). From this frame, curriculum is conceptualized and embodied as relations with others and the world in a manner that transforms identities and knowledge construction (Fifield & Swain, 2002; Lave & Wenger 1991; Steinberg, 2001). Identity and what counts as knowledge intersects (Fifield & Swain, 2002) and shapes how curricular projects are enacted. For instance, Giroux (1997) advocates for democratic schooling and curriculum innovation that is informed by varied people's knowledge and interests. Grounding this volume in an autobiographical and biographical framework answers the call for scholarship that centralizes the voices of scholars and communities of color within a U.S. context. Moreover, an added strength of this volume is our exaltation for linguistic diversity and diverse epistemologies in scholarship, particularly for 21st-century educators and researchers who are committed to equity and social justice. Thus, this collection responds to the need for research and curriculum that raises the following questions:

1. What type of society/world do we want, and what role should curriculum, if any, play in achieving this goal?

2. What constitutes knowledge and who decides?

3. Whose voices should be present at the table when talking curriculum development, implementation, and assessment?

4. What core discourses and philosophies shape prepackaged curriculum in use within classrooms and textbooks?

5. How might institutional values, policies, and practices disrupt family and community needs and values?

6. What practices and public forms of scrutiny should be utilized in curriculum lesson study, as well as teacher evaluation?

7. How should we develop and organize curriculum, particularly for historically marginalized and underrepresented populations in K–14 education? Higher education? In teacher education?

8. What ideas, representations, values, norms, and judgments about childhood and youth, learning and teaching, life and culture should be represented in curricular goals?

9. In what ways should families, elders, and communities shape knowledge construction for children and youth?

10. How do institutional policies perpetuate oppressions that intersect with race, class, language, nationality, etc., and how do these areas of difference interconnect as they are produced or silenced in curriculum?

11. How are educators guiding learners to understand the sociopolitical, philosophical, historical, ethical, and moral forces behind the development, sustainability, and implementation of emancipatory curricular goals?

12. What alternative and dissident curricular projects are generated in community spaces that can be harnessed by educators to enact culturally responsive curricula?

To provide some insights into these questions, the contributors to this volume employ qualitative research methods that provide thick descriptions of the power dynamics that shape curriculum and praxis. Hence, the current political climate mandates that we magnify the varied spheres of conflict related to curriculum and the varied sites (home, school, and third space) where emancipatory curriculum engagement is undertaken in spite of it. In this spirit, this collection illuminates the sociopolitical, philosophical, ethical, cultural, and moral dimensions of curriculum implementation within K–14 education, higher education, and teacher education training.

Furthermore, lived experience has taught us that the dialectics of the teaching self and the culture that produces the teacher is complex and dynamic. As such, the depth and breadth of curriculum implementation are chronicled through narrative, descriptive, interpretive, ethnographic, autoethnographic, autobiographic, case study, essay, and visual work utilizing prose and poetry that is accessible, multiperspective, multi-genre, multilingual, and multicultural—theory-based, intersectional research that elicits inquiry and self-reflection.

The breadth and depth of this work contributes to the interdisciplinary field of scholarship within the three aforementioned contexts: (1) research on home lives (Heath, 1983; Moll, Amanit, Neff, & Gonzalez,1992; Moll & Gonzalez, 1994); (2) school-based curricular projects (Barton, 2001; Morrell & Duncan-Andrade, 2002; Morrell, 2002; Morrell, 2004; William-White, Muccular, & Muccular, 2012; Cook, 2004; Mahiri, 2004; Larson, 2005; Barret & Noguera, 2008; Fischer, 2005, 2007; Hill, 2009; Akom, 2009; Rodriguez, 2009); and (3) community-centered projects and/or agency (Moje, 2000; Carillo, 2000; Moje, Ciechanowski, Kramer, Ellis, Carrillo, & Collazo, 2004; Dimitriadis, 2001/2009; Dyson, 2005; Fisher, 2003; Heath, 1983; Mahiri, 2004; Dredger, Woods, Beach, & Sagstetter, 2010).

We organize this work in this way and exalt scholarship that contributes exploring third-space learning contexts as important sites for knowledge construction and curricular examination. Theoretical perspectives on third space and hybridity theory shape the discourses presented in this volume because they extend the ways that critical consciousness is shaped—by location, time, and ideologies. For instance, scholars such as Bhabha, (1994), Soja, (1996), and Moje et al. (2004) discuss how people within communities draw upon multiple funds of knowledge and discourses to make sense of the world and texts.

Hybridity, then, applies to the integration or disintegration of knowledges based on social and cultural practices as they are shaped by the curricular context. Supporting the importance of space or place is the work of Kincheloe and Pinar (1991) who remind us that place and human feeling are intertwined; and learning is situated within experience and emotion that is manifested through curriculum encounters. Thus, third space is not only about a "place" for learning or a "time" for learning, but is also an ideological embodiment that illuminates how learning is positioned and situated within a historical and political moment (Kincheloe & Pinar, 1991; Steinberg, 1992), which shapes critical consciousness. Consequently, within curricula, like other texts, "third space is produced in and through language as people resist cultural authority, bringing different experiences to bear" in the learning contexts (Moje et al., 2004, p. 43). Third space then is born through collision—a hybrid space that brings forth a new area of negotiation of meaning and representation—a space where new identities are formed. It is a symbolic space where past experiences, emotion, and location converges. Hence, an autobiographical understanding of pedagogical practice and curriculum is clearly informed by not only the "complexity of place" (Pinar, 1995, p. 533), but is also shaped by third space.

Finally, the diverse contributors to this volume come from communities whose cultural epistemologies and world views are largely invisible in K–14 education discourse and curricular contexts; invisible within higher education and teacher education discourse; and within academic scholarship focused on curriculum studies. Giroux (1997) posits that language is inseparable from lived experience and how people create their distinctive voice, a voice meaningful to legitimating particular ways of life. Like Giroux (1997), Reynolds (2003) suggests that privileging "academic discourse over the discourse that speaks to the public is one way that power operates" (p. 64). Consequently, we envisioned a volume that reflects contributors' bilingual, bi-dialectal, bi-cultural, transnational, and multicultural competencies within the research act. Such a text decolonizes and disrupts the ways of *doing* research. And, it is revolutionary in that it is localized and grounded in the specific meanings, traditions, customs, and community relations that operate in each diverse setting (Denzin, 2010). In addition to disrupting authoritative models of qualitative research on curriculum theory, this collection merges "grounded, critical, pragmatic, and indigenous theories" (Denzin, 2010) with intentionality.

In this spirit, we hope that readers of this text will be called to reflect on their lived experiences and background, including how they have been shaped by the current historic moment.

References

Akom, A. A. (2009). Critical hip hop pedagogy as a form of liberatory praxis. *Equity & Excellence in Education, 42*(1), 52–66.

Barret, T., & Noguera, P. A. (2008). Makin' it real: Rethinking racial and cultural competence in urban classrooms. In K. M. Teel & J. E. Obidah (Eds.), *Building Racial and Cultural Competence in the Classroom* (pp. 97–110). New York: Teachers College Press.

Barton, A. C. (2001). Science education in urban settings. Seeking new ways of praxis through critical ethnography. *Journal of Research in Science Teaching, 38*(8), 899–917.

Bhabha, H. K. (1994). *The location of culture.* New York: Routledge.

Carrillo, R. (2000). Intersections of official script and learners' script in third space: A case study of Latino families in an after-school computer program. In B. Fishman & S. O'Connor-Divelbiss (Eds.), *Fourth International Conference of the Learning Sciences* (pp. 312–313). Mahwah, NJ: Erlbaum.

Castenell, L. A., & Pinar, W. F. (Eds.). (1993). *Understanding Curriculum as a Racial Text: Representations of Identity and Difference in Education.* Albany: State University of New York Press.

Commission on Effective Teachers and Teaching. (2011). Transforming teaching: Connecting professional responsibility with student learning. National Education Association. http://www.nea.org/home/49981.htm

Common Core State Standards Initiative. (n.d.). *About the Standards.* http://www.corestandards.org.

Cook, J. A. (2004). Writing for something: Essays, raps, and writing preferences. *English Journal, 94*(1), 72–76.

Denzin, N. K. (2010). Grounded and indigenous theories and the politics of pragmatism. *Sociological Inquiry, 80*(2), 296–312.

Dimitriadis, G. (2001/2009). *Performing Identity/Performing Culture: Hip Hop as Text, Pedagogy, and Lived Practice.* New York: Peter Lang.

Dredger, K., Woods, D., Beach, C., & Sagstetter, V. (2010). Engage me: Using new literacies to create third space classrooms that engage student writers. *Journal of Media Literacy Education, 2*(2), 85–101.

Dyson, A. H. (2005). Crafting "The humble prose of living": Rethinking oral/written relations in the echoes of spoken word. *English Education, 37*(2), 149–164.

Emery, K., & Ohanian, S. (2004). *Why Is Corporate America Bashing Our Public Schools?* Portsmouth, NH: Heinemann.

Fifield, S., & Swain, H. (2002). Heteronormativity and common sense in science (teacher) education. In R. M. Kissen (Ed.), *Getting Ready for Benjamin: Preparing Teachers for Sexual Diversity in the Classroom* (pp. 177–189). Lanham, MD: Rowman & Littlefield.

Fisher, M. T. (2003). Open mics and open minds: Spoken word poetry in African Diaspora Participatory Literacy Communities. *Harvard Educational Review, 73*(3), 362–389.

Fisher, M. T. (2005). Literocracy: Liberating language and creating possibilities. *English Education, 37*(2), 92–95.

Fisher, M. T., (2007). *Writing in Rhythm: Spoken Word Poetry in Urban Classrooms.* New York: Teachers College Press.

Freire, P. (1970/2000). *Pedagogy of the Oppressed.* New York: Continuum.

Giroux, H. A. (1997). *Pedagogy and the Politics of Hope: Theory, Culture, and Schooling*. Boulder, CO: Westview Press.

Grumet, M. (1976). Psychoanalytic foundations. In W. Pinar & M. Grumet, *Toward a Poor Curriculum* (pp. 111–146). Dubuque, IA: Kendall/Hunt.

Harvard Business School (2008). The role of social entrepreneurship in transforming U.S.A. public education. Breakout session, Harvard Business School Global Business Summit. http://www.hbs.edu/centennial/businesssummit/business-society/the-role-of-social-entrepreneurship-in-transforming-usa-public-education-2.html

Heath, S. B. (1983). *Ways with Words: Language, Life, and Work in Communities and Classrooms*. Cambridge, UK: Cambridge University Press.

Hill, M. L. (2009). *Beats, Rhymes and Classroom Life: Hip-hop Pedagogy and the Politics of Identity*. New York: Teachers College Press.

Jobrack, B. (2012). Tyranny of the Textbook: An Insider Exposes How Educational Materials Undermine Reforms. Lanham, MD: Rowman & Littlefield.

Kincheloe, J., & Pinar, W. (Eds.). (1991). *Curriculum as a Social Psychoanalysis: The Significance of Place*. Albany: State University of New York Press.

Kincheloe, J., & Steinberg, S. (1993). A tentative description of postformal thinking: The critical confrontation with cognitive theory. *Harvard Educational Review, 63*(3), 296–320.

Kincheloe, J., & Steinberg, S. (1997). *Changing Multiculturalism*. Philadelphia: Open University Press.

Ladson-Billings, G. (1994). *Dreamkeepers: Successful Teachers of African American Children*. San Francisco: Jossey-Bass.

Larson, J. (2005). Breaching the classroom walls: Literacy learning across time and space in an elementary school in the United States. In B. Street (Ed.), *Literacies Across Educational Contexts: Mediating Teaching and Learning*. Philadelphia: Caslon Press

Lave, J., & Wenger, E. (1991). *Situated Learning: Legitimate Peripheral Participation*. Cambridge, UK: Cambridge University Press.

National Opportunity to Learn Campaign. (2009). Lost opportunity: A 50 state report on the opportunity to learn in America. http://www.otlstatereport.org/

Mahiri, J. (Ed.). (2004). *What They Don't Learn in Schools: Literacy in the Lives of Urban Youth*. New York: Peter Lang.

Moje, E. B. (2000). To be a part of the story: Literacy practices of gangsta adolescents. *Teachers College Record, 102*, 652–690.

Moje, E. B., Ciechanowski, K. M., Kramer, K., Ellis, L., Carrillo, R., & Collazo, T. (2004). Working toward third space in content area literacy: An examination of everyday funds of knowledge and discourse. *Reading Research Quarterly, 39*(1), 38–70.

Moll, L. C., Amanti, C., Neff, D., & Gonzalez, N. (1992). Funds of knowledge for teaching: Using a qualitative approach to connect homes and classrooms. *Theory into Practice, 31*, 132–141.

Moll, L. C. & Gonzalez, N. (1994). Critical issues: Lessons from research with language-minority children. *Journal of Reading Behavior, 26*(4), 439–456.

Morrell, E. (2002). Toward a critical pedagogy of popular culture: Literacy development among urban youth. *Journal of Adolescent & Adult Literacy, 4*(1), *97–111*.

Morrell, E. (2004). *Becoming Critical Researchers: Literacy and Empowerment for Urban Youth*. New York: Peter Lang.

Morrell, E., & Duncan-Andrade, J. (2002). Promoting academic literacy with urban youth through engaging in hip-hop culture. *The English Journal, 91*(6), 88–92.

Murrell, P. C. (2002). *African-Centered Pedagogy: Developing Schools of Achievement for African American Children*. Albany: State University of New York Press.

Murrell, P. C. (2007). *Race, Culture, and Schooling: Identities of Achievement in Multicultural Urban Schools*. New York: Routledge.

National Center for Education Statistics. (n.d.). Postsecondary Remedial Education. http://nces.ed.gov/ssbr/pages/remedialed.asp?IndID=15

Pinar, W. (1974). *Currere*: Toward reconceptualization. In J. Jelinek (Ed.), *Basic Problems in Modern Education* (pp. 147–171). Tempe: Arizona State University, College of Education.

Pinar, W. (1975). *Currere:* Toward reconceptualization. In W. Pinar (Ed.), *Curriculum Theorizing: The Reconceptualists* (pp. 396–414). Berkeley, CA: McCutchan.

Pinar, W. (1988). Time, place, and voice: Curriculum theory and the historical moment. In W. Pinar (Ed.), *Contemporary Curriculum Discourses* (pp. 264–278). Scottsdale, AZ: Gorsuch Sacrisbrick.

Pinar, W. (1991). Curriculum as social psychoanalysis: On the significance of place. In J. Kincheloe & W. Pinar (Eds.), *Curriculum as Social Psychoanalysis: Essays on the Significance of Place.* (pp. 167–186). Albany: State University of New York Press.

Pinar, W. (1995). *Autobiography, Politics, and Sexuality: Essays in Curriculum Theory, 1972–1992*. New York: Peter Lang.

Pinar, W. (2004). *What Is Curriculum Theory?* Mahwah, NJ: Lawrence Erlbaum.

Pinar, W. (2012). *What Is Curriculum Theory?* (2nd ed.). New York: Routledge.

Pinar, W., & Grumet (1976). *Toward a Poor Curriculum*. Dubuque, IA: Kendall/Hunt.

Pinar, W., Reynolds, W. M., Slattery, P., & Taubman, P. M. (1995). *Understanding Curriculum*. New York: Peter Lang.

Reynolds, W. E. (2003). *Curriculum: A River Runs Through It*. New York: Peter Lang.

Rodriguez, L. F. (2009). Dialoguing, cultural capital, and student engagement: Toward a hip hop pedagogy in the high school and university classroom. *Equity & Excellence in Education, 42*(1), 20–35.

Soja, E. W. (1996). *Thirdspace: Journeys to Los Angeles and Other Real-and-Imagined Places*. Malden, MA: Blackwell.

Steinberg, S. (1992). Critical multiculturalism and democratic schooling: An interview with Peter McLaren and Joe Kincheloe. *International Journal of Educational Reform, 1*(4), 392–405.

Steinberg, S. (2001). *Multi-Intercultural Conversations: A Reader*. New York: Peter Lang.

U.S. Department of Education. (2004). Four pillars of NCLB. http://www2.ed.gov/nclb/overview/intro/4pillars.html

U.S. Department of Education, Office of Planning, Evaluation and Policy Development. (2010). *ESEA Blueprint for Reform*. http://www2.ed.gov/policy/elsec/leg/blueprint/blueprint.pdf

Vandal, B. (2010). *Getting Past Go: Rebuilding the Remedial Education Bridge to College Success*. Boston: Education Commission of the States.

William-White, L., Muccular, D., & Muccular, G. (2012). Reading, writing, and revolution: Spoken word as radical "literocratic" praxis in the community college classroom. In B. Porfilio & M. Viola (Eds.), *Hip-Hop(e): The Cultural Practice and Critical Pedagogy of International Hip-Hop Inquiry* (pp. 197–219). New York: Peter Lang.

PART ONE

Home

We all grow up with the weight of history on us. Our ancestors dwell in the attics of our brains as they do in the spiraling chains of knowledge hidden in every cell of our bodies.[1]

The notion of culture is a dynamic entity, not simply a collection of foods, clothes, and holidays, but a way of using social, physical, spiritual, and economic resources to make one's way in the world.[2]

If I were really asked to define myself... I would start with stripping down to what fundamentally informs my life, which is that I'm a seeker on the path.[3]

---

1   S. Abbott (1983). *Womanfolks: Growing Up Down South.* New York: Houghton Mifflin.

2   M. Genzuk (1999). "Tapping into Community Funds of Knowledge." In *Effective Strategies for English Language Acquisition: Curriculum Guide for the Professional Development of Teachers Grades Kindergarten Through Eight* (pp. 9–21). Los Angeles: Los Angeles Annenberg Metropolitan Project/Arco Foundation.

3   b. hooks (July 13, 1994). "Point of View." *Chronicle of Higher Education, 40*(45), p. A44

CHAPTER ONE

Grandma's Brer Rabbit Wasn't the Fool You So Admire

Teaching to Oppose the Conveniences Blackness Affords Whiteness

JANICE TUCK-LIVELY & AYANNA F. BROWN

Shakespeare's Jaques (1623/1937) proclaimed, "all the world's a stage, and all the men and women merely players; They have their exits and their entrances; and one man in his time plays many parts, His acts being seven stages (*As You Like It*, Act II, Scene VII, 139–143). It is sometimes laughable, although usually after the fact, that we wonder if our experiences are being penned by a playwright or cajoled with strings, as if we are puppets of the academy, being toyed with by the imaginative dramaturgical whims of another. However, rather than following the roles scripted for us by the writer, we seek to use these experiences, our "currere," as tools to reconstruct the monocultural positivistic pedagogies that seem to cast us as props, essential for the mainstage where dominance is reinscribed and ignorance and oppression are conveyed as naturalistically inevitable characteristics for blackness. As Morrison (1992) purports, these representations of power are embodied in American literature, where authors carefully craft and coopt our racialization.

> Through significant and underscored omissions, startling contradictions, heavily nuanced conflicts, through the way writers peopled their work with the signs and bodies of this presence—one can see that a real or fabricated Africanist presence was crucial to their sense of Americanness. And it shows. (p.6)

Morrison reminds us that blackness matters in American literature because even the silent presence of the black shadowed body gives definition to whiteness. We offer our audience a tapestry of narratives to examine several questions: (1)

What is yielded for Black children in reading American literature, where black-ness is depicted in consortium with powerlessness and/or sociocultural deficien-cies? (2) As blackness is commodified (Brown, 2010) and linguistically repre-sented in American literature, are there spaces for Black children to oppose these commodities in academic spaces where the literature is being presented? (3) How might the identity of the teacher facilitate the reading and responses to reading of the depictions of blackness in these literatures? We present these questions as guideposts to disentangle a multilayered set of narratives based on Janice's experi-ences. The "we" voice in this text represents our reflective teaching discussions, analytical processing, and sometimes "black therapy,"[1] sessions that have become critical. The "I" in the text represents Janice's voice that shepherds the experiences in two contexts, familial and school.

Uncle Remus Flashback

Janice sits in Ayanna's office sharing with her a conversation she had with a White male colleague in her department, and her response to his teaching Joel Chandler Harris's *Uncle Remus: His Songs and His Sayings* in his Issues in Diversity graduate seminar. This casual conversation with him struck a nerve and opened a wound that Janice had long since forgotten she'd acquired. He understands why the texts could possibly be problematic for Janice as an African American, and to help defuse her agitation, he informed her that Alice Walker had a similar negative response to the collected tales, then gave her a copy of her article "The Dummy in the Window: Joel Chandler Harris and the Invention of Uncle Remus."

"Ayanna, I know he means well, but as he talked about how valuable Joel Chandler Harris's Uncle Remus was, I listened quietly but was still angry." Janice feels exhausted in trying to describe the conversation with our colleague but also perplexed by her own response to the text, as well as his knowing he is an educa-tor committed to anti-racist education. "I know his points were valid, but I don't think he really understood where I was coming from."

"What did he say?" Ayanna inquired with a furrowed brow and a sure tone.

"I'm too tired to explain, but the Uncle Remus tales he extols as a literary gift were conspired narratives to reproduce and reinforce ignorance. While he was forwarding the idea of how these tales represented how Black enslaved life was captured for a wider audience, I pressed the possibility of seeing this literature as a slap in the face to Black people. I believe these tales are the 'same chain, with a different name.'" Janice's eyes are heavy but through her rhyme scheme, a smile creeps onto her face. We high-five as our laughter fills Ayanna's office.

---

1   We often gather in a "white-free zone" to release how we are feeling while simultaneously engag-ing analytical and strategic approaches for moving forward as professors who rely on American literature for myriad purposes, but also as half of the full-time Black faculty at a PWI.

After calming down and reminding Janice that the office walls are thin, Ayanna asserts, "Use the power of the pen. Spend time reflecting on what you were trying to explain to him and then advance it to our larger discussions of curriculum and pedagogy." Janice nods in agreement and then extends an offer Ayanna can't refuse.

"Let's do this together. Your experience in curriculum and pedagogy will allow me to engage this on multiple levels." Yet, Janice remains uneasy and even unsure as to whether her childhood reflections, school experience, and a labored conversation with a colleague will make sense placed in prose.

Ayanna reassures Janice: "Your story is an important one to share, especially for folks teaching these texts."

"Teachers have to lay the appropriate foundation," Janice says. "These aren't just quaint little folktales like Harris makes them out to be; traditional folktales were developed to instruct the population in the values and behaviors deemed acceptable to the dominant White culture or at least the assumed reader. The Brer Rabbit tales were cautionary tales and tales of survival, but those lessons as survivalist stories are dependent upon the framing."

"What is appropriate, Jan? If I am a White teacher, what must I do to handle this text? See, I am not sure if your term *appropriate* suggests there is only one way to teach. Be careful, girl—you need to explain this," Ayanna cautions.

"Listen. I am a product of Black education in the 1960s. I moved to the Westside of Chicago in 1963. I only saw White people when in school and they were teachers. Our community was Black. Chicago in the 1960s was post–Emmett Till, and Fred Hampton who lived two blocks from me was killed in 1969. So, appropriate teaching is being 'mindful' of who Black people were and who they were striving to be. Ignoring that sociopolitical landscape makes teaching these texts no different than listening to Fractured Fairytales or watching minstrel-laced Bugs Bunny cartoons."

Ayanna reaches for her handbook on sociolinguistics and tosses it to Janice as she speaks. "Linguists from Labov, Rickford, Smitherman, Ball to Alim, and Williams have taken apart Black language showing how Black talk was and still is purported to denote ignorance and deficiency despite its creativity and structure. Debates are unceasing as to whether it is a dialect, slang, or a language and how *this talk* hinders social mobility. For a language that is not taught in school, Black children across this nation all know what "She be trippin'" and "I'm finnsta go" mean. Despite how times have changed, very little has changed what people think about Black language and subsequently Black people. Case in point was Obama's presidential candidacy—'Obama isn't Black enough. He doesn't sound Black.'"

We both want to make a connection to the larger culture and socially constructed ways of "seeing" that impacts "being." Ellis (1999) posits:

Our lives are particular, but they also are typical and generalizable since we all participate in a limited number of cultures and institutions. We want to convey both in our stories. A story's generalizability is constantly being tested by readers as they ask if it speaks to them about their experience or about the lives of others they know. (p. 674)

Authoethnography allows me to share that part of my experience that was unique to me, but as I analyze the experience, and "zoom backward and forward, inward and outward, distinctions between the personal and cultural become blurred, sometimes beyond recognition" (Ellis, 1999, p. 673). Ellis sees it as "social science prose" that through my first-person narration, "concrete action, dialogue, emotion, embodiment, spirituality, and self-consciousness are featured, appearing as relational and institutional stories impacted by history and social structure, which themselves are dialectically revealed through actions, feelings, thoughts, and language" (p. 673). Some subject matters are especially suited for analysis through the qualitative perspective that autoethnography provides. In using autoethnography, I am able to not only validate but also analyze an experience that initially resulted in my shame—via the presumptiveness of my White male fifth-grade teacher, Mr. S., and now over 40 years later—ignited by a conversation with my colleague—the lingering roots of frustration that have evolved into anger. Neither of them could grasp how a Black child could feel ignorant, ugly, and illiterate, because the Africanist presence in these texts is taught to appeal to the Eurocentric purview. I was angry because their discourse of "the preservation of Black culture" only reflected an image of "The Happy Darky." If my colleague is going to teach Uncle Remus to our largely White middle- to upper-class students, I wanted to be sure he would convey the alternative framing for Uncle Remus so this reproduction of whiteness layered my adolescent-rooted anger. Unbeknownst to my colleague—and probably an irrational expectation on my part—I really wanted him to reconsider teaching Uncle Remus as a way to amend my fifth-grade teacher's irresponsibility to me. He taught the text. And so, I am still angry.

We use autoethnography as a way "to convey the *meanings* attached to the experience" (Ellis, 1999, p. 674) and to "tell a story that readers could enter and feel a part of" (ibid.), "experience the experience we are writing about." (ibid.). Autoethnography thus becomes a way of working through the incident and constructing some meaningful social implications inherent in it. Like any good narrative, it is a way of making meaning out of the human existence. We suggest that the lived experience serves as a foundation for pedagogies and considerations for curricula. What would be the consequence for schooling if it were not?

Literary Historical Context for Harris's Uncle Remus

In 1880, Joel Chandler Harris introduced his classic folktale collection *Uncle Remus: His Songs and His Sayings*, based on animal folktales he had heard told by the slaves on the Turnwold Plantation in Putnam County, Georgia. The collection was an immediate success. It has been estimated that the book sold 7,000 copies in its first month in 1880, and 4,000 copies annually for two decades. The audience for the collection of tales told by Uncle Remus—the kindly old Black slave created by Harris to narrate the tales about the comings and goings of Brer Rabbit on the Old Plantation—was predominately White.

Image 1: Uncle Remus: His Songs and His Sayings

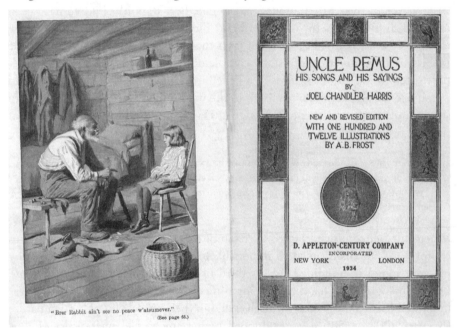

"Brer Rabbit ain't see no peace w'atsumever."
(See page 63.)

UNCLE REMUS
HIS SONGS AND HIS SAYINGS
BY
JOEL CHANDLER HARRIS

NEW AND REVISED EDITION
WITH ONE HUNDRED AND
TWELVE ILLUSTRATIONS
BY A.B. FROST

D. APPLETON-CENTURY COMPANY
INCORPORATED
NEW YORK   LONDON
1934

Harris (1880/1934) intended his tales for the enjoyment of children. He said in the introduction to the fifteenth anniversary edition to the collection:

> I seem to see before me the smiling faces of thousands of children and not an unfriendly face among them. And out of the confusion, and while I am trying hard to speak the right word, I seem to hear a voice lifted above the rest, saying: "You have made some of us happy." (pp. iii–iv)

Harris did, in fact, make "some" children happy, for *Uncle Remus: His Songs and His Sayings* is ensconced in the literary tradition of children's literature. Frey and Griffin (1987) support that "there is no denying that they [the tales] had great impact on child audiences over the past century" (p. 103). However, while these tales indeed brought smiles to the faces of countless White children, the same cannot be said of countless Black children's engagement with the tales. Through Harris's use of a framed narrator—Uncle Remus—and the impenetrable dialect he constructed, the tales have been a source of shame and have lost the "teaching" power with which they—like most traditional folktales and fables—were originally imbued in the oral tradition, contributing instead to a distorted view of African Americans. The Brer Rabbit folktales evolved from the tales that African slaves brought with them to America and reflected a composite of memories of the parables and stories they learned in Africa and their new experiences in slavery on antebellum plantations. An example of the impact of Harris's dialect to impede the transmission of generational knowledge can be seen in the tale "A Story about the Little Rabbits." In the tale, Brer Rabbit's children have been captured by Brer Fox. In order to obtain their freedom and keep from being eaten, they must complete a series of tasks that Brer Fox assigns them. The little rabbits are only able to successfully complete each challenge because they carefully listen to the guiding words of a little bird. The tale represents a parable to encourage the slave children to listen to the wisdom of their elders if they are to survive in their environment. A passage of Harris's (1880/1934) transcription of this tale reads:

> Brer Fox, he sot dar en study w'at sorter skuse he gwineter make up. Bimeby he see a great big stalk er sugar-cane stand'in' up in de cornder, en he cle'r up his th'oat en talk biggity: 'Yer! You young Rabs dar, sail 'roun' yer en broke me a piece er dat sweetnin'-tree,' sezee, en den he koff (p. 108).

When I first encountered Harris's version of this tale at age ten, my inability to comprehend the dialect made it impossible for me to understand the tale or any inherent moral it contained. In his third book, *Uncle Remus and His Friends*, Harris apologized for his dialect being difficult to read concluding that he was interested only in the stories themselves and in their revelations of human nature (Keenan, 2008, p. 58). I would doubt whether any true characteristics of "human nature" can be ascertained if the exaggerated dialect prevents comprehension, and what type of human nature is being represented. Since speech is often judged as reflecting intelligence, Moore and MacCann (1986) question whether Harris's dialect is a real representation or a misrepresentation of Black speech when Uncle Remus calls Atlanta "Lantmatantarum" (p. 86).

My Grandma's Brer Rabbit: Janice's Familial Bond

As an African American child growing up in the late 1960s, my first encounter with the Brer Rabbit folktales came in the form of the oral tradition via my grandmother. Sitting around the kitchen table after supper in the evenings in our small Westside Chicago apartment—much like the slaves who originated the tales, I imagine—or sometimes just before bedtime, my Nana told me, my sister, mother, and father the colorful tales of Brer Rabbit. Brer Rabbit was always the center of the tales, along with the other animals that populated his community; Nana never mentioned a character named Uncle Remus. She was the granddaughter of former Alabama slaves and sharecroppers. The stories had been handed down to her from them, and they flowed from her tongue in the everyday English of one who had "some schoolin'" peppered with the quintessential phrases and witticisms indicative of Southern speech, and I understood it perfectly.

When my Nana recounted her tales to me, there was always a gleam in her eyes and laughter in her voice; she loved Brer Rabbit unconditionally. On the other hand, while I enjoyed Brer Rabbit's escapades, I was not as comfortable with him, preferring "High John the Conqueror." High John could be considered the first African American superhero. According to legend, High John was a whisper of hope and a wish for something better that put on flesh and became a man. He came from Africa, walking across the waters following the slave ships and watching over his people. Even though he was really a prince, he assumed the role of a slave when he arrived here, protected his fellow slaves and constantly outwitted his masters. It is thought that the while the Brer Rabbit tales originated during slavery, the High John narratives emerged after the Civil War and freedom. In her essay on "High John de Conquer" from her folktale collection, Zora Neale Hurston (1943) asserts that High John was Brer Rabbit in disguise:

> When Old Massa met him, he was not going by his right name. He was traveling, and touring around the plantations as the laugh-provoking Brer Rabbit. So Old Massa and Old Miss and their young ones laughed with and at Brer Rabbit and wished him well. And all the time, there was High John de Conquer playing his tricks of making a way out of no-way. (p. 452)

The difference for me and what made me like High John so much was because he was human, a Black man who was strong and smart—something that was seldom seen in literature during my childhood—while Brer Rabbit was an animal, making it hard to ever imagine that he was anything more than a make-believe comedic character. And even though he usually got the upper hand, his behavior seemed a little too shady and self-serving to me at times; I couldn't exactly figure him out. Was he a hero or a rascal? I was impressed with his ability to outwit Brer Fox, Brer Wolf, or Brer Bear, but his methods often left me wondering.

Being young myself, I identified with his smallness, his vulnerability, and his ability to gain the upper hand among the larger, stronger animals in spite of his size, but sometimes he accomplished these feats through behavior—lying, cheating, stealing—that I had been instructed against. When I questioned my Nana about Brer Rabbit's dubious conduct, she chuckled and simply said, "Brer Rabbit was a rascal, baby; but them was hard times back then and Brer Rabbit was doin' the best he could to make it." For a while I never quite understood what she meant by "doin' the best he could to make it" given the moral incorrectness of his behavior, but I trusted the wisdom of it because my Nana said it was appropriate.

Even if I didn't know about the hard-time circumstances of Brer Rabbit, my grandmother, mother, and other family members had made me very aware of the conditions for Black people living in the racist South via our family history and instilled in me a consciousness of similar circumstances in the so-called free North. African Americans had migrated to the North believing they were escaping the oppressive racist conditions of the South and gaining greater economic opportunities. What they usually found were the same discriminatory conditions only more subtle in their presentation. I remember my grandmother taking my mother, sister, and me to lunch one afternoon to a nice restaurant in downtown Chicago. While we were allowed to enter and be seated, we sat for an hour without ever being waited on. I watched as White family after White family who had entered after us were seated and waited on. We finally got up and left and settled for lunch at Woolworth's. I came to understand that Brer Rabbit's "need" to trick prissy Miss Cow out of some of her milk in order to feed his family was no different from my great-great grandfather's need, as a Black sharecropper, to hide a few bushels of his corn crops from the landowner who systematically cheated him out of his fair share through fees and incidentals at the end of each season. In his essay "The Origins of Southern Sharecropping," economic history scholar Ralph Shlomowitz (1979) states that based on reports filed with the Freedman's Bureau regarding disputed labor contracts between Black sharecropping farmers and the White planters who were their landlords, the farmers alleged that:

> [The] planters had swindled them at the division of the crops. The most frequent complaint related to the inaccurate planter accounts. They alleged being charged for goods which they had not bought from the planter and having deducted from their earnings forfeitures for lost time during the year which they had not incurred. (p. 559)

For me, my Nana's Brer Rabbit tales were a form of humorous entertainment and became "parables for livin'" as Nana would call them. There was usually a "Now, what you think about that?" at the end of each tale from Nana, thereby giving my sister and me an opportunity to share our thoughts on the outcome of the tale. Some of the things I remember learning were the dangers of pride from the tale of the Tar-Baby; the folly of laziness from the tale of Brer Rabbit going fishing; and the importance of listening to my parents from the tale of Brer Rabbit's little rabbits' encounter with Brer Fox. My experiences with the Brer Rabbit tales achieved the desired outcome that Nana (and probably the original tellers of the tales) planned based on scholar Mikkelsen's (1983) observations about their intent:

> Throughout the years of slavery the animal fables had been transmitted orally by storytellers to members of the black culture both to entertain and to inculcate social values; the most effective devices of humor and language pattern had been preserved and refined in

many cases through numerous telling, and characters and events had evolved as symbols for power struggles among individuals and institutions. The black child and adult were thus taught such survival tactics as passive resistance, no-work "work" ethics, and the value of entertaining a white audience, all through the safety of allegory. (p. 4)

Eventually, as a result of my Nana's constant tutelage, I gained a greater appreciation for what Brer Rabbit and his exploits really represented, and he assumed his rightful place of honor in my mind, along with High John the Conqueror.

It was my Nana's telling, and her sly grin as she recounted Brer Rabbit's escapades—his ability to outwit, and outmaneuver in dangerous situations—that helped me to appreciate him. I sensed she knew something about him I needed to know. Even when I did not completely understand his ways, eventually, I felt as though I understood him. Mikkelsen (1983) articulates my feelings of Brer Rabbit in her description: "Neither superhuman nor possessing magic powers, Brer Rabbit is quite frequently all too human, guilty at times of foolish and prideful actions, at other times of illegal or amoral ones. Yet, always he survives, for small and defenseless as he is, his more powerful opponent invariably exercises less intelligence" (p. 3). Nana, through the tone in her voice and the emphasis on Brer Rabbit's amazing cunning, helped me to see that Brer Rabbit was what scholar Robert Cochran (2004) calls a "Signifying Rabbit in the fullest sense of that term…" (p. 21).

In his seminal text *The Signifying Monkey*, Gates (1988) traces the practice of signifyn' back to the trickster figure in African folklore. The trickster was usually a god, goddess, spirit, or anthropomorphic animal who plays tricks or otherwise disobeys normal rules and societal norms (pp. 44–45). The tricksters' power seemed to lie in his/her disregard for the rules and those who create them. Within the African American community signifyin' is a form of verbal wordplay utilizing the strategy of indirection in its discourse rather than direct confrontation. The verbal battles are playful assaults involving loud talking, bragging, and teasing putdowns. The messages are usually encoded, decipherable by other members within the community. For African Americans, it became a means by which to establish credibility/status within their community, release anger, and frustration through their masterful wordsmithing. And if I didn't know anything else, as a Black child on the Westside of Chicago, I knew the power that those adept in signification possessed and respected it. Brer Rabbit was all right with me. But my Nana's Brer Rabbit was not the one I found in school.

Searching to Oppose Your Construction of My Culture

My second encounter with Brer Rabbit came in the form of Harris's folktale collection *Uncle Remus: His Songs His Sayings* when I was in fifth grade. My fifth-grade teacher, Mr. S., was a very kind White man who seemed truly committed to the education of his Black students in Chicago's Lawndale community. He constantly sought creative ways to convey concepts and knowledge to us. He taught us to make and fly kites in order to understand the science of aerodynamics and turned the learning of timetables and arithmetic into competitive games with the incentives of prizes and candy for our efforts. He even rearranged all the desks in our classroom to replicate streets and had us draw maps of the routes we took from our homes to school to learn the significance of geography. Mr. S. was an engaging teacher, and I was one of his best students. One of his biweekly class assignments was book reports; students visited the school library, selected a book, and turned in a written report the following week.

On one particular occasion when I was sick with the flu and unable to go to the library and select a book, Mr. S. selected a book for me to read and write about. The book was *Uncle Remus: His Songs and His Sayings*. When Mr. S. presented me with the book, he was extremely excited and told me that he knew I would enjoy it because it was one of his favorites. I took it as a personal compliment and embraced the book, assured that I would get an "A" because he said these were the tales of Brer Rabbit, and I already knew all about him from my grandmother's stories.

I did not recognize Harris's tales as the same ones my Nana recited to me, and found the text incomprehensible. The first obstacle to my understanding was the stories' frame—the character Uncle Remus who I knew nothing about. *Why was he at the beginning and end of the stories if they were tales about Brer Rabbit? Why was he always talking to a little White boy?* I could make this out from the pictures in the book. I took the book to my grandmother, hoping she could enlighten me.

"Nana, who was Uncle Remus?"

She was quiet at first, her brow furrowed as if she was thinking, then she quietly said, "He was an old Black man who told lots of lies."

Her answer didn't get to the heart of my confusion—Uncle Remus's relationship to Brer Rabbit—so I pressed her. "But what did he have to do with Brer Rabbit and the stories you tell us?" I think I must have made her mad with this question because her answer came quick this time and her tone was terse. She sounded the same way she did when she was correcting me for doing or saying something wrong.

"He ain't got nothin' to do with Brer Rabbit and you need to remember that."

"But he's got to have something to do with him," I insisted. "Uncle Remus' name is right here in the title of the book about Brer Rabbit."

Nana was silent. Still looking for connections, I asked her another question. "Well, have you ever heard of Joel Chandler Harris? He's the author of the book— the book about Uncle Remus and Brer Rabbit." My grandmother and mother gave each other knowing looks, then laughed. Not a laugh of amusement or humor, but a short snide exhalation of disgust.

"Yeah, he was the White man that put the lies in Uncle Remus' mouth. And, he ain't got nothing to do with Brer Rabbit either." Her responses only compounded my confusion.

As previously stated, the second obstacle that made the tales unreadable was the language; they were not written in any English that I knew, and I couldn't understand why Mr. S. had given me—a 10-year-old—a book to read that was written in what I perceived as a foreign language:

> "'Oh, he in dar, 'sez Brer Buzzard, sezee. "He mighty still, dough. I speck he takin' a nap," sezee. "Den I'm des in time fer ter wake 'im up," sez Brer Fox, sezee. En wid da the fling off his coat, en spit in his han's, en grab de axe. (Harris 1880/1934, p. 37)

As hard as I tried, I could not find the Brer Rabbit tales that my Nana told me embedded in these tales even though the story headings indicated that the stories were about him. As I struggled to read what I now know was a construction by Harris of African American speech, I could decipher Brer Rabbit's name on the pages as I flipped through them: "…en he sorter broach 'about Brer Rabbit's kyar'ns on" (Harris, 1880/1934, p. 54), "'…en don't you say nothin' twel Brer Rabbit come en put his han's onter you,'" (p. 55), "W'y, ders er old gray rat w'at uses 'bout yer…" (p. 69). However, the fractured dialect used in both the narration by Uncle Remus and the dialog of the characters made the stories themselves incomprehensible. Fry and Griffin (1987) posit that, "Not only is the Black Southern dialect in which [the tales] are written sometimes difficult for a modern reader to understand, it is unhappily reminiscent of minstrel-show humor" (p. 103). The dialectic nature of the text was a source of shame and embarrassment to me. Instinctively, without being told through the use of dialect, I recognized the characters, *though animals*, as representing Black people. With the absence of my grandmother's smile and conveyance of pride in Brer Rabbit's cunning, the written presentations of the animals in these texts were symbolic of a people who were constructed as scheming, dishonest, illiterate, and ignorant by hegemonic educational and moral standards. I saw them in the same way John Herbert Nelson (1999) described them in 1926 in his chapter "Uncle Remus Arrives" published in the book *The Negro Character in American Literature*:

> We are not long in discovering, what Harris and many others pointed out, that the animals are the negroes themselves, and that Brer Rabbit represents the ideal hero of their primitive dream world—an individual able, through craft and downright trickery, to get the better of a master class seemingly unbeatable. The ideals of the animals are the negro's; their prying dispositions, their neighborliness, their company manners, their petty thefts, their amusements are all the negro's…. Even the hopeless incongruity of this animal world—the rabbit and the fox owning cows, and hurting their "hands," and feeling an elementary kind of responsibility for their families—is part and parcel of the negro spirit.

It is a product of his primitive outlook on life, of a poetical feeling that takes no account of the hard logic of consistency. (p. 76)

I sensed that the Brer Rabbit on the pages of Harris's tales was absent of all the nobility and cunning versatility that my grandmother had imbued in him. He was reduced to a court jester and lazy con artist always looking to get over, avoiding a hard day's work, none of which were traits that this Black child had ever been encouraged to emulate. And it seemed to me that Uncle Remus was the worst of all because he was the one speaking and in his telling circumscribing Brer Rabbit and all of his kin to this representation.

As I continued to engage Harris's book, I realized that Uncle Remus was the shameful portrait of blackness that my family had taught me to avoid, the ever-smiling, dutiful, accommodating "Uncle Tom"; abhorred not for his ways but because rather than his ways being a means to an end, as in the case of Nana's Brer Rabbit, his ways were the end. He was the ideal Negro that the antebellum South desired us all to be. According to Nelson (1999), Uncle Remus was "eminently typical of his [my] race," "always consistent, a genial exponent of the psychology of the negro" who "brings the past so vividly into the present" (p. 77). The ever-devoted servant, Uncle Remus, "never forgets the immediate moment—with its duties, its dinners, its 'sunshine niggers,' its talk, and its leisure" (p. 77).

Since I was unable to decipher the tales in a meaningful way, the book report that I submitted to Mr. S. focused on my impressions of the book's use of dialect and my rejection of the tales based on this. I thought my White teacher would be pleased that I recognized that the book reflected forms of ignorance and illiteracy that should not be modeled. I did not mention my feelings of shame. My White teacher did not understand my negative response in my book report to his beloved book of folktales.

When Mr. S. returned my paper to me, he did so after class, once all the other students had received their papers and had left. I was excited because I assumed Mr. S. wanted to compliment me in private on the great job I had done. As he handed me my paper, I smiled as I looked up into his face. "Janice, I'm really disappointed in you," he said. "This book report is very poor work." I was surprised by his words and suddenly noticed that his face was red and filled with a restrained anger as he spoke. I dropped my head and stared at the floor, too embarrassed now to look Mr. S. directly in the face. "This book," he said, pointing to the copy of *Uncle Remus: His Songs and His Sayings* lying on his desk, "is an American literary classic, and I don't understand why you didn't like it." Mr. S. truly seemed genuinely perplexed by my lack of appreciation for the book, especially since it had been established that it was a book worthy of appreciation. I remained silent, not knowing how to explain to him my inability to decipher the language in the book, believing he would think I was dumber than I now felt since he obviously thought that I should have understood it. I nodded my head while my eyes remained fixed on the floor, not hearing much of what Mr. S. was saying. I was trying to figure out how I was going to redeem myself in his eyesight. Mr. S. finally said in a very frustrated voice, "Janice, this book represents your people's history, and you should be ashamed of yourself for not appreciating your culture. These stories are something you should be proud of." I looked at the big red "D" on the top of my book report. "I'm sorry, Mr. S., I guess I should have tried harder," I said. As I turned and left the classroom, I choked back tears and was washed with shame as I began to internalize my perceived failures—my failure to make any literal sense of the text, my failure to see any connection between my history and my people as presented in the text. On my slow walk home, my disdain for the Uncle Remus tales cemented with each step because they were the source of my shame, and I wondered, where were my champions, Brer Rabbit and High John, now when I needed them the most?

The Politics of Identity and Education

As African American professors, one in literature and one in education in 2012, we can now articulate a different appreciation for the significance of the Brer Rabbit folktales. We understand how they represent a bridge between the tales that enslaved Africans brought with them from Africa, the blending of those tales as the cultures intermixed, and the new messages they embodied as they developed and advanced the slave experience. They are in fact artifacts that preserve a culture and depict mechanisms for survival. But within higher education, there is a continuum of reconciliation that is both perplexing and rewarding. Ayanna's research in language, literacy, and sociology is pressed when teaching her predominantly White middle-class students about language access and the discourses that can constitute knowledge in different communities. The challenges in teacher education are dynamic and constant; teach language and literacy so students understand the power of access coupled with preserving language and literacies; in this way, students can continue to value who they are and the knowledge possessed within that identity. For example, Janice's grandmother's appreciation for Brer Rabbit acts as a gateway to Janice's remembering the pride and value of the Black oral tradition. There are bonds that are reinforced across generations, reminding Black children of the sanctity of time spent with elders. Yet, even within Harris's time, there may have been a sense of shame his dialectic tales evoked for Black students. What did they need or have to reconcile as they heard or read text allegedly *representing* who they were? We wrestle with the notion that there may not have been an alternative or oppositional third space for those Black children to develop their own view of these tales alongside their own positive identities; the tension between how Black people are represented as an absolute static whole then and now remain a problem.

As a folklorist, Harris may have been well-meaning in his intent to preserve "authentic" African American folktales, and several scholars believe that without his efforts many of the folktales would have been lost. However, the fact that in 1966 in a Westside kitchen in Chicago amidst the turbulence of the Civil Rights Movement Janice's grandmother was still telling these stories attests to the power of the tales outside of Harris's efforts. What should also be carefully considered is how Harris's dialectic affectations themselves began to hamper the effort of formal preservation among Black people. Moore and MacCann (1986) report that:

> Alice Bacon, the leader of the folklore society at Hampton Institute, described (in 1898) how difficult it was to procure new examples of folk traditions in the schools. It was 'almost impossible for (teachers) to gather from their pupils any folklore at all, so certain are they, if they have any, that it is something only to be laughed at…'" (p. 98)

Bacon's students, like Janice, found that when the entertaining "parables for livin'" of our foremothers and fathers moved from our cabins and quarters into the larger public sphere via Harris's interpretations, they were mocking mirrors of our true selves and became talismans of shame bound to our necks. So, "contrary to the claim that without Harris the tales would have been lost, it can be argued that his minstrel-evoking dialect made them objects of mockery and hence more difficult to collect after 1880" (Moore & MacCann, 1986, p. 98).

It would be easy to villainize Mr. S. and our colleague; they articulate and work within a progressive construct that espouses an appreciation for Black culture, while simultaneously upholding a topography of blackness in its most fictitious form. Thus, as Black professors, what is our most important task? We believe it is a commitment to preserving the self so that we are bearers of the oppositional stance, illuminating multiple perspectives of reading texts that we most need. Maybe we need to be "Nana," and Mr. S, and our colleague all in one—reading, writing, and living evolved curricula to explore the multiplicities of text.

Ayanna was tickled to admit in a quiet moment after reading Jan's prose, "I now understand why my mother could not stand for us to watch *Good Times* and *Sanford and Son*. 'Turn that mess off,' Mommy would shout from beyond the living room and into our consciousness. Mommy would grumble at the mockery of poverty and oppression, ignorance, and alley-cat struttin' that seemed to iconize Black family life on television."

It didn't matter that on each of these shows, there were engaged communities, where neighbors looked out for and advocated for one another, and where children sought out advice from community members to help them make choices, and there was evidence of resistance when forms of class- or race-based oppression impacted the community itself (e.g., *Good Times*, *What's Happening*, and *That's My*

Mama).There was also the presence of dual-headed households (*Good Times* and *The Jeffersons*) and a visible Black middle class (*The Jeffersons*), despite the saturation of images of poverty and the "deteriorating" of Black family life. Rather, the deficits within these shows embodied in the performativity of Black ignorance (e.g., language use and behavior) were enough for Mommy to understand the power of the images. She knew Black people could recover from the onslaught of images that feed the White imagination byway of the television; however, she also did not subscribe to those same images as a source for entertainment. To subvert the potential destruction she saw seeping through the television, she managed to hyper-correct our grammar, enunciation, and sentence structure—reminding us at every turn that Mommy "pays the cost to be the boss." We understood this to mean that when we would leave the house, we represent her, and the world would see and hear intelligent children—because she has already suffered for our benefit. More important than whatever would be televised, Mommy would not allow her daughters to accept the images as templates; they were the lies White folk created and wanted us to accept as mirrors.

Maybe Mommy and Nana were teaching us something about ourselves to prepare us for this very moment—watch quietly, listen loudly, question boldly, and write uncompromisingly. Teach fiercely.

References

Brown, A. F. (2010). "Just because I am a Black male doesn't mean I am a rapper!": Sociocultural dilemmas in using "rap" music as an educational tool in classrooms. In D. Alridge (Ed.),*Message in the Music: Hip Hop, History, and Pedagogy*. Wyomissing, PA: Tapestry Press.

Cochran, R. (2004, Spring). Black father: The subversive achievement of Joel Chandler Harris. *African American Review, 38*(1), 21–34.

Ellis, C. (1999). Heartful autoethnography. *Qualitative Health Research, 9,* 669–683. doi:10.1177/104973299129122153

Frey, C., & Griffin, J. (1999). Joel Chandler Harris: The Uncle Remus stories. In *The Children's Review of Literature* (Vol. 49, pp. 103–105). Detroit, MI: Gale Research.

Gates, H. L. (1988). *The Signifying Monkey: A Theory of African American Literary Criticism*. Oxford, U.K.: Oxford University Press.

Harris, J. C. (1880/1934). *Uncle Remus: His Songs and His Sayings*. New York: D. Appleton-Century Company.

Hurston, Z. N. (1943, October). High John de Conquer. *The American Mercury*, pp. 450–458.

Keenan, H. T. (2008). Joel Chandler Harris and the legitimacy of the reteller of folktales. *Short Story Criticism* (Vol. 103, pp. 56–61). Detroit, MI: Gale.

Mikkelsen, N. (1983). When the animals talked—a hundred years of Uncle Remus. *Children's Literature Association Quarterly, 8*(1), 3–5.

Moore, O., & MacCann, D. (1986). The Uncle Remus travesty. *Children's Literature Association Quarterly, 11*(2), 96–99.

Morrison, T. (1992). *Playing in the Dark: Whiteness and the Literary Imagination*. Cambridge, MA: Harvard University Press.

Nelson, J. H. (1999). Uncle Remus arrives. In *The Children's Review of Literature* (Vol. 49, pp. 75–77). Detroit, MI: Gale Research.

Shakespeare, W. (1623/1937). As You Like It. In *The Works of William Shakespeare Complete* (pp. 251–280). Roslyn, NY: Black's Readers Service Company.

Shlomowitz, R. (1979). The origins of southern sharecropping. *Agricultural History, 53*(31), pp. 557–575. http://www.jstor org/stable/3742755

CHAPTER TWO

De-Pathologizing Urban Spaces Through Dense Inquiry

GARY MUCCULAR JR.

Inner City Streets as a Site for Disciplinary Study

I grew up in the inner city and attended inner-city public schools in Richmond, California. I was a rowdy, loud, head-strong, and mischievous child. I was also a constant talker and a class clown. However, during my elementary school years, I had teachers whom I felt actually cared about me. Some looked like me (racially), and some didn't. They praised me, despite my shortcomings, and disciplined me when I needed to be. These educators would be considered culturally relevant instructors, as articulated by Ladson-Billings (1994). I had a certain connection with some teachers in each grade, which made me feel like I was important; they knew where I was coming from. I felt like a mutual understanding existed between the teachers and me. They knew that it was my job to be a child; to talk, to joke around, and even cause mayhem, at times.

It was natural for me to be a little rowdy sometimes because many of the kids in the neighborhood were that way. It was a survival tactic and a way of socializing in our community. For example, my teachers understood (especially those who grew up in the surrounding inner-city areas— Richmond and Oakland) that growing up in the inner city and growing up as a black male in these environments mandated that one be tough and street smart, or one would be picked on and bullied by his peers. "Soft" kids were labeled as such and constantly ridiculed by peers, so that the whole school population (or at least it felt like it at times) picked on a kid until he or she proved himself by fighting back or "kicking up a little dust." This usually meant displaying a couple of acts of defiance towards authority, or engaging in one purposeful act that would make the class stand up and take notice (like beating up or hitting someone known to be way tougher than the kid was thought to be). One didn't have to win the fight, but only needed to let it be known that if messed with (harassed), there was going to be a real battle. Physical jousting (wrestling and play fighting) was also done with one's friends to see where one stood in the order of toughness. This is where one learned self-defense and learned how to be successful (or unsuccessful).

These were survival tactics, coping skills, and most importantly a form of acculturation for this environment. Though this type of social "learning" was frowned upon by school authorities, and was against school rules, (something teachers were expected to act upon in the form of discipline), my culturally conscious teachers knew that this socialization was essential to survival in many urban contexts. Their consciousness and practices inverted the deficit discourse utilized in education research that propagates the notion that certain minority youth and inner-city youth cannot learn, or do not have the capacity to learn; or that some do not have the desire to learn.

For many inner city youth, like myself in the later 1980s and 1990s (Muccular, 2007), the street is a secondary classroom. Overall, my knowledge of urban street culture was shaped by experiential learning that can be described as follows:

Table1: Street as Metaphoric "Classroom"

"Period" as a Metaphor for the Organization of Study	Knowledge and Skills Under Study	Learning Outcomes Forged by Societal Factors
1st period: English for varied contexts	Proper code-switching techniques for varied audiences; usage of slang vs. Standard American English.	How to communicate effectively, both in academia, and in suburban/urban social arenas.
2nd period: Logic	Proper decision making based on social context and creative problem solving.	Calculation of time needed to hang out with friends and get home without drama (i.e., being bullied, mugged, shot, etc.); contemplating whether to sell drugs or not. Understanding and navigating personal and group boundaries.

continued next page

"Period" as a Metaphor for the Organization of Study	*Knowledge and Skills Under Study*	*Learning Outcomes Forged by Societal Factors*
3rd period: Geography	Community awareness and utilization: "Turf" or street survival—represent yo' city.	What/who do I align myself with for safety (possible options: guns, cliques, gangs, set, street or block loyalties vs. family loyalties)?
4th period: Lunch	Peer deliberation, discourse, and interaction.	Critical thinking and socio-emotional awareness
5th period: Intra- and Intercultural Studies	Perfecting my swag (character or identity); how to stunt. (show off) to build reputation.	Establishing street identity; learning how to dress, what appropriate car to drive; and what music to listen to. Developing the appropriate attitude adjustment to interact with people (how to perfect your "game," i.e., pick up/talk to opposite sex).
6th period: Ethics	Christian world view vs. the "secular" world view.	How to navigate daily issues and relationship with varied people and personalities who have different values, mores, and morals.

These structures of interdisciplinary study are part of an embodied curriculum that the streets offered. And, the streets have high expectations for "students." For example, as a youth, my life and that of many of those around me depended on success in surviving within and navigating this terrain. Additionally, my success in the streets directly correlated with my status in this environment. And while there was valuable knowledge and skills to obtain in this setting, I had to also develop interpersonal, ethical, and moral knowledge and skills to learn to navigate through tumultuous and sometimes contradictory messages related to street culture and survival. For example, three very important elements helped to shape and develop my identity: growing up in the church (my stepfather and biological father were both pastors); participation in academia; and watching/listening to urban music videos (hip-hop culture). In essence, my attitude, personality, and identity development derived from a mix of church culture, academia, and Bay Area hip-hop culture. Similar to many others in my community, scholarship argues that identities are situational and continuously developing under constraints of privilege, status, and performance demands (Murrell, 2002). In other words, individuals are constantly negotiating their sense of self, where their perception of self leaves off, and where the rest of the world's perceptions begin.

The informal classroom (like street culture) shapes the intelligence of a people who grow up in urban communities and those who live active lifes that sometimes includes dealing with adversity born of economic inequality. For example, I was primarily raised in a single-parent family home (in the earliest part of my life). Yet, beyond the learning that occurs in the formal setting of schools, shaped by knowledge and skills that derive from textbooks focused on discrete bodies of information from various disciplines of study, students' lives in the inner city are also influenced and shaped by learning in informal ways—ways that reflect embodied knowledge forged by a larger sociopolitical field of experience (see Appendix). This curriculum coincides with our daily lives and activities, given the larger sociopolitical context that produces an unequal distribution of resources within and between communities, and unequal learning opportunities between schools. For example, African American students are overrepresented on all indicators of school failure (low test scores, high suspension rates, and high dropout rates), and they are routinely compared to Caucasian students, many of whom are middle class (Ladson-Billings, 1994). In addition, Ginwright (2004) states that urban youths' identity, working-class communities, and schools cannot be isolated from the struggles from which it emerges (p. 34). This may account for why fewer than 10 percent of African American men go to college, yet they constitute 76 percent of the nation's prison population (Murrell, 2002).

Marginalization, institutional racism, discrimination, and lack of cultural understanding and sensitivity (among other factors) have been cited as the cause of these ills. Therefore it is no surprise that academic failures will manifest themselves in many different ways such as suspensions, expulsions, dropouts, and truancy.

This reality shapes the lives of many poor and working-class students in our nation, and certainly shaped the circumstances of many of those in my neighborhood while growing up. And these lessons were applied directly to our daily lives. This reality helped to influence our value systems, influences that must be examined within a historical and culturally shaped landscape of economic and racial subordination. For instance, Tatum (1997) suggests that some youth refuse to learn from instructors due to the lack of care in classrooms, or due to instructors (largely white and female) who do not affirm their students' backgrounds. And as a consequence, some youth display what some may interpret as an "attitude" where they refuse to learn; or they may reject the mainstream culture that in turn rejects them. This can be yet another form of survival to affirm one's personhood and identity.

American culture, too, romanticizes all of the characteristics of what it means to be Caucasian and economically successful (which seem to be used interchangeably). That was a measuring stick that I, as an African American male, could never reach. I could dress in Caucasian-influenced attire, speak *proper* English, and reach financial success, yet I would still *only* be considered a prosperous African American. As I grew older and my knowledge of class differences, society, and perceptions of me (and others who looked like me) grew, the more I began to rebel against and question society. Society's outlook on blacks made me angry; therefore I did not want to adhere to society's perception of normalcy. To me, society was saying that to be normal was to be white, and to be white was to be American. Furthermore, it seemed to me that the more I was taught to emulate Caucasian persons, the more my own ethnicity would have to be sacrificed. And the thought of sacrificing myself or ethnicity to be a part of a society that I felt would never totally accept me as an equal was not worth the sacrifice. For example, my perceptions of hip-hop culture, was that this was culture centered on the concepts of revolution against what society deemed "normal"; as society would never perceive me or anyone from my community to be normal. Furthermore, I had come to the conclusion that in order for me to have pride in myself and my culture, I had to denounce what the masses perceived as normal.

One possible reason for the rejection of curriculum and academic culture by youth, like me, is the lack of discussion of class in education. hooks (2009) suggests that class is rarely talked about in the United States. In fact, hooks indicates that individuals from class backgrounds deemed undesirable are expected to surrender all vestiges of their past, which creates a "psychic turmoil" (p. 137). Additionally, hooks suggests that silencing enforced by bourgeois values is sanctioned in the classroom by everyone (p. 136). Nowhere is there a more intense silence about the reality of class differences than in educational settings. In particular, class differences are significantly ignored in classrooms (p. 135), which shapes the purpose of my chapter.

Examining Class in the Classroom

In this text, I utilize a community college student's autobiographical essay of lived experience, community, and issues stemming from social class status, informed by my sociopolitical consciousness as an educator and as someone who grew up in an urban cultural context. The student, Natasha, tells a story of her experience within her community; and I, Gary, raised in a nearby neighboring community, respond to Natasha's story through an inquiry process called *dense questioning*.

Here, I model the process of dense questioning to illustrate a way to examine the social and economic complexities of home place in an urban community, while magnifying the micro- and macro-level factors that circumscribe the lives of low-income people. As I read, I engage in a dense questioning strategy to show how critical questioning practices can enable deep thinking and reading of community and society. While I engage in this process of examination, I also engage in a further understanding of myself as an educator and as an African American man who grew up in a very similar urban context.

At face value, Natasha's story can be used to propagate myths about inner-city youth or about an inner-city youth's academic experience as a writer; or it can contribute to the curriculum conversation to reconceptualize ways to understand students' self-stories *as the curriculum*, while understanding how stories enable study of the sociopolitical issues shaping people and their communities.

Figure 1: Dense Questioning Strategy

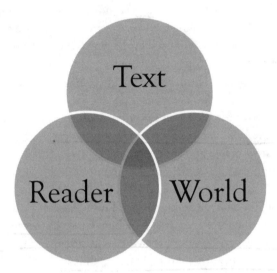

It is important to note that good readers build meaningful links between what they read, think, and the world in which they live. Thus, this process helps one to generate a basic question that the text can answer, then one can link what one reads to one's own experiences, thoughts, beliefs, and opinions. Ultimately, dense questioning as a process enables modeling of ways to engage critically with texts, while using critical literacy questioning to disrupt and de/pathologize our understandings of urban lives and the spaces people inhabit. For example, when a student reads text, there are connections that a student is encouraged and expected to make.

Through the dense questioning strategy, a teacher and his/her students are able to make links between the text, one's knowledge of self, and one's knowledge of the world around him/her (macro- and micro-level examination of society). Consequently, by examining students' writing on their personal experience, this same strategy can be utilized to legitimate students' writing as being worthy of study (bringing in their home and community knowledges), while also enabling opportunity to delve into the private worlds of students' lives, often far removed from classroom inquiry.

Table 2: Description of Dense Questioning Process

Categories (in sequential order)	Description
1. Text	1. Information found in the text
2. Reader	2. Reader's experience, values, and ideas
3. World or Other Literature	3. Knowledge of history, other cultures, other literature
4. Text-to-Reader	4. Combines knowledge of text with knowledge of history and other cultures
5. Text-to-Other Literature	5. Combines knowledge of text with knowledge of other pieces of literature
6. Reader-to-World	6. Combines knowledge of reader's own experiences with knowledge of other culture and peoples
7. Reader-to-Other Literature	7. Combines knowledge of reader's own experiences with other pieces of literature
8. Dense Question	8. Combines knowledge of all three areas into one "dense" question

Essay: "Some People Never Learn" by Natasha

I used to live deep in "East Oakland" on a turf called "Greenside." Of course when I went to look at the apartment on 77th and Bancroft Ave, I had no idea what I was getting myself into.

At this time I just needed a place for myself and my children to live, so when the Oakland Housing Authority called me and offered me a place, I took it. Under better circumstances, I would have never chosen this as a place to live. My life would never be the same after that [living there], and there would be many sleepless nights during my stay at 2509 Bancroft Ave.

Living on a "spot" or a "turf "isn't like living anywhere else. Greenside was a drug spot and there was a lot of foot traffic constantly through the building. You are subjected to whatever the criminal element puts out there. If the "corner boys" are having conflict with other turfs, the chaos will be brought to the building. Frequently, the quarrels would be amongst those selling drugs. A fight could break out at any time without a moment's notice, and you can get caught up in whatever was going on, being at the wrong place at the wrong time. I can recall one night when I was on my way to work at UPS, and as I was walking down the stairs to the parking lot. There was a group of men who were attacking a man with the butt of an AK 47. They yelled at me to "go back in the house" and terrified, that's exactly what I did! My heart was hammering in my chest like a jack hammer on cement. I was so scared that something would happen to me as a result of what I had witnessed. I prayed to God that none of them came to knock on my door to talk to me, or that they didn't mess with my car. I would later learn that there was a code among those who hustled there, and those who resided there. As long as you kept your mouth shut and minded your own business, you would be okay.

Table 3.

Gary's Dense Questioning
• What historic and contemporary knowledge do you currently have about the City of Oakland?
• What is a Housing Authority? When and why were they established? What government agency oversees subsidized housing and why?
• What factors should be examined and considered when county housing authorities place single parents and their children in communities?
• What strategies should be used to educate educators about the cultures and populations that are marginalized in urban public housing communities?

Table 4.

Gary's Dense Questioning
• In what ways might Natasha's community resemble or differ from the community where you reside?
• What factors do you believe helped to produce this community?
• What psychological and emotional ramifications would this environment produce?
• How do you think long-term residence in this area would affect Natasha's academic performance, as well as relationships with classmates or professors?
• In what ways should we (educators, policymakers, parents, citizens) address the social, moral, or economic needs of young people who reside in community spaces like the one Natasha describes?
• What ideas and concepts does this environment raise for you about spirituality, interpersonal relationships, and personal/moral development?

I've seen many terrible things living there: drugs being sold, fights, kids playing in trash, people wandering aimlessly—high on drugs. People having sex outside, people being arrested, sideshows, people being shot and shot at. None of those things prepared me for what I saw happen to Tee-Tee.

2002 was a crazy year on Greenside, especially during the summertime. More youngstas were hitting the block and selling drugs, and the O.G.'s were getting more money than ever, having so many people working for them. The hustlas started having these parties in the courtyard in the front of the building, with a DJ and all. They acted as if they owned the building, and were doing us a favor by letting us stay there. They did whatever they wanted, with no regard for the residents. Some of the resi-

dents would actually participate with them, but I just looked on from my porch. On this particular evening, there was too much drinking and drug use. I could tell that something was going to happen, but I didn't know what. Angry words started to be exchanged between people, but with the music so loud, I couldn't tell what was being said. Once I saw that the situation might escalate, I went back inside my apartment.

One of the people among the throng was a chick named Tee-Tee, and she was a factor out there on the block. She had two chicks working under her and they were her entourage. I rarely saw her without them. I have to admit; she is the main turf chick who was out there getting her money. Her boyfriend, who we will call "Shot Caller," was the one who started that drug spot anyway, so Tee-Tee had pretty much been out there from the beginning. There was nothing remarkable about her look; she was of average build and height, didn't wear makeup and usually had her hair braided in singles. She was nice enough and on occasion she and I exchanged a few words, mostly small talk. I mentioned to her to "be safe" or "stay out of trouble" and her reply was usually the same,

"I'm cool, ain't nothin' goin' to happen to me over here." How wrong she was and didn't even know it.

On this particular night as I mentioned earlier, people were really intoxicated and "feeling themselves." The music was loud, and the drinks and drugs were flowing. A little while later, I was in my bedroom and it sounded like they [the people hanging out] were moving from the courtyard to the street side of the building. The bedrooms of my apartment faced the parking lot, and when I heard commotion out there, I wanted to see what was going on to make sure that nothing was happening to my car. As I looked out the window, I heard loud voices (a lot of what was being said I could not make out because too many people were talking at once). Then I saw that one man was being bullied by several people, one of which was Tee-Tee. All of a sudden, she took off her belt and started hitting the man with it. I am shocked to see her behaving this way, as I have never known her to be physically aggressive. This was an intrepid crowd and they were inciting her to continue with what she was doing. Then the man snaps and calls Tee-Tee a "Bitch" and says to her "You are going to get it."

The next thing I know the man runs and gets in his car. I'm thinking he was just trying to get away from being assaulted. The tires screech loudly, and he began backing up faster than he should have been, particularly with the amount of people in the parking lot. He continued to back up and he hit a lady who was there, but not involved; and, then hits Tee Tee, backing up over her body.

"Oh my God" somebody screams, but this angry driver isn't through. He drives forward over her body and backs up over her a second time. He was dragging her body on the ground, the way a sleepy child drags a Raggedy Ann doll. My bedroom window is closed but I'm able to smell the burning rubber and the burning flesh. I'm paralyzed with fear and disbelief as my mind was trying to figure out what my eyes had just seen. Did I just witness a murder?

Her body was lying lifelessly on the sidewalk. Lots of screams, people crying, people hitting the car, chasing it on foot as it drove away. Tee-Tee was lying there on the ground in an unnatural position with her body twisted and her butt was now located below her chest. I'm horrified at what I just saw. It all happened within minutes and I was in my bedroom shaking like a leaf on a breezy day.

Somebody outside was yelling "Help, please help. Somebody call an ambulance." Others were yelling "Oh my God, Tee-Tee is dead!"

I am praying for the Lord to save her life and I am going numb at the surreal event I had just witnessed. My son was asleep on my bed through the entire ordeal and I just lay on the bed with him, crying and praying.

Shortly thereafter, I hear the ambulance siren approaching, followed by the police outside telling people to move out of the way. I hear what sounded like a whole lot of confusion. I lay there very quietly on my bed, and when the police knocked on my door, I know it is for a witness statement and I don't answer. I just let them knock until they are satisfied that nobody is home or that we are asleep.

Table 5.

Gary's Dense Questioning
• What circumstances produce the culture of "hustling"?
• What psychological issues might this type of violence and bullying have on developing youth or adults in the area?
• What economic and political circumstances can you think of that produce the types of issues described in the text?
• What ideals do you glean from this story about the author's concept of parenting?

Believe it or not, Tee-Tee lived! She was taken to Highland Hospital. Sometime later, my neighbor, Lulu, and I decided to go and see her. I am nervous about seeing her after what happened. All the way to the hospital, I have knots in my stomach. It seemed as though the palms of my hands had become a fountain because they were sweating so much. My mouth was as dry as a desert as we approached the room, and I'm coming close to not going in. Part of me wasn't sure if I could handle seeing her if she was disfigured. I gird up my loins and go inside the room, and to my great relief she doesn't look as bad as I had imagined. She laid there on the bed all casted up and bruised, but talking mostly like normal. I started to cry as I tell her what I witnessed and how I prayed that God would let her live. She too begins to cry and thanks me for praying for her.

The doctor said that Tee-Tee would recover; however, she would not be able to have any kids since her pelvis was crushed, and that she would most likely walk with a limp for the rest of her life, being aided with a cane. I asked Tee-Tee what she was going to do when she got out and she assured me and the others in the room that she was moving away from Oakland and leaving the streets alone. Lulu and I talk with her just a few more minutes and then give our well wishes and leave.

About three or four months later as I was walking home from the store, I noticed Tee-Tee on the block with her walker. I was flabbergasted to see her out there after her promise in the hospital, but I just hugged her, shared a few moments of small talk and continued on my way. Sometime after that, I see her and now she was driving again. I began to notice her more and more back on the block. Pretty soon she was no longer using her walker and she was once again almost full-fledged out on the block. I didn't say much to her after that, but I was and still am puzzled when I see her out there.

About one or two years later I saw her at a grocery store. The baby with her in the car seat is cute and before I could even inquire about who the baby belonged to, she tells me that this was the baby the doctors told her she would never have. I am filled with joy for her at that moment, but it was short lived when she tells me how she was still light weight on the block. I was kind of surprised, but not really. We chat until it was her turn in line and that was the end of that.

Some people never learn. Tee-Tee was so fortunate that God spared her life, and not only that, He allowed her to do all of the things the doctors said she would never do. Yet despite all of that, she couldn't leave the streets alone. Her near-death experience wasn't enough to wake her game up. God spared her and it would seem like she would want to do something more productive with her life than wasting it in the streets. The streets don't care about nothin' but the streets. As traumatic as this event was, it wasn't enough to keep Tee-Tee off the block, and out of harm's way.

Unfortunately, there are many, many people who don't learn from situations as severe as this one. What do I know? I'm on the outside looking in. Maybe hustlin' is all that she knows, and didn't see any other way to make it. Next time she may not be as fortunate.

I ride through there from time to time on my way to my destination; I notice that much has changed. The building is closed down, gated and boarded up. That hasn't stopped the drug activity though, just slowed it down. I see her [Tee-Tee] on occasion and think to myself: "Is this place worth their lives to them?" I may never know the answer to that question. What I do know is that she is still out there now and again… Some people never learn.

The Socioeconomic Context of Natasha's Community

It is important for educators to use students' writing as a vehicle to examine, analyze, and explore the circumstances within communities, placing emphasis on sociopolitical dynamics mediating students' worlds.

Many urban challenges and adaptive responses by individuals have stemmed from a history of disenfranchisement within communities, and how this history impacts families and youth. For example, the visual imagery and circumstances described in Natasha's essay are partly shaped by the economic structure in the city of Oakland, which also correlates with class relations, complicated by racial and class conflict. For instance, in the early 1900s, Oakland experienced expansive black business growth and population growth despite racial discrimination in housing and lending practices. Between 1900 and 1910, the number of blacks nearly tripled (Ginwright, 2004, p. 37). During this time, blacks created strong cultural and economic communities, largely concentrated in West Oakland.

World Wars I and II provided black populations in Oakland with job opportunities (largely in the shipyards, manufacturing, service, and industry), and financial stability that were previously denied on racial grounds. However, the unemployment rate among black men rose from 28.6 percent in 1950 to 50 percent by 1970. What was once a hub of black businesses (barbershops, restaurants, nightclubs, and bars) became areas of expensive rent, deteriorated facilities, and the beginning of systematic poverty.

Additionally, the city also experienced "white flight." Between 1960 and 1970, Oakland's white population declined by 21 percent, while the black population increased by 41 percent (Ginwright, 2004, p. 40). The shift in the racial composition of Oakland is complicated by the fact that discriminatory practices in housing eliminated the possibility for blacks in Oakland to relocate to the suburbs where many of the manufacturing jobs had gone. Moreover, in the 1960s, public transportation to the surrounding suburbs was limited, and blacks were further alienated from the job market.

Currently in West Oakland there is an absence of essential retail services such as banks, grocery stores, and drug stores (Ginwright, 2004, p. 46). The majority of buildings and office space along West Oakland's major streets are vacant and in poor physical condition. The city also has some of the oldest homes and contains 1,359 vacant and boarded-up structures.

This year (2012), when the Oakland Police and the mayor's staff analyzed both historical and current data on shootings and homicides, it was found that 90 percent of shootings and homicides occurred in 5 percent of the city—or approximately 100 city blocks (City of Oakland, 2012).

Not surprisingly, these same 100 blocks have some of the highest joblessness and school dropout rates. Many of these areas straddle economically depressed commercial corridors that attract prostitution and open-air drug markets. These "hotspots" are also in, or near, the same areas where children under the age of six lost their lives to senseless gun violence in 2011.

As violent crime rates increase, housing values decrease and taxes increase to meet the growing strain on police and social services. Additionally, when cities develop a negative reputation due to violent crime and drug abuse, businesses are less willing to invest anywhere in Oakland (City of Oakland, 2012). These circumstances shape and help produce the lives of those who inhabit the community that Natasha describes.

A Final Word

Educators must know the history of communities in order to provide culturally relevant curriculum, and to engage in supporting dialogue about historic community issues and socioeconomic change. Talvacchia (2003) also suggests that developing relationships, as well as the development of the heart and mind is a foundation and fundamental aspect of a teacher's identity, practice, and spiritual formation. In other words, as an educator, the way one teaches and how one teaches (one's integrity) should be parallel (Muccular, 2007). Talvacchia (2003) further suggests that a more multicultural and sensitive pedagogy allows instructors to see those they teach more fully and completely as human beings. This type of pedagogy not only affects the students, but also places moral responsibility on the instructor. Dense questioning is one approach to facilitate an engaged pedagogy that allows for the examination of class-based issues.

Many students who reside in inner-city environments experience trauma or violence stemming from historic and economic issues. So in order to teach these students, educators need to learn to meet them where they are. They need to understand the plight of urban communities and how students have learned to relate to each other based on their circumstances; people develop in cultural and historic contexts. That is to say, children and adolescents are embedded in a sociocultural context that affects their development (Schaffer, 2000).

Just as education and life in the academy is valued, so is the way of life for people/students who grew up impoverished or in inner-city surroundings. When teaching students, it is important for instructors to understand where their students are from and bring students' stories into the classroom for dialogue and as sites for learning about sociopolitical issues. Certainly, students' life-writings can also allow for exploration of traditional learning goals, such as asking:

- How do you view this writer's paper?

- What recommendations would you offer the writer to strengthen the essay?

- What are the writing assessment possibilities that Natasha's paper provides?

- What other learning possibilities might this paper offer for classroom and community learning?

Yet, instructors cannot expect students to buy into their teaching style (or content) unless the teachers display *care* along with a willingness to dialogue with students and engage them about issues that are pertinent in their informal learning contexts. This engagement can, as illustrated, take place through the utilization of dense questioning strategies that enable dialogue, critical thinking, and critical consciousness. This statement begs the question about how educators are trained to engage in this manner. Thus, there are questions that must also guide programs that engage in teacher education:

- What training or learning is needed to assist educators in their ability to reach students whom they have had limited knowledge of and experience with their culture or those who grew up in urban environments?

- What skills are needed to aid teachers in their ability to teach youth disciplinary knowledge in formal education, while also being attentive to the daily issues that shape students, particularly those living in constant survival mode?

Moreover, educators must learn to understand and appreciate the resiliency, talents, and gifts that people from lower socioeconomic communities have used historically and continue to use to live within and transcend adverse circumstances.

In sum as an educator, I have been challenged by the different environments I have had the pleasure of experiencing while developing the early stages of my identity, as it placed me in environments where I learned many life lessons about my class standing, values, and character. And, my journey helped to develop my thinking about pedagogy, particularly when examining students in the context of their environment. Thus, for me, teaching about class is a vital and important component of curriculum for critical consciousness.

References

Adksion-Bradley, C., Johnson, D., Lipford Sanders, J., Duncan, L., & Holcomb-McCoy, C. (2005, January). Forging a collaborative relationship between the black church and the counseling profession. *Journal of Counseling and Values, 49*, 147–154.

Banks, J. (2000). Multicultural education: Characteristics and goals. In J. A. Banks & C. A. M. Banks (Eds.), *Multicultural Education: Issues and Perspectives* (3rd ed., pp. 3–31). Boston: Allyn & Bacon.

Chinn, P., & Gollnick, D. (2006) *Multicultural Education in a Pluralistic Society*. Upper Saddle River, NJ: Pearson

City of Oakland (2012). http://www.oaklandnet.com/contactmayor.asp

Comer, P., & Poussaint, A. (1992). *Raising Black Children*. New York: Penguin.

Davis, P. (2005, Spring). The origins of African American culture and its significance in African American student academic success. *Journal of Thought*, 43–58.

Enns, C., & Forrest, L., (2005, Spring). Toward defining and integrating multicultural and feminist pedagogies. In C. Z. Enns, & A. Sinacore (Eds.), *Teaching and Social Justice: Integrating Multicultural and Feminist Theories into the Classrooms* (pp. 3–23). Washington, DC: United States American Psychological Association. *Journal of Thought*, 43–58.

Galloway, A. (2003). Psychology at work inside and outside the church: Bridging the gaps between emotional, physical, and spiritual health. *Journal of Psychology and Christianity, 4*, 343–347.

Gardiner, H., Kosmitzki, C., & Mutter, J. (1998). *Lives Across Cultures: Cross-Cultural Human Development*. Needham Heights, MA: Allyn & Bacon.

Ginwright, S. (2004). *Black in School: Afrocentric Reform, Urban Youth, and the Promise of Hip-Hop Culture*. New York: Teachers College, Columbia University.

Hale, J. (2001). *Learning While Black*. Baltimore, MD: Johns Hopkins University Press.

hooks, b. (2009). Confronting class in the classroom. In A. Darder, M. R. Baltodano, & R. D. Torres (Eds.) , *The Critical Pedagogy Reader* (2nd ed.). New York: Routledge.

Ladson-Billings, G. (1994). *The Dream Keepers: Successful Teachers of African American Children*. San Francisco: John Wiley & Sons.

Muccular, G. (2007). *The Case for the Need for Spiritual Development in Education* (published thesis). Sacramento: California State University - Sacramento

Murrell, P. (2002). *African-Centered Pedagogy: Developing Schools of Achievement for African American Children*. Albany: State University of New York Press.

Schaffer, (2000). *Social and Personality Development*. Belmont, CA: Wadsworth/Thomas Learning.

Talvacchia, K. (2003). *Critical Minds and Discerning Hearts: A Spirituality of Multicultural Teaching*. St. Louis, MO: Chalice Press.

Tatum, B. (1997). *Why Are All the Black Kids Sitting Together in the Cafeteria?* New York: Basic Books, Perseus Books Group.

CHAPTER THREE

Найти Себя[1]

An Autobiographical Journey of a Russian Teacher in America

LILIYA ZHERNOKLEYEV

> The fact that Russians can easily blend in and start living an American life speeds the process of assimilation, loss of identity and loss of some cultural traits. That is why parents are worried because they understand how quickly their children can lose something that actually sets them apart from Anglo-Americans, something that belongs to them and makes them unique. (Liliya's journal reflection)

Recently there has been major immigration from former Soviet Union countries due to the unstable economic position in varied countries. Slavic people come to the United States hoping to gain better opportunities and have access to a more stable financial life for their children and grandchildren.

Some people, like those in my family who left countries in the former Soviet Union to seek a better life, feel the impact of having to make the difficult decision to become part of the United States. One such challenge Russian immigrants face is that they are expected to sacrifice their culture and language when they come to America (first generation), and many feel vulnerable about abandoning what identifies them with their culture and language. This is due to the ideology that a strong sense of cultural belonging and knowing one's heritage may end up in the "melting pot" of American society. This thinking aligns with Calderon (1998), who points out that "acculturation involves painful, sometimes unconscious decisions, such as what is to be saved or sacrificed from the old, evaluating what one wants and needs to adapt from the new, and integrating these into a comfortable sense of self" (p.10). Consequently, in order to adapt and fully participate in the new culture (America), some of the old traditions and ways of thinking or doing may be sacrificed.

This proves challenging for several reasons. First, I am from a very white European country where everyone spoke one dominant language (Russian), some Latvian, and the other languages we heard (those not spoken by other Baltic ethno-linguistic groups) were from tourists. The issue of cultural adaption is challenging as well because there is a tendency for adult members of the Russian community to isolate from all that is American for the sake of keeping all that is Russian alive in the lives of children (language, customs, traditions, patriotic teaching). On the other hand, there is the other cultural extreme (mostly from the youth), which is the tendency to cling to all that is American—watching only American movies, speaking only English, or forgetting cultural traditions such as the importance of taking care of elderly members of the family. All are attempts to assimilate, of course. So it holds that in either case, opportunities to become acculturated and hone one's home language while gaining advanced communication skills in the home language is compromised (скомпрометировано). Yet the ability to become enriched by language exposure and to understand могущество языка (the power of language) in the world beyond one's immediate environment is compromised as well. In sum, and as one might imagine, either example would seem to sabotage a positive immigration experience and would impact positive identity development. Thus, the key is то найти баланс (find a balance) between two languages and cultures, so that identity conflicts and discomfort due to assimilation can be avoided. From this standpoint, a person's effort to better understand him/herself and others can be enriched when one becomes conscious of the need to develop a bicultural and bilingual approach to living, particularly in an English-dominant environment. As a first-generation immigrant[2] from Riga, Latvia (located in a northern part of Europe and a former Soviet Union country), and as an elementary school teacher, I see a significant need for Russian immigrant children to keep their native language while learning English; and while learning about the diversity of culture within the United States. This is salient because Russian parents too are facing their own challenges inherent to their immigration experience and adjustment within a new cultural, at the same time trying to support their children's English language development.

Having observed the speech of three generations of Russians—within my family, amongst my friends and their children, and within other Russian families; and having studied language maintenance and loss among Russian children in a community in California (Zhernokleyeva, 2011), I have come to the conclusion that with each new generation, native-language retention catastrophically decreases. This is due to a variety of factors such as the level of acquired English

---

2   My family origin is of mixed-Slavic ancestry (Siberian, Polish, Belarus, Ukrainian, and Russian).

used by immigrants, the type of communities they live in, their employment circumstances, and their level of access and exposure to the English language; all are factors that shape language maintenance and loss.

And for first-generation immigrants, no matter how much English they use every day, their first language is still their dominant language. This holds true in my own case. When I came to this country in 2001 as an 18-year-old, I never had any pressure from my parents about not using enough Russian language. In fact, they were more worried as to whether or not my siblings and I would be able to learn enough English to be successful; they wanted us to practice. The language chosen for our conversations was English and we would often code-switch. However, for second-generation immigrants, using their primary language as their dominant language is not always the case. Second-generation immigrants typically adapt more easily to the dominant language of the new country and tend to choose it as their dominant language for everyday conversations and communications, even in their households, as documented in Valdes and Figueroa (1994, pp. 15–17). J. A. Fishman (1965) states, that "by the fourth generation, immigrants become monolingual in English, the language of the majority society" (p. 26). The first language is almost always lost to the fourth generation.

Given this generational pattern of language use, I ask myself: *In what ways should the curriculum shape language maintenance? What role should curriculum play in developing bilingualism and biculturalism?* These issues are important in an age when we are steeped in nationwide dialogue about curriculum. Clearly, issues such as immigration (illegal and legal), and dwindling support for bilingual education (in the state of California particularly) are at issue. And though the United States is a linguistically and culturally diverse nation of immigrants, language *is the least robust element of the generational legacies to survive in the process of adaptation* (Nesteruk, 2007, p. 30). Hence, the curricular lives of bilingual learners are issues that must be explored. Consequently I embrace Silova and Brehm's (2010) challenge for academics to "reflect on their own role of reconfiguring existing education spaces and constructing new intellectual spaces…open to a multiplicity of voices, critical inquiry, and a true dialogue in a spatial politics of knowledge production" (p. 467). Thus, here begins my contribution to the language curriculum landscape and critical inquiry— this is my story.

Об Иммиграции и Приспосабливании[3]

People must have the right to choose how they want to raise their children and they must have a voice in determining what they want to see for their children's future within the bounds of democracy and societal well-being. (Liliya's journal reflection)

---

3   On Immigration and Adjustment

Back in Latvia, my stay-at-home mom had five children to care for. My father, who was born in Siberia in 1955, immigrated to Latvia in 1980. He had a small car-washing business, which was enough for my parents to live on and retire. However, they worried about my siblings and me because they knew that we all needed to complete our education, which was very expensive. Due to the dissolution of the Soviet Union, the creation of sovereign nation states with fledgling economic systems, and the unstable economic situation in the country of Latvia, nearly all the young people, even those who held university degrees, would leave Latvia in order to find jobs in other European countries. Consequently, my parents chose to immigrate to the United States so that we could all be together in one country, rather than spread throughout Europe. Thus, leaving Latvia for America, I was full of excitement and dreams about seeing the world, and having the chance to travel to another continent to start a new life.

Like that of my parents, the objective of many other Russian people for immigrating is the continuous progress of Russian children. Many Russian people remain hopeful about children being brought up with a Christian spiritual base (Baptist, in the case of my family), and having a clear sense of the cultural group to which they belong. Yet, losing something as defining as one's home country is the tradeoff that many parents, like mine, make. It is said that the "process of 'growing up American' ranges from smooth acceptance to traumatic confrontation, depending on the characteristics that immigrants bring along and the social context that receives them" (Portes & Rumbaut, 2001, p. 19).

Language is vital to identity, no matter the culture. Likewise, to understand and achieve academic success opens the door to inclusion. If our children do not acquire Russian-language fluency, they cannot fully participate in the culture. It can often be heard among Russian elders that their grandchildren learn the American language and culture quickly, and this leads to disassociation from Russian history and tradition. Это может привести к непониманию и разделению между поколениями (This can lead to separation and misunderstanding between generations). To some extent, Russian parents and elders (like mine) have to allow faith and hope to guide their children in their search for a new bicultural or even multicultural identity and acceptance in America.

Преодаление Трудностей[4]

I had a college professor who printed out some letter that made fun of Russian traditions and culture, and instead of giving it just to me, he gave a copy to everybody in class. He wanted to have a discussion about it and laugh in a joking way, but I felt it was unfair and disrespectful. He found the use of language and content amusing and thought that since I was in his class, we could have a discussion about it.... Every time I hear people [like my former professor] say something in a joking way about the Russian culture, I feel

---

4   Overcoming Challenges

very defensive and hurt, like someone is *making fun* of my parents. Of course among my Russian friends we joke about the way Russians mix languages when communicating in Russian, or we joke about the Russian traditions and culture in general. However, when an "outsider" does the same thing, a self-defense mechanism clicks in to protect what is dear to one's heart. (Liliya's journal reflection)

As a new immigrant and an 18-year-old teenager just out of high school, I tried to fit into the American college system, while at the same time learning the language and culture. As one might imagine, all the ethnic and linguistic diversity in America was very interesting and unusual to me. Yet, I started losing myself, forgetting what I believed in and what identified me (or who I was) in terms of my cultural upbringing. I felt lost and no longer understood what was right or wrong for me as I acquired some degree of cultural assimilation. My journey included living with a roommate with whom I could not communicate. I would spend hours trying to memorize some English sentences to say to her, so it would feel like we had some kind of communication; but most of the time, I would not understand her reply because she spoke fast and used many words unknown to me. Still, I would not give up. I asked my Russian friends who had been in the U.S. longer and developed more English for how to say something, and then I would try to approach my roommate again. Yet, through this process, it was painful to realize that I could not express myself on the same intellectual level as native English-speaking students because of the language barriers. The social barriers I experienced were even more pronounced in academic settings. Every time it was my turn to speak in class, I would sweat, trying to find the right words to express myself. The lack of English-language vocabulary prevented my intellect from showing. Consequently, I always felt I was missing out on information taught in class because I was trying to learn English and the curriculum at the same time, while wanting desperately to earn passing grades on my assignments.

My language challenges did not end with English. I thought I was very proficient with Russian until I took the Russian language test that would lead to a credential to teach Russian as a second language. After seven years living in the country, I still needed to practice my academic Russian. I had gone to the Russian language test very confident, and yet I still struggled on the speaking portion. Like many language learners, when one is under pressure on an exam, this confounds one's performance. Consequently, I mixed both languages in my oral communication and could only make one clear, fluent sentence in Russian. It made me feel embarrassed and ashamed of myself. This was an eye-opener and a challenge for me as well. That experience forced me to take a second look at my language proficiency, and I realized that if I did not seriously work on my first language, I might lose a very big portion of it. Это было бы разрушительным потерять Русский язык, так-как это все что у меня осталось из прошлого. (It would be devastating to lose the Russian language because it is one of the few things I have left from the cultural life I lived in Latvia).

My journey has taught me that, in any language, if speech is not properly developed, the ability to think collapses and self-expression suffers. It leads not only to emotional stress, but also to the loss of ability to have meaningful dialogue with others. With language proficiency, a person develops self-esteem and confidence in the ability to think, cope with the basic challenges of life, and have the opportunity to be successful and happy within a language community. As bell hooks (2003) posited, "the feeling of being worthy, deserving, entitled to assert our needs and wants, achieving our values, and enjoying the fruits of our efforts" (p. xii) is connected to our voice and speech.

Inherently, I desired to be a language advocate. I enrolled in a credential program focusing on bilingual and multicultural education because I wanted to help children like myself—those who are new to the system, who need support, and who need someone who will understand them and what they are going through in a school system that often does not affirm their identity as immigrants and language learners. The more I became exposed to the American school system, and to different cultures and different students, the more I understood that it was not a mistake that I was enrolled in a program focused on equity issues. Everything happens for a reason. In my teacher education program, I developed a growing consciousness about being a member of an immigrant language minority population, albeit not a member of a minority group that has experienced historic racial, linguistic, and economic oppression *in* the United States. Nonetheless, my studies were very meaningful because I could use my experience to serve my community.

There is an absence of scholarship focused on the Russian population in the United States, particularly in the field of bilingual education, so reflection enables me to learn more about myself and my community while allowing me to think more deeply about identity and culturally responsive language curriculum. When examining my journey throughout college—completing my undergraduate work, a teaching credential, and working towards a master's degree—I came to better understand the evolving person I am. Кто я теперь и что именно определяет меня? К чему я действительно принадлежу? (Who am I now and what really identifies me? Where do I really belong?). Through my education and my professional life as a teacher—my *currere* (Pinar, 2012)—I have begun to answer these questions.

Воспоминания Учебной Программы и Обучения: Краткое Сравнение Между Латвией и США

My memories of schooling in Latvia are quite naturally a comparison between the two school systems I had experienced—what I had taken from my experience in Latvia, and what I was gaining from my experience in becoming a certified teacher in the U.S. For example, the physical school year in Latvia is very similar to the American system; all the schools in the country start September 1st and end in June 1st. Yet this is where the similarities stop.

In Latvia, the typical school day started at eight in the morning and ended at three or four o'clock in the afternoon, with six periods a day. Students can elect additional classes. Every class period from first through twelfth grade is 45 minutes long, with a recess for five to ten minutes between periods.

The typical school week for a student contained 16 school subjects (some of the classes were only once a week, some twice, some every day): math, Russian language, Latvian language, literature, biology, chemistry, physics, economics, ethics, history, art history, philosophy, physical education, shop, art, geography, German language or English language. Also, all schools were bilingual—every student took some classes in Russian and some in Latvian (without Latvian language fluency, people cannot gain citizenship rights in the country; they cannot vote and cannot make any decisions that would affect them). Moreover, Latvia has become an increasingly ethno-linguistically diverse country, thus there exists an intensified discourse on bilingual education (Silova, 2002), and in the Russian-majority state secondary schools, instruction must be at least 60 percent in Latvian (Breggin, 2009).

I never felt privileged or special that I had all those classes; I complained. Yet, I thought everyone needed to take those classes in order to graduate and be admitted to the university. However, I am not proud to say that I came from a very traditional school system where the teacher's авторитет (authority) was not questioned. In terms of our behavior, our teachers were очень требовательные (very strict). For much of the time, the Russian educational structure followed the lines where the teacher did most of the speaking while the students sat quietly at their desks listening and taking notes. However, teachers would encourage us to "think outside of the box" and created time and structure for us to do so, including discussion. We were encouraged to use the information we obtained every day from the news, the community, and other people in order to think critically and to shape our independent thinking. The teachers would try to teach us to think critically about politics and everything we saw in our lives. For example, we would discuss political or life-situations that were occurring at the moment in other countries or our own, and would reflect on the issues, asking what we, as citizens, would change or like to see changed. They would challenge us to have our own opinion, asking whether we agreed or disagreed with what was going on around us.

My literature teachers (5th–12th grade) always encouraged us to connect literature with the situations that were taking place in the world in this present time, including how the issue relates to our own lives; then we would write essays about the topic and its connection to our experiences. My history teacher encouraged us to watch the nightly news. Later we would discuss the stories in class, and share our personal views about the news. Overall, the main goal of our teachers was to teach us to use and process information around us and to be independent and critical thinkers (иметь независимое, критическое мышление). As a student, I neither questioned why the system was designed this way, nor did I wish for anything else because I never knew or thought that there were other ways to structure learning or implement curriculum.

My whole perspective on education and particularly the type that I was exposed to changed tremendously once I was introduced to an American school system during my student teaching experience. I was placed in an ethnically diverse, low-income, Title 1 school where all the programs were cut due to budget problems. From my studies in my credential program, I explored how there are class distinctions in neighborhoods—lower-class people, middle-class people, and upper-class people—which shapes student access to quality schooling. Traditionally, a student is limited to the school in that neighborhood. Within a poverty-ridden neighborhood there may be high-performing schools as well as schools that have substantial economic needs. Latvia, however, is different: middle-class families lived next to very poor people and very rich people. We all attended the same school. We all had the same access to primary education.

Of course later in one's education, a person in Latvia would have greater access to a university if s/he has more money and connections. In Latvia after regular school, those from wealthy and poor families are well-prepared for the best universities in the country, unlike here in America, particularly after a student attends a Title 1 school. Many American children are destined for failure in a system that does not focus on their needs.

When I was student teaching, I was astounded (удивлена) to learn that at my school and throughout the district, the majority of the American public school day was focused on learning language arts and there was little time for all the other subjects. The fact that students only spent 30 minutes on math, or 20 minutes on either science or social studies during a week left me speechless. It shocked me that elementary students did not have music or art classes; it equally astounded me that they neither had a physical education (PE) teacher, nor did the administration even allow time for PE. Some classroom teachers would just take time and teach PE on their own, understanding how crucial physical activities are for children. Yet, it was customary for teachers to "kill and drill" language arts all day, and students would still have difficulties reading and writing because they did not get any support with their other needs; not to mention that they did not get a chance to be well-rounded in their studies.

These conditions have implications in the Russian community. Many Russians are displeased with most public schools, with the level of learning in public schools, but also with the requirement that children attend schools in the district in which they reside (an issue raised by Reklama, 2007). We cannot give up on neighborhood schools because so many children might lose any chance of getting any education. However, neighborhood schools need to be closely examined to determine what works and what doesn't to support student learning for diverse populations; this includes what needs to be changed in order for our children to attain higher education, and/or if they desire an education that simply enables them to be well-rounded in the world at large. Many in the Russian community believe that the American K–12 school system is not good enough and fails its own students, while ironically the university system is known worldwide as the best system. Thus, it feels like both systems contradict each other since the K–12 school system must prepare students for university. The two systems should be more like partners because one cannot survive without another.

Interestingly, I was not able to value my Russian educational experience and curricular journey until I started an American system and understood how well prepared I was, despite my lack of English proficiency. I had earned "A" and "B" grades. The fact that foreign students who come to study in American universities have a better chance to succeed than our own students should make us embarrassed about this situation. Portes and Rumbaut (2001) tell us that educated immigrants are "in a much better competitive position and are more likely to succeed occupationally and economically in their new environment" (p. 46). In my case, when I came to America, I was very well-educated in my first language and academically well-rounded having been educated in a wide range of subjects within an extended curriculum. This proves that knowledge is transferable no matter which language one chooses to continue one's education in. The lesson here is that one can never overlook the major role that background knowledge plays in every student's life.

Unfortunately, not all English Language Learners (ELL) in the United States come to an American school system with both a strong educational background and language support. The lack of academic and language support places ELLs in a very difficult place, particularly when there is not enough time or sincere dedication to developing those language competencies within the structure of the curriculum. It is easy for ELL students to fall behind to the point where it is difficult to catch up. In addition, the strengths of bilingual, bicultural children are often not recognized as talents in the U.S. school system. The ability to translate from one language to another at a young age should be seen as a valuable skill and an asset to build upon.

Because the American school system does not support second-language learning, there is insufficient time given to the skill of bilingualism and cultural knowledge. As such, the language learner is in a learning environment that is shaped by conditions and methods of training based on priorities, attitudes, interests, and demands not necessarily in the best interest of students. Students would really benefit from learning another language, and if English is their second language, they should have an option to keep learning their first language. Yet in California, Proposition 227 supports English learners by providing initial short-term placement for no more than one year in intensive, sheltered English-immersion programs. For children who are not fluent in English, this policy is detrimental; the law, which was approved in the 1990s by California voters, dictates instruction and the types of curricular support given to language learners.

Shockingly, from my personal observations, the American school system works against those who are language minorities and the system is designed for them to fail. The school system works only for a small group of people, and it discriminates and alienates the rest of the groups who cannot be called successful (Ellis, 1995). For example, students who lack the knowledge of the language that is broadly used in their everyday lives may feel unsafe and threatened. In some schools, some students may develop the mentality that, because they are bilingual or since English is not their first language, they are less valued. This sharply contrasts with research that suggests that immigrants who possess knowledge of their mother tongue and the language of the country they are presently living in have a very great chance of succeeding (Portes & Rumbaut, 2001).

As a bilingual kindergarten teacher, I know that Russian children learn conversational English quickly and it seems that the children are still using the Russian language; yet they do not know how to grammatically speak, write, or read in their language. They know some basic phrases that they may use with their parents, survival skills (навыки выживания). Thus, in order for children to become proficient in both languages, they need to be provided with dual-immersion bilingual education. The best scenario would be to have a teacher who speaks both languages fluently, making smooth transitions from one language to another.

In addition, it is also important to create new programs and educational possibilities for students to develop globally, since we live in a world with a mixture of all cultures and traditions. The world we live in is constructed on social interaction; thus, we cannot be separated from each other. We cannot survive by living in isolation; we need each other to interact with and learn from. Moreover, social interaction is fully and completely dependent upon our cultures, history, and customs. When we learn about different cultures and customs, it helps us to enrich our own knowledge and way of living (Vygotsky, 1962, 1978).

Мой Взгляд на Будущее[5]

It is important to teach children methods for exploring their lives through curricular content, to learn about different cultures, and where they fit into the social fabric of America. This is a very difficult job for educators in a climate that focuses

5   My Vision for the Future

on standards only. Yet, students must see their native culture and language as the vehicle for learning, rather than viewing their language as something that holds them back. Educators, too, must integrate all the possible techniques to help their students to succeed and gain self-awareness and self-esteem. Linguistically and culturally diverse students face additional barriers in school, such as a lack of role models or a lack of someone who understands how to meet their everyday learning needs.

Bilingual teachers and educators can help to address these issues and be role models to enable students to become successful. Unfortunately, from my observations, there is a lack of skilled personnel capable of providing programs and support necessary to help those students gain important skills needed for a meaningful and useful education. In order for students to get meaningful lessons that they can use in their everyday lives, they need someone from their own community and with the same background or the same language to become that role model for them.

Moreover, language cannot be taught separately from culture because language cannot be separated from culture. The possibilities of language are boundless. Certainly, a common language supports unity of a society. Yet people who speak the same language and share the same culture typically look for support and understanding from a person with the same or similar background. (Kasatkina, 2009; Nesteruk, 2007). Language, too, is the most powerful cultural indicator that identifies us with our families and communities, and language gives us a sense of belonging. Thus, it is very important to create a deep understanding of inner self or self-consciousness that will help one better understand the world. For instance, "how do we create an oppositional worldview, a consciousness, an identity, a standpoint that exists not only as that struggle which opposes dehumanization but as that movement which enables creative, expansive self-actualization" (hooks, 2003, p. 15)? The only way to understand and respect other cultures and traditions is to understand and respect one's own. Similarly, the only way to understand other people is to understand and love one's self.

I have an opportunity to work in a unique setting with only Russian students that allows me to use the knowledge of my first language to help my students adapt more easily in America. I teach kindergarten in a K–12 charter school, providing home-school and independent study in a variety of configurations that include classroom instruction, lab support, tutoring, and student and family services. My classroom pupils are 100 percent Russian. It is an American charter school that requires that all curriculum and instruction be taught in English language; however, I use and encourage my students to express themselves in Russian. By doing so, I have the chance to use my first language to help affirm my students while building their confidence in both languages. Speaking Russian also helps them to develop as thinkers, and using their first language supports their learning. Furthermore, developing students' love and appreciation for both Russian and English and culture is my goal. This is important because I value my students individually, which includes their ability to think and share their thoughts. Consequently, I do not put an emphasis on the language they choose to use, rather I want them to not fear sharing and participating in class. And if they cannot yet use English, it is okay and expected for them to use Russian. To the contrary, in my previous position in another district, the traditional public school schedule focuses on time, and doesn't allow teachers to include any extracurricular activities or spend extra time focusing on bilingual students. It does not include activities that will allow teachers to reach the broader community. Moreover, language learners require much slower pacing, lots of visuals, hands-on activities that require more work, and flexibility in the schedule.

By and large, I look to incorporate into my teaching the knowledge that I possess though academics and my immigration experiences—knowledge that I can share with my students without losing a sense of who they are, or losing their mother tongue, culture, and traditions. It is also the case that since all my students are Russian, it is important for me to include the backgrounds of the students' knowledge and translate necessary academic information for them. This helps to decrease their stress and anxiety level. I want them to know that I respect and love their first language, which happens to be mine as well. And even though I learned language as an adult and accepted all the difficulties of school life, the feelings of insecurity and not belonging were still there. It does not matter the age when one starts a new journey. There is always the fear of being misunderstood, or laughed at for making a mistake, even being rejected. Никто не хочет испытать это. (No one wants to feel rejected.) That is why, as a teacher, I make it a habit to make my newcomers' lives easier, more enjoyable, and less stressful. So, it is my belief that all students can learn and achieve if we first ensure that basic needs and support systems are in place. Though our core mission and curricular objectives are to emphasize standards-based curriculum, we also privilege the following:

- Providing high-quality curriculum, instructional support, and community and social resources to families and students in our community

- Providing parents and guardians instructional guidance and support

- Identifying student instructional needs and providing individualized education plans

- Assessing student learning style, modality, and achievement

- Providing access to district/social/community services and support as well as mentoring opportunities

We work to create multiple pathways to meet the divergent needs of our student population, such as seeing every child as an individual learner and finding strengths by enriching them through technology, visuals, and manipulatives. In every lesson, I try to use students' background knowledge and connect my lessons to their Russian experience by showing short clips from Russia or pictures that would connect the Russian experience to that of America and more specifically, California. We use songs, dance, and music. We create art projects for every science, social studies, and language arts unit, so students who are visual and kinesthetic learners get to experience learning by making things with their hands or body movements in dance.

Character development and civic engagement is equally important in school and is another part of the curriculum. Recently, students participated in the Homelessness Awareness Project, exploring what factors might cause homelessness. Students learned that despite race, class, or status, we humans should have empathy for each other. We discussed the unpredictability of homelessness and how we never know when we might need help. Students also learned about different cultures and traditions through acquiring new languages, by celebrating the holidays that our country celebrates, by reading stories (such as *The Lorax, I'm Thankful Each Day, April Foolishness, The Christmas Blessing*), by watching movies, and by participating in project-based learning. Projects included a series in which we compared worms and snails, growing them in the classroom and watching them change; and another hands-on project where we learned about water. I focus on science, which is not a priority in most traditional public elementary schools, since literacy and math are privileged disciplinary foci under No Child Left Behind.

Building character is helping others to find their strengths, to know and use their abilities, and taking pride in helping others. These are crucial elements to meeting our objectives in teaching kindergarten. By and large, children tend to enjoy their schooling experience and grow to be confident and happy. One unknown author said, "Only if a child feels right can he think right." I have that saying in big print on my wall to remind me every day what kind of teacher I must be.

I can truly say that my life and my curriculum studies have helped me to realize that I want to be the kind of teacher who helps students to see their bilingualism as their strength, help them to value themselves, and help them to succeed. I want to be the kind of teacher who builds strong relationships with students—ones that give them strength to not be afraid to try and not be the one who breaks. I want them to have a memorable kindergarten experience, in a good way. In the long run, this includes independent thinking along with a healthy dose of critical thinking to raise their self-confidence and self-esteem; tools needed на протяжении всего процесса обучения (throughout the whole learning experience).

References

Breggin, B.(2009). Intercultural language trends at a quadriethnic English-medium university in the Baltics. *Journal of Intercultural Communication*. http://www.immi.se/intercultural/nr21/breggin.htm

Calderon, M. (1998). Adolescent sons and daughters of immigrants: How schools can respond. In K. Borman & B. Scheider (Eds.), *The Adolescent Years: Social Influences and Educational Challenges*. Chicago, IL: University of Chicago Press.

Ellis, C. (1995). The other side of the fence: Seeing black and white in a small, southern town. *Qualitative Inquiry, 1*(2), 147–167.

Fishman, J. A. (1965). Who speaks what language to whom and when? *La Linguistique, 2*, 67–68

Fishman, J. (1991*). Reversing Language Shift: Theoretical and Empirical Foundations of Assistance to Threatened Languages*. Bristol, PA: Multilingual Matters.

Heleniak, T. (2006). Latvia looks west, but legacy of Soviets remains. Migration Information Source. http://www.migrationinformation.org/Profiles/display.cfm?ID=375

hooks, b. (2003). *Teaching Community: A Pedagogy of Hope*. New York: Routledge.

Hornberger, N. H. (2002). Language shift and language revitalization. In R. B. Kaplan (Ed.), *The Oxford Handbook of Applied Linguistics*. Oxford, U.K.: Oxford University Press.

Kasatkina, N. (2009). Analyzing language choice among Russian-speaking immigrants to the United States. Ph.D. dissertation, University of Arizona, United States. Dissertation and Theses: The Humanities and Social Sciences Collection. (Publication No. AAT 3402029).

Nesteruk, O. (2007). Parenting experiences of eastern European immigrant professionals in the US: A qualitative study. Ph.D. dissertation, Louisiana State University. http://etd.lsu.edu/docs/available/etd-03292007-102554/unrestricted/Nesteruk_diss.pdf

Pinar, W. (2012).*What Is Curriculum Theory?* (2nd ed.) New York: Routledge.

Portes, A., & Rumbaut, R. G. (2001). *Legacies: The Story of the Immigrant Second Generation*. Berkeley: University of California Press.

Reklama, R. (2007). How happy Russian immigrants are in the U.S.? Voices that must be heard. http://www.indypressny.org/nycma/voices/280/briefs/briefs_1/

Silova, I. (2002). Bilingual education theater: Behind the scene of Latvian minority education reform. *Intercultural Education,13*(4), 463–476.

Silova, I., & Brehm, W. C. (2010). An American of European education space. *European Educational Research, 9*(4), 457–470.

Silova, I., Moyer, A., Webster, C., & McAllister, S. (2010). Re-conceptualizing professional development of teacher educators in post-Soviet Latvia. *Professional Development in Education, 36* (1–2), 357–371.

Valdes, G., & Figueroa, R. (1994) *Bilingualism and Testing: A Special Case of Bias*. Norwood, NJ: Ablex.

Vygotsky, L.S. (1962). *Thought and Language*. Cambridge, MA: MIT Press.

Vygotsky, L. S. (1978). *Mind in Society: The Development of Higher Psychological Processes*. Cambridge, MA: Harvard University Press.

Zhernokleyeva, L. (2011). *Home Language Maintenance Among Russian American Children*. Lambert Academic Publishing.

CHAPTER FOUR

The "Not-So-Silent" Minority

Scientific Racism and the Need for Epistemological and Pedagogical Experience in Curriculum

NICHOLAS DANIEL HARTLEP (KOH MOIL 고모일)

CRT represents a space of both theoretical and epistemological liberation. (Ladson-Billings, 2003, p. 11)

This chapter describes my development of a dual consciousness as a transracial adoptee and the unique ways that this dual consciousness informs my teaching about race and identity; especially the topics of family structures and transracial student identity, while working with pre-service teachers. To me, my dual consciousness refers to the duality of being perceived as culturally White, but racially/ethnically Asian. However, many understand dual consciousness to be based on the work of W. E. B. Du Bois (1903). This duality—being perceived as culturally White and racially/ethnically Asian—operates while I struggle to assert my own self-actualized identity and voice in a racially hostile society. As an Asian (or Korean) American transracial adoptee, I have to "balance two worlds": the adoptive (my racial "yellowness") and the non-adoptive (my cultural Whiteness) (Garrod & Kilkenny, 2007).

Purpose of This Chapter

Informed by the work of Asian American critical theorists (e.g., see R. S. Chang, 1999; Hartlep, 2010a; Takaki, 1989; Wu, 2003), and in order to describe my development of dual consciousness as a teacher educator who is a Korean American transracial adoptee, my chapter is written using an Asian critical race theory (hereafter AsianCrit), autoethnographic framework (H. Chang, 2008; R. A. Chang, 1993; Gotanda, 1995). The purpose of my chapter is to point out the unique ways that my ability to "read the word and the world" (Freire & Macedo, 1987) informs my teaching and supervision of pre-service teachers at the University of Wisconsin–Milwaukee, a Midwestern "Urban 13" University.[1] Using AsianCrit, the aim of my chapter is the theoretical and epistemological liberation that according to Ladson-Billings (2003) is represented by critical race theory (hereafter CRT). My chapter also tackles how and why the existence of scientific racism necessitates what I am calling "ethnoracial" epistemologies and pedagogies for K–12 teaching and learning.

As a transracial adoptee, I am positioned in a unique place provided that my adoptive parents are, from my perspective, "White liberal racists" (Kailin, 2002). Kailin (1999) defines "White liberal racism" as less obvious and/or covert expressions of racism that are prevalent and present in White "progressive" social circles. My position as a transracial adoptee presents me with the opportunity to have a unique perspective on race and racism given that my upbringing has been in such a colorblind milieu. Since historians have not done an adequate job recording Asian American history, the experiences of Asians in America remain rendered invisible (e.g., see Loewen, 1995; Takaki, 1989). As a Korean in America, this is why I take it as my personal (ethnic and adopted) and professional (clinical) duty to implore the early-childhood pre-service teachers that I work with and supervise in public urban elementary schools to better understand their own epistemologies and biases (Howard, 2006; Malewski & Jaramillo, 2011; Sensoy & DiAngelo, 2011).

What I am calling an "ethnoracial" epistemological or pedagogical approach to teaching and learning, thus, requires teachers to know the history of oppressed, marginalized, and colonized people (Hartlep, 2012; Naber, 2002). I believe that adopted Asians in America constitute such a group of people. Consequently, ethnoracial epistemology and pedagogy necessarily requires that teachers become "cultural citizens" of, and for, their students (e.g., see Hartlep, 2011b; Yoshimura, 1989). Previously I have written that cultural citizenship requires citizens to change their behavior. This means that teachers and students must learn and experience things that they have not experienced due to their inhabitation of segregated settings. White teachers (and also student teachers) must socialize and enter spaces they have never been before. By default, this means that how they teach about family configurations (adoptive, mixed, blended, single-headed, nuclear, step, foster) must change also.

But how does curriculum transformation—turning a colorblind curriculum into ethnoracially sensitive curriculum—occur? Especially when the general public tends to believe that colorblindness is the best approach for all things related

---

1   The Urban 13 is a research-sharing association between 13 public urban universities in major metropolitan areas of the U.S.

to adopted children (e.g., see Likins, 2011)? How do teachers teach (using what pedagogy) about families and identities in culturally sensitive ways? R. S. Chang (1999) asserts that Asians are "disoriented" because of their positioning in the Black-White binary contextualized within a racist world. He is right; but I would argue that adopted Asians who grow up in transracial environments are disoriented and dually conscious because of the mismatch between their identities (self and perceived) and the identities of their adoptive parents (self and perceived). Adopted Asians' disorientation and dual consciousness should cause teachers to teach about family structures and adopted student identities in culturally relevant (Gay, 2010; Ladson-Billings, 2009) and socially just ways (Ayers, 2004). The first step in accomplishing this is that teachers must understand that their own epistemologies are biased, which in turn impacts their teaching and the learning of their students.

Asian Critical Race Theory

There are numerous epistemological walls that prevent White female teachers from using *emic* as opposed to *etic* explanations within their teaching practice. While the emic paradigm appreciates non-White culture, the etic paradigm depreciates non-White culture, favoring materialist and Eurocentric understandings for teaching and learning (Harris, 1976; Padilla, 2004). Indeed, the mainstream curriculum and instruction that is used in public schools tend to rely on etic explanations and understandings. One such example is how schools narrowly focus on achievement (excellence), rather than on equity. Another is the increased standardization of content and curriculum within K–12 education (Swope & Miner, 2000). These things, cumulatively speaking, are based on Eurocentric standards and principles of teaching/learning. Urban public schools are laden with not only Eurocentric tendencies, but also rely on a teaching force that is highly female (Toldson, 2011). This unbalanced teaching force has been written about and addressed as a key issue for anti-racist educators and education (e.g., see Kailin, 2002). Suffice it to say, White female teachers lack experiences and epistemologies allowing them to understand since they lack experiential knowledge (Hayes & Juarez, 2012).

This partially explains why as a male Asian American adoptee, past elementary school teacher, and current assistant professor of educational foundations, I feel that it is incumbent to write from an AsianCrit perspective (R. S. Chang, 1993, 1999; Gee, 1999; Liu, 2009; Teranishi, 2002a). Since the world is racially hostile to people of color and because racism is ordinary, CRT (and AsianCrit) provides marginalized people with tools and methodologies they can use to describe their feelings all while in a safe environment (Chapman, 2011; Delgado & Stefancic, 2001; Dixson & Rousseau, 2006; Taylor, Gillborn, & Ladson-Billings, 2009). Gee (1999) explains the following: "Critical Race Theory, in its purest form, is best understood as the antithesis to the traditional belief in color-blindness" (p. 764). As a result, AsianCrit is important for Asian Americans because the "Black-White" racial binary (Gee, 1999; Wing, 2007; Wu, 2003) prevents their needs from being recognized. Insidiously, while attention is given to issues related to the needs of the African American community, rarely are the needs of Asian Americans acknowledged and/or addressed since society has classified Asians as being "model minorities" (Hartlep, forthcoming-b; S. J. Lee, 1996, 2005).

CRT has been broken down into several hybrid branches (See Figure 1). In this chapter, I elect to use AsianCrit (one branch of CRT), which moves discourse beyond the binary of Black and White, and acts as a counter-narrative to the model minority stereotype (Paek & Shah, 2003; Teranishi, 2010; Yang, 2004).

Figure 1. Branches of Critical Race Theory (Adapted from Yosso, 2005, p. 71)

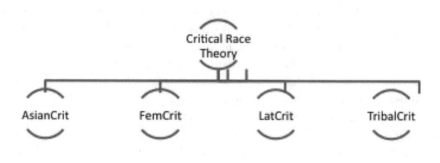

Reports and Rhetoric on Asian Americans

The message of the "model minority" stereotype is that Asian Americans are succeeding in schools (e.g., see S. J. Lee, 1996, 2005; Teranishi, 2002b; Tran & Birman, 2010; Victoria, 2007; Wallitt, 2008; Weaver, 2009; Yang, 2004). At odds with this message, however, are reports that indicate otherwise. The Coalition for Asian American Children and Families' (CACF, 2011) "'We're Not Even Allowed to Ask for Help': Debunking the Myth of the Model Minority" underscores how the model minority myth is a burden for students and conceals Asian Pacific American heterogeneity. Using mainly 2007–2008 data provided to them from the New York City Department of Education (DOE) and the New York State Education Department (NYSED) for over 1,500 schools, much of the report's findings are disaggregated and presented in quantitative and qualitative ways.

In "Asian American and Pacific Islanders. Facts, Not Fiction: Setting the Record Straight," the National Commission on Asian and Pacific Islander Research in Education (CARE, 2008) reports that the model minority label obscures Asian

Americans' true achievement and struggles. The report shares three falsities pertaining to Asian Americans success, while sharing 11 facts that debunk and set the record straight in respect to Asian Americans. Related is Redondo, Aung, Fung, and Yu's (2008) report, "Left in the Margins: Asian American Students and the No Child Left Behind Act" which shares the following: "Contrary to stereotypes that cast Asian Americans as model students of academic achievement, many Asian American students are struggling, failing, and dropping out of schools that ignore their needs" (p. 1).

The Education Trust-West's (2010) "Overlooked and Underserved: Debunking the Asian 'Model Minority' Myth in California Schools" reports on the performance of Asian American students in California, highlighting the incredible diverse set of students. The report sets forth various recommendations for improving the way data are collected and analyzed on and for Asian American communities in California, as well as across the nation.

Despite their publication, the aforementioned reports have done little to quell the belief that Asian Americans are model minorities. For this reason, teaching and learning about Asian Americans' lives is extremely difficult due to the immensity and profundity of political and propagandistic rhetoric. The conservative rhetorical message disseminated through state-sponsored and state-owned news is that public city schools are failing at their mission of educating students. However, if the public would invert this rhetorical message, they would see that the reality is that the original mission of urban schools has always been to "mis-educate" them (Woodson, 1990). City schools are extremely successful at their mis-education mission, leading to social and economic inequality reproduction (Duncan-Andrade & Morrell, 2008). Another conservative message is that Asian Americans are model minorities who are successful and succeed without the use of social welfare programs. Indeed, scientific objectiveness is a tool that is used for the social reproduction of inequality and the perpetuation of the model minority stereotype.

Biased Epistemologies

To me, the scientific method and scientific objectiveness do not exist. I feel that the scientific method is subjective rather than objective based on the fact that its underpinnings are racist. It has been documented that the scientific method rests on Eurocentric and positivistic epistemologies that are biased and that favor a White, middle-class, Judeo-Christian, and androcentric perspective (Scheurich & Young, 1997; Zuberi & Bonilla-Silva, 2008). The scientific method's ontological moorings are biased against minorities, especially poor populations of people of color, holding that science must follow strict and "objective" procedures. Accordingly, the scientific method is driven by the false understanding that objectiveness can be reached by removing biases in the form of subjective researchers and protocols, making it a very colorblind paradigm. CRT, on the other hand, is based more upon a phenomenological- or experiential-based knowledge/understanding paradigm (Parker & Lynn, 2002). CRT emphasizes experiential knowledge, and values existential reasoning over empirical and scientific objectivity. CRT asserts that "to know" both means, and requires, to have experienced the particular phenomenon under discussion. The assertion or belief that there is not one universal human experience runs counter to, and is antithetical to, what colorblindness portends. Colorblindness and a belief in cultural universality refuses to recognize diversity and difference, which produces essentialized, racist, homophobic, and capitalistic lenses in which to read and interpret the world. As a result, unequal and inequitable outcomes are deemed the result of cultural inferiority or a lack of effort (read: victims are blamed).

CRT and "ethnoracial" epistemologies are endarkened, raced, classed, gendered, queered, non-normalized, non-universalized, non-essentialized, while *emic* paradigms return voice to the silenced, muted, and oppressed populations of society (Bernal, 2002; Gordon, 1990; Wright, 2002). Given that ethnoracial epistemologies are conflictive with much of the mainstream discourses, and certainly neoliberal education (Kovacs, 2011), it stands to reason that CRT is frequently at odds with traditional education, which is colorblind.

Curriculum Devoid of Adopted Asian People Like Me

Whenever I examine educational curriculum materials, I always examine them using my lens as an adopted person because being a transracial adoptee has caused me to have unique schooling experiences (R. Lee, 2011). As a result, my assessment or judgment of curriculum emanates from a subjective standpoint about how curriculum should validate the experiences of not only Asian Americans generally, but Asian adopted people specifically. Apple (1995) asks simple, yet extremely profound, questions about schools and their curriculum: "What do schools teach (curriculum)?" "How do they teach it (pedagogy)?" and "Why do they teach it (value)?" Apple arrives at the ultimate question, "Who is best served by this teaching and learning?" These three key questions are important for teachers to ask themselves since it is imperative that teachers understand that the foundation of U.S. education was (and has been) inequitable, and race and class based for non-dominant cultures and people (Mayer, 1997; Sandel, 2012). To me, then, Apple's (1995) questions insist that school curriculum must include the voices of adopted people, certainly not a dominant group.

For me, several questions remain beyond Apple's (1995) four. First is the matter of curriculum: Why should, or should not, Asian Americans and Asian adoptees be represented? If educational curriculum is objective, then why aren't the voices of adoptees heard? Second is the issue of legitimacy: What makes a school curriculum academic, and who is allowed to make such judgment? Third is the question of voice: What people are listened to in the curriculum, and what people go unheard?

Does the school classroom and its curriculum allow for alternative perspectives and/or voices from those unseen and unheard? Last is the debate over a colorblind curriculum, which consists of three parts: (1) What function does a colorblind curriculum play in the reproduction of social marginalization and exclusion? (2) How do adopted Asian Americans fit into a school curriculum that is largely Eurocentric, androcentric, and paternalistic? and (3) How can Asian Americans' presence in curriculum be written off because they are revered as "model minorities," especially in the face of numerous reports that indicate otherwise?

The curriculum that my K–12 teachers followed when I was a student was devoid of adopted Asian people like me and paid little to no attention to Asian Americans at all. Never did I read or hear about what it meant to be an adopted Asian American in my textbooks, or within my school materials. Compounding the colorblind curriculum I received were my adoptive parents who raised me in a colorblind fashion. I lived in, and attended schools, in communities that were predominantly White, which seriously and profoundly shaped my epistemology and my experiences. Being socialized in a colorblind fashion, unfortunately, caused me to internalize racism. Adding insult to injury, up until I was eight years of age, I believed I was White. Not surprisingly, then, most of my friends during my adolescence were White, middle-class or working-class boys and girls. Now as an adult, when reflecting back upon my childhood, it is fairly safe to label my adoptive parents as "liberal racists" (Kailin, 2002). For this reason, being an adopted Asian American was extremely difficult for me because I could not share my feelings about race with my parents who were supposedly not racist (Bonilla-Silva, 2010). As a young person, I felt as though my White parents could not relate to the things that I was experiencing on a day-to-day basis inside and outside school; therefore, I felt as though I had no one to confide in.

One example of racial difficulty was my inability to explain to my adoptive White parents that I was experiencing "microaggressions" and "micro-insults" (Sue, Capodilopa, Torino, & Bucceri, 2007). My intense feelings and experiences and the suffering in silence continued well into my college years (both undergraduate and graduate). Interestingly, during my high school years, I attempted to fit in by being a "model minority" (Tayag, 2011). I would be quiet and unassertive (Tateishi, 2007). I would not voice my concerns and I was passive during social encounters. It was not until I was completing my doctoral coursework that I became aware and actively sought to reject such a stereotypical label. This rejection of the model minority, and my adherence to my own empowerment as an Asian American adoptee caused me to critique not only society and schools (Hartlep, 2010a), but also to read various reports on Asian Americans (Palmer, 1999, 2011). I now understand that the model minority stereotype stymies Asian American students in numerous ways and holds many social and educational implications for Asian American teaching and learning (Weaver, 2009). Colorblind curriculum that is devoid of people like me—adopted Asians—merits transformation and AsianCrit allows Asian Americans to counter-narrate the model minority stereotype. Suffice to say, K–12 curriculum needs to honor the experiences of adopted individuals.

Ethnoracial and Epistemological Pedagogies

As an early childhood teacher in the Milwaukee Public Schools, I frequently "read the word and the world" (Freire & Macedo, 1987). I would not automatically assume that the parents of my first-grade students operated from a culture of poverty as espoused by Payne (2005), but rather, I got to know my students and their families through "authentic" relationships and caring over time (Valenzuela, 1999). Freire and Macedo (1987) write that "Reading the world always precedes reading the word, and reading the word implies continually reading the world" (p. 35). While I was a public K–12 classroom teacher, I had to recognize that many outside forces were vying for my attention and time. These forces were extremely adamant about telling me what was wrong with my students, but as Gorski and Landsman (forthcoming) indicate, "The Poor Aren't the Problem."

Now, as a current teacher educator (professor of educational foundations), my role has changed somewhat. For instance, I believe now that being in the field of teacher education requires me to use a pedagogy that is infused with epistemologies and pedagogies that allow my undergraduate students to begin to learn to "read the word and world." This task is formidable, especially since many of the pre-service teachers that I instruct believe in Payne's (2005) "framework for understanding poverty" and utilize what can only be described as a "pedagogy of poverty" (Haberman, 1991), a "test-prep pedagogy" (Rodríguez, 2011), and/or a "free and reduced pedagogy" (Fasching-Varner & Seriki, 2012). Moreover, the great majority of the pre-service student teachers that I supervise come from White suburban cities and come from families that tend to be different than those that they will teach in urban public schools (Howard, 2006). It is apparent why their perspectives are different and many times at odds with the experiences of urban youth. Much of their biased epistemologies shine through their comments about the requirement that Milwaukee Public School teachers must live in the Milwaukee in order to teach (the residency requirement): many oppose the residency rule, believing that they should not have to live where their students live. This is also apparent in the fact that many of these same pre-service teachers, while in the college of education, live in suburban cities (not in Milwaukee).

Teaching About Families

Du Bois (1903) wrote that a dual consciousness was the "sense of always looking at one's self through the eyes of others, of measuring one's soul by the tape of a world that looks on in amused contempt and pity" (p. 9). As a Korean adoptee, my identity as a transracially adopted person has been colored by the books that I have seen in early/elementary classrooms—both when I was a student and while I was an in-service teacher. One children's book that troubles me is Nina Pellegrini's (1991) *Families Are Different*, which tells the story of Nico[2] and her sister Angel, both adopted girls from Korea.

Both sisters, understandably, look different than their transracial (White) adoptive parents. What disturbs me most about this book is that it romanticizes the reality of being an adopted Asian (Korean) child. The premise of the story is that all families are different, which if argued well, is certainly true. Unfortunately, this story does not discuss other configurations of adoptive families—gay or single-sex families, or gay adoptive families—which alienates children who live in different sets of circumstances. These omissions are not slight, nor are they surprising given the majority of the family books that I have seen in early/elementary classrooms are "adoption-blind" as well as colorblind (e.g., Hoberman & Boutavant, 2009). Most frightening, though, is that Pellegrini's (1991) book maintains the status quo since it is highly paternalistic and insensitive.

Another problematic book that many elementary teachers use for teaching about families that also disturbs me is *We Adopted You, Benjamin Koo* (Walvoord & Shute, 1989), which fulfills the "master narrative" (Payne, 2012; Swartz, 1992) of a loving Korean biological mother abandoning her child in Korea, but who "loved" her son so much that she did it. The book narrates from the perspective of a White savior and is much too idyllic to be accurate or truly sincere. None of these children's books truly tells the side of the story from the biological mother's perspective. It is important to mention that more accurate testimonies of biological Korean mothers who have given up their child(ren) for adoption exist (e.g., see Dorow, 1999; Han, 2010). These texts should be used in the classroom whenever possible.

It is vital that teachers understand why they feel the way they do about a host of educative issues. For instance, why do children learn or fail to learn? Why is there an achievement gap? Why do they teach students the way that they do? Critical reflection is necessary for practitioners because "racist epistemologies are deeply embedded in the meaning-making structures that inform the naturalization of oppression and the normalization of racial inequality in public schools" (Duncan, 2005, p. 102). I am reminded of the Tom Paxton song, "What Did You Learn in School Today," which begins with the lyrics, "What did you learn in school today, dear little boy of mine? What did you learn in school today, dear little boy of mine?" and ends with the following stanzas:

> I learned that Washington never told a lie.
> I learned that soldiers seldom die.
> I learned that everybody's free,
> And that's what the teacher said to me.

---

2   Coincidently some of my friends call me "Nico," derived from a shortening of the Spanish spelling of my name Nicholas, Nícolas.

I learned that policemen are my friends.
I learned that justice never ends.
I learned that murderers die for their crimes
Even if we make a mistake sometimes.

I learned our government must be strong;
It's always right and never wrong;
Our leaders are the finest men
And we elect them again and again.

I learned that war is not so bad;
I learned about the great ones we have had;
We fought in Germany and in France
And someday I might get my chance.

Most of the student teachers whom I have supervised at the University of Wisconsin–Milwaukee have been White women.[3] This is a statistic that is not anomalous, and follows the national trend of White teachers in multiracial schools (e.g., see Kopkowski, 2006; Toldson, 2011), commonly referred to as the "demographic imperative." What I have learned from my family and my White pre-service teachers who are previous students, is that their epistemological and pedagogical experience is one of Whiteness and middle class (Howard, 2006). I will share two such examples that illustrate a lack of awareness.

My Family and Movies

Mainstream media, society, and school marginalize the racial and cultural realities of adopted people (Smith, Jacobson, & Juárez, 2011). Insidiously, adoptees have been depicted harshly and inappropriately by Hollywood. For instance, I watched the movie *Hop* (2011) with my wife and four-year-old daughter this past Easter. In the beginning of the film, there is a scene where a White family is sitting around the dinner table eating and discussing their day's events. During this dinner-table conversation, an "Eastern Asian"-looking young girl utters the following comment: "Mom, Dad, sometimes I think the only reason you adopted me was because my brother is incompetent." This scene, and the little girl's statement, steamed me. When I asked my wife if she caught the intensive scene, she was at a loss for what scene I was referring to. My wife not catching the insensitive scene illustrates to me how adoptees have become the butt of jokes and relegated to comical cinema within children's entertainment. I made an explicit learning opportunity out of this scene for my four-year-old daughter, rewinding the DVD to this particular scene and discussing why not only did it hurt my feelings and marginalize my lived reality, but also how families are diverse. I informed my

3   While I do have two non-White female students (one Japanese and one Mexican), the only reason is because I am bilingual and was intentionally placed as their supervisor. Moreover, the other five supervisors whom I worked with were White women. I am an ethnic and gender "double minority" (Hartlep, forthcoming-a).

daughter that she was an Amerasian, the product of me, an Asian, and her mother, a White American. I also informed her that families came in various forms, constituting many different races, sexual orientations, and marital configurations. I did this because I want my daughter to be conscious of the diversity of family dynamics. This story relates to my own upbringing because my adoptive parents were oblivious to the experiences I faced as a transracial adoptee.

My Students, Reading Across America, and Teaching Other People's Children

"Reading Across America," an initiative on reading created by the National Education Association (NEA), occurs on March 2nd of every year. My student teachers, as many in-service teachers around the United States, celebrated this day through formally recognizing Dr. Seuss's birthday. This ubiquitous children's literature author is universally known. Lesser known by many practicing K–12 teachers, however, was his xenophobic sentiments toward Asians, particularly Japanese.

Minear wrote and published *Dr. Seuss Goes to War: The World War II Editorial Cartoons of Theodor Seuss Geisel* in 1999. Ten years later, in 2009, Schiffrin wrote and published, what was considered to be Minear's sequel and companion: *Dr. Seuss & Co. Go to War: The World War II Editorial Cartoons of America's Leading Comic Artists*. Both books, Minear's (1999) and Schiffrin's (2009), document stereotypical caricatures, and rhetorical, albeit, incendiary commentary, that is anti-Japanese. As an adopted Korean and as a teacher educator, it is my belief that Seuss's political beliefs and previous illustrations ought to be considered when K–12 teachers use his literature. For this reason, I found it morally responsible to email my student teachers background information on Theodor Seuss Geisel (Dr. Seuss). Most of the student teachers were surprised of his past and were unaware of his xenophobic stance.

A second example, like "Reading Across America," illustrates how the student teachers whom I work with lack an understanding that they are privileged. A sense of paternalism pervades the psyches of many of the student teachers I supervise. During one observation, I witnessed how one particular non-White student continued to be ridiculed in front of his classmates by the student teacher. After the lesson, as I commonly do, I debriefed and had a feedback session with the student teacher. I asked her about Tu (a pseudonym) and why she continued to marginalize and ridicule him. She pushed back, and dismissed my feedback and what I observed. I responded to her rebuttals by giving examples of why I felt she did not serve his educational needs. A series of exchanges were made about how she taught and treated Tu. She relented and eventually began to cry as she felt guilty of bad teaching.

This illustrated to me that she was unaware of her own hidden assumptions, biases, and privilege. I base this on two insensitive comments that she made to me when resisting my constructive criticism. Statement 1: "Well, you know Tu is a refugee. They don't even know how old he is because in his culture they don't have records like we do in the U.S. All I know is that he is not a first grader." Statement 2: "Well, the cooperating teacher does that [read: reprimands and punishes him]. If he cannot sit still and pay attention, he knows that he has to lay his head on his desk and be quiet."

In response to Michelle's (a pseudonym) first statement, I asked her if she knew what country Tu was from. She did not know. I asked her to do some investigating and find out. At the time of writing this chapter, I have still not been notified by Michelle. Michelle's statement was wholly paternalistic, as she does not know anything about Tu's culture, yet is very willing to demonize him through faulty comparisons with her culture. By minimizing Tu's culture and critiquing it as inferior, her status as a White women was made superior, damaging the teacher-student relationship. Her unreflective thoughts are apparent.

In regard to Michelle's second statement, I informed her that "teacher-centered pedagogy" is much more concerned with student compliance and subordination than it is with student learning. I reminded her that UW–Milwaukee, as an urban teacher preparation program, has strict guidelines about professionalism and culturally relevant best practices. I told her that if I saw her treat my Amerasian daughter, who is a kindergartener, in a similar way, that I would try and get her fired. I asked Michelle if she would want the teacher of her child to treat and teach her in such a way. She replied almost immediately, no. I reminded her of Delpit's (1995) *Other People's Children* and asked her why she had an uncritical acceptance of the pedagogical and professional practices of her cooperative teacher and did not cultivate her own. I used a problem-posing technique and centralized race and her White privilege during our debriefing session. I asked her if she would be more critical of her cooperating teacher's teaching practice if she was an Asian or African American. She could not answer my question. She did answer, though, that she would try and teach as though her students were her own children, next time.

Concluding Thoughts

It was my intention to use an AsianCrit autoethnographic framework in my chapter in order to produce counter-stories that show that Asian Americans are not model minorities, that colorblind curriculum is problematic, that the scientific method is not objective, and that scientific racism is a reason that ethnoracial epistemologies are necessary in curriculum and instruction. As a result, I feel curriculum must be transformed since it does not adequately meet the needs of Asian Americans and Asian American adoptees. Scholarship informs teachers that Asian stereotypes abound at an unremitting rate in children's literature (see, e.g., Aoki, 1981; Interracial Books for Children, 1976; Salvador-Burris, 1978), which impacts the education of all students, but especially Asian Americans. Unless teachers actively resist using curriculum that is adoption blind and colorblind, they are complicit in the subordination and mis-education of their students. As an adopted person, I actively resist problematic curriculum because I do not want to re-victimize the children and students I serve. Curriculum that is socially just and justice oriented should serve as a "window" and a "mirror" for students. According to Style (1988), curriculum must "function both as *Window* and as *Mirror*, in order to reflect and reveal most accurately both a multicultural world and the student herself or himself" (p. 6, italics added).

As an Asian American adoptee, my dual consciousness informs how I teach and what I feel is important to teach. Since adoptee voices are not heard, nor are ethnoracial epistemologies/pedagogies valued (Lowe, 2001), curriculum remains Eurocentric and hetero-normative (Adams, 2010). Not only does curriculum need to be transformed, the teaching force needs to reflect the students taught in our nation's schools. In order to build our nation's Asian American teaching force, more programs like Concordia University-Saint Paul's Southeast Asian Teacher (SEAT) Program[4] are necessary. Unbalanced education is a byproduct of a largely White and female teaching force as indicated by the demographic imperative. As a transracial Korean adoptee professor of educational foundations who works with predominantly White women, it is noticeable and perceptible, to me, that "ethnoracial" epistemologies are necessary to appropriately transform curriculum and teacher practice. In order for this to occur, teachers must begin to become "cultural citizens" (Hartlep, 2011b) and acknowledge and be acquainted with their Whiteness (Hayes & Hartlep, forthcoming).

Acknowledgments
Many thanks to Subini Annamma for reading various iterations of this chapter.

References

Adams, M. (2010). *Readings for Diversity and Social Justice* (2nd ed). London: Routledge.

Aoki, E. M. (1981). Are you Chinese? Are you Japanese? Or are you just a mixed-up kid? Using Asian American children's literature. *The Reading Teacher, 34*(4), 382–385.

Apple, M. W. (1995). *Education and Power* (2nd ed.). New York: Routledge.

Ayers, W. (2004). *Teaching the Personal and the Political: Essays on Hope and Justice.* New York: Teachers College Press.

Bernal, D. D. (2002). Critical race theory, Latino critical theory, and critical raced-gendered epistemologies: Recognizing students of color as holders and creators of knowledge. *Qualitative Inquiry, 8*(1), 105–126.

Bonilla-Silva, E. (2010). *Racism without racists: Colorblind racism and the persistence of racial inequality in the United States.* Lanham, MD: Rowman & Littlefield.

CACF (Coalition for Asian American Children and Families). (2011). *"We're not even allowed to ask for help": Debunking the myth of the model minority.* New York: Pumphouse Projects. http://cacf.org/resources_publications.html#We'reNotEvenAllowed

Chang, H. (2008). *Autoethnography as Method.* Walnut Creek, CA: Left Coast Press.

4   http://www.csp.edu/academics/areas-of-study/teacher-education/post-bacc/seat/

Chang, R. S. (1993). Toward an Asian American legal scholarship: Critical race theory, post-structuralism, and narrative space. *California Law Review, 81*(5), 1243–1323.

Chang, R. S. (1999). *Disoriented: Asian Americans, Law, and the Nation-State.* New York: New York University Press.

Chapman, T. K. (2011). Critical race theory. In S. Tozer (Ed.), *Handbook of Research in the Social Foundations of Education* (pp. 220–232). New York: Routledge.

Delgado, R., & Stefancic, J. (2001). *Critical Race Theory: An Introduction.* New York: New York University Press.

Delpit, L. D. (1995). *Other People's Children: Cultural Conflict in the Classroom.* New York: New Press.

Dixson, A. D., & Rousseau, C. K. (Eds.). (2006). *Critical Race Theory in Education: All God's Children Got a Song.* New York: Routledge.

Dorow, S. (Ed.). (1999). *I Wish for You a Beautiful Life: Letters from the Korean Birth Mothers of Ae Ran Won to Their Children.* St. Paul, MN: Yeong & Yeong Book Co.

Du Bois, W. E. B. (1903). *The Souls of Black Folk.* Chicago: A.C. McClurg & Co.

Duncan, G. A. (2005). Critical race ethnography in education: Narrative, inequality and the problem of epistemology. *Race Ethnicity and Education, 8*(1), 93–114.

Duncan-Andrade, J. M. R., &Morrell, E. (2008). *The Art of Critical Pedagogy: Possibilities for Moving from Theory to Practice in Urban Schools.* New York: Peter Lang.

Education Trust-West. (2010). Overlooked and underserved: Debunking the Asian "model minority" myth in California schools. Oakland, CA: The Education Trust. http://www.edtrust.org/west/publication/overlooked-and-underserved-debunking-the-asian-%E2%80%9Cmodel-minority%E2%80%9D-myth

Fasching-Varner, K., & Seriki, V. D. (2012). Moving beyond seeing with our eyes wide shut: A response to "There is no culturally responsive teaching spoken here." *Democracy & Education, 20*(1), 1–6. http://democracyeducationjournal.org/cgi/viewcontent.cgi?article=1049&context=home

Freire, P., & Macedo, D. (1987). *Literacy: Reading the Word and the World.* New York: Continuum.

Garrod, A., & Kilkenny, R. (Eds.). (2007). *Balancing Two Worlds: Asian American College Students Tell Their Life Stories.* Ithaca, NY: Cornell University Press.

Gay, G. (2010). *Culturally Responsive Teaching: Theory, Research, and Practice* (2nd ed.). New York: Teachers College Press.

Gee, H. (1999). Beyond Black and White: Selected writings by Asian Americans within the critical race theory movement. *St. Mary's Law Journal, 30*(3), 759–799.

Gordon, B. M. (1990). The necessity of African American epistemology for educational theory and practice. *Journal of Education, 172*(3), 88–106.

Gorski, P., & Landsman, J. (Eds.). (Forthcoming). *"The Poor" Aren't the Problem: Insisting on Class Equity in Schools.* Sterling, VA: Stylus.

Gotanda, N. (1995). Critical legal studies, critical race theory and Asian American studies. *Amerasia Journal, 21*(1&2), 127–135.

Haberman, M. (1991). The pedagogy of poverty versus good teaching. *Phi Delta Kappan, 73*(4), 290–294.

Han, S. (Ed.). (2010). *Dreaming a World: Korean Birth Mothers Tell Their Stories.* St. Paul, MN: Yeong & Yeong Book Co.

Harris, M. (1976). History and significance of the emic/etic distinction. *Annual Review of Anthropology, 5,* 329–350.

Hartlep, N. D. (2010a). *Going Public: Critical Race Theory and Issues of Social Justice.* Mustang, OK: Tate.

Hartlep, N. D. (2010b). Predicting eugenics and education: Rethinking an educational fault line. *Academic Exchange Extra.* http://www.unco.edu/ae-extra/2010/3/hartlep.html

Hartlep, N. D. (2011a). Review of *The Myth of the Model Minority: Asian Americans Facing Racism* by Rosalind Chou & Joe Feagin. *Critical Questions in Education, 2*(2), 105–107.

Hartlep, N. D. (2011b, Summer). Cultural citizenship, not color-blindness: A Korean adoptee's plea to parents. *Korean Quarterly, 14*(4), 18.http://www.koreanfocus.org/wp-content/uploads/2011/10/Cultural-citizenship-not-color-blindness-Nicholas-Hartlep.pdf

Hartlep, N. D. (2012). A "lost generation": The inadequacy of love in colorblind Korean transracial adoptive families. *Korean Quarterly, 15*(2), 17–19.

Hartlep, N. D. (Forthcoming-a). A "double minority": Insights from an Asian American male early-childhood teacher educator. In N. E. Johnson & S. A. Wilson (Eds.), *Teaching to Difference*. New York: Peter Lang.

Hartlep, N. D. (Forthcoming-b). *The Model Minority Stereotype: Demystifying Asian American Success*. Charlotte, NC: Information Age Publishing.

Hayes, C., & Hartlep, N. D. (Eds.). (Forthcoming). *Unhooking from Whiteness: The Key to Dismantling Racism in the United States*. Boston, MA: Sense Publishers.

Hayes, C., & Juárez, B. (2012). There is no culturally responsive teaching spoken here: A critical race perspective. *Democracy & Education, 20*(1), 1–14.

Hill, T. (Director). (2011). *Hop* [motion picture]. Los Angeles, CA: Universal Pictures.

Hoberman, M. A., & Boutavant, M. (2009). *All Kinds of Families!* New York: Little, Brown.

Howard, G. R. (2006). *We Can't Teach What We Don't Know: White Teachers, Multiracial Schools* (2nd ed). New York: Teachers College Press.

Interracial Books for Children. (1976). Asian Americans in children's books. *Interracial Books for Children Bulletin, 7*(2&3), 1-39. http://www.eric.ed.gov/PDFS/ED123315.pdf

Kailin, J. (1999). How white teachers perceive the problem of racism in their schools: A case study in "liberal" Lakeview. *Teachers College Record, 100*(4), 724–750.

Kailin, J. (2002). *Antiracist Education: From Theory to Practice*. Lanham, MD: Rowman & Littlefield.

Kopkowski, C. (2006). It's there: Talk about it. *NEA Today, 25*(3), 26–31.

Kovacs, P. E. (2011). *The Gates Foundation and the Future of U.S. "Public" Schools*. New York: Routledge.

Ladson-Billings, G. (2003). It's your world, I'm just trying to explain it: Understanding our epistemological and methodological challenges. *Qualitative Inquiry, 9*(5), 1–12.

Ladson-Billings, G. (2009). *The Dreamkeepers: Successful Teachers of African American Children* (2nd ed.). San Francisco, CA: Jossey-Bass Publishers.

Lee, R. (2011). Same and different: Supporting transracially adopted Asian Americans. *Independent School, 70*(2), 74–81.

Lee, S. J. (1996). *Unraveling the "Model Minority" Stereotype: Listening to Asian American Youth*. New York: Teachers College Press.

Lee, S. J. (2005). *Up Against Whiteness: Race, School, and Immigrant Youth*. New York: Teachers College Press.

Likins, P. (2011, November 19). Celebrate adoption and color-blindness of the open heart. *USA Today*. http://usatoday30.usatoday.com/USCP/PNI/NEWS/2011-11-19-PNI1119opi-my-turn-likinsPNIBrd_ST_U.htm

Liu, A. (2009). Critical race theory, Asian Americans, and higher education: A review of research. *InterActions: UCLA Journal of Education and Information Studies, 5*(2), 1–12.

Loewen, J. W. (1995). *Lies My Teacher Told Me: Everything Your American History Textbook Got Wrong*. New York: New Press.

Lowe, L. (2001). Epistemological shifts: National ontology and the new Asian immigrant. In J. Chuh & K. Shimakawa (Eds.), *Orientations: Mapping Studies in the Asian Diaspora* (pp. 267–176). Durham, NC: Duke University Press.

Malewski, E., & Jaramillo, N. (Eds.). (2011). *Epistemologies of Ignorance in Education.* Charlotte, NC: Information Age Publishing.

Mayer, S. E. (1997). *What Money Can't Buy: Family Income and Children's Life Chances.* Cambridge, MA: Harvard University Press.

Minear, R. H. (1999). *Dr. Seuss Goes to War: The World War II Editorial Cartoons of Theodor Seuss Geisel.* New York: The New Press.

Naber, N. C. (2002). So our history doesn't become your future. *Journal of Asian American Studies, 5*(3), 217–242.

National Commission on Asian American and Pacific Islander Research in Education (CARE). (2008). Asian Americans and Pacific Islanders. Facts, not fiction: Setting the record straight. http://professionals.collegeboard.com/profdownload/08-0608-AAPI.pdf

Padilla, A. M. (2004). Quantitative methods in multicultural education research. In J. A. Banks & C. A. Banks (Eds.), *Handbook of Research on Multicultural Education* (2nd ed.) (pp. 127–145). San Francisco, CA: Jossey-Bass.

Paek, H. J., & Shah, H. (2003). Racial ideology, model minorities, and the "not-so-silent partner": Stereotyping of Asian Americans in U.S. magazine advertising. *Howard Journal of Communications, 14*(4), 225–243.

Palmer, J. D. (1999). From the "yellow peril" to the "model minority": Asian American stereotypes from the 19th century to today. *Midwest History of Education Journal, 26*(1), 33–42.

Palmer, J. D. (2011). *The Dance of Identities: Korean Adoptees and Their Journey Toward Empowerment.* Honolulu, HI: University of Hawai'i Press.

Parker, L., & Lynn, M. (2002). What's race got to do with it? Critical race theory's conflicts with and connections to qualitative research methodology and epistemology. *Qualitative Inquiry, 8*(1), 7–22.

Payne, C. M. (2012). Countering the master narratives: The "why?" of education for liberation. *Voices in Urban Education, 34,* 6–14. http://www.annenberginstitute.org/VUE/countering-the-master-narratives-the-%E2%80%9Cwhy%E2%80%9D-of-education-for-liberation

Payne, R. K. (2005). *A Framework for Understanding Poverty.* Highlands, TX: aha! Process.

Pellegrini, N. (1991). *Families Are Different.* New York NY: Holiday House.

Redondo, B., Aung, K. M., Fung, M., & Yu, N. W. (2008). Left in the margins: Asian American students and the No Child Left Behind Act. New York: Asian American Legal Defense and Education Fund. http://www.aaldef.org/docs/AALDEF-EE-Left-in-the-Margins-NCLB-2008.pdf

Rodríguez, L. F. (2011). Challenging test-prep pedagogy: Urban high school students educate pre-service teachers using liberatory pedagogy. In B. D. Schultz (Ed.), *Listening to and Learning from Students: Possibilities for Teaching, Learning, and Curriculum* (pp. 87–100). Charlotte, NC: Information Age Publishing.

Salvador-Burris, J. (1978). Changing Asian American stereotypes. *Bridge, 6*(1), 29–35.

Sandel, M. J. (2012). *What Money Can't Buy: The Moral Limits of Markets.* New York: Farrar, Straus & Giroux.

Scheurich, J. J., & Young, M. D. (1997). Coloring epistemologies: Are our research epistemologies racially biased? *Educational Researcher, 26*(4), 4–16.

Schiffrin, A. (2009). *Dr. Seuss & Co. Go to War: The World War II Editorial Cartoons of America's Leading Comic Artists.* New York: The New Press.

Sensoy, O., & DiAngelo, R. (2011). *Is Everyone Really Equal?* New York: Teachers College Press.

Smith, D. T., Jacobson, C. K., & Juárez, B. G. (2011). *White Parents, Black Children: Experiencing Transracial Adoption.* Lanham, MD: Rowman & Littlefield.

Style, E. (1988). Curriculum as window and mirror. In M. Crocco (Ed.), *Listening for All Voices: Gender Balancing the Social Curriculum* (pp. 6–12). Summit, NJ: Oak Knoll School Monograph.

Sue, D. W., Capodilopa, C. M., Torino, G. C., & Bucceri, J. M. (2007). Racial microaggressions in everyday life: Implications for clinical practice. *American Psychologist, 62*(4), 271–286.

Swartz, E. (1992). Emancipatory narratives: Rewriting the master script in the school curriculum. *The Journal of Negro Education, 61*(3), 341–355.

Swope, K., & Miner, B. (Eds.). (2000). *Failing Our Kids: Why the Testing Craze Won't Fix Our Schools*. Milwaukee, WI: Rethinking Schools.

Takaki, R. T. (1989). *Strangers From a Different Shore: A History of Asian Americans*. Boston: Little, Brown.

Tateishi, C. A. (2007). Why are the Asian-American kids silent in class? Taking a chance with words. *Rethinking Schools, 22*(2), 20–23.

Tayag, M. (2011, Spring). Great expectations: The negative consequences and policy implications of the Asian American "model minority" stereotype. *Stanford Journal of Asian American Studies, 4*, 23–31.

Taylor, E., Gillborn, D., & Ladson-Billings, G. (Eds.). (2009). *Foundations of Critical Race Theory in Education*. New York: Routledge.

Teranishi, R. T. (2002a). Asian Pacific Americans and critical race theory: An examination of school racial climate. *Equity & Excellence in Education, 35*(2), 144–154.

Teranishi, R. T. (2002b). The myth of the super minority: Misconceptions about Asian Americans. *The College Board Review, 195*, 16-21.

Teranishi, R. T. (2010). *Asians in the Ivory Tower: Dilemmas of Racial Inequality in American Higher Education*. New York: Teachers College Press.

Toldson, I. A. (2011). Diversifying the United States' teaching force: Where are we now? Where do we need to go? How do we get there? *The Journal of Negro Education, 80*(3), 183–186.

Tran, N., & Birman, D. (2010). Questioning the model minority: Studies of Asian American academic performance. *Asian American Journal of Psychology, 1*(2), 106–118.

Valenzuela, A. (1999). *Subtractive Schooling: U.S.-Mexican Youth and the Politics of Caring*. Albany: State University of New York Press.

Victoria, N. A. (2007). A+ does not mean all Asians: The model minority myth and implications for higher education. *The Vermont Connection, 28*, 80–88.

Wallitt, R. (2008). Cambodian invisibility: Students lost between the "achievement gap" and the "model minority." *Multicultural Perspectives, 10*(1), 3–9.

Walvoord, L., & Shute, L. (1989). *We Adopted You, Benjamin Koo*. Niles, IL: A. Whitman.

Weaver, S. (2009). Perfect in America: Implications of the model minority myth on the classroom. *Colleagues, 4*(2), 8–11.

Wing, J. Y. (2007). Beyond black and white: The model minority myth and the invisibility of Asian American students. *Urban Review, 39*(4), 455–487.

Woodson, C. G. (1990). *The Mis-Education of the Negro*. Trenton, NJ: Africa World Press.

Wright, H. K. (2002). An endarkened feminist epistemology? Identity, difference and the politics of representation in educational research. *Qualitative Studies in Education, 16*(2), 197–214.

Wu, F. H. (2003). *Yellow: Race in American Beyond Black and White*. New York: Basic Books.

Yang, K. (2004). Southeast Asian American children: Not the "model minority." *Future of Children, 14*(2), 127–133.

Yoshimura, E. (1989). How I became an activist and what it all means to me. *Amerasia Journal, 15*(1), 106–109.

Yosso, T. J. (2005). Whose culture has capital? A critical race theory discussion of community cultural wealth. *Race Ethnicity and Education, 8*(1), 69–91.

Zuberi, T., & Bonilla-Silva, E. (2008). *White Logic, White Methods: Racism and Methodology*. Lanham, MD: Rowman & Littlefield.

CHAPTER FIVE

Nrhiav Kuv Lub Suab, a.k.a Finding My Voice

A Hmong Student-Teacher's Curriculum Story

KAYING HER

Family Influences and Lessons

As far back as I can remember, my parents have always said "UvUv, nthiaj li tua zoo" (Bear with it, good things will come). This is the mantra my parents would use whenever my seven siblings or I would encounter any problem, disagreement, or mistreatment in school, such as name calling by other kids and problems in the larger society. Even as a child when I experienced difficulties, each time I heard these words from my parents, I would think: "What do they *know*? They're not the ones going through it." Yet though I thought this, I still listened and practiced what my parents advised because they were older. Wiser. My parents are peaceful people who don't want trouble from anyone, so they taught my seven siblings and me to prevent and avoid altercations. My parents raised me to honor and value my elders—my culture—so my parents' advice must carry wisdom.

My parents based their mantra on the way they lived their lives. They lived in Laos during the Vietnam War; the Laotian countryside became battlefields for skirmishes between Hmong soldiers (supported by American Central Intelligence agents) and the communist Laotians (supported by Vietnamese), which became known as the Secret War. My parents learned to survive by bearing all hardships and mistreatments that came their way by not speaking. This was how they survived in Laos, and after fleeing Laos to become refugees in Thailand. Since coming to America and living in the country for over 20 years, my parents still believe that not speaking or voicing an opinion is the best way to survive. They believe this because that is how they survived, and that was their best advice for their children. My parents' mantra followed me throughout my 16 years of schooling and throughout other aspects of my life, such as in the workplace and relationships. However, at one point I did not feel I would need their advice, "UvUv, nthiaj li tua zoo" (Bear with it, good things will come). Little did I know how right I would be in thinking how little my parents' way of thinking reflected the strategy needed for dealing with some of the people around me, or within the society in which we now live. I will explain.

Curricular Field Placement for Teaching

In 2011, I enrolled into a teaching credential program (bilingual focused) at a state university. Here, teacher candidates are instructed in teaching students of diverse ethnic and cultural backgrounds, bilingual students, and students who are English learners. How perfect it was that after 16 years of schooling from elementary through college, I had finally found a place where I felt like I belonged.

My cohort was small, consisting of 16 pre-service teachers: one male and 15 female students, including myself. We were definitely a multicultural group with students of Egyptian, Mexican, El Salvadorian, Vietnamese, Mien, African American, Caucasian, and Hmong backgrounds. I was also working with a co-ordinator (Dr. Smith) who understood me; I was taking classes with a cohort-turned-friends who accepted me for who I am, a petite Hmong woman who loved watching Spanish telenovelas (soap operas), though I do not understand them; and I was enrolled in a department where the mission statement articulates an ideal in which I believed:

> Advocate a social justice perspective across schools, communities and political contexts. Work towards preparing students to take an active role in the reconstruction of the education system into one that is equitable for students from linguistically and culturally diverse backgrounds.

And I loved this feeling of being a part of a group where diversity and being unique was embraced and show cased. This was evidenced through our community interaction: we were a close bunch who ate lunch together and walked together to every class.

The feeling here was unlike my early-elementary school experiences where I initially felt out of place. At that stage of my life, the teachers wanted to hear me regurgitate from their lectures and were not interested in what I really thought or felt. As an English-language learner (EL), I was also a quiet student. This meant that at times, I also felt that my cultural background and experiences could not contribute to the topics taught since everything was American-focused and American culture only. That eventually shifted.

In addition, I have always wanted to be a teacher, shaped by the influence of my fourth-grade teacher who noticed my struggles, particularly with reading and who made the extra effort to support me with English language development (ELD). Since that time, I saw becoming a teacher as my way of paying it forward, making a difference in someone else's life. Now in my credential program, I could share my cultural heritage and identity related to topics discussed in class, including how to incorporate diversity into the curriculum. It was also liberating to be able to share my thoughts and ideas *aloud* and with my cohort.

Moreover, I was thrilled because it was the final semester in the credential program and I was finally going to specifically study methods of teaching English learners (ELs). This was a special feature of the department I was enrolled in, one that the *regular* department (a euphemism for mainstream education department in the college) did not have. Moreover, many schools and colleges of education do not adequately prepare future and practicing teachers to teach language-minority students (Nieto, 2009). So this class would help me to better help my students, especially in a nation where there are many languages and cultures. Diaz-Rico (2008) further states that teachers who make attempts to build on students' prior language expertise will model expert learning, so I was ready to attempt this. As such, I felt fortunate to have the coursework and the fieldwork hours because it would help me to develop lessons that would enable all my students to be equally successful.

The Field Placement

My cohort had class on Mondays and classroom fieldwork on Thursdays. The first Monday's class filled me with inspiration and ideas about ways to adapt the standardized curriculum to an appropriate curriculum using ELD methods and strategies such as visual aids, sentence frames, gestures, and body language (total physical response) to meet my students' needs and support their language development. I was eager to engage students in fun learning activities and games (such as rhyming words and bingo) to build interest and use the English language. I was also full of anticipation for my fieldwork because I would have a chance to actually teach ELs with the knowledge I acquired from class and my knowledge from lived experience. Here would be an opportunity to show my skills in adapting the lessons in order to provide cognitive academic language instruction (Collier, 1987; Cummins, 1981; Diaz-Rico, 2008) that would ensure student success with learning English language forms and functions (Diaz-Rico, 2008).

I was also excited about the possibility of serving as a role model due to my positionality as a former EL student who learned English and went to college. I wanted my students to know that it is positive to be bilingual because you have two unique languages and cultures that will benefit you in the future, especially in the workplace.

The First Day

That first day at my assigned placement at the dual-language immersion elementary school was a new experience. The course instructor chose this elementary school to provide a placement to complete the fieldwork requirements to work with ELs. Yet, two things that I noticed instantly were that the majority of the student population was of Hispanic background, as well as the majority of the faculty and staff.

As I looked around, I felt a bit concerned because the methods course I was enrolled in was for English learners (ELs)in general, yet we would be working at a Spanish-immersion school. So I began to ask myself questions:

- What about the other non-Spanish ELs?

- How will I and my classmates know if we can teach other ELs students if there is no diversity?

- Why were we required to teach at this school and not an elementary school that had diverse groups of ELs?

Though I raised these questions in my head, I felt that I could not ask them of my placement coordinator because she had been using this school for her course's fieldwork for years.

As school started, Dr. Smith, the course instructor and fieldwork supervisor, greeted our cohort in a room onsite that was designated for our use at the school. The cohort was then divided into five groups of three and assigned to different elementary grade levels and classrooms for student teaching. Elementary students were grouped by developmental levels: beginner, intermediate, advanced English language development (ELD), and they would work on the curriculum at their levels. Along with my cohort-mates Angela and Esmeralda, I was assigned to teach ELD for a first- through third-grade cluster group of students based on their English proficiency levels:

Level 1: Beginning/Preproduction

Level 2: Beginning/Production

Level 3: Intermediate

Angela, Esmeralda, and I were assigned to work with a classroom teacher named Ms. Lopez. Upon arrival to Ms. Lopez's classroom, we introduced ourselves as state university students who would be working with her in her classroom. Then we individually gave Ms. Lopez our names, which she acknowledged with a smile and a nod. She then informed us that we would be able to observe that day's class for ELD.

While she was informing us where we were to sit for the day's observation, she spoke Spanish only, which caused me to be a bit confused. Why was Ms. Lopez speaking in Spanish only; where is the English? I did not understand. I thought to myself, any second now she will switch to English. I suppose I expected that she would see the confused look I had and repeat her words for me in English, so I did not say anything. Yet, this did not happen; she continued to speak in Spanish.

All along, Angela and Esmeralda nodded their heads and took in what Ms. Lopez said while I politely smiled, waiting. I looked to Angela then Esmeralda, but they just smiled back at me. And Ms. Lopez, while she spoke, did not even look at me. It was so weird that she was seemed to ignore me, like I was not even there. I was alert and listening, wasn't I?

Later, I asked Angela what Ms. Lopez said because I didn't understand her instructions, and Angela informed me that Ms. Lopez would like us to observe her ELD lesson from the back table. Angela added that Ms. Lopez would like us to note her use of sentence frames and repetitions of the dialogue with each student.

"Was that all Ms. Lopez said?" I asked.

"Yes," Angela replied.

I accepted the notion that Angela shared all the information I missed. Angela, Esmeralda, and I then found our way to the back of the room as the homeroom students left, and while ELD students entered into the classroom.

During the observation, Ms. Lopez taught the students how to greet and ask other how they were feeling. She did not interact with Angela, Esmeralda or me, which provided me time to reflect on the earlier events. I glanced at Angela and Esmeralda, both of whom were clearly enjoying the lesson and were quietly discussing the teaching strategies they observed.

Withdrawing myself from the present, I questioned further:

- Why am I completely excluded from Ms. Lopez's instruction?

- Am I supposed to know Spanish since this is a Spanish–English immersion school?

I suddenly did not feel welcome in the classroom at all. How come? I questioned that maybe my feelings were unfounded—it was just me, perhaps, because Angela and Esmeralda looked fine; they were smiling and enjoying the lesson. And the Spanish instruction.

After the ELD lesson, the homeroom students returned to class. The students read silently as Ms. Lopez approached the back table. She stood next to me, facing the three of us and started talking. She spoke in Spanish again.

Again, I did not understand a word she was saying; but it seemed very important and informative by the way Angela and Esmeralda replied in Spanish while nodding their heads. And Ms. Lopez continued to look back and forth toward Angela and Esmeralda as she spoke, while I stood there, right next to her, looking at her.

"UvUv, nthiaj li tua zoo"
(Bear with it, good things will come)

To raise critical consciousness means first of all to notice the linguistic and cultural imbalance and contradictions in everyday social and cultural practices that are taken for granted, and to critically reflect on the values attached to those practices. (Kubota, 1998, p. 303, as cited in Diaz-Rico, 2008)

> Attitudes toward second-language teaching and usage in schools overlap with other kinds of attitudes, such as…racial prejudice against speakers of other languages. (Diaz-Rico, 2008, p. 31)

I may have felt shy or uncomfortable in classrooms throughout elementary school and even into college, but I had never felt like I didn't even exist before. This feeling of alienation was so new to me that I was not sure what the feeling was. Suddenly, I was fuming, simmering in my anger as I stood in that classroom, in my student-teaching field placement, completely ignored, alienated, and excluded from the conversation that was taking place right before me; with not a single word offered to me and certainly not one word that I understood. I felt inhuman, unworthy because there I was next to Ms. Lopez, right in front of her; yet, she did not even look or acknowledge my presence. I felt crushed and close to tears. Ms. Lopez then turned her attention back to the elementary school students, signifying the end of our observation and debriefing.

- Why was this happening?
- Was it so hard to acknowledge my presence, even though I may not understand the dialogue taking place?
- And why was I hurt and close to tears when no one actually said anything bad or did anything bad to me physically?

These questions compounded as I hurried back to the safety of our designated classroom. Furthermore, though I felt ostracized, an outcast from the circle, I was overwhelmed by the feeling that I should not say anything because it was not my place, along with the thought that speaking would be negative for me. I thought of my parents. They learned to survive by bearing all hardships and mistreatments that came their way by not speaking. This was how they survived in Laos. Moreover, my culture had emphasized that a respectful woman was one who listened and remained silent because she has a good heart.

- Is this what it takes to be a good, respected woman?
- Does it mean that I am not good, but a troublemaker if I speak up?

I was in a bind since addressing this conflict was out of my comfort zone and outside what I had been taught, which was that questioning something should be avoided; it's better to bear one's confusion in silence. More so, would I be labeled a bad student for making such an issue out of the fact that Ms. Lopez's instruction was in Spanish and I did not understand? The hardest part about not speaking up was not wondering why she would not speak English and include me, but why she ignored me. Yet I feel obligated to make a good impression. I try to rationalize what I felt: maybe today was just a bad day for her. So I chose to not say anything to Ms. Lopez. Instead, I hastily walked out the classroom door without Angela and Esmeralda.

Debriefing

Arriving into the designated classroom, Angela, Esmeralda, and I were the first students there, so I asked Dr. Smith: "Why did Ms. Lopez speak only Spanish to us?" Dr. Smith's smile faded then she recomposed herself. She was surprised by my question and at first she just stared at me.

Before Dr. Smith could answer, I said: "I don't understand Spanish. I was confused and probably looked like it too. I queried further: "But why was she talking in Spanish only? There was nothing in English for me to understand."

Dr. Smith, who kept nodding her head to suggest that she was listening while I was talking, replied "the school has a language model. The teachers are not supposed to talk in English in front of students. So that is why Ms. Lopez spoke in Spanish only."

As Dr. Smith informed me of this, I felt stupid for bringing this issue up because it was a part of their school policy to speak Spanish. Yet, I was not satisfied with her answer because this was the first time I had heard of this policy. It was neither mentioned in the course syllabus nor was it mentioned by Dr. Smith prior to fieldwork that the language would be in Spanish, or Spanish only.

And though I am not satisfied with Dr. Smith's answer, I could not find any fault with it either. It would be unprofessional, even petty for me to question the school's language policy since it was an immersion school. Yet, I questioned whether or not this school was an appropriate placement for me, particularly if the language was to be Spanish only because my comprehension of Spanish was far below basic. Notwithstanding that, the approach to my training as an emergent teacher was to be "sink or swim."

What about my needs/culture as a student? Would this negate my learning?

As a last attempt to find an answer to make the fieldwork placement make sense, I let Dr. Smith know that I did not want anything to be lost in translation as a learner, and as one who was learning how to teach ELs. I thought my comment merited serious consideration. Yet Dr. Smith's response was to inform me that Angela and Esmeralda were good students and would help translate for me in class, so I should not worry.

Translate?

I sat down at an empty table, fuming inside. There seemed to be no appropriate answer or fix to change the situation. The logic of Dr. Smith's response made sense, yet it was inadequate in alleviating the issue because I would not be able to learn in this situation without real-time comprehensible input. What was being communicated instead was that my learning was to take place based on what my eyes could observe, and from another student's intake of knowledge, and interpretation of the information. I felt cheated out of an education, paying for a teacher education program that I felt was the right fit to allow me, in theory, to use my experience and cultural background to help me teach; yet, my needs were set aside and relegated to a you-can-observe-only status. And here also was my last chance as a final phase student teacher to interact with students and use my ELD knowledge and language in a meaningful context. Yet I would be limited because I would not have the same access to information for structuring the lessons, and would not have direct access to instruction from my fieldwork classroom teacher in the same manner as my Spanish-speaking classmates.

Angela and Esmeralda overheard the conversation with Dr. Smith and kindly tried to cheer me up as they saw my tear-filled eyes. They informed me not to worry; that they would translate for me. I felt better knowing they would be there to help me.

I tried to reassure myself that this was the first day of class observation and fieldwork at the school, so "UvUv, nthiaj li tua zoo" (Bear with it, good things will come). I told myself this so I would not cry.

I had looked forward with eagerness to the fieldwork because the onsite field class gave so many strategies to help students develop language. The class emphasized the uniqueness of each language and culture and how these features should be used to make the lessons culturally relevant (Ladson-Billings, 1992; 1995). Yet after that observation, I was not sure there really was room for the inclusion of cultural relevancy for me as a student-teacher in this "real-world experience" of fieldwork because there was no place for cultures and languages other than Spanish. The dominant culture and language of the school and the policy of my placement coordinator took precedence, with little regard to other cultures and languages.

My Field Placement Journey

This first day at the Spanish–English school set the pattern for the weeks to come. Each Thursday, I felt increasingly discouraged as I went into Ms. Lopez's classroom. She neither acknowledged my presence nor did she communicate in anything other than Spanish. And each Thursday I became more invisible. My eagerness and motivation for the onsite course dwindled as well.

During the observation, the elementary students worked on their preferences of various activities in ELD and participated in different types of grouping configurations and learning tasks. However I was never informed about the reason for structuring learning in varied ways, or the reasons for varied instructional methods being utilized for lessons. These observations did not help me gauge or understand the use of each teaching strategy because I received minimal instructional information.

Both Angela and Esmeralda tried their best to translate for me at every opportunity; however it was usually after our fieldwork and the information would be brief. Thus, each week, I felt like I was missing a big chunk of the big picture (the direct information given by Ms. Lopez about her teaching and management strategies seemed very detailed and informative). From indirectly observing Ms. Lopez's lessons, what I was learning (or piecing together) was not what was discussed by Ms. Lopez. When I compared what I observed with Angela and Esmeralda, the information often contradicted.

Still each Thursday, I would wait patiently with Angela and Esmeralda as Ms. Lopez explained *something*, hoping she would just turn to look at me and say something to me, anything. I became the quiet shadow that hovered nearby.

I started asking others in the cohort if their classroom teachers spoke only Spanish to them. Surprisingly the answers I received from all of my cohort members contradicted what I was told. All the other classroom teachers spoke English to my cohort members, even when in front of the students because the teachers were providing information and teaching strategies. Upon hearing this, I felt outraged at the unfairness of being the only one who could not communicate with the classroom teacher and I felt cheated. Everyone was learning, growing, and developing while I was not learning anything. All of these weeks, I just observed and accepted what happened and what was told to me. I was not progressing, but regressing because of my mistreatment and my misery. And though I smiled and attend fieldwork every Thursday, deep down I was dying, trying to cope. I even wondered what good would await me at the end of this experience. I clung so hard to hope and what my parents had always hoped would happen if you just bear it.

The Student-Teaching Takeover

I saw the last three days of fieldwork as my opportunity to demonstrate not only my teaching skills, but that I was a capable human being with a voice and goals. Inside I hoped I had not waited too long to be active in the class. I had also hoped Ms. Lopez would be supportive of my lesson plans and would provide feedback. For my take-over lesson, Ms. Lopez had not included me in the communication about what she wanted to see for our individual lessons. Nonetheless, I consulted with my cohort members.

For three days of class, my two cohort members and I were to develop individual lessons, instructions, materials, and lead each day's ELD lessons in English.

I would have a day to teach while the other two student teachers would act as aides, and vice versa.

Angela was the first lead teacher to instruct, and I planned my ELD lesson based on Ms. Lopez's written feedback on Angela's evaluation sheet. I thought it was ironic that Ms. Lopez communicated the feedback in English. However, I was glad to be able to have some direction to help me plan my lessons.

For my 30-minute ELD lesson, the students would practice how to express things that they liked using adjectives. The students would be using language frames and sentence prompts to develop a dialogue:

Line 1: I like your ____ (noun). It is ____ (adjective).
Line 2: Thank you. I like your__ (noun) because it is ___ (adjective) too.

Each student would be given a picture card so that they would know what the noun would be for their oral communication. The adjectives were written next to the adjective space, so the students could use it as a visual aid to assist with their oral communication. The structure of the lesson was whole class–small group–then whole class to ensure that the students would know what they would be doing in their small groups and to ensure that they would have ample opportunities to practice. The students would be assessed using an observation checklist for completing the dialogue, since the lesson would only be 30 minutes.

The morning of my teaching, I arrived at school very early due to my excitement for the opportunity to teach ELD and also because I was nervous about the lesson going as planned. When I arrived at the school, Angela and Esmeralda were not yet there. So I waited for a nerve-wracking 15minutes. I thought about going to the classroom to prepare for my lessons. I sat hoping that the lesson would go smoothly. I thought how bad it would be if I forgot my instructions. I hoped that students would be able to understand my lesson and would be successful on the independent practice.

It was 10 minutes before 8 a.m. when my cohort-mates finally arrived. We then hurriedly walked into Ms. Lopez's class where she was in deep conversation with a parent. We quietly set up my materials and posters, and I reviewed what I wanted my cohort members to help me with during the lesson. I asked Angela to lead my small group of second graders, while Esmeralda would lead the small group of third graders. This would leave me with the first graders (for 10-minute segments). I would signal with "Amigos" (the school uses this word as a signal to get students' attention) and the small groups would rotate to the next station or group. Thus, each group of students would have opportunities to practice their dialogue with three teachers.

Finally, I began to teach my lesson. While I taught, Ms. Lopez observed and circulated; however, she spent only seconds observing my group of students during small-group practice, then went to observe the other small groups. As she was observing the other small groups, I thought: "Oh, no. You only observed 10 seconds of my small group!" My students did not even get to independent practice using the language frames (sentences that I want them to use) in a dialogue yet. And as the lesson ended at the allocated time, Ms. Lopez filled out my evaluation form while I dismissed the students back to their homerooms.

By this time, Ms. Lopez's homeroom students entered the classroom. She walked over to them and instructed them to read silently. While all of this occurred, I waited patiently for her to end instruction and provide me with feedback. However, her feedback never came. Instead, she started to talk with her classroom aide and students as they read.

Taking a minute to pack my materials, I continued to wait for my feedback from Ms. Lopez. However, she still did not approach me; yet she did walk up to my cohort-mate Angela, and handed her my evaluation sheet, then she walked us out of her classroom. I wondered: "Why is Ms. Lopez not handing my evaluation sheet to me and why is she not providing me with any feedback, as she did for Angela?"

I was dumbfounded.

- Did I offend Ms. Lopez somehow?
- Did I look too busy and that was maybe why Ms. Lopez did not hand me my evaluation?
- Will she have enough time to go over her comments with me?

I was glad that she took time to write her comments, yet she still had not said anything to me.

As I walked back with Angela and Esmeralda to our designated classroom, I pondered what could have gone wrong during the lesson. Then Angela handed me my evaluation and I saw the score I received along with Ms. Lopez's written comments. She gave me a score of 7 out of 10 and wrote:

- Arrived five minutes late, which did not give you time to prepare for the lesson.
- Materials did not provide enough choices for students to select their answers.

How could I have received a low score? I planned my lesson using Ms. Lopez's feedback to Angela and the instruction she taught a day earlier. I further thought:

- How could I be deducted a point for time when I was in the classroom 10 minutes before class started?
- How could I be deducted two more points for materials because I provided each student with a picture card to help answer the language frame?

I limited the students' language frame choices because Ms. Lopez said Angela had too many choices, and the students became confused during the prior lesson.

The more I tried to find reasons for the score I had received, the more upset I became. All my thoughts ran back and forth between what I had been experiencing since the first day of observation until this moment. Then suddenly it all made sense, a piece of puzzle falling into place.

This was not about how I taught the lesson, or what I did and/or did not do; it had nothing to do with me. This was prejudice. Discrimination. I was treated differently and scored based on a different standard than my cohort-mates. Suddenly, it all made sense—the way I was alienated on the first day of observation, how I was made to feel like I did not exist. Running through my mind were words, definitions, and examples of prejudice and discrimination that I had experienced, had learned about, and had heard of throughout my years of school. Images flashed and played over and over in my head.

My head was spinning. I had this feeling of nothingness that I had heard about and had read about in firsthand accounts in historic texts in history class. Maybe this was what African Americans felt before the civil rights movement? Or like the many women who worked the same jobs as men during World War II but were told they could not work once the war was over because the jobs belonged to men. Or Native Americans who held countless treaties with the American government to keep their lands, but then were told their treaties were meaningless. Or like the gay and lesbian community who had been an active part of society as taxpayers, laborers, and citizens, yet are denied the right to marry.

Then experiences from my childhood in the refugee camp in Northern Thailand flashed: the wired fence around the camp; the curfew; the soldiers guarding the entrance of the camp; the way Thai people treated Hmong refugees and the look in their eyes as they spoke to us; the way my parents were talked to as if they were children when asking Thai doctors in the refugee camp for help. Now, in this day and age, how can prejudice and discrimination happen, especially under a program where social justice is the ideology? I felt so much anger that I cried.

- Why is this happening to me?
- Did I do something to offend Ms. Lopez?
- Is this why she does not like or cannot even respect me?

I was so emotional that I walked out of the classroom during instruction, and sat crying in my car. When I was able to compose myself, I returned to the classroom. Dr. Smith had noticed that I had walked out and had asked Angela and Esmeralda if they knew what upset me. They both had observed and witnessed the different treatment I received from Ms. Lopez. They saw the way Ms. Lopez would not talk to me and would not look at me as she provided information. They were also confused about Ms. Lopez's refusal to speak English to the three of us, while they saw her communicate openly in English to her classroom aide.

When I returned, Dr. Smith asked to speak to me outside. I told her all that had happened to me since that first day in my placement—how I had been treated and was made to feel since that first day. Dr. Smith apologized for not following up on the incident after the first day of observation, and for the way I was treated and made to feel.

I felt disappointed however. Here was a department instructor who is supposed to be teaching my cohort about being advocates for EL students and advocating against prejudice. How contradicting and hypocritical to say one thing and do another. That was all she said to me, nothing else, nothing more!

Holding my composure through the remainder of the class, I did not know what to do, or how I was supposed to accept this treatment. It was not until I returned to the university campus that I realized and found my resolve: I have to speak up and voice this mistreatment. I have to say something because if I do not, then it will happen again to someone else. I must speak up because I do not want another person to go through what I went through.

My Resolve

> Language is a chief vehicle for deploying power, whether constructively or destructively. Language is a kind of social asset, and schools are agencies in which language is often used to benefit the privileged and disenfranchise the powerless. Schooling practices can empower or disempower, depending on the language and cultural policies of the school. (Diaz-Rico, 2008, p. 29)

Prejudice and discrimination is unjust. To treat another person like he or she does not exist is immoral. My mistreatment should have not happened, especially in a program that embraces diversity and emphasizes social justice. For me to just ignore my mistreatment and the discrimination against me is not social justice.

Though Dr. Smith apologized for this occurrence, that did not make it okay. The Spanish–English Immersion School has a contract with the credential program to allow their student teachers to teach and include their multicultural social justice emphasis in the lessons. Yet I, a student of that credential program, was informed by an instructor within the program that my feelings of alienation were unfounded because the school had a language model to uphold. This made no sense. Why would a program contract with a school that did not respect or agree with the program's mission statement?

Finding my resolve and my voice based on the fact that I was discriminated against and that it should never have occurred in a place where social justice and equality are entwined, I composed an email to Dr. Smith, explicitly calling my mistreatment as it was: discrimination. I also explained my feelings, my mistreatment, and the importance of why I chose that credential program (because of the social justice focus, which was violated):

> I feel Ms. Lopez is being discriminating towards me because from the first day I stepped in her classroom, not once did she talk or interact with me. Angela and Esmeralda have noticed this too. She has never bothered to try to communicate with me, even when we are outside her classroom. Outside her door numerous times, waiting with Angela and Esmeralda, I do attempt to talk to her…but she continues in Spanish without making eye contact with me. She has ignored me and she neither had the courtesy to even look at me nor hand me the evaluation sheet for my lead teaching today. I feel all of this has contributed to how she has viewed me. I am not a picky student who cannot accept my actions and the grade I received for it, but I feel no person should be made to feel this way. After careful thinking, I am bringing this up in the hopes of saving another student from the same experience that I had. We are in this program for a reason—social justice…

Dr. Smith might have brushed off my words on the first day of observation, or when she noticed I was upset on the day of my evaluation, yet she could not ignore my voice.

The email I sent Dr. Smith, my voice, ignited action. Dr. Smith immediately replied that: "social justice is the ideology of our program." She asserted that I was correct to point out this fact, and that she would talk with Ms. Lopez about resolving the issue and would report back to me. She wrote,

> You are so right, no one should be treated the way you were, and I have an email in to Ms. Lopez so I can talk with her about this situation. I very much appreciate your calling this to my attention, and I will definitely address the issue before your next class period. Please accept my apology for not bringing it to her attention earlier. (Smith, 2011)

Over the weekend, Dr. Smith emailed me to report what was discussed; and Ms. Lopez emailed me to apologize for the way she treated me and made me feel:

> I am emailing you to apologize for not communicating with you and making you feel bad. That has not been my intention at all. I explained to Dr. Smith how it has been difficult for me because you arrive when my students are there and I'm in the middle of taking roll…. We have not had much time to talk before or after your lessons because when you arrive, I have my students and when you are leaving, my students are coming in. I try to stick to the language model as much as possible (at least in front of my class). When I need to talk to English-only parents, I always try to do that to the side, but many times I also talk to them in Spanish. The day you taught your lesson was a difficult morning for me because I had to go over things with parents and I felt very rushed, so I apologize that I did not make contact with you prior to your lesson. (Lopez, 2011)

It was not the best letter of apology or well thought out, but it was an apology. How can I be a good social justice teacher and believe in social justice if my instructor and supervisor (who teaches about social justice) do not practice what they preach? Throughout all this, I realized that I must have courage and find my voice. I learned to speak up and stand up for social justice, which I have realized is one of the most powerful things a person can do for themselves.

Moreover, what my parents have always advised: "Uv Uv, nthiaj li tua zoo" (Bear with it, good things will come) was not applicable in my mistreatment. My parents imparted their advice based on their own understanding, their own view, and from the goodness of their hearts because they did not want conflict for themselves or for their children. Their advice reflected their experience in the refugee camps and being immigrants in America.

It saddens me to realize my parents have been so mistreated that they feel they have no voice. They have rights, feelings, dreams, and hopes, just like anyone else. Yet they will not stand up and fight against prejudice and discrimination because of the vulnerability of being an immigrant in a society where your voice is often ignored. Maybe this was why my parents always taught my siblings and me to bear any hardship. I realize they did not literally mean bear all mistreatment and negativity, but they silently taught each of us, their children, to be optimistic and keep moving forward; they also taught us, whether they realized it or not, to not let the bad things hold us down because the future holds opportunities and good things.

My Development and My Future

I finally understand the silent message behind my parents' words of wisdom. I realize I have found my voice through bearing the mistreatment that I was dealt. I had hoped I would be treated better in my field placement and program, and I tried bearing the alienation and hurt I felt and burying these feelings deep in my heart. Yet it is not right for me to bear discrimination and suffer it. No person should be made to feel like they do not exist and are not good enough to be spoken to, acknowledged, and respected.

From this experience, I have learned that to be a teacher is a big responsibility. Your actions will affect your students.

Teachers are individuals too. They each have different skills and knowledge to pass on. In teaching my future students to deal with such issues, I would use my personal experience as a lesson in speaking up. Issues of discrimination should not be present, yet these issues still occur.

As for my skills and knowledge, I hope to pass on the wisdom of my experience as a person who embodies the will to speak up though one may be scared or the only one raising her voice. As for social justice, according to Sleeter (1993), social justice is the goal that students would leave school with skills to change the inequalities in society. This model emphasizes teaching students to analyze inequality and oppression in society, while helping them develop skills for social change. Therefore, teachers who are teaching in multicultural education programs that emphasize social justice must be able to practice what they say. In my experience, I had to be my own teacher of social justice because if I did not speak up and advocate for change, it was not going to happen. To ensure that no future student of mine has to go through what I experienced, I now have my own mantra: "Listen to your voice; be the change that you want to see."

References

Collier, V. (1987). Age and rate of acquisiton of second language for academic purposes. *TESOL Quarterly, 21*(4), 617–641.

Cummins, J. (1981). Age on arrival and immigrant second language learning in Canada: A reassessment. *Applied Linguistics, 2*(2), 132–149.

Diaz-Rico, L.T. (2008). *Strategies for Teaching English Learners.* (2nd ed.) Boston: Pearson Education.

Ladson-Billings, G. (1992). Liberatory consequences of literacy: A case for culturally relevant instruction for African American students. *Journal of Negro Education, 61,* 378–391.

Ladson-Billings, G. (1995). Toward a theory of culturally relevant pedagogy. *American Educational Research Journal, 32,* 465–491.

Lopez, A. (personal communication, April 17, 2011).

Nieto, S. (2009). Bringing bilingual education out of the basement and other imperatives for teacher education. In A. Darder, M. P. Baltodano, & R. D. Torres (Eds.), *The Critical Pedagogy Reader* (2nd ed., pp. 468–484). New York: Routledge.

Sleeter, C. E. (1993, March). Multicultural education: Five views. *Education Digest,* 53–57.

Smith, B. (personal communication, April 15, 2011).

PART TWO

School

There is the pain and indignation over the schools and their imprisonment in politicians' rhetoric, in business thinking, in seemingly ever-intensifying forms of control; there is the struggle to teach students and prospective and practicing teachers about the history and politics of their situation; there is the movement at once phenomenological and political, to articulate a conception of curriculum beyond present institutional constraints, a curriculum of compassion, and the search for pathways to an uncommon ground, a ground of integrity, inclusion, and caring.[1]

Children learn more from what you are than what you teach.[2]

The function of the university is not simply to teach breadwinning, or to furnish teachers for the public schools, or to be a centre of polite society; it is, above all, to be the organ of that fine adjustment between real life and the growing knowledge of life, an adjustment from which forms the secret of civilization.[3]

---

1   W. Pinar as cited in W. E. Reynolds (2003). *Curriculum: A River Runs Through It*. New York: Peter Lang.

2   W. E. B. Du Bois, http://www.lucidcafe.com/library/96feb/dubois.html

3   W. E. B. Du Bois (1903/1994). *The Souls of Black Folk*. Chicago: Dover. Inc.

CHAPTER SIX

Curriculum Transformation Through the Study of Hmong Culture

YA PO CHA

Molded by My History

I am *Hmoob* (Hmong), a descendant of the indigenous people of southern China, dating back thousands of years. My ancestors survived with an ancient culture on subsistence farming. They lived in isolation on high mountaintops hidden away from civilization. In the 1800s, Hmong started migrating into Laos and Vietnam due to Chinese oppression and relentless warfare with the Chinese. As late as the beginning of the 20th century, formal education was still a foreign concept to Hmong people.

The French were the first westerners to encounter the Hmong in Laos at the turn of the 20th century as they colonized Southeast Asia and started collecting tax from the Hmong people (Cha, 2010a). In the 1950s, Hmong were drawn into the Cold War when the United States Central Intelligence Agency (CIA) recruited them to head off the Ho Chi Minh Trail and rescue downed pilots. It was about this time that Hmong parents started sending their children to Laotian schools in the city. Young children were sent in small groups to live in Laotian towns, entrusted to their teachers who were also Laotian. Meanwhile, the parents continued to live traditional agrarian lifestyles in the mountains.

To Hmong parents, sending their children to school meant giving them the opportunity to *kawm txawj kawm ntse* (to acquire knowledge and intelligence). In actuality, Hmong students were taught everything from a second or third language (Laotian and French) to math and science. As part of the education they received in school, they learned personal hygiene as well as western philosophy.

Hmong children had not been formally educated in their primary language until the end of the 1900s. That is because a Hmong writing system was not created until 1952 (Vang, 2008). Even so, the Hmong language was not widely used until recently. Another reason is that Hmong people do not have a country of their own.

By the early 1970s, there were young Hmong men and women in Laos who had obtained an education and started working in various fields, including education and health. At the same time, several Hmong students were sent to study abroad. This was a surreal opportunity for young men of a tribe the Chinese called "barbarians" since the dawn of time, because until then Hmong people had been illiterate and uneducated. But education became real when Dr. Yang Dao obtained his doctorate degree in social science and became the first Hmong ever to earn the title "doctor" (Moua, 2008).

Family Influences

My father never had the opportunity to attend school. The Laotian government was reluctant to establish schools in Hmong villages in the mountains. Like most Hmong men, my father was a soldier and a farmer. However, he realized the potential benefits of an education, and he lobbied long and hard to bring a school to our village, so I would not be sent away to school. As a result, in the fall of 1973, I was enrolled in first grade at a Laotian grammar school within a stone's throw from my house. I still remember the exact words used by my first-grade teacher when he taught my classmates and me how to eat. His words were *nyung jin nyum sa sa* (Laotian in English phonics meaning "eat patiently, chew slowly").

In May of 1975, the Americans pulled out of Southeast Asia, and Laos became a communist republic. General Vang Pao, the American connection and Hmong military leader, was airlifted to Thailand. His soldiers and their families were left to be persecuted by communist Laotians, known as the Pathet Lao. The majority of the Hmong chose to surrender to the communists, but tens of thousands fled to Thailand. My family was among the latter, because my father had been a soldier fighting for the Americans. To the communist regime, my father was an American *tub teg tub taws* (accessory) or *yeeb ncuab* (the enemy). Thus, there was no telling what the communists would do if my father were to surrender. On the other hand, if he was caught fleeing the country, my father would have faced persecution for certain. If we made it to Thailand, we became *neeg thoj nam* (refugees of war), with an uncertain future and there was no telling what was going to happen once we reached Thailand. That is because we were the first group of refugees to make the attempt to flee to Thailand from our region.

The sentiments in my family at the time were fear and uncertainty, but my father chose to flee Laos.

Members of my family along with about 200 members of our village fled to Thailand. My family and 200 other villagers had to do what we call *khiav nyab laj* (flee from communist soldiers). The last thing I remember about Laos was the never-ending *nraim nruab zoo nruab tsuag* (hiding and waiting on the jungle floor); there, all kinds of critters were crawling on the ground, and mosquitoes were swarming in the air. I remember being very hungry, wet, and cold. The trip that was no more than 50 kilometers took us five grueling days of walking, carrying only the absolute necessities on our backs. It was a dreadful journey out of Laos.

Fortunately, my family made it to Thailand safely. Life in a refugee camp, however, turned out to be nothing short of misery. At the height of the population boom in the refugee camp, there were about 1,000 Hmong and Laotian refugees living within an area of a couple square miles. Additionally, the camp was secured with barbwire and round-the-clock soldier patrol. There was only one entrance into the camp, and permission to go in or out of the camp was constantly being scrutinized by Thai soldiers at the gate. However, our camp, Refugee Camp of Ban Hoiyot, was one of the most lax and peaceful among a half-dozen refugee camps in northeastern Thailand, near the Laotian border.

In the refugee camp, everybody would wait for international aide. Rice, processed food, and the occasional stale meat and fish were brought in twice a week. By the time the next truckload arrived, some people had gone for days without a decent meal, because we were not allowed to venture out of the refugee camp to work or gather food. There was no life, no future, and no hope in the camp until the United States and France started accepting refugees into their countries.

For five years, my family made the refugee camp our home. I was fortunate enough to have the opportunity to go to school. I attended a Thai school in the nearby town where I made the four-mile roundtrip on foot every day. I managed to finish the fourth grade by the time we boarded a bus to the airport bound for America in December 1979.

Schooling in America

In the United States, I started school in the sixth grade in Portland, Oregon, knowing only three English words: *yes, no,* and *table* (*yog, tsis yog,* and *rooj*). Middle school was a struggle. For a couple hours a day, I was placed in a class with other newcomers where I learned English as a second language. Most of the day, I sat in regular classes without any assistance or tutoring. Except for typing class, I just sat and watched others learn. I was not getting any support at home either, because my parents were clueless about how the educational system in the United

States worked. By the time I got to high school, however, I was making good progress.

In high school, I came to know a wonderful teacher, Mr. John Rhoe, whom I had for English and geography. I would go to class early just to talk to him, even during the cold mornings of winter without a coat. One day, he took me to Mervyns and bought me a coat. Then, he asked me to help him with yard work, and he paid me for it. During the summer of my junior year, Mr. Rhoe helped me get a job at his friend's landscape nursery.

On the second day at work, I was instructed to sweep the parking lot after a customer had loaded some gravel. After what seemed like *ib tiam neej* (a lifetime), I managed to sweep about a shovelful of sand and gravel back into the holding stall. I was sweating profusely and experiencing shortness of breath. The combination of hard work and the triple-digit temperature of Fresno, California, was a rude awakening. This was my first real job.

Faced with the reality of having to work for a living, I started thinking about my future. As a teenager, I knew welfare was not for me. I grew up on it. Manual labor work and farming wouldn't work for me either. I picked cherry tomatoes, strawberries, and grapes in my early teens, and I couldn't cut it. In addition, I dreaded using food stamps. Food stamps made me feel degraded and second class. Because we were on welfare, my parents couldn't afford to buy me the things I wanted. In fact, I was not able to eat out until I started working. Thus, when Mr. Rhoe paid me $20 for helping him with his yard work, I went straight to Burger King and bought my very first Whopper. I wanted the American dream.

As I contemplated my future, I regretted being born into a poor and lowly family. I was not just poor. I felt awkward and unfit for American society; as Mike Wallace of *60 Minutes* put it: "they [Hmong] belong to another age" (Lando, 1979). In fact, during a class discussion about immigrants in my high school literature class, a Caucasian girl openly told everybody that Hmong were the most awkward ethnic group, and I couldn't even defend the Hmong name. The truth is, I didn't know much about myself, and neither did she.

I went to California State University–Fresno upon graduating from high school, determined to succeed in higher education. In my spare time, I learned everything I could about Hmong culture from my father and by getting involved in various cultural events, because there were no books on Hmong culture in those days. I started helping to conduct weddings and helped out at funeral rituals.

I graduated from CSU–Fresno with a degree in biochemistry. I went on to work as a clinical lab assistant at the University of California–Davis Medical Center. Working as a lab assistant was so boring. Not only that; it was a dead-end job and I wanted a career, so I went back to college. As I worked the night shift, I attended CSU–Sacramento during the day. I wanted to obtain a single-subject teaching credential in physical science, because I had always been fascinated with science. Furthermore, I only had to take two more classes to fulfill the requirement.

On Teaching

Teaching science involved a very diverse student population with instructions strictly in English. In addition, the goals were prescribed in the standards that students would ultimately be tested on in standardized exams. I enjoyed teaching chemistry, because it was an elective class and students were quite engaged; although in physical science, there were always some students who were not cooperative and didn't seem interested in the class. However, I enjoyed teaching science. After all, teaching is a profession that is highly valued and well respected by Hmong elders. And, I was among the very first Hmong college graduates to enter the teaching profession, and the first in my large extended family to graduate from college. As a result, relatives and family friends often compliment me on the accomplishment. In addition, I have been asked to give speeches and give advice to young people on countless occasions and at different events. I learned to value my culture and people, and I was able to take part in cultural events in great depth. That put me in a strategic position to bridge the Hmong world to the modern world; as a cousin and fellow teacher recently told my wife: "He [Ya Po] is kinda weird. He is very Americanized, but he is *so* Hmong."

For the last 15 years, I have been teaching at Luther Burbank High School, a highly diverse inner-city school. The student population varies from year to year, but the average is about 2,000. And within this environment, the Hmong student population has been around 30 percent since I started teaching here.

At the turn of the millennium, Luther Burbank High School, a Title I school, was at a low point. Gang fights were rampant and student performance suffered. That was because Luther Burbank High School was located in one of the poorest areas of south Sacramento where there were many street-gang factions from many ethnic groups including African American, Hispanic, and Asian gangs.

The school's Academic Performance Index (API) in the late 1990s and early 2000s was so low that the school was placed on program improvement. Consequently, school administrators were eager to try new strategies. So, when my colleague Patrick Vang wanted to teach Hmong language classes, our principal at the time was receptive to the idea. Thus, Mr. Vang started teaching Hmong language class as an elective, while he wrote the course of study and presented it to the district. Our administrators saw the potential benefit of the courses, and they stood behind him. It was soon converted into a foreign-language course beginning with only one level.

By the fall of 2004, Mr. Vang had turned the classes into four levels of fully accredited world language classes meeting college A through G California State

University and University of California requirements. The course descriptions are as follows:

Table 1: Levels of Hmong Language

Levels of Hmong	Description and Goals
Level 1	Basic phonology, grammar, and literacy skills. Introduction to Hmong history, culture, and population diaspora.
Level 2	Develop greater efficacy in reading, writing, and speaking skills. Explore Hmong history and culture further and in greater depth.
Level 3	Develop effective communication skills in oral and written forms. Introduction to academic writing and reading. Student will learn to decode the more sophisticated language usage such as poetry, folksongs, translating, and essays.
Level 4	Develop the knowledge and academic skills to take the Hmong language to the next level by studying the most complex of Hmong language, analyzing Hmong poetic chants, developing academic writing skills and creative writing, honing public speaking skills, etc.

It was at that time also that I was approached by the coordinator of bilingual education to help teach the Hmong language classes. I felt honored that I was going to be able to share my knowledge with Hmong students. Moreover, it was an extraordinary opportunity for me to work with the nearly 800 Hmong students on our campus. Through this experience, I would be able to teach a subject that was dear to my heart while being able to help shape the future of Hmong students and our community in a significant way. I felt like I was being empowered by the school to educate, guide, and be a role model to the next generation of youth. I wanted to help improve my students' chances of becoming successful in this world.

Thus, I took the California Subject Examinations for Teachers (CSET), obtained the authorization to teach Hmong language, and started teaching Hmong. Being authorized to teach my home language was so thrilling that I didn't mind teaching summer school and six classes, instead of the usual five during the 2005–2006 school year. Consequently, I have been teaching Hmong language full-time since.

When I first started teaching Hmong, I had mixed reactions from my colleagues. A science teacher whom I had collaborated with and had gone on countless field trips with said that my move to foreign language was a big loss for the science department. The French teacher didn't seem too happy either, because most of the potential French students signed up for Hmong instead. Even the Spanish teachers didn't seem too happy, because there were fewer Hmong students taking Spanish, and they had to cut back on their offerings.

Members of the Hmong community seemed pleased however with the idea of teaching their children how to read and write their native language, because there has never been such a program in our region. Many Hmong parents moved their children from other schools to Luther Burbank High School just so they can take the Hmong classes. Even 12th-grade students would voluntarily sign up for Hmong instead of other electives, so they could learn to read and write Hmong. In sum, most of the responses I received since moving to language and cultural teaching have been quite positive.

Table 2: World Language Standards

California World Language Content Standards
Content — Language users address a wide variety of topics that are appropriate to their age and stage.
Communication — Real-world communication takes place in a variety of ways.
Cultures — Culturally appropriate language use requires an understanding of the relationship between the products and practices of the culture and its underlying perspectives.
Structures — The content standards use the term *structures* to capture the multiple components of grammar that learners must control in order to successfully communicate in linguistically and culturally appropriate ways.
Settings — Language users need to carry out tasks in a variety of situations representative of those they will experience in the target culture.

Transitioning to Hmong language classes has been empowering, at best. That was because nearly all my students are Hmong and have varying language capabilities. The outcome, in addition, was not going to be measured by the California Standardized Test or Golden State Exam, but *raws qhov muag pom* (in the eyes) of the administrators and *hauv nruab siab* (in the hearts) of my students. And, of course, I have to be mindful of the California curriculum standards for world language.

Curriculum-as-Planned

The curriculum standards for all world language classes were set by the California Department of Education (2009). The main objectives to be met are language and culture. Thus, I am expected to develop lesson plans that meet these standards. To achieve this goal, my colleague Mr. Vang and I worked together to write relevant curriculum and lesson plans that conform to the standards and to improve Hmong students' personal and academic outlook.

We made sure the main objectives were met, which helps legitimize our courses, because the administrators were firmly behind our curriculum and the things we did with our students. Our curriculum was experimental at the beginning, but we kept realigning and improving the classes and instructional materials over the years. We proofread each other's instructional materials, paid attention to student responses to each lesson, and did student evaluations at the end of the school year. We also find it necessary to modify our curriculum to fit the students' needs as each successive generation seems to have lost more of the language and culture.

Because Hmong as a world language is a fairly new concept, a comprehensive textbook has not been written. There are advantages and disadvantages to not having a textbook. One of the challenges is that I am unable to solely concentrate on teaching because I must plan the curriculum. And it takes a lot of time to prepare my own teaching materials, as I have to keep seeking out ways to refine instruction during instruction. Furthermore, there are no existing instructional materials that have been proven to be effective. On the other hand, the lack of a textbook does not stifle what I can do in the classroom and what reading materials I offer to my students. Consequently, I write most of the reading passages I share with my students. The content of the reading materials I generate focuses on cultural themes such as folktales and legends. I write stories that touch on students' everyday lives, Hmong values, and contemporary issues such as polygamy, drug abuse, racism, domestic violence, street gangs, etc.

Furthermore, I often plan activities that are student driven to get students to become more involved. Such activities include question-and-answer sessions, speeches, and oral presentations. Being able to shape not only the course curriculum but also the content of my teaching materials has been a privilege. As an added bonus, my students hardly ever misbehave, prompting my colleague to keep reminding me that *txoj hauj lwm no yog nws txoj kev npau suav* (this is his dream job).

I want to help Hmong students build cultural capital by acquiring the skills and knowledge to succeed socially and academically as indigenous involuntary immigrants living in the United States. I was in the shoes of these students not so long ago, so I know what they are going through and I am able to anticipate what their needs are. This, I hope, will help our youth becoming contributing members of society, if not the leaders of tomorrow.

Hmong children are typically raised to not speak their minds and to not question authority. Many of them are often at a loss when it comes to self-identity, but they are not able to seek out answers. They have no knowledge of their own history and cultural traditions. That is because Hmong children do not receive formal education on their own history; it is not taught in school. They also do not know much about their own cultural traditions, because nobody sits them down and explains to them *why* certain things are being done, and done in certain way.

It is imperative that students understand who they are and what being Hmong is all about. Hmong youth these days are not culturally and linguistically fluent. What they know about mainstream American culture is what they see on television. Many of them are out of touch with both Hmong and American worlds. They are at a loss. This is one issue they are faced with, and they need to develop a clear understanding to help them come to terms with their self-identity.

Hmong students also need to overcome obstacles that hold them back. These obstacles include socioeconomic setbacks, lack of motivation in school, lack of academic support at home, and lack of educational guidance. When I first began teaching these courses, I felt an urgency to help them overcome these issues to gain self-confidence and raise their self-esteem. These are not prescribed in the standards, but they are the things Hmong students need from a cultural standpoint. I need to invigorate these students and remind them of the reasons they should be proud of themselves. This is important because of the salience of community and cultural issues, particularly Hmong parents' cultural norms.

On Parents and Community

Hmong parents possess many talents and knowledge. Yet they are not able to help their children academically. They also have neither the ability to articulate nor the patience to explain their cultural practices and rituals to their children. Students have been told frequently that education and cultural fluency are important, but they don't know *why* these things are important. As such, some of my lessons are developed with the intention of connecting my students with their parents. These lessons also serve as opportunities for Hmong parents to help their children academically. In Hmong 2, for example, students have to do an oral presentation on their family history, so getting the information from their parents is a must.

In the Hmong world, adults are highly opinionated, and children are not encouraged to express their opinions freely. When Hmong parents tell their children to do certain things, they usually don't give very good instructions (by Western standards) nor do they offer to explain why. As my father has always put it, "*Kuv kom koj mus ces cia li mus xwb yeej tsis tuag li*" (When I tell you to go, just go, it will not kill you). No explanation is offered to assure the children about what they are being told to do. Hence, Hmong courses not only teach students literacy and cultural history, but also serve as a forum for students to voice their opinion and get their questions answered.

The cultural practices and traditions can, at times, be confusing and perceived by some to be demoralizing for our students, thus, lowering their self-confidence. In my classroom, however, students learn the reasons why cultural events or rituals are being carried out. They learn how things are supposed to be done in the Hmong cultural practices and understand the importance of these practices. Take the tying of a string around the wrist as an example. Hmong children grow up seeing it being done without knowing much about it except the fact that it is an important part of the Hmong culture. In class, students learn that is a form of blessing bestowed upon individuals, a practice adopted from Laotian customs.

Sometimes, the expected outcomes are laid out; sometimes not. As such, most discussions end up with an "aha" moment. For instance, every Friday, I usually provide space for students to ask any question. That is because at home, students rarely get to ask questions about the things they see and do. The question-and-answer sessions usually serve as a great forum for dialogic interaction and meaningful discussions. During this time, I make a point to allow students to answer questions from their peers, and when an answer from a student is satisfactory, I just validate it. When nobody seems to have a decent answer, I will offer the best answer I can come up with. On occasion, students come up with questions that I don't have an answer to, and I would simply tell them "I don't have an answer" and then we can research it further. There are also days in which we just talk the whole period, and I don't think this is wasted class time.

Over the years, my students have asked all kinds of questions. Students would bring up a wide variety of issues, ranging from racism to politics and Hmong culture to higher education. Students have asked questions such as: What do I need to do when I am *niam tais ntsuab* (maid of honor) or *phij laj* (best man) at a wedding? Why do Hmong people *ua neeb* (practice shamanism)? Why do my parents always want to hook me up with my first cousin? I came to realize that when a student asks a question, there are a dozen or so students who stand to benefit from it. I focus on what they want to know. And as they advance into higher-level courses, I guide them to use critical thinking and question the status quo.

These experiences are not only practical and relevant information for students, but are also satisfying for me, the teacher, as well. Overall, and in my opinion, when Hmong youth are given the opportunity to speak their minds freely, it is quite empowering.

Over the centuries, Hmong people have been acclimated into a subordinate culture, having a language that is insignificant to the host society. So the commonly held perspective is that there is nothing to be educated about in Hmong. In fact, when I told my friends that I was teaching Hmong, they often asked if I had to "invent new words and concepts" to teach. The assumption here is that there is no formal education to be gained in Hmong, so I have to invent academic words and ideas to teach to the students. My response has always been, "I just teach what is already there." Although there has never been a formal education for the language, and culture and history have not been contextualized, there is a wealth of knowledge that can be shared with the students.

The Hmong language is well structured, so teaching students how to read, write, and speak the language properly can be overwhelming. Essentially, to teach the language formally is to simply contextualize and educate students on how the Hmong language works and what Hmong culture is all about. Also, since there is no authority and credible text on the content, I have to structure the class with a total departure from the traditional banking model of teaching (Freire, 1970).

I can't just shove the information down their throats. I have to get students more involved and get them to buy in to the lessons and information.

My students' language skills and knowledge of Hmong vary widely. I usually have two or three non-Hmong students in every class who do not know anything about Hmong. And the Hmong students have language skills ranging from speaking very little to being fluent in Hmong. This proves challenging because the administrators would not separate students into different classes based on level of language skills. As a result, if I am going to teach these students how to read, write, and speak Hmong, I need to reach out to all of them. In the words of our current principal, I need to make the content accessible to all students, a teaching concept that has been proven effective in second-language acquisition by leading researchers in the field (Diaz, Justicia, & Levine, 2002)

Making sure all my students understand my instructions is crucial in my class. I believe that only when I reach out to every student will those who want to succeed have an equal opportunity. That is particularly important in an education system where success is measured with standardized test scores and bilingual education has been nearly abolished. That is because the use of a language other than English in the classroom has been restricted in California by Proposition 227, an initiative passed by voters in 1998 requiring public schools to provide instruction to English learners strictly in English, and without the aid of their primary language (BallotPedia, 2012). This law has been instrumental in shaping the way I have been teaching.

To meet the main objectives of reading, writing, and speaking Hmong, I place a heavy emphasis on the basic literacy skills in level one. I drill them on the phonetics and composition of words. With lesser emphasis on language acquisition, I often have to code switch between Hmong and English to make sure I communicate to all students with varying language levels. If code switching seems insufficient, I resort to translating between the two languages. That has been my mode of communication to reach out to all my students. It is time consuming and repetitive, but I have the luxury of doing so, because I don't have to worry about rushing through the content to prepare my students for the standardized examinations.

Another means to bring all students along is to have my students sit in groups of four at each table. I also group students with varying language skills and abilities so they can help each other. Students who learn fast are grouped with students who are slow to catch up. And I emphasize cooperation rather than competition among students. An example of how the students help each other is when we do reading-aloud activities in class. I will carefully write my reading passages so that the paragraphs contain four or five lines. I assign each group to a paragraph. Then members of each group can decide how they read the paragraph out loud to the class. The following is an excerpt from one of my reading passages entitled "Paub Kev Cai Hmoob" (Hmong Social Etiquette):

Table 3: Excerpt of Hmong Writing and English Translation

Hmong Social Etiquette Excerpts	English Translation
Excerpt A	Excerpt A
Tsis hais yog kab lis kev cai ntseeg xws li kev cai dab qhuas los puas kev tab qhua, Hmoob yeej coj tau kev cai ruaj nreeg. Kab tshoob kev kos, ib siab ob qeg los ib yam, Hmoob yeej tseem cia cov txiv neej leg thiab npaj ib puas tsav yam. Cov poj niam Hmoob uas paub tab yeej paub ntsoov tias thaum twg lawv tsis nce tsum.	Whether it is religious rituals or social customs, Hmong people have rules and structures firmly in place. Take traditional Hmong wedding ceremonies and funeral rituals as examples; the men are in charge of the preparations, and they preside over everything. Hmong women who know Hmong customs know when and where to not get involved.
Excerpt B	Excerpt B
Thaum muab ua tib zoo tshuaj ntsuam los mus, Hmoob cov kev cai tob heev, tsuas yog tias nws tsis tshua ncaj ncees rau txhua tus xwb. Qhov no yeeb vim lub neej txheej thaum ub raug rau txiv neej tswj hwm. Txiv neej Hmoob tuav hwj chim nruj nreem ua rau poj niam mi nyuam ua nwj. Tab sis los rau tiam no peb yuav tsum rov nug peb tus kheej tias nws puas ncaj ncees.	When carefully evaluated, Hmong customs carry profound meanings, but they are just not fair to everybody. This is because long ago, Hmong men were dominant. Hmong men used to have complete control, forcing women and children into subordinates. But these days, we need to ask ourselves whether or not this is fair.

The most common way students would approach the reading has been reading together simultaneously. The next best alternative is to divide the paragraph up and each member reads solo, but everybody works together to help each other pronounce every word beforehand. Few students opt to have one person read and the rest repeat. The objectives are for everybody to take part in the reading and every word has to be read correctly, or they have to read it again and again until these two objectives are met. I don't just group my students based on language and academic skills; I make sure each group contains both male and female students. That is because there has been gender inequality instilled in most of these students. In my classroom, I have students work with classmates of both genders, so boys and girls learn to think of each other as equals and intelligent human beings to promote gender equality. In traditional Hmong families, men are dominant in every aspect of life. Men make the major decisions and women are responsible for childrearing and household chores. Women's opinions and dreams are often disregarded. In the United States, the majority of older Hmong men and many young men still treat their wives in this way. It is amazing to see young men from a male-dominated world accept the opinion of their female counterparts and Hmong girls are able to stand up for their personal beliefs and defend their positions. They learn to accept each other's opinion without personally attacking one another. In the end, Hmong students become more comfortable and accepting of each other.

Moreover, I use a variety of group activities to engage students to practice reading, writing, and speaking Hmong. Oral presentation is a common routine to not only work on their ability to speak the language, but to speak with confidence. I give my students a rubric to work on public speaking, including maintaining eye contact with the audience and speaking clearly and loudly. Here too is where students need to work cooperatively with each other. The rubric specifically evaluates students as a group and not as individuals. Thus, if a student underperforms, the whole group's grade is affected. Initially, there is some resistance to the idea, but students eventually learn to work with each other.

Another activity that I believe is an invaluable teaching tool for my students is debate. In a debate, I usually move all the girls to one side of the classroom and all the boys to the other. I would focus on a topic that is highly gender sensitive and have the students discuss it. I would play the moderator, and sometimes, the devil's advocate. Topics I have brought up for discussion include Hmong customs that are gender biased, issues related to gender roles, and dating outside of the ethnicity. At first, I will have students speak only in Hmong. However, as the debate continues, they are allowed to use English. The dynamics usually starts slow with only the most fluent Hmong speakers and outspoken students talking. Then, others will join in as the debate continues. And there are always the few who are quiet and do not speak their minds. Yet, I make a point to bring every student into the conversation. And, I usually get a lively discussion when the topic is hot and dear to their hearts. A debate is an activity in my class that gets the usually shy and quiet Hmong students talking and is a chance for the girls to make their voices heard.

History and Relevant Curricular Innovation

An important component of my Hmong lessons is Hmong history. My students usually learn about history in the form of folktales and war stories from decades earlier told by their parents or grandparents. When I take Hmong students back several thousand years into the past, and they realize that our ancestors have been able to hang on to our ancient cultural practices for that long, their eyes light up. After all, who would not have pride in themselves when their ancestors have persisted as ancient civilizations like the Romans and Aztecs rose and fell. When students learn that the reason Hmong people remained much the same for more than 4,000 years was no accident, they learn to be proud of their ancestors. In one of the history lessons last year, I compared Hmong people's practice of animal sacrifice to western practices that precede the birth of Jesus, discussing the fact that our ancestors were able to retain practices in the face of some extreme adversities. In addition, the Chinese have conquered and totally assimilated many ethnic groups in China, but they had not been able to do so with the Hmong. Our ancestors put up a good fight against Chinese oppression and remained isolated and independent until the 20th century. In learning this, one of my students, Tommy X., yelled, "that's Hmong power!"

My Hope for the Future

My experiences growing up helped to shape my teaching style, especially the teaching of Hmong as a world language. For the last seven years, I have had the privilege to teach Hmong language to high school students. I have taught Hmong students how to read, write, and speak their native tongue formally, which very few of prior Hmong generations have had the opportunity to learn. I have also helped Hmong students learn about their past to help them understand who they are, and hopefully, help them prepare for the future.

Many Hmong students come in as freshmen, with very low motivation to do well in school; and have improved their behavior and academic performance drastically by the time they become juniors and seniors (Cha, 2010b). Students who went through multiple years of our language program have gone to college and started great careers. In fact, two former students of our language program are now Hmong language teachers at a local charter school. In sum, as a teacher it is gratifying to know that I have positively influenced many young lives in my community.

My colleague Mr. Vang and I have changed the way Hmong students see themselves, Hmong people, and our culture more than anybody had anticipated. The students themselves seem surprised too when they can read Hmong better than their parents, and when they know more about Hmong cultural history than their peers. Recently, a parent told me after attending my workshop on Hmong history that *"peb yuav tsum qhia li no rau txhua txhua tus mi nyuam Hmoob"* (we need to do this for every Hmong child out there).

References

BallotPedia. (2012), California Proposition 227, the "English in Public Schools" Initiative (1998). http://ballotpedia.org/wiki/index.php/California_Proposition_227,_the_%22English_in_Public_Schools%22_Initiative_(1998)

California Department of Education (2009). *World Language Content Standards for California Public Schools.* http://www.cde.ca.gov/be/st/ss/documents/worldlanguage2009.pdf http://www.clta.net/standards/standards.pdf

Cha, Y. (2010a). *An Introduction to Hmong Culture.* Jefferson, NC: McFarland & Company.

Cha, Y. (2010b). *Hmong Heritage Language Program at the Secondary Level and Its Impact on Hmong Student Academic Achievement* (Master's thesis). http://csus-dspace.calstate.edu/xmlui/bitstream/handle/10211.9/397/YaCha%20MA%20Final%20Thesis.pdf?sequence=1

Diaz, D., Justicia, N., & Levine, L. (2002). A research report for the U.S. Department of Education. Making Content Accessible to Promote Second Language Acquisition: The ESL Intensive Program at Hostos Community College. http://www.eric.ed.gov/PDFS/ED477556.pdf

Freire, P. (1970). *Pedagogy of the Oppressed.* New York: Herder & Herder.

Lando, B. (Producer). (1979). *CBS 60 Minutes: Our Secret Army.* Available at http://www.youtube.com/watch?v=hIDca-4ksAE

Moua, W. (2008). Dr. Yang Dao. Learn Hmong Lessons and Traditions. http://hmonglessons.com/the-hmong/hmong-leaders/dr-yang-dao-yaj-daus/

Ng, F. (2008). From Laos to America, the Hmong community in the United States. In H. Ling, *Emerging Voices: Experiences of Underrepresented Asian Americans* (p. 20), New Brunswick, NJ: Rutgers University Press.

Vang, T. S. (2008). *A History of the Hmong: From Ancient Times to the Modern Diaspora.* Lulu.com.

Vang, W. (2004, Summer). Closing the achievement gap of Hmong, Mien, and Lao students. A District Commissioned Studies Report for Sacramento City Unified School District.

CHAPTER SEVEN

In Pursuit of Social Justice

My Socialization in Becoming a Social Studies Civics Educator

MAGGIE BEDDOW

D elving deep into my own lived experiences as a learner and a teacher, I begin a phenomenological examination of the dynamic stages or situated episodic changes I have encountered across three critical periods of time in my socialization process and journey of becoming a social justice civics educator—first, as a young girl growing up in the 60s and 70s; second, in the 80s and 90s as a pre-service and middle school teacher; and third, as a university teacher educator in this new millennium. I focus on this temporal space to make meaning of my unforeseen journey that led me to become a social studies civics educator, something I did not foresee, particularly because I have come to realize that my currere is not typical of many teachers I have come to know in higher education.

I encountered many detours along my journey and I often say that I was a late bloomer in life. I earned my teaching credential at age 31; I married at 36 and had my daughter at 37; I earned my Master's degree at 39, remarried at 46, and finally earned my PhD at 52 while struggling with cancer and my second divorce. But as Dall'Alba and Sandberg (2006) remind us, understanding is not limited to cognitive content or activity, but rather is "embedded in dynamic, intersubjective practice…[that] integrates knowledge, acting, and being. Understanding of practice, then, is enacted in and through practice. Such embodied understanding of professional practice constitutes an unfolding 'professional way-of-being'" (p. 7); similarly, Heidegger (1927/1962) posits an *unfolding circularity* that develops over time through interpretations of encounters within a person's current embodied understanding of practice. Hence, I reflect upon my own evolving understanding of my past and present, and how this journey is interwoven between the way I actually live my life now, both personally and professionally, and what I understand and believe as a result of my past experiences. I analyze these events in terms how they have influenced my currere as a social justice civics educator.

Episode 1: Growing Up in the 60s and 70s

To begin my journey, I take note of some key events that have shaped my embodied understandings and regress to a place in my mind that I have not visited for many years. I am always consciously aware that as a White female educator from a so-called middle-class family, it may be perplexing for "Others" to fathom how and why I am able to relate to those who have been oppressed due to their race, class, and ethnicity. Yet, I painfully recall experiencing socioeconomic challenges due to the sudden loss of our family's income, which resulted from my father's suicide when I was five years old; as well as being a product of the 1960s Civil Rights era, and having grown up in Los Angeles where I became aware of racial tensions and unrest that occurred during the 1965 Watts Riots.

I was born and raised in Sacramento, California, but after my mother remarried, we relocated to Los Angeles in the summer of 1965 due to my stepfather's job transfer. We lived in a middle-class Van Nuys community in the San Fernando Valley in Southern California for one year where I attended fourth grade. My memories of that year are quite unremarkable, and the following year we moved up to a higher-class community in Studio City where the majority of inhabitants were White and identified as Jewish. I attended the local public schools with students who were primarily from middle- to upper-income families. Two of those schools—Walter Reed Junior High and North Hollywood High—were known for many of their famed students from the entertainment business, as well as Ron Unz, the notorious proponent of California's Proposition 227 (English for the Children), which unfortunately passed and virtually dismantled bilingual education in California. I mention the latter as it would be years later that I would find myself in complete opposition to Ron Unz's stance on bilingual education.

In 7th grade I remember becoming interested in being bilingual. My Spanish teacher, Mr. Victor Galindo, introduced me to acquiring a second language, and I continued to take both Spanish and French classes in high school. But it was my experiences working at a Sizzler Restaurant near Ventura and Laurel Canyon Boulevards where my multilingual currere truly began. I began to interact with the restaurant cooks, Rios and Hector, whom I credit for teaching me *real* Spanish. In 1974, after graduating from high school, I decided to move with my Mexican boyfriend to Juárez, Mexico, near the U.S. border of El Paso, Texas. Looking back, I cannot believe the manner in which I informed my mother of my intentions through a written letter, which, needless to say, did not sit well with her. I truly did not have a plan for myself other than to explore life and postpone any college plans, so off I went. Unlike today, Juárez was safe then and Jaime's family owned a reputable pharmacy called Farmacia de los Ríos. They embraced me as one of their family members, and after living with them for over a year, I became quite fluent in Spanish and familiar with Mexican customs and traditions through my lived experiences. After breaking off this relationship and returning to Sacramento, I decided to enter a study-abroad Spanish program in 1977 at El Colegio Cervantes in Guadalajara, Mexico.

I became immersed in Mexican culture, history, and the Spanish language; so after returning to the United States, it was no surprise that I would pursue a path towards earning a bilingual teaching credential and a supplementary secondary credential in Spanish (described in the next section). I later pursued graduate studies in Spanish as I considered becoming a Spanish teacher; hence, I studied abroad for three more summers in Spain, Peru, and Guatemala. Soon after, I met Rolando DeLeón from Guatemala and we married in the Catedral Primada Metropolitana de Santiago, the main cathedral of Guatemala City. We lived in Sacramento and I fulfilled my dream as a bilingual teacher in Washington Unified School District. Our daughter, Maya, was born on my birthday in 1992 and although my marriage to her father did not endure, I was determined to raise Maya to be bilingual, despite the challenges that we faced due to my decision to have her attend our neighborhood school rather than a bilingual one.

Episode 2: Pre-Service and Middle School Teacher

Pre-Service Experiences
To set the context for my continuing journey—my currere, I unveil the influences that helped me to reconceptualize my teachings. I digress to January 1988 when I embarked on my journey to become an educator by entering a social-justice-oriented teacher education pre-service program. According to its 1996 Bilingual/Multicultural Education Department's Mission and Goals (BMED, n.d.), its espoused philosophy states that:

> The faculty and staff of [BMED] view our mission as synonymous to the mission of [Sacramento State University], which is providing and facilitating access and equity for an ethnically diverse student population that is reflective of the state's diverse population. Our primary goals are to prepare outstanding teachers of bilingual and multicultural education who in turn prepare their students to fully participate in a democratic, pluralistic society. Outstanding bilingual and multicultural teachers give their students the means to: 1) Advocate a social justice perspective across school, community and political contexts; 2) Use and further develop students' cultural funds of knowledge, bilingualism, biliteracy; 3) Lead students to achieve at academically high standards across the core curriculum; 4) Guide students to explore issues of prejudice towards people of different ethnicities, socioeconomic classes, language and language varieties, abilities and disabili-

ties, sexual orientation, and; 5) Promote school transformation toward equity and social justice on multiple levels.

I intentionally chose this program, not only for its focus on cultural diversity, multiculturalism, bilingualism, social justice, and educational equity, but also for its commitment to its pre-service students to serve in low-income, culturally and linguistically diverse K–12 schools.

One of the professors who had a lasting impact on me was my social studies methods instructor, Dr. Duane Campbell. From day one, I remember his passion when describing himself as critical democratic socialist whose personal philosophy was to stand up against the social injustices of society. He was not timid about proclaiming his political bent, and each week it was clear his course objectives were guiding us to transform and develop an understanding about our own educational philosophy as a way to become critical educators and change agents. I remember Dr. Campbell instilling in us how multicultural education was an outgrowth of the Civil Rights Movement with a goal to reform society; thus, being a product of this era, what I remember as a young girl during the Watts Riots began to finally make sense as it was never clear to me why there were such intense racial tensions. I began to realize that some of what I observed and experienced in relation to racism and prejudice were real, even in my own family. I say that because being the youngest sibling of two older brothers and a sister, I was often teased to the point where I could not distinguish between what was done in jest or what was done in seriousness; but shamefully I remembering one of my brothers telling me through his laughter that because I had invited my African American friend to our house to swim, that we would have to now drain the pool. Further, I also remember hearing derogatory comments about our Jewish neighbors, which was conflicting to me as my best friends were Jewish, and as a Christian I was raised to accept others. Dr. Campbell challenged us to critically define and ponder on how we address diversity while creating curriculum that was inclusive and representative of marginalized voices. I especially remember him emphasizing that education is not neutral and that we needed to stand up against oppressive policies and inequities and dismantle what Bourdieu and Passeron (1990) would argue is a type of an unbalanced education that perpetuates the cultural reproduction theory. These types of practices are harmful to poorer, lower-performing students as they favor the privileged and perpetuate status quo inequities for the subordinate masses by keeping people uninformed. Further, those with access to knowledge about how democracy fundamentally works possess a form of cultural capital that rewards people with both political and economic benefits. I began to critically examine my own place in society as a White person and realized that Bourdieu and Passeron's (1990) message truly resonated for me in terms of how cultural capital is provided to privileged individuals who have an ability to function in society where class legitimacy and domination is reproduced over a lengthy period of time, causing negative implications to ordinary people.

Hence, concepts, critical thinking, values, and the development of my own multicultural education philosophy began to take shape in Dr. Campbell's class. As he began to prepare us students for the major assignment—creating our two-week curriculum project—he told us with such strong conviction his disappointment in the lack of curriculum that focused on César Chávez. Much of what he shared in our class was about his own experiences in organizing and volunteering in support of César Chávez and the United Farm Workers' movement. He stated in dismay that here in California, where one would think he would be acknowledged, there was little known about César Chávez's efforts to improve the lives and working conditions of migrant farm workers. This sparked my own memories of a happenstance meeting with César Chávez some ten years back while driving from Los Angeles to Sacramento. I had taken an interest in learning about the plight of the United Farm Workers and decided to take an impromptu detour off of Highway 5 to the UFW headquarters in La Paz, California, outside of Bakersfield. I wanted to see for myself what Chávez and his supporters were doing to organize the farm workers in protest against the powerful and oppressive land owners and farmers. In that brief encounter, I was able to talk with César who, in his low-key manner, convinced me that what he was doing was the ethical and right thing for migrant farm workers. I wondered what I could do to help the cause, but little did I know that in due time, I would become a bilingual teacher at Elkhorn Village Elementary School where many of my students' parents were migrant farm workers. It was at that time that I realized it was clear it was my duty to include my students' history and backgrounds in my curriculum, and that is what I did.

Middle School Teacher Experiences

After completing my pre-service credential program in the late 1980s, I began my journey as a bilingual teacher in a small, rural school district in West Sacramento where many of my students were Spanish-speaking children of migrant farm workers. In 1992, while teaching in a sixth-grade bilingual class at Golden State Middle School, I followed closely the United Farm Workers' protest against California grape growers. About that same time, I became aware of Luis Moll's (1992) study about incorporating students' funds of knowledge and experiences into classroom curriculum. Data from the studies' surveys revealed that families with rural backgrounds had a great deal of knowledge about the cultivation of plants, animals, ranch management, mechanics, carpentry, masonry, mining, electrical wiring, and medical folk remedies, as well as entrepreneurial and science-related skills. Thus, at the beginning of the school year I inquired with my students and their families as to what they were interested in learning that year. Many of them expressed a desire to learn more about César Chávez and the UFW, so it didn't take long for me to create a civics-oriented curriculum unit that would teach my students not just about the man himself, but about his principles, values, and contributions toward improving the lives of migrant farm workers.

As we began the unit, I showed my students news clippings that described how consumers across the state of California were boycotting grapes and lettuce as a way to take a stand and support the farm workers' cause. I then showed them a video that had been produced by the UFW showing the cause and effects of harmful pesticides to farm workers in the fields and to the environment, which had a lasting impact. We had several class discussions about what the farm workers endured, and many of the students opened up about how their own family members were impacted by the poor working conditions in the fields. We brainstormed ways that we might be able to support the UFW's efforts as my students expressed an interest to get actively involved with *La Causa*. After much deliberation, the students decided to write letters directly to Chávez to persuade him to continue *la lucha*. We had been following the news closely through current events activities and knew that Chávez was struggling in his efforts; the students did not want him to give up his fight until conditions and policies had improved for the farm workers. I was in full agreement with my students, and after providing a template letter to my students, they articulated their views, while asking César to please write back. We carried our letters to the local post office and mailed them to the UFW headquarters in La Paz, California. See samples of our letters below.

Soon after mailing our letters to César Chávez, I was on maternity leave until March 1993. When I returned to the classroom, my students would periodically ask me if we had received a response from Chávez. I kept them informed about the boycott by resuming our weekly current events activities, and the students learned shortly thereafter that César had been fasting as a way to bring attention to the cause. Sadly, we would also learn that just months after we wrote our letters, the hunger strike had gravely weakened Chávez, resulting in their hero and role model passing away on April 23, 1993.

Although we never did receive a response from Chávez, letter writing still proved to be a simple yet powerful act of civic participation as it provided an authentic voice to my students who were passionate to stand up for the rights of the oppressed farm workers—an issue that directly related to them and their families. The notion of letter writing to public leaders, legislators, newspaper editors, and other similar mediums is a form of critical pedagogy as it intersects social, political, and economic aesthetics across multiple dimensions of society. It is a genre of writing that serves as a persuasive and empowering communicative tool to counter injustices, and hopefully to enact change for the oppressed and underprivileged in the world at large.

Figure 1: Teacher Letter

Golden State

Middle School

Catherine Bardo, Principal
Ronald Hashisaka, Vice Principal

1100 Carne Street
West Sacramento, CA 95605
(916) 571-0173

December 1, 1992

United Farm Workers of America AFL-CIO
P O Box 62
La Paz Keene, California 93531

Attention Cesar Chavez

RE SAY NO TO GRAPES

Dear Mr Chavez

Our 6th grade bilingual class is studying the environment and the effects of pesticides Many of our students' parents are farmworkers and after showing your educational film, my students have become very aware of the devastating results after using pesticides in the fields

We support your efforts in improving conditions for farmworkers and we have written letters in support of your grape boycott We would appreciate a reply from you and if we can be any of further help, please let us know

Very truly yours,

Maggie DeLeón
6th Grade Bilingual Teacher

Figure 2: Student Letter

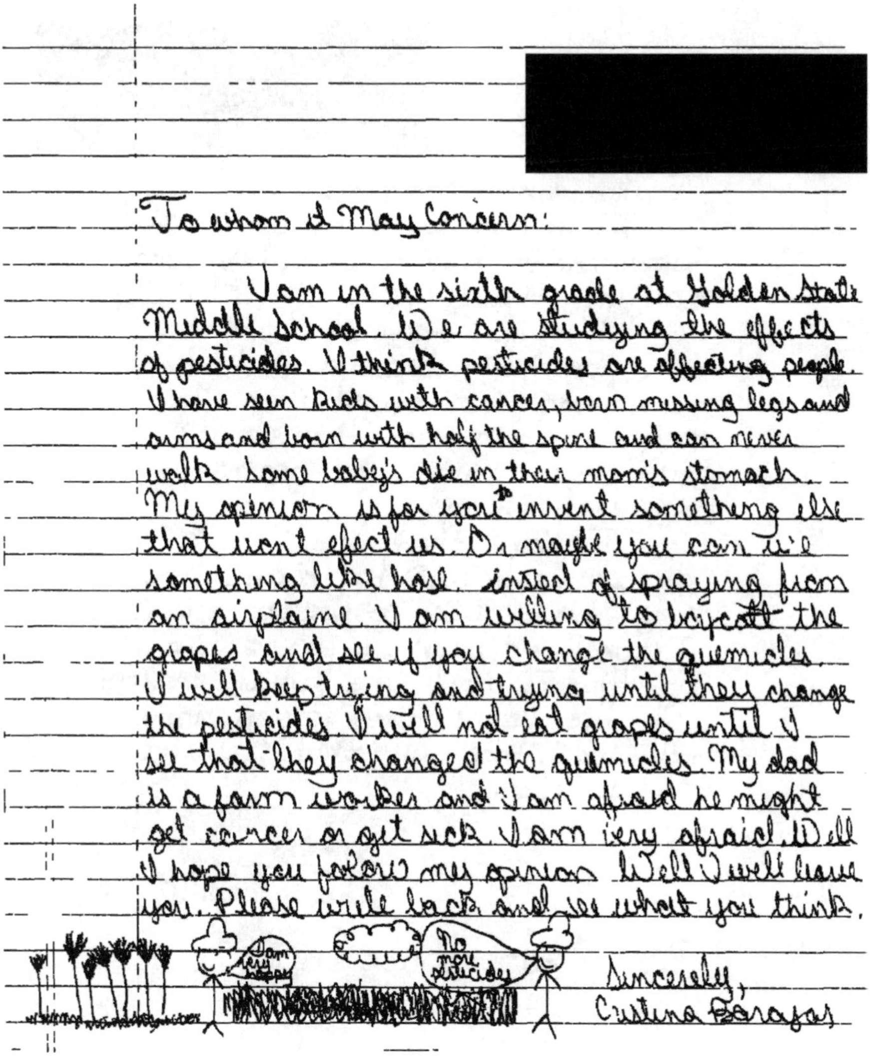

To whom it May Concern:

I am in the sixth grade at Golden State Middle School. We are studying the effects of pesticides. I think pesticides are affecting people. I have seen kids with cancer, born missing legs and arms and born with half the spine and can never walk. Some baby's die in their mom's stomach. My opinion is for you to invent something else that won't efect us. Or maybe you can use something like hose. instead of spraying from an airplane. I am willing to boycott the grapes and see if you change the quemicles. I will keep trying and trying until they change the pesticides I will not eat grapes until I see that they changed the quemicles. My dad is a farm worker and I am afraid he might get cancer or get sick. I am very afraid. Well I hope you folow my opinion Well I will leave you. Please write back and see what you think.

Sincerely,
Cristina Barajas

Figure 3: Student Letter

To who it may concern:,
    I am in the sixth grade at
Golden State middle school. We are
studying the effects of pesticides.
    I think pesticides are not
good for people. Because pesticides
are making people get sick. And
they are efecting the whole world
and other things like grapes, water
and other things.
    I think that they should
not use pesticides too many times
They should use pesticedes only once
of month or year. I would like to
say that I dont like whats hapening
with the people that work in the
field. Well thas all that I wated
to tell you.

           Sincerely,
           Judith Calvillo

P.S. Please write back.

Figure 4: Student Letter

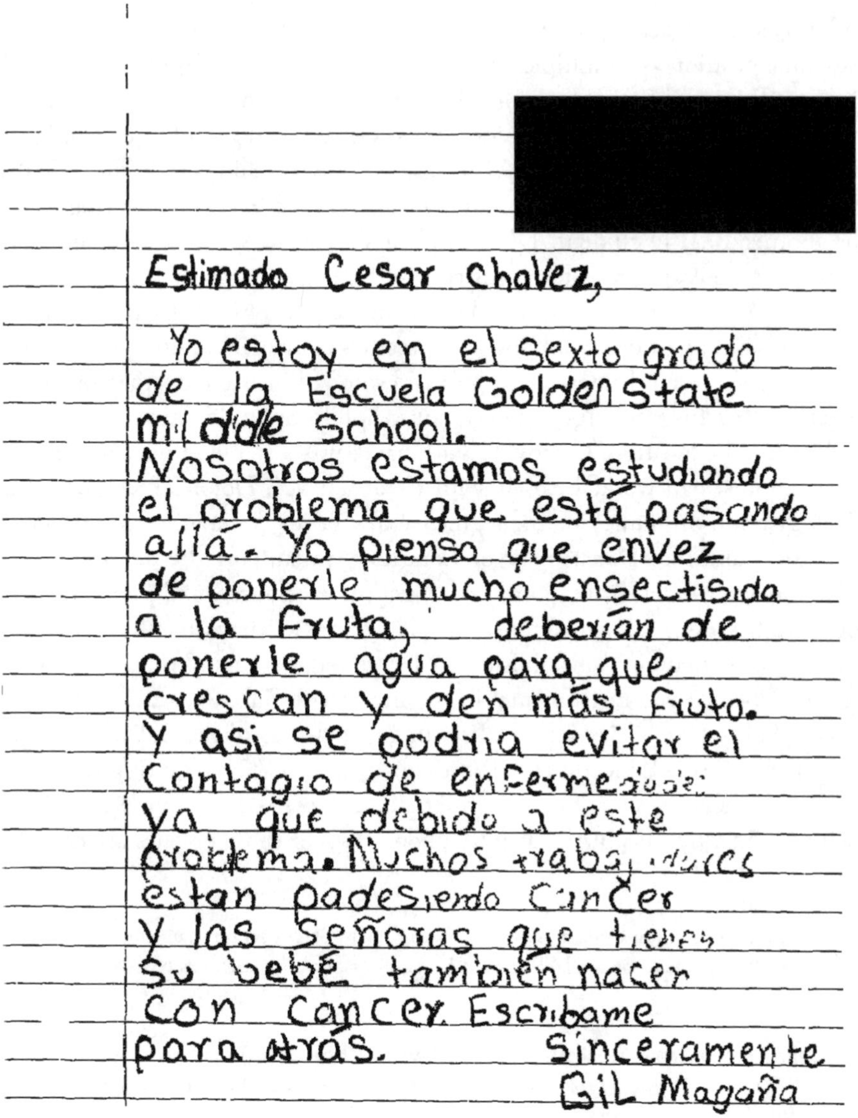

Estimado Cesar Chavez,

Yo estoy en el sexto grado
de la Escuela Golden State
middle School.
Nosotros estamos estudiando
el problema que está pasando
allá. Yo pienso que envez
de ponerle mucho ensectisida
a la Fruta, deberían de
ponerle agua para que
crescan y den más Fruto.
Y asi se podria evitar el
Contagio de enfermedade
ya que debido a este
problema. Muchos trabajadores
estan padesiendo Cancer
y las Señoras que tienen
su bebé también nacer
con cancer. Escribame
para atrás.   Sinceramente
                 Gil Magaña

Episode 3: University Teacher Educator

In 1997, after a brief appointment as a middle-school vice principal, I accepted a part-time position as a multiple-subjects social studies methods instructor for the Bilingual/Multicultural Education Department. I was mentored by Dr. Duane Campbell to teach what was considered his course. I had the advantage of having already been his student and he had observed my teachings at Elkhorn Village Elementary School, where he recommended that I serve as a cooperating teacher for another BMED student. Dr. Campbell shared his syllabus with me, and I spent time observing him teach his course. In 1999 I began my doctoral studies at the University of California–Davis, pursuing a PhD in language, literacy, and culture. As part of my ethnographic studies course, in addition to observing Dr. Campbell teach, I interviewed him and some of his students to gain an emic perspective on his teachings and his espoused philosophy about social justice and multicultural education. Clearly, César Chávez was a staple in his curriculum as Dr. Campbell had worked closely with César Chávez, Dolores Huerta, and the UFW. Around this same timeframe, the César Chávez Foundation began to work with the California Department of Education to support the development of César Chávez Model Curriculum, a compilation of resources and standards-based social studies lessons designed for students in grades kindergarten through twelfth grade. The curriculum was published in 1999, and on August 18, 2000, Senator Richard Polanco was instrumental in passing Senate Bill 984, which established César Chávez Day of Service and Learning. Provisions of the Bill were inserted into the California Education Code Sections 37220-37223, requiring K–12 public school teachers in California to teach about César Chávez on March 31st of each year, marking his birthday as a holiday. Two of those policies are described below (CDE, 2001):

> California Education Code 37220.5. The State Board of Education shall adopt a model curriculum guide to be available for use by public schools for exercises related to César Chávez Day.

> California Education Code 37220.6. (a) There is hereby created the César Chávez Day of Service and Learning program to promote service to the communities of California in honor of the life and work of César Chávez.

In 2003, Dr. Campbell decided to accept an early retirement package called FERP (Faculty Early Retirement Package). I interviewed and was hired full-time to teach the social-studies methods course that Dr. Campbell had cultivated for many years in the BMED Department. It was instinctive for me to model my course curriculum after Dr. Campbell's syllabus and what he had been teaching for a number of years as I had included César Chávez both in my teachings in my former middle-school classroom and at the university. But around this same time, shifting priorities narrowed the role of teaching social studies and civics in certain learning contexts. Since the 2001 passage of the No Child Left Behind Act (NCLB), one of its unintended consequences was the omission of social studies from its accountability system, resulting in the narrowing of instruction in math and language arts in underperforming elementary schools (Leming, Ellington, & Porter, 2003). According to the May 2007 National Council for the Social Studies Position Paper (NCSS, 2007), there has been a

> a steady reduction in the amount of time spent in the teaching of social studies, with the most profound decline noticed in the elementary grades. In addition, anecdotal information indicates that many American children are receiving little or no formal education in the core social studies disciplines: civics, economics, geography, and history

I soon became aware of the negative impact of leaving social studies behind at the elementary level. While supervising out in the field at several schools that had been identified as lower performing, K–6 principals and teachers told me they would either spend very limited time teaching social studies, or just leaving it out altogether to focus on improving the language arts and math scores. This phenomenon significantly impacted my social studies methods course in terms of field-based assignments that had typically been conducted with our school partners in lower-socioeconomic communities as my university pre-service students would tell me that their cooperating teachers—many of whom were BMED graduates—told them that there was no time in the school day to teach social studies. This was disconcerting to me; my students and graduates who had been deliberately socialized to reject oppressive policies and practices that would perpetuate the status quo for marginalized students had been completely disregarded, for it is social studies where students learn about how society and the government function, and ways that our future citizens can get involved in the democratic system so as to elect politicians who would represent their positions and political views. But what stunned me the most was when I heard from several BMED students that their cooperating teachers—again, many of whom were BMED graduates—said it was "illegal" to teach social studies and civics as the focus would now be on basic literacy skills and math.

Hence, despite my numerous attempts to push back on this way of thinking, the marginalization of social studies teaching in our partner schools was real. So as a way to get around this limitation, I decided to reconceptualize my social studies curriculum with a targeted focus on César Chávez as I knew that it would be supported by the Polanco legislation and education codes. I empowered my students by providing them this policy knowledge and then created an interview assignment for my credential students as I wanted to survey their cooperating teachers' knowledge about the César Chávez legislation. In addition, I also wanted to learn how many of these teachers in our partner schools were teaching about César

Chávez; by providing this assignment, I could survey how many of our field cooperating teachers were teaching about César Chávez in context with other activist role models who professed similar ideals such as Dolores Huerta, Dr. Martin Luther King Jr., and Mahatma Gandhi. Although some of the cooperating teachers did know about this legislation, disappointingly most teachers did not, including our former BMED graduates who had been teaching in the field for a few years. This was very telling to me and made me even more resolved to include César Chávez in my curriculum as a social justice educator. Below is my referenced assignment, which I continue to include in my social studies curriculum.

Figure 5: César Chávez Day Cooperating Teacher Interview and Analysis

---

César Chávez Day Cooperating Teacher Interview and Analysis

Directions: Access the California Department of Education César Chávez website: *http://chavez. cde.ca.gov/ModelCurriculum/*. Scroll to the link "Law" and print out the 1-page Authorizing law. Then scroll to the "Model Curriculum" link and peruse the site to select a grade-level lesson to print out and attach to this paper. Schedule a brief time to review these documents with your CT. Interview your CT, using the two prompts below. Take notes during the interview, and then summarize your CT's response. Type up those summaries below (single-spaced). Write *your own* reaction to your CT's responses and explain what *you* will do as a future teacher with regard to teaching about César Chávez.

CT Interview Prompts

Name of CT: _____

1) Does your school principal and colleagues recognize and teach about César Chávez on March 31st, as mandated by legislation? If so, how?

2) Have *you* made any changes in your curriculum in response to the César Chávez legislation? If so, what?

3) Explain why you have or have not modified your curriculum in response to this legislation.

My Reaction to My CT's Responses

1) What will I do as a future teacher with regard to the teaching about César Chávez?

2) Why do *you* think teachers should include the teaching about César Chávez in their curriculum? Why?

Once I received the interview assignment from my credential students, I introduced them to the César Chávez Model Curriculum on the California Department of Education website (http://chavez.cde.ca.gov/) and had them peruse the site to become familiar with the lessons and available resources. We found that each grade-level lesson was supported by the California K–12 History/Social Science Academic Content Standards. For example, the sixth-grade lesson called "Farming as a Way of Life" was aligned to Standard 6.2.2, calling for students to "trace the development of agriculture techniques that permitted the production of economic surplus and the emergence of cities as centers of culture and power." When reading the lessons from the website, it brought back memories of the letters that my sixth-grade students had written to César Chávez back in 1992. I told my pre-service students about that letter-writing assignment, and one of them alerted me to one of the resource links on the César Chávez Model Curriculum page. To my amazement, the letters that my sixth-grade students had written to César Chávez back in 1992 had been posted to this California Department of Education César Chávez website that was established in 1999 (see http://chavez.cde.ca.gov/, under "Resources for Teachers"). I felt so proud to show my university students these artifacts because even though César was not able to directly respond to our letters, his family and the foundation sent a message loud and clear to the public that these letters were indeed important and valuable for all educators to read.

After years of unremitting efforts to convince my future social justice teachers that social studies and civics indeed should and must be taught in elementary schools, in July 2008 the California Commission on Teacher Credentialing added a new mandate that was a blessing in disguise. K–12 pre-service teacher candidates must successfully complete a teaching performance assessment in order to earn a preliminary credential, and our institution decided to adopt the Performance Assessment for California Teachers (PACT), a comprehensive assessment directly linked to the California Teaching Performance Expectations (TPEs). The PACT consists of four tasks (planning, instruction, assessment, and reflection), with special attention given to the development of academic language. But for multiple-subject elementary teacher candidates, the blessing was that they now had to also demonstrate competencies in different content areas by successfully completing three content area tasks (CATs) in one of the following three domains: planning, instruction, or assessment. As the social studies methods instructor, I oversaw and guided my students through the History-Social Science (H-SS) Planning CAT, giving special attention to academic language development. In one of the lessons, I went online to the California Department of Education website and showed my students the letters my sixth-grade students had written to César Chávez. Although it was not required, I did share that writing persuasive letters is a powerful tool for getting students engaged in their communities and the world around them. I also shared the following National Assessment Education Program report entitled "What does the NAEP Writing Assessment Measure?" (NAEP, 2012), which stated:

> **Persuasive writing** seeks to influence the reader to take some action or bring about change. It may contain factual information, such as reasons, examples, or comparisons;

however, its main purpose is not to inform, but to persuade. The persuasive topics in the writing assessment ask students to write letters to friends, newspaper editors, or prospective employers, as well as to refute arguments or take sides in a debate.

We discussed how writing persuasive letters develops critical thinking skills, empowers students to become active citizens, provides an authenticate audience, and develops persuasive academic literacy skills and civic participation. Because of that, I encouraged my students to consider including a persuasive letter-writing assignment in their H-SS CAT performance assessment.

After spending two class sessions on the background of César Chávez's principles and values, the students were given six weeks to complete their mandated Performance for California Teachers (PACT, 2010–2011) social studies performance assessment called the History-Social Science Content Area Task or H-SS CAT (see http://www.pacttpa.org). Because this was a culminating performance assessment, I guided the students but followed the provisions insofar as providing limited feedback. Although it was not mandatory for my students to actually teach their two César Chávez lessons, many of the students did and asked their university supervisors to provide them feedback on their teaching. I was pleased to hear from many of the supervisors how well prepared the students were in implementing social-justice-based lessons about César Chávez. After my students submitted their assignments, I was anxious to evaluate their final teaching performance assessments, not only to know how they did in accordance with the History/Social Science Teaching Event rubric, but also to see how they addressed my specific instructions on social justice and multiculturalism in their learning segment, based on Sleeter and Grant's *Multicultural Approaches* (2009), which the students had focused on throughout several of their courses in the program, as well as in their field experiences. The continuum of those approaches included human relations; single-group studies; multicultural education approach; and, the multicultural and social reconstructionist approach.

Over the past four years since I have implemented this assignment, there was one student named Melisa who made a lasting impression on me in terms of her ability to reach the multicultural/social reconstructionist level of teaching. After she submitted her History-Social Science CAT and PACT, I learned she had effectively made connections between teaching about César Chávez's social activism and developing her students' academic literacy through an assignment similar to the one I had assigned to my sixth-grade students back in 1992. After teaching a unit about the late César Chávez and Dolores Huerta, co-founder of the UFW who was a speaker at our university in 2008, Melisa had her own sixth-grade students write letters to a local school district board member who was in charge of school safety. The students inquired about the district and school's anti-harassment, anti-bullying policies. Melisa selected this assignment as she knew that a couple of her students were being bullied at school and she wanted this to become a civics lesson. She was convinced that the best way to combat this social injustice would be to take action through writing persuasive letters to those responsible for overseeing her students' safety at school.

Melisa scaffolded this assignment in various ways such as having them brainstorm ideas in groups, use various graphic organizers to support their writing, and write draft and final copies of their letters. Based on a rubric that she had created, Melisa assessed her students' content and writing skills. Through this intensive analysis, the credential student was able to monitor her students' learning while reflecting upon her own teaching abilities. As evidenced by her students' letters, Melisa demonstrated an effective way to develop content literacy using civics-based lessons that promoted persuasive letter writing. She aligned her assignment both to the History-Social Science sixth-grade standards, and also to the California English Language Development standards (grades 6–8) related to writing business letters and persuasive compositions. Her assessment served multiple purposes as she integrated the teachings of history/social science content and academic language development, while also promoting social action through letter writing. I was so pleased that Melisa "got it" that I subsequently invited her, along with her cooperating teacher Lydia Cruz, to present alongside me at the California Council for the Social Studies annual conference. When a student is provided knowledge about policies such as the César Chávez legislation, history/social studies content, and standards-based lessons that justify the teaching of social studies and civics-based curriculum, they are bolstered to create social justice curriculum as Melisa did when she required her students to write persuasive letters to a board representative about a real problem that existed at their school, i.e., bullying.

Thus, Melisa's assignment met her social justice civics goals and the students received a response from the school board member indicating that he would like to come to their class to speak directly with the students about safety policies. The students were thrilled as they felt empowered and important enough that a local official had actually read their letters and would take the time to address their concerns in person. It was a lesson that would go far beyond developing academic literacy as it would demonstrate to the students that it was worth their time to become informed and take action about social injustices affecting them at local and national levels.

Below are examples of the students' letters to Board Member Houseman:

Sample #1

March 19, 2010

Dear Mr. Houseman:

My name is Adolfo, and I am a sixth grade student at Clayton B. Wire Elementary. I want to take a stand against bullying. In the 1960's Latino and Filipino migrant farm workers were being mistreated and bullied by growers and police officers. In 1965, Cesar Chavez decided to join the Filipino workers in a strike, in Spanish a huelga. He also created the United Farm Workers, a union that fought to help all field workers. This union fought to get workers water, restrooms, and better pay. Cesar Chavez also marched and striked so that he could take a stand against the unjust treatment of workers. My hero Cesar Chavez stood up against unfair and unjust treatment of the farm workers, and I want to stand up for something I really believe in. I believe that every student should not only be safe, but feel safe at school. Bullying is a big problem and something needs to be done about it.

I believe that there should be an anti-bully policy at Clayton B. Wire, and at all schools. Everyone disagrees with others from time to time, and that's just human nature. In some extreme cases some people may even be pushed into a fight, and that's not cool. But a bully is someone who continues to intimidate or fight his or her victims over and over again. I know that the students who are being bullied need help, but I think that the bully needs help too! I saw a movie about a boy who was being bullied, and it turned out that the bully was being bullied by an older brother. So, maybe a bully becomes a bully, because he or she is being bullied. I think a good anti-bullying policy will help all.

If we had an anti-bullying policy students would get better grades. I use to get bullied a lot last year and sometimes this year. When I was being bullied it was hard to think about school and I would get bad grades. Being called names made me feel bad and that was all I could think about.

Also, if we had an anti-bullying policy more students would come to school. When students are being bullied they are afraid to come to school. Sometimes I was afraid of being pushed, made fun of or beat up. I would try to stay home sick so that I would not have to go to school.

Therefore, I would like it if you and your safety committee could develop an anti-bullying policy. A good policy would help the bullied victim be safe and feel safe, because there would be steps to follow to complain against a bully. The victim would know that his or her complaints are being heard. Most importantly, the victim would not feel alone, or feel that no one cares about his or her safety. Additionally, good policy would make certain that a bully get some help to stop his or her bullying behavior. A good policy would say what would happen next if a bully continues to be a bully. Finally, a good policy would have training for teachers, and others, so that they know how to handle a bullying situation.

I know that making an anti-bullying policy might take too much time, and cost too much money, but if everyone felt safe at their schools I think grades, and attendance would improve. Students would be able to concentrate on their school work instead of worrying about the bully. Students wouldn't be afraid to come to school. I also know that many of the students who snapped and went on a shooting spree at their schools were victims of bullying. So, is it really too expensive to do nothing?

Respectfully yours, Adolfo

Sample #2

March 19, 2010

Dear Mr. Houseman,

My name is Cristal and I am writing to you about a very important issue that affects me and all the students of the world. I am talking about bullying, and it's time to take a stand. Just like Martin Luther King Jr. who stood up against discrimination and stood for civil rights, I am writing to you, because I want to stand up against bullies. During the Civil Rights Movement, African Americans were bullied and told what they could or couldn't do. They were called names, beat up and sometimes even killed just because of the color of their skin. Martin Luther King knew that this was not right and that someone needed to take a stand against this racism and injustice, Dr. King boycotted, marched and spoke out. Dr. King made many sacrifices like risking his life in order to take a stand against injustice. Like Dr. King I am taking a stand by telling you that I think each school should have a policy to stop bullying.

First, many students feel unsafe, because bullies are bullying them, and there is no one to stop them. If we had a policy, the students would know who to talk to, or where to go for help; this would make our school and all schools a safe place. The victims would know that they would not get in trouble or get hurt anymore if there was an anti-bullying policy. Last year there was a student in my class who bullied a lot of people. Many times nothing was done about it. Students would tell teachers and yard duty aids about the bullying, but I'm not sure that anyone ever listened to us. Feeling like no one was listening or trying to help us made school feel unsafe. After a while the bully finally got suspended when he started yelling at the teacher, and the social worker. But, he never got suspended when he threatened the students, or at least that's the way it appeared to us. I think that students being threatened are just as important as teachers, and staff being threatened. The teacher kept telling us to ignore him, but sometimes it was really hard to ignore his threats; this made school a scary place to be sometimes. Each school year is different. Some teachers seem to know how to handle a bullying situation, and other teachers don't seem to know what to do. That's why I think, if we had a school wide and a district wide anti-bullying policy everyone would know what to do and school would always feel like a safe place.

Second, when students are being bullied it is hard to do well in school. When the bully in my class was picking on me it was hard to focus on my class work. This was part of the reason why I got bad grades. If my school had an anti-bullying policy I would have a way to talk about what is happening; then, I could focus better.

Also, I think there should be anti-bullying classes given to teachers and school staff, so that everyone knows the policy, and know what to do when faced with a bully. My teacher told me that when she was a little girl there was a colorful poster with a house on it. Every house in the neighborhood that had that poster in their window was a safe house. A safe house was a house you could run to if you were being chased or followed by a stranger. Perhaps we could have a similar type of poster in the windows of the teachers who were trained in anti-bullying. Then the students would know who they could go and talk to if they are having trouble with a bully. Lastly, there should also be a way to report bullying so that students can have confidentiality and not be afraid to speak up. I know that training teachers and making a policy are hard work and will take a lot of time but it's important to remember that students are just as important as teachers and staff.

When students are listened to, they feel like they are respected, and like they are important. I think an anti-bullying policy will allow the students to be heard. It would make our schools a safer place where students can learn; feel respected, and listened to. Thank you for taking your time to listen to me. I am feeling very important and respected by you right now.

Sincerely, Cristal Giles

Sample #3

March 19, 2010

Dear Mr. Houseman

My name is Kayla and I am a sixth grade student at Clayton B. Wire Elementary. I'm writing this letter to you, to persuade you into doing something important for my school and all the schools in our district. First of all, Nelson Mandela tried to stop racism and tried to fight for rights of all. In 1948, there was an apartheid which legalized racial segregation in South Africa. This apartheid kept white citizens with all the power and control while segregating black South Africans. Nelson Mandela understood the inequities of this legal segregation and he decided to take a stand. Though, the outcome for all of that was that he went to prison for nearly 3 decades; he was always fighting for something bigger than himself. After being released from prison Mandela was elected President of South African in 1994. Nelson triumphed over injustice, and not in a small way. Nelson Mandela fought for the rights of others and gave them a voice and a way to take a stand, like Mandela I am taking a stand. I am writing this letter and giving a voice to those that have been bullied and to ask for an anti-bullying policy.

Bullying and racism affect kids emotionally and sometimes physically. Emotionally, when children are called names they sometimes start believing these names and they lose their self-esteem. My mom stays that names can't hurt but when kids believe them they can be extremely hurtful. When being hurt emotionally, people won't forget it easily, it stays with them. But, physically the pain only hurts for a while; bruises and scrapes heal and disappear.

Furthermore, bullying is a cycle. Bullying can affect many people because sometimes the person who is being bullied might become a bully in the future. I would like to have an anti-bullying program. First, while in school I have seen many students being bullied and this makes our school an unsafe place. One girl in my class was made fun of and she would cry. School was not a safe place for her because she was being hurt emotionally. Secondly, when students are bullied it is hard for them to learn. The emotional effect of name calling and low self-esteem make it hard to learn. Name calling stays inside and it follows you all day; when this happens it is hard to focus and learn because you mind is too busy thinking about what you are feeling. Thus, bullying needs to be stopped so that students can feel safe and learn.

I would like to have an anti-bullying program. In this policy the school would have a way to handle bullying. Students could fill out a report that would allow them to talk about the bullying. Our policy could also include a way to help the bully so that they stop what they were doing. Also, teachers could be trained so that they would know what to do and how to help everyone involved in bullying. Lastly, there should be a way to let parents know what is happening so that they can work with the school to make everything better for all students.

In conclusion, you might say, it cost too much or it's too difficult to do. Well, it's for the kids, because bullying and racism may continue, if we don't put a stop to it. And, the most important part of all, school will be a better place, and kids will want to come. Thank you for reading this letter and I'd appreciate it if there was an anti-bullying system.

Sincerely, Kayla

Writing persuasive letters, such as those that my sixth-grade students wrote to César Chávez as well as those Melisa's students wrote to the local board member, proved to be a powerful teaching tool for getting students civically engaged in their communities and the political world around them. It empowered them to become active citizens, provided them an authenticate audience, and developed persuasive literacy skills. But what was most exciting for me was how Melisa understood the overarching goal of my assignment, which was something that not all of my students *got*. Melisa embodied understanding about how to integrate social justice into a writing assignment, which was remarkable given the political climate that ignored the teaching of social studies to the very students who needed it most: those who were often marginalized in society due to their socioeconomic status and the fact that many of them attended poorer and lower-performing schools. Melisa used her letter-writing assignment to teach about César Chávez's principles in standing up against injustices, and she also was able to make that connection with her students that their voices could be a powerful way to promote anti-bullying policies to a local school official.

Conclusion

Running the course of my own journey as a social justice civics educator, these episodes serve to demonstrate how the socialization and mentoring processes helped my own transformation toward becoming a social justice civics educator. I was guided along my unforeseen journey to use facts and policies as a way to justify the teaching of social studies in a time when it is often left behind in elementary curriculum. I did not always feel empowered to stand up for injustices, but from my own experiences as a young person and particularly from my socialization process in the BMED department, both as a pre-service teacher and later as a cooperating teacher and university teacher educator, I view myself as a social justice practitioner who can empower others to do the same. I have been fortunate along the way to meet the co-founder of the UFW, Dolores Huerta, and have included her as a key person in my lessons about César Chávez. I now practice and utilize the act of writing as a tool for teaching civics to an authentic audience and to make it one of the simplest yet complex staples of my curriculum. Through my own lived experiences, I have found that I have expanded my currere and reconceptualization repertoire. I am piloting a blog assignment in my university courses, requiring students to regularly discuss current events topics related to education, and then write a letter to the newspaper editor and/or to Duane Campbell's *Choosing Democracy* blog to articulate his or her views on timely issues. My goal is to engage my students in civic engagement as a way of supporting them in thinking critically about an issue, and to take a stand for social justice.

References

BMED (Bilingual/Multicultural Education Department Mission Statement). (n.d.) http://edweb.csus.edu/bmed/mission.html

Bourdieu, P., & Passeron, J. C. (1990). *Reproduction in Education, Society and Culture*. London: Sage.

California Department of Education. (1999). César Chávez Model Curriculum. http://chavez.cde.ca.gov/

CDE (California Education Code). (2001). 37220.5-37220.6. http://law.onecle.com/california/education/37220.5.html

Dall'Alba, G. & Sandberg, J. (2006). Unveiling professional development: A critical review of stage models. *Review of Educational Research, 76*(3), 383-412.

Dewey, J. (1938). *Experience and Education.* New York: Macmillan.

Heidegger, M. (1927/1962). *Being and Time.* Oxford: Blackwell.

Leming, J., Ellington, L., & Porter, K. (2003). *Where Did Social Studies Go Wrong?* Washington, DC: Thomas B. Fordham Foundation.

Moll, L. (1992). Bilingual classroom studies and community analysis: Some recent trends.*Educational Researcher, 21*(2), 20–24.

NAEP (National Assessment Education Program). (2012, August). What does the NAEP writing assessment measure? http://nces.ed.gov/nationsreportcard/writing/whatmeasure.asp

NCSS (National Council for the Social Studies). (2007, May). Social studies in the era of No Child Left Behind: A position statement of the NCSS. http://www.socialstudies.org/positions/nclbera

PACT (Performance Assessment for California Teachers). (2010–2011). Elementary history/social science teaching event candidate handbook. PACT Central: Stanford University.

Polanco, R. (2000, August 18). *California Senate Bill 984.* http://chavez.cde.ca.gov/ModelCurriculum/law.html

Shulman, L. S. (1987). Knowledge and teaching: Foundations of the new reform. *Harvard Education Review, 57*(1), 1–22.

Sleeter, C. E., & Grant, C. (2009). *Making Choices for Multicultural Education: Five Approaches to Race, Class, and Gender* (6th ed.). Hoboken, NJ: Wiley.

CHAPTER EIGHT

A Writer, a Reader, and a Rape

Responsible Pedagogy Through Dialogue and Self-Study

DANA MUCCULAR

The Journey of a Reader

In this chapter, I merge autobiography and descriptive modeling of teacher practice through an account of my experience as a reader for an online college composition class. When I first undertook employment as a "reader" (a person employed by the community college to assist faculty in reading student writing), I did not realize that a curriculum foundation would be established for me to explore an important part of pedagogical practice—*currere* (Pinar, 2012). Currere encompasses multiple facets of academic theory for the sole purpose of engaging in discourse about one's reflective past, present, and future. This becomes the synthesis of curriculum development and education. Carson (2006) indicates that curriculum, or currere, makes "sense of the course of life, [and] is a complicated conversation that has enlisted multiple discourses," (p. 189). Schubert (2009) confirms this notion by indicating that "curriculum studies addresses… questions about what is worthwhile to study in many different venues, including schools" (p. 137). This questioning can be achieved through participating in, and actively reflecting on one's subjective lived experience, which in turn provides for an effective relational curriculum that constructs a new sense of self and understanding. From this standpoint, a curriculum is not "dead," lackluster, or "corpse-like," due to the fact that it is a "complicated conversation" (Pinar, 2012). Thus, it is through this subjective that I examine an autobiographical narrative about an experience that significantly shaped a student's identity, while simultaneously allowing for the examination of my identity and experience. Most importantly, the action of writing about lived experiences has not only assisted in the process of my healing (i.e., revealing the self behind the mask of "educator"), this process has also assisted in enriching my approach to strengthening the study of the self in a writing course.

Dialogue Journal as a Visual Representation for Research

Through reading a student's personal writing, reflecting on the process of her writing, validating her feelings through active dialogue journals, a teacher will be better able to assist students in building both academic and personal skills related to self-concept and their own learning goals. Scholars such as Freire (1970/2000) and hooks (1990) would not only place the construction of students' experiences as curriculum for the attainment of academic knowledge, but this construction would also allow for the teachers to become students, as well as the students becoming the teachers.

In reviewing a particular student's essay (Nicole), it became obvious to me that there is a need for educators to use the currere to build relationships with students that enable students to write feely about their lives. This can only take place in an environment where trust and communication have been established. In addition, in previous work I assert that educators are not addressing the multiple ways to relate to their students (Jones, 2008), which includes addressing students' cultural beliefs, morals, and norms (even those indicating biases), and engaging in the practice of critical pedagogy (Freire, 1970/2000) to analyze power dynamics within the learning environment and society. Thus, as teachers we can experiment with ways to establish learning spaces that reflect critical pedagogy's goals of having a continuous cycle of unlearning, learning, relearning, reflection, and evaluation. This cycle has contributed to the transformative student-teacher relationship.

As an educator, I desired to demonstrate my engagement and understanding of Nicole's autobiographic essay through a dialogue journal. Peyton and Staton (1993), indicate that:

> A dialogue journal is a written conversation in which a student and teacher communicate regularly...[t]he teacher is a participant in an ongoing, written conversation with the student, rather than an evaluator who corrects or comments on the student's writing.

Peyton and Slayton (1993) further explain the process of dialogue journaling by indicating that the purpose of the dialogue journal is to concentrate on the content of student work, versus concentrating on the context of student work. The written language the teacher utilizes serves as a vehicle for assessing the student's knowledge base, as well as challenging the student to work beyond the boundaries of their knowledge base. The teacher moves beyond a mere voyeur and moves more towards being an educator who is relatable, accessible, and one who validates the students' experiences.

I used this methodology to provide student support with literacy development, and as a means of active pedagogical praxis. In describing Pinar's views, Henderson and Kesson (2009) indicate that too often curriculum is turned into superficial monologues, and "attribute[ed]…to…shallow narcissism and corporate thinking in the academy" (p. 132). Rather, curriculum through this process of engagement is righteously alive, humble, non-traditional, illuminating and thought provoking.

Furthermore, this methodology allowed me the opportunity to read students' work more intently; and to offer a medium to give students feedback during their enrollment in an online composition course. I highlighted and responded to the portions of the writing that resonated with me. This process builds relationships, supports communication, develops critical dialogue, and allows me as an educator "to become" the student, essentially, creating an atmosphere of "good curriculum" (Henderson & Kesson, 2009, p. 133).

Here I show how I utilize a story of trauma as a site for personal catharsis and as an artifact to engage in responsible pedagogical practice that allows for student voice, while raising awareness about the racialized and gendered myths that bind our imaginations. Within the classroom, educators must negotiate the tensions of challenging students' views, while adhering to a responsible and nurturing pedagogy that rejects the voyeur's gaze. This means that a humanistic approach to literacy is essential to serve as a vehicle for developing critical consciousness related to human experience. Moreover, Lewison (2002), as cited in Miller (2009), states that the field of critical literacy is defined by "disrupting the commonplace, interrogating multiple view points, focusing on sociopolitical issues and taking action and promoting social justice" through texts (p. 201). Therefore, I decided that magnifying the content is necessary to utilize the writing classroom as a site for emancipatory praxis.

Moreover as a researcher, this visual process and method reveals my thinking process and my model for pedagogical engagement within a writing context.

A Dialogue Journal Visual Process

Some suggested ways to embark upon reading this piece are:

1. Reading Nicole's story first, then reading my dialogue journal;

2. Reading my dialogue journal then Nicole's story; and/or

3. Alternating between reading Nicole's story and my dialogue journal.

Overall, either process will enable readers to gain insight into both the writing and thinking of two people engaged in a pedagogic situation.

"A Writer": Nicole's Story

People look at me. They think I have it all. I am beautiful, smart, lucky to be light-skinned, have confidence that shows, always surrounded by people and fortunate to have two jobs. They look at me and think I am "fake" because of the clothing I choose to wear. They look at me and think I am a "whore" because I walk with confidence. They look at me and think I am a "slut" because I smile a lot and get a lot of attention from a lot of people. They look at me; don't give me a chance, a chance to explain. They look at me; don't give me an opportunity, an opportunity to defend myself. They do not ask about me or my story. They look at me. They judge me.

Yes, I am the new girl in town. I am new to the city life in general, I am new to the City, and I am new to college. I walk on campus with my new tight green dress, my favorite white stilettos, and I am wearing the most expensive make-up product that I own. I let the curls of my Hawaiian hair naturally flow past my exposed shoulders. And I make sure I walk tall, with my head high, and shoulders back. I am excited and thrilled for the new chapter that has finally begun in my life. However, I will not lie to you or myself. It is true. I anticipate changing this year. I just want to be a woman for once. This was going to be the year for me, I just know it. I want to feel what the other girls feel. I want to tell stories about the way my boyfriend touched me and how amazing it felt and how much I enjoyed it. But, what I really want is to stop hallucinating. Although I have done it my whole life, and it has grown to become normal for me, I know it is not normal at all. And what I need in life is for this to end. My plan? To force myself to continue on no matter what, to suffer if I need to, to continue on no matter how sick or nauseated I am getting. But most importantly, I will not let fear consume me no matter how real the appearance of this man I once knew seems to be. But I will do what it takes. I will always do what it takes to be normal and to let the past finally go.

"A Reader": Dana's Dialogue Journal

I like that you affirm yourself through your physical characteristics. However, I find myself unable to relate. You stated, "lucky to be light-skinned." Are you indicating that darker skin is not socially acceptable or desirable in discussing your lucky light-skin? What luck are you speaking of in being light-skinned? I ask these questions because initially growing up in the Black community in Oakland, California, I was exposed to every "shade" of Black person there was. I felt like I belonged and saw no differences from who I was, versus who they were. Yet, as I grew older, I became increasingly aware of my identity as a young, dark-skinned Black girl, as I was submerged in a culture of unyielding skin-color awareness. The lighter one's skin was, the more accepted that individual was in the community. Second, segments of my family magnified their love of light-skinned, long-haired, fair women—the epitome of beauty at its best. I heard the consistent "ohhs" and "ahhs" related to "how gorgeous she/they are!" specifically while watching television or reading a magazine.

Some scholarship documents "light-skinned" women/ biracial women in discussing the "mulatto" through American films, alluding to light skin as being most desirable. This juxtaposes my position as a darker-skinned Black woman, because society teaches us that the lighter one's skin pigmentation, the more socially accepted they are. Conversely, dark-skinned Black women were representative of women who were overweight, and so dark that it is preposterous even to suggest that she be a sex object. This stereotypical ideology of the dark-skinned Black woman has been portrayed for generations, and has led to modern beliefs.

Additionally, what defines a person as a whore? Is it merely a walk that substantiates a person being labeled as such (as you have stated)? It's interesting that you have paired "confidence" with the label of "whore."

It is a Friday night. I gave this handsome guy my number about a week ago. And we are finally spending time together. We saw a movie, ate dinner, went to Coldstone, laughed the whole night, flirted and temporally bonded. You can sense the attraction from miles away. As the night ended we end up in his car, then shortly after we are at his house. We then make it to the couch and soon to his bedroom and onto his bed. He starts to kiss me. I kiss back.

"It's ok. You can do this, Nicole, he is different. I'm sure of it this time."

He grabs my body, placing mine against his, firmly and demandingly.

"Breathe, Nicole, breath."

He begins to undress me.

"Nicole, don't let fear consume you. Stop shaking. This must end now."

"Girl, you ok?" He asks in a concerning manner.

"What? Oh, yea. Sorry. Your hands are cold is all." That was my most famous reply.

"Oh. Then warm them up then, girl!" He flirtatiously replies.

We laugh.

He lays me down. He kisses my body. He touches my thighs. He spreads my legs. He places his body on top of mine. He begins to thrust his body slowly. Now he is starting to breathe deeply. I then close my eyes and release a soft, fake moan.

"Wow, am I actually doing it? It is working." For the first time, I feel ok. Am I normal now? Am I a true woman now? Can I handle a man being on top of me without wanting to cry? I knew it. I knew this was the year for change. I knew my plan would work. Just takes practice.

I then start to relax. I could feel the breeze come through the window which was partly opened.

Which people are you smiling at? Who are you getting attention from? Is the attention you seek warranted? You outlined sociocultural expectations which deem certain attire as acceptable, or "fake"? You have specifically dedicated your description of your appearance to discussing your apparel, and cosmetics; this in turn, makes you appear to be increasingly aware of other's perceptions of you. Are these perceptions validated? Do these particular aspects make you feel more of a "woman for once"?

What makes a woman "feel" like a woman, and what stereotypical perceptions have you projected onto yourself? I get the sense that you are wearing a mask for the masses surrounding you. Who are you hiding from? Why is the mask, which you choose to wear, a necessity?

Simply having an intimate relationship with a male does not make a woman feel like a woman. What are the silences outlined in this text? Society over-sexualizes women, and convinces us that we should "dress to impress," but I am getting the sense that you are either dressing to impress, or encouraging yourself. I sense an internal conflict here. It appears that you want to be noticed, but at the same time you seem angered by the negative recognition you perceive you are receiving. Are you seeking approval?

Your writing is engaging. You switched subject matter on me; you are drawing me into what you are doing. Your language reminds me of Shange's (2010) choreopoem, "For Colored Girls." You tell the story, but with a lyrical "flow." Your writing has a fluidity and it seems to dance between vivid scenes; and from voice to emotion.

You seem to "pump" yourself up, or force yourself to be with someone? There is an escalated level of anxiety, with the elevated level of intimacy. The date began positively, but now you are working to encourage yourself to get through the process of initiating, and completing sexual activity. Further, there is increased inner dialogue that is placing you in a defensive state of mind. Why are you fearful? This depiction is erotic in nature; however, I see a missing piece. Where is your voice? Where are your thoughts in this depiction? I am only seeing at the

I can hear the leaves hit each other and make beautiful music as the birds flap their wings and chirp so innocently. I have never been so comfortable with a man before. His skin is so soft, like a baby who just received a bath from its brand new mother. We are both breathing together; sharing a heartbeat that almost has the same beating rhythm. My legs are comfortably wrapped around him as if he was protecting me and I never wanted him to leave. His breath smelt so good, like he just ate a freshly mint leaf and sweetened it up by eating chocolate. I am very relaxed. However, a few minutes go by. His motion and vibe begins to change. He grabs my hands and holds them tightly over my head.

His body is moving faster. His moans are becoming louder. He finally releases me. The opened window is now banging atrociously against the wall. The wind was a gentle breeze that is now coming in horrifically as if it was scared to be outside and was coming in, in need of protection. The once innocent chirping birds now fight viciously with such anger and hatred. I no longer feel relaxed. I am feeling scared.

What's happening?

Fear is beginning to fill me. I then hold this guy closer to my body, refusing to let this scenario happen to me again.

"Nicole, you were doing so well…it's ok…you got this."

I shut my eyes tighter as I bury my face into his muscular chest and grab his naked shoulders tightly. His skin is changing. It's becoming rough. It's no longer the texture of baby skin, but the texture of an adult alligator—rough, dried, and with cracks all over, like a lake that has been dried up for years. His breath was no longer freshened with mint and sweetness. I can smell and see the thick yellow film that covers his teeth which was destroyed from him doing heroin and cocaine. His touch was no longer kind and soothing. It was now forceful, demanding, and controlling.

I release my body from his and open my eyes.

end how you give a "soft, fake moan." Have you been victimized in the past? Where is your sense of authority over your body within this act?

Your inner dialogue is amazing to me! What happened to you for you to ask yourself these specific questions?

Good usage of metaphor. You are feeling comfortable with him. It appears you have never been this comfortable before. You are relaxed, but are you in control? Comfort and control are two different states of mind.

Your language changed; instead of being wrapped in comfort and protection, you are now portraying an image of imprisonment here by using the phrase "releases." There is conflict here. There is instantly a different scenario happening. Why are you afraid? What's coming? What's about to happen?

It seems that your inner dialogue is most present when engaged in a conflict. With the enjoyment of the date prior to this conflict, your voice was not present; however, I now hear vividly a "victim's voice" crying to NOT fall victim to the same incident. Who are you fighting? An event that occurred in your past, yourself, or both?

Wow, this is insightful. Who are you describing? The imagery that you are presenting is deep. This is someone else. There are now two distinctively different men presented here. What is happening right now? Who are you seeing? Why are you seeing this? Who are you feeling? How much do these visions haunt you?

You are drawn back to your past when you are most vulnerable. The image that you are portraying is powerful, who is this that you see? This man you are with is significantly different from the slender, handsome, well-built man that you presented previously. This man is: overweight, bad breath, drug addicted, and powerful. But powerful in a different way; he is gaining power from a response that you are giving him. This is evident in his "smirks [with] that ugly smile." I am assuming at this time that you are being victimized by this man, because of the previous inner dialogue of anxiety that you

Oh shit. It's him again. "Nicole, this is not real. Remember. You are hallucinating. This is just a memory. Let it go."

My date has turned into that man I once knew. I try to convince myself that it was not real. I begin to cry. My stomach is turning. I feel extremely nauseous, as if I was on the Titanic that is racing to the bottom of the ocean. The room is spinning. My tears are causing my mascara to smear. The skin around my eyes is turning pitch black while dark streaks are running down my face. I am now staring at a man who is three times bigger than me. He is beginning to thrust his sweaty body faster and rougher as he smirks that ugly smile down at me. I know this is not real, but I cannot control my past. It is too powerful and it enters my mind at such ease when I am in a vulnerable state. I look into this man's eyes with fear. It is flaming with hatred and violence. His yellow and glossy eyes are allowing me to see my reflection. All I see is me as a scared little girl who is being touched where I should not be touched. All I see is my innocence being stolen by this ugly Black man. All I see is me being told to smile and to tell him I am enjoying what he is doing to me. All I see is this huge man hovering over my young, innocent body and telling me that if I repeat this, he would kill me. All I see is me at the age of five. Helpless.

All I see is…
Me, and my father.
The man I once knew.

Again, I could not handle it. I asked my date to get off of me and told him I needed to leave. His confused face causes me to apologize and I falsely tell him I will try this again next week. Little does he know I will come up with every excuse in the book as to why I cannot have sex with him again, and I will keep doing so until he gets bored of me and decides to lose my phone number. This happens every time. I actually thought that this year would be different. I thought that I would meet a college boy that would help me overcome my past and the hallucinations that I get when I am having intercourse—the memories of my father molesting me. I just want to be a woman

spoke of while intimate with the young man. How long have you been a victim of your past?

You are a little girl in this scene! There is a plethora of emotions that I am feeling at this moment. One of many of the emotions that I am feeling right now is anger, the second emotion is sadness.
Child sexual abuse occurs with both males and females in every culture, every sociopolitical entity, and on every socioeconomic level. Child sexual abuse usually goes unaddressed within these diverse communities. With these silences, children are left victim to their abusers, and are left to deal with the emotional disturbances that develop from their victimization. Along with this continuous perpetuation of victimization, the only help that this population is left with is assistance from human services (e.g., social workers, foster family homes, physicians), and clergy (if the instances are reported); yet there are a great number of children that are dealing with this issue.

The story of sexual abuse for people is an experience of learning in the world that must be named, examined, shared, and challenged to strive for a more just and equitable society. It is increasingly important to allow for that voice to be shared through dialogue. Do you have other outlets to share your experience with others?

You have actually drawn me back to an incident that happened to me when I was six years old; the pain, humiliation, depression, and shame that I felt was insurmountable, and haunted me for many years into adulthood. Was it my father? No? Did I feel pain the same? Yes! I dealt with consistent mental montages of a family member molesting me.

This was your father! The man that you once knew, but this was not the same man that was raping you!

I have noticed that the issue of color is once again prominent. You are speaking of this "ugly Black man." I am struck by the image of the violent, big Black man that longs for the light-skinned flesh of his child, while being challenged by the same stereotype of the oversexed and savage, violent and for once. I want to feel what the other girls feel. I want to tell stories about the way my boyfriend touched me and how much I enjoyed it. All I want is to be normal. And I will do what it takes.

It is now weeks later since my Friday-night date. I am ready to try this again. I am ready to attempt to be a woman, to be normal. Fourth week of school: I now walk on campus with my baby-blue dress, my Black heals and my sparkly make-up. I walk tall with my head high, and shoulders back as always. I exchange eye contact with another good-looking gentleman. Can he help me over my problem? I give him my number. The cycle repeats.

Yes. There are other girls out there like me. They dress like me. Act like me. Get attention like me. But next time, look at her and me; give us a chance, a chance to explain. Look at her and me; give us an opportunity, an opportunity to defend ourselves. Ask about us or our stories. Look at me, look at her. Sure, ask yourselves why. But do not judge us. Do not judge me. Do not judge her. Do not judge that whore, the way you judged me.
Because you will not know....you will never know what it is like.

We are not perfect, lucky or as beautiful as you think.

frenzied Black man who is constructed as lusting for white flesh. You have clearly made a significant distinction between this man (your father), the other young man (that you are dating); you made mention of the texture of his skin (the date), but not the color of his skin, which has become salient. I am left with the imagery of your abuser being a very large, dark-skinned man, which perpetuates in other's imagination pejorative issues of dark-skinned Black man in media. There is an author named bell hooks (1990) who indicates that, "Images of Black men as rapists, as dangerous menaces to society, have been sensational cultural currency for some time. The obsessive media focus on these representations is political. The role it plays in the maintenance of racist domination is to convince the public that Black men are a dangerous threat who must be controlled by any means necessary, including annihilation" (p. 61). How can you speak your truth while also allowing people to realize that this imagery is co-opted and utilized in ways that also harm Black men? I ask because Black men are used to perpetuate racial stereotypes and racism. However, sexual abuse and misogyny must be viewed as a male issue of domination, power and control, not merely a Black male issue, right? Rape is not just a Black male issue, It is a societal pathology. And, we must be careful to unpack these issues without reproducing false constructions of Black male deviancy (only).

Do you feel that this rape has caused you not to have meaningful relationships? Are you afraid of intimacy, or the ability to have a committed relationship, because of what happened to you?

You said you "thought this year would be different," what were you expecting? Did you receive counseling, spiritual guidance, or speak with a close friend about your experiences? How have you healed, or sought to heal from this experience? This is a long journey...

Do you feel alone? What do you feel that it takes in order to be "normal"?

So, it looks as though it takes you a few weeks to "recuperate" from your relapse of victimization. It is fascinating that you identify and acknowledge that there is a cycle happening; do you desire to break that cycle? Do you desire to respond differently than you have been?

How do you feel in writing your experiences in this essay? Has it helped you with your road to recovering from this event that occurred in your life?

This piece has affected me on various levels, during the analysis process:
1) I was able to relate to what you were going through mentally and emotionally.
2) You engaged me in this story with these seemingly compartmentalized scenarios that explain your actions.
3) This piece made me question sociopolitical stereotypes of what being a woman meant—I was challenged to examine the definitions of such terms as "beauty," "sexy," and "normal."
4) I was challenged to understand the process of healing through writing.

Humanizing Pedagogy and Critical Literacy

We Wear the Mask

We wear the mask that grins and lies,
It hides our cheeks and shades our eyes,
This debt we pay to human guile;
With torn and bleeding hearts we smile,
And mouth with myriad subtleties.

Why should the world be over-wise,
In counting all our tears and sighs?
Nay, let them only see us, while
We wear the mask.

We smile, but, O great Christ, our cries
To thee from tortured souls arise.
We sing, but oh the clay is vile
Beneath our feet, and long the mile;
But let the world dream otherwise,
We wear the mask!
— Paul Laurence Dunbar

Initially upon reading Nicole's essay, I wore my own mask, a mask that portrayed a message of disconnecting from my surroundings. This mask indicated that as a reader, I am to separate my emotions from what the students write about. Historically, I observed my own teachers' inability or unwillingness to relate to me or my experiences. So I initially thought that this was the most appropriate action to take in reading student essays. My goal when I first began as a reader was not to read student writing for *content*, but instead to read student writing for *grammatical and sentence errors*. However, as I read Nicole's essay, I was viscerally provoked, and emotionally drawn into this student's raw memoir. This evoked personal memories of sexual abuse in my own life that I have not had to confront in quite some time, and I was not quite sure I was prepared to confront. However, as Rodriguez (2006) stated, it was time for me to "unmask my identity."

There is an increasing need for responsible pedagogy, which demands that one remove the mask as an educator. People consistently wear masks on a daily basis. These masks, which are meant to project an image based on societal expectations, have actually lead to an "inauthentic self." In reviewing authenticity and self-determination theory, Kernis and Goldman (2006) summarize that "people are authentic when their actions reflect their true- or core-self, that is when they are autonomous and self-determining," (p. 11). Kernis and Goldman further this review in indicating that when an individual is autonomous and self-determining, one will encounter and receive consistent and varied experiences with "openness" without "distorting or attempting to avoid" the varied and new experiences that will take place. It is through the inauthentic self that individuals attempt to hide, remain closed to new opportunities (that would assist in healing); and they may silently suffer from pain, depression, a sense of defeatism, rejection, loneliness, and hopelessness. They may suffer silently from rape, molestation, and/or emotional, mental and other forms of physical abuse. These manifestations of authentic emotions are dynamic, shaped by societal, cultural, and inter/intrapersonal factors. And these factors act in concert to shape the individual, particularly the individual who participates in school and curriculum.

In turn, there must be risk-taking by educators to make a conscientious effort to not be a voyeur within the classroom, but to allow for personal issues to be revealed. An educator must be transparent through the dialogue with the student. Miller (2009) indicates that:

> the dualism of the mind/body split can render a…teacher helpless if the individual does not understand the sociopolitical implications of the separation. If a teacher blindly accepts particular curriculum or ideas without completing background research, s/he may be sabotaging her/his agency (p. 195).

It is significant to establish deep inquiry and embodied practices to make a connection between the real-world issues that shape all of our lives as we run the course. Students are not objectified or alone; there is a more pronounced population on the macroeconomic level that has experienced similar situations of rape and/or molestation.

The effort of using a dialogue journal can help to support the development of a community of care. This context then necessitates that educators take risks in pushing students and themselves to explore sociopolitical issues that shape their socialization and experiences.

In this age, there is an incredible push for educators to homogenize learning and not allow students the freedom to explore their lives within a learning space. Similarly, it is just as significant (if not more) for an educator to be vulnerable with his/her students. This supports teacher/student relationships as well as fostering a positive learning community. Greene (2009) states:

> We cannot negate the fact of power. But we can undertake a resistance, a reaching out towards becoming persons among other persons, for all the talk of human resources, for all the orienting of education to the economy. To engage with our students as persons is to affirm our own incompleteness, our consciousness of spaces still to be explored, desires still to be tapped, possibilities still to be opened and pursued. At once, it is to rediscover the value of care, to reach back to experiences of caring and being cared for (p. 95)

Greene (2000) discusses how this affirmation of our own incompleteness in part can be accomplished through the ability of telling stories. It is in this process of "becoming" through telling stories that individuals become aware that their self-identity is not merely a construction of gender, ethnicity, and/or socioeconomic caste systems; one's identity also encompasses the construction of relating to one another through meaningful lived experiences; creating and realizing human relationships; and examining the spaces in which these entities are constructed. This knowledge and the themes embedded in Nicole's story helped me to explore my own lived experiences of sexual abuse, and the relationships that I have cultivated through a poetic reflection of my past experiences, present realities, and hopes for the future:

Dear seed of my womb [to come]:
If I am to be the best mother/grandmother I can ever hope to one day be,
Then let me be as real to you, as my Savior, the Lord Almighty, has been to me.
Because at this point in my life, I know no other way.
Let me share my journey;
What was, what is, and what I pray to come.

What was:

Weeping… for interrupted memory's childhood
A past, once upon a time, that I attempted to forget.
A past encompassed with sorrowful blue notes, darkness, and loneliness.
A past enveloped with gorging my temple to suppress unspoken truths,
Because skeletons were supposedly better left in a dingy deserted closet.
A past that haunted me with cold-sweat nightmares, a piss-burned nose, and a urine taste in my mouth.

With the secrets…
I died a little bit each night as I laid my head on my pillow,

I wished that death's slumber would enter my door.
What is:

I have spent many years...
Healing and releasing,
Being delivered continuously from the bondage of a past that was not warranted,
But instead was placed upon me.
Perpetually worrying what world you will be born into.
I never want you to experience...
Hurt, pain, depression, discouragement,
Which rests at the hands of a perverted man-child and/or woman-child
But I know that the world deals blows that I cannot control

What I pray to come:
But if any such emotions, or occurrences take place in your life,
Know that you are more than a conqueror.
Speak the silences that hide in corners and closets;
Release those entities which attempt to enslave your mind, and hold hostage your heart;
Allow joy to create vulnerability within you;
Choose to be free
Choose freedom as your way of life.
— Dana Muccular

Currere as a Practice of Healing

Stories about sexual abuse need to be told, as the writing space is a site for critical consciousness and healing in curriculum. And consciousness-raising can lead to emancipatory action within the classroom, instead of propagating voyeuristic approaches to students sharing their lives. Students are empowered to speak their truth; and educators, in turn, must resist the tendency to engage in pedagogy that is withdrawn and that does not delve into students' worlds. Lorde (2007) states:

> Change means growth, and growth can be painful. But we sharpen self-definition by exposing the self in work and struggle together with those whom we define as different from ourselves, although sharing the same goals...this can mean new paths to our survival. (p. 123)

For years following my sexual abuse, I experienced: betrayal, anger, anxiety, shame, humiliation, depression, and literal self-destruction. As a child, I gorged my body with food. As a teenager, I had so much hate in my heart—an utterly bitter, cantankerous soul that no one could see from the outside, because I had the perfectly pleasant quiet and smiling mask to fit any situation I was in. I was at the brink of what seemed to be "no return"; it was at this point that I cried out to Jesus in the most genuine of prayers to help deliver me from my oppression. What seemed to be a supernatural intervention was my saving grace. It was at this point that I sought a different route than the journey that I was initially on. I finally realized that I was/am a victor, not a victim. I was, in essence, "struggling to reconceptualize my own identity" (Lastica, 2009, p. 55), and who I truly desired to be. Most importantly, I knew I did not want to remain as I was; I wanted a new life, a fresh perspective.

hooks (2005) indicates that students desire to be healed from psychological, emotional, and physical issues. I also wanted to be "healed," to be free from the hate, the mental montages that played in my psyche. I did not want negative aspects of my past to determine my future. I did not want to be "trapped in [the] space between my [my present life] and [my] former life" (Lastica, 2009, p. 56). I was in between the spaces of my past as well as my present, uncertain of my future to come. However, I understood that I desired a greater purpose to dive "into the depths and recess and caves of the private self-into the 'window of the soul,'" (Martin, 2009, p. 104). My ability to aggressively confront my past through reflection is what caused my healing to occur; and the process allowed for me to forgive, to be delivered in my newfound Christian walk; and to write experiences that I did not feel comfortable speaking about. This is what ultimately set me free.

With this in mind, it is imperative for educators to cultivate and evaluate their ability to foster student learning. It is necessary to challenge the a priori notions that may stem from social-emotional issues related to trauma. Equally important as well is making the effort to study the self in order to understand the world surrounding the teaching self. It is through the study of self that personal and academic knowledge is deepened (i.e., becomes meaningful, purposeful, and fulfilling). Consequently, I developed further understanding of my position as an employed "reader" in the community college composition classroom. In this pedagogic instance, I was called to raise awareness about the complexity of gender as it intersects with race and with notions of female sexuality and sexism, whether external or internalized; and no matter how painful.

Thus, as I finished reading Nicole's essay, I reflected on my past and the factors that shaped who I have become as an educator, and who I desire to be in the future. Martin (2009) indicates that reflection on this positionality is an "instinct…to interpret myself, my journey, and my present position in life by the standards that defined my past…" (p. 105). Thus, in evaluating my journey, I have learned that I can and do choose to be free.

References

Berry, T. R. (2009). Women of color in a bilingual dialectical dilemma: Critical race feminism against a curriculum of oppression in teacher education. *International Journal of Qualitative Studies in Education, 22*(6), 745–753.

Bogle, D. (2001). *Toms, Coons, Mulattoes, Mammies, and Bucks: An Interpretive History of Blacks in American Films* (4th ed.). New York: Continuum.

Carson, T .R. (2006). Help without giving advice: Pinar, curriculum studies, and Canada. In B. S. Stern (Ed.), *Curriculum and Teaching Dialogue* (pp. 185–192). Greenwich, CT: Information Age Publishing.

Childhelp (2012). National child abuse statistics. http://www.childhelp.org/pages/statistics

Darder, A., Baltodano, M. P., & Torres, R. D. (Eds.). (2009). Critical pedagogy: An introduction. In A. Darder, M. P. Baltodano, & R. D. Torres (Eds.), *The Critical Pedagogy Reader*, (2nd ed., pp. 1–20). New York: Routledge.

Dunbar, P. L. (1993). *The Collected Poetry of Paul Laurence Dunbar* (Joanne M. Braxton, ed.). Charlottesville: University Press of Virginia.

Freire, P. (1970/2000). *Pedagogy of the Oppressed*. New York: Continuum.

Greene, M. (2000). Lived spaces, shared spaces, public spaces. In L. Weis & M. Fine (Eds.), *Construction Sites: Excavating Race, Class, and Gender Among Urban Youth* (pp. 293–303). New York: Teachers College Press.

Greene, M. (2009). In search of a critical pedagogy. In A. Darder, M. P. Baltodano, & R. D. Torres (Eds.), *The Critical Pedagogy Reader*, (2nd ed., pp. 84–99). New York: Routledge.

Henderson, J. G., & Kesson, K. R. (2009). Curriculum work at the intersection of pragmatic inquiry, deliberation, and fidelity. (Review of Pinar [2012], *Intellectual Advancement Through Disciplinarity: Verticality and Horizontality in Curriculum Studies*). *Educational Researcher, 38*(2), 132–136. http://edr.sagepub.com/content/38/2/141.full.pdf+html

hooks, b. (1990). *Yearning: Race, Gender, and Cultural Politics*. Boston: South End Press.

hooks, b. (2005). *Sisters of the Yam: Black Women and Self-Recovery*. Boston: South End Press.

Jones, D. (2008). *Teaching Means Learning Me: A Critical Examination of Effective Implementation of Multicultural Education and the Cultural Identities of Teachers in Private Preschools* (published thesis). Sacramento: California State University–Sacramento.

Kernis, M. H., & Goldman, B. M. (2006). Multicomponent conceptualization of authenticity: Theory and research. *Advances in Experimental Social Psychology, 38*.

Kissel-Ito, C. (2008). Currere as transformative storytelling in religious education. *Religious Education, 103*(3), 339–350.

Ladson-Billings, G., & Tate, W. F. (2009). Toward a critical race theory of education. In A. Darder, M. P. Baltodano, & R. D. Torres (Eds.), *The Critical Pedagogy Reader*, (2nd ed., pp. 167–182). New York: Routledge.

Lastica, J. R. (2009). This is my crossroads. *High School Journal, 92*(3), 54-60.

Lorde, A. (2007). *Sister Outsider*. New York: Crown .

Martin, J. V. (2009). Currere and the hours: Rebirth of the female self. *Journal of Curriculum Theorizing, 25*(1), 100–109.

Miller, S. J. (2009). (Dis)embedding gender diversity in the preservice classroom. In S. R. Steinberg (Ed.), *Diversity and Multiculturalism: A Reader* (pp. 193–209). New York: Peter Lang.

Peyton, J. K, & Staton, J. (1993). *Resource Guide: A Dialogue Journal Bibliography*. Washington, DC: NCLE.

Pinar, W. F. (2012). *What Is Curriculum Theory?* (2nd ed.). New York: Routledge.

Rodriguez, D. (2006). Un/masking identity: Healing our wounded souls. *Qualitative Inquiry, 12*(6), 1067–1089.

Schubert, W. H. (2009). Currere and disciplinarity in curriculum studies: Possibilities for education research. *Educational Researcher, 38*(2), 132–143. http://edr.sagepub.com/content/38/2/136. extract

Shange, N. (2010). *For Colored Girls Who Have Considered Suicide/When the Rainbow Is Enuf: A Choreopoem*. New York: Scribner.

CHAPTER NINE

"We Will Understand It Better By and By"

Sojourning to Racial Literacy

AYANNA F. BROWN

Farther along we'll know more about it,
Farther along we'll understand why;
Cheer up, my brother, live in the sunshine,
We'll understand it all by and by.
— From a hymn by W. B. Stevens, 1911

Why does there seem to be opposition in associating the legacy of racism in the United States with the current educational climate? Is it absurd to discuss openly the historic and persisting deficit beliefs about African Americans, which are grounded in de facto and de jure racist practices? If racism was so powerful that it gave birth to a nation and its economic prosperity for over 346 years, would not that same racism be strong enough to influence epistemologies promulgating in K–12 schools and in teacher education? What types of measures could be taken to eradicate nearly three and a half centuries of hate? I use these questions as guideposts to examine and interrogate why it is critical to understand racism and education despite Civil Rights laws and efforts to achieve social and political equality. Delgado (1995) suggests:

> Civil rights laws efficiently and smoothly replicate social reality, particularly black-white power relations. They are a little like the thermostat in your home or office. They assure that there is just the right amount of racism. Too much would be destabilizing—the victims would rebel. Too little would forfeit important pecuniary and psychic advantages for those in power. So, the existing system of race-remedies law does, in fact, grant

minorities an occasional victory…. Particularly in areas where concessions are not too costly… (p. 80)

Race and racism are not accidental products of individualized ideologies. Delgado reminds us of the legally constructed significance of inequity, which makes race and conversely racism not only normal in the United States but reinforced through the law. As one of my students, Darcy,[1] wrote in a course journal: "Racism is as American as baseball and apple pie." I believe efforts to unveil these complex and nuanced structures require an intellectual activism (Bell, 1980; 1987; Crenshaw, 1995; Stovall, 2006). I regard intellectual activism as sojourning, intentional choices and actions made to debase a centric purview in efforts to generate new questions and concomitantly create new spaces for discussing lived realities as a form of literacy—racial literacy.

Sojourning to Racial Literacy: Event 3

I still remember the pain and abhorrence I felt in graduate school when I used an analytic racial lens to discuss Freire's (1970/2000) notion of oppression as a pedagogical journey shared by the oppressed and the oppressor. During a class discussion, I suggested, that oppression in the United States is multifaceted and based on a racial hierarchy; and the liberation of which Freire speaks seems impossible because racial oppression is psychologically coercive and has evolved to include the rhetoric of colorblindness. I furthered my analysis to discuss the inevitability of racial oppression in the United States by suggesting some Whites rely on racism in a multitude of forms to both construct and maintain identity. As my peers listened, some nodding in agreement and others with inquisitive expressions, an exchange of reasonable discussion began to brew among us. There was interest in looking at Freire in a U.S. context, and as I attempted to provide a scenario to color my analysis, my professor, sitting beside me, interrupted me in mid-sentence by yelling, "Shut up!"

Believing I was in a mad-woman's dream (*I know she isn't yelling at me*), I continued to complete my point.

But the yelling continued, only louder and shook me into that present moment. "Ayanna, Shut up!"

My peers' silences were hollow.

The heat from my own body radiated and yet stunned, I worked to pierce my lips shut forbidding a reply to exude from me.

I felt and tasted salty water as it rolled down the contours of my face and I was boiling with anger and embarrassment.

And my classmates remained silent.

---

1 Students' names used throughout this chapter are pseudonyms. Permission was granted by students to use their journals for research and reporting .

My eyes were then fixed on an irrelevant image in the room.

The pale faces of graduate students all seemed to be gazing at my beaten-down brown spirit, like the curious faces you see in those old postcards of a lynching—not disgusted or saddened by the event but motionless, gazing and wondering when the branch will break.

I felt hung.

My first semester in graduate school wasn't my first event in "reading the world" with an analytic racial lens. Unfortunately, I had many encounters as an adolescent where I had to advocate for my own educational needs, which either pitted me against authority figures or an entire system. I saw structural racial inequality easily—it was either my literacy gift or curse. Battles with "The Academies: Event 1" involved fighting to be admitted into an Advanced Placement course, arguing with guidance counselors, and eventually, the superintendent of the city schools, who called my home one Tuesday afternoon about my college choice ("Black College or University of California schools: Event 2"). *Do all superintendents call all high school seniors on their home telephones to berate them about their college choices? He should have been calling all the Black and Latino kids in E.P.A. apologizing for their forced destiny to community colleges while he was at the helm of instructional leadership for the district.* Ladson-Billings (2009) posits, "[T]he experience of oppressions such as racism or sexism has important aspects for developing a CRT analytical standpoint (p. 21). Critical race theory (CRT) was my reality, and while I could not name it in a scholastic way, I knew my educational experiences and opportunities were based on my work to displace what the system had planned for me.

Today, I regard these events as my "Welcome Mat" for entering the journey towards elevating an understanding of race as systematic, interactional, discursive, reactive, and most importantly, a transformative reality. I entered secondary education and ultimately college teaching with my own insights as to how race and discussions of race functioned (Bonilla-Silva, 2002; Brown, 2008; Reisigl & Wodak, 2001). The absence of discussions of "race" in curricula and pedagogy serve as a catalyst for my teaching and learning. Critical analysis of our sociopolitical world and its subsequent impact on diverse communities isn't included on standardized testing on any level. Critical perspectives are also not constituted as needed, necessary, common or core to what is promulgated in teacher education. This critical absence forces me to question, "Are our teacher candidates growing any critical roots? Will we 'understand it better by and by'?"

My Teaching Contexts

My students, most of whom are White and female, have accepted "raceless" identities (Morrison, 1992; Fordham, 1988). Most of them had not been encouraged to see themselves as White—they just "be." Leonardo (2009) suggests, examining the social, political, and cultural contexts for how whiteness has influenced their own educational experiences is an odd concept and a disturbing experience. Discussions of difference either begin with great distance from themselves, or contrastingly, they situate their own experiences or views as frameworks for thinking about other people and communities. So, when talking about education, their frames of references become the center for how they think about learning and communities. Giroux (1997) regards this as a "third space for whites," where "White righteousness" and "the White hegemonic oppressor" are located and then nuanced and entangled to reveal the reproductive nature of race, power, and oppression in education, which are discursively activated (Brown, 2012). I created the Race and Equity course to develop a supportive, yet critical space where teacher candidates could actively locate their own journeys and deconstruct the relationship between race and education; and quite frankly, to combat the consequences of the White paradigmatic center that is so entrenched. Bhabha's (1994) inception of the third space is an articulation of meaning conveyed through cultural knowledge, which is dynamic and continually under construction.

> It is only when we understand that all cultural statements and systems are constructed through [this] contradictory and ambivalent space of enunciation… It is that Third Space, though unrepresentable in itself, which constitutes the discursive conditions of enunciation that ensure the meaning of symbols of culture have no primordial unity or fixity; that even the same signs can be appropriated, translated, rehistorized and read anew. (Bhabha, 1994, p. 37)

I purport a third space to be the opportunity to make college academic courses dynamic, where reinterpretations and lived experiences guide learning. There is value if courses can work to disrupt positivistic rationalities, which all too often frame the epistemological stance for pedagogy. I believe there must be both alternative and oppositional ways of thinking, doing, and teaching that can lead toward a reconceptualization of education, and a "third space," undefined yet supported in its manifestation during praxis, is critical.

I present my deliberative choices to cultivate racial literacy among White teacher candidates through my course development and teaching. I use an active reflective approach in the course alongside critical questioning because it appropriates opportunity for my students to process their ideas and to embrace questioning as a tool for development (Howard, 2003). Alongside using reflection as a tool for self-improvement, I use narrative as an equally important cornerstone to support how the class community both "names" and "owns" their experiences as relevant for sense-making and analysis. Gilborn (2008) reiterates:

> A particularly striking aspect of some CRT is the use of storytelling and counterstorytelling. Here myths, assumptions and received wisdoms can be questioned by shifting the

grounds of debate or presenting analyses in ways that turn dominant assumptions on their head. (p. 31)

Throughout the course, we use and encourage narratives to support autonomy while simultaneously developing a community (Brown, 2008). Narrative is empowering, and invites a reflective process and practices that allow students to receive perspectives of race and racism as much as they offer them. The course goals then are to: (1) support students' abilities to be both critical and analytical about race and use those insights to raise questions about how and when ideologies determine epistemologies; and (2) develop a voice to advocate with research and action for students who are oppressed by educators and educational processes that create systems. Using data from student reflective journals, I illustrate how White teacher candidates respond to racial literacy *in situ* of education and praxis.

Racial Literacy?

We've all heard those racially rooted scenarios like, "If you are a Black male driving down the street with your friends in the car and you are pulled over by the police, keep your hands on the steering wheel and look forward. And don't reach for your license until you are asked." Or, "When you are followed by store security or employees, act undisturbed by their presence. It will more quickly dissipate their paranoia." And, "When you are the only Black person or non-White in class and don't understand material, wait until after class to ask your questions or meet with your professor during office hours." Or conversely, "If you are *the only one* in your class and you understand material, make an effort to demonstrate that knowledge in clear ways. Stand out!" These scenarios did not originate with journalist John Quinones and the producers at the American Broadcast Company (ABC); they are seeds planted by parents of Black children preparing their children for racism in the real world. Teaching Black children how to handle race-related prejudice or overt racism is common in Black families. Unfortunately, for many Black families, being familiar with these types of events and ways to react is necessary. What do we call the intelligences, knowledges, or practices needed by Black youth to turn on their "racial radar"? What competencies are required for Black youth that allow them to read a racial world that enables them to respond to potential problems and retain a healthy self-concept? Twine (2004) coined the term "racial literacy," which emerged from the parental labor of White mothers who train their non-White children to develop racial consciousness and the ability to respond to racism in the United Kingdom. I find it interesting that within this concept, White mothers equip their biracial children to deal with racism, and it is accepted as a literacy—a skill; conversely, Black families who strive to do the same are quick to be labeled as paranoid or having hypersensitive imaginations. The reality, however, according to Twine's work, is Black children must be equipped "with resources that assist them in countering everyday racism," (p. 882). The concept of racial literacy is not limited to Twine's scholarship, as Frabutt, Walker, and MacKinnon-Lewis (2002) discuss similar postulations as racial socialization. "Parents of children in racial/ethnic minority families face unique challenges and complexities throughout the family life course" (p. 200). Part of these challenges include the additional responsibilities minority families bear in "socializing their children to function competently in the broader society (p. 201). This task for minority families is reflective of the necessary knowledge of "race" and difference that parents believe will impact their children, if acquired and used properly. So my research in understanding the degrees to which non-White families work to prepare and protect their children in a racist society created questions for me. Mainly, what do we call White people (not necessarily children) who have no knowledge, understanding, empathy, or ability to critique race-related events? Would they be labeled racially illiterate? Goldberg (1993) states,

> Racial knowledge consists *ex hypothesi* in the making of difference; it is in a sense and paradoxically the assumption and paradigmatic establishment of difference. An epistemology so basically driven by difference will "naturally" find racialized thinking comfortable; it will uncritically (come to) assume racial knowledge a given (p. 150).

I listen patiently to my White teacher candidates process information about "race," and there is a painful moment for me because I know they will soon enter the classroom where the faces that will peer up at them are hues of brown and with languages of rich histories. And my teacher candidates might be compelled to follow their scripts, consume their curricula, and reproduce narratives of those kids who can't and won't learn. Rather than becoming numb to this pain, I decide that I can offer an intervention. What if I change the familial rooted context of racial literacy from mothers to their Black children? What if the context for racial literacy is teacher education and the audience is teacher candidates who embrace racelessness or colorblindness as if these ideologies are advancing the schooling experiences of non-White students? Would racial literacy skills manifest themselves differently in school settings than in family life or within implications for social policy? "Failing to discuss, describe, and account for issues of race in learning settings and educational processes renders us blind to the ways that racialization can play an important role in learning and schooling" (Nasir, 2012, p. 5).

I don't see my own teacher practices akin to a mother nurturing and protecting her children, so the core of racial literacy to this end is not analogous. However, there seems to be an epistemological chasm for Black and White children. First, it is critically necessary for Black children to understand race and how it functions in everyday life in order to survive and prosper. Conversely, White children are privileged in not being required or even remotely aware of racism and the extent to which non-White children don't share this same luxury. The privilege of whiteness disables White children, and ultimately, White adults from grappling with these issues and their roles within it. The absence of opportunity to develop a racial analytic lens or literacy contributes to the development of active, passive, or dysconscious forms of racism. The tenets for racial literacy applicable for an educational context are grounded in developing a racial analytic lens:

1. Teach students about "race" and its function in multiple contexts;

2. Use discussions of "race" as a means to interpret and analyze texts, including everyday life;

3. Encourage student inquiry into how their own racial identities are influenced or impacted by their educational experiences;

4. Promote racially literate thinking (e.g., reading, writing, discussion, listening to music, and engaging in producing art) as a tool for high academic performance.

The Inception of EDU 331

I began my position as an assistant professor in 2007 and my initial responsibility was to revise the Foundations of American Education course (EDU 104). With great enthusiasm, I pursued developing a course that would explore the culture of education in the United States alongside the propaganda of education in the United States. So rather than limiting my curriculum to Jefferson and Mann as the roots of public education, I positioned ideology, ethnocentricity, hegemony, and discourse as stapled concepts used to interrogate, for example, Jefferson and Mann, among a host of other educational architects and philosophies. To this degree, my students would be able to explore philosophies of education in a social context rather than as isolated perspectives for teaching and learning. Because this was a required course for our teacher candidates, I was confident that this oppositional approach to the romantic narratives of education in the United States might inspire my students to raise new questions throughout their programs; in many ways, it did just that. Here's an example of my approach:

Jefferson advocated for a meritocratic system in education. He espoused that if you work hard, you will succeed and be rewarded and that everyone deserved an equal opportunity to participate in education. Class, if Jefferson believed this, why were Black people excluded from education? What was the risk in American society to exclude women from education beyond the third grade? What is Jefferson's ideology on equality based on his writings in *Notes on Virginia*? What do these notes tell us about education for non-Whites?

Despite the success of the revised course for the department, students moved through their remaining methods and content area courses disconnected from sociocultural and sociopolitical issues and an opportunity to apply to the pedagogy.

Unconsciousness, dysconsciousness (King, 1991), and unquestioned consumption of "the American idea" were common embodied student dispositions as they completed their programs, for there were no other courses after 104 that pushed them to examine the quality of education for students subjugated by power and ideology. Whiteness as an ideological dominance saturated our teacher education program! Earick (2009) asserts, "Our public education system supports White power and privilege that manifests itself in White supremacy. This is accomplished through the reproduction of White racial ideologies in our schools" (p. 11). How could I get students to discuss the correlations between racism and education as a reality and not a myth of my own "Black conspiracy theory"? Not to mention help unsuspecting students deconstruct it, and have it move in their pedagogical considerations during a 15-week course? I used Howard's (2003) charge to teacher educators as a nucleus for the development of the course:

> In order to provide more meaningful knowledge and skills for teaching in today's cultural context, teacher educators must be able to help preservice teachers critically analyze important issues such as race, ethnicity, and culture, and recognize how these important concepts shape the learning experience for many students" (p. 195).

As the only African American in my department, I felt a pressure to address the absence of discussion of racism and education (Brown, 2008). I was inspired and excited, discontented and isolated—my observations and thoughts were only mine; there were no collegial discussions I might align with to create a toolkit to dismantle "the master's house" (Lorde, 2007). So I wrote.

> New course. New course goals. Extend. Push. Identify self in relationship to education. How do you participate in cultural reproduction? What are we producing in education in the United States? What do we envision as the educational outcomes for non-White students? (Brown & William-White, 2010)

While the course was offered for spring 2009, no one signed up (Brown & William-White, 2010). I marketed the course and recruited former students from my previous 104 classes, for they had experienced my oppositional approach to thinking about issues and text. I worked to have the course cross listed within the minors of Sociology and our Intercultural Studies program. If anything was going to change, I needed an audience.

In spring 2009, nine students enrolled, all White females. In fall 2009, eight students enrolled: one White male, one Latina, and five White females. In fall 2010 there was one African American female, one White male, two Latinas, and seven White females. In fall 2011, six White females enrolled.

Course Description: This course identifies race and equity as constructs for analysis and interrogation rather than isolating race as a variable by which educational outcomes are measured. As such, this course will develop a broader understanding of race that includes examining social constructs like "whiteness," "blackness," "othering," and teacher identity that often remain unexamined in many teacher education programs.

Inadvertently, as I developed the course curriculum based on the absence of discussions of "race" within my students' discourses and among my colleagues as we did departmental planning, I found that my framework for what students should learn in the class had teaching tenets for a racial analytical pedagogy I espoused. Table 1 illustrates the alignment of the course objectives with the tenets for racial literacy.

Table 1: Alignment of Course Objectives and Racial Literacy Tenets

Course Objectives	Alignment of Racial Literacy Tenets with Course Objectives	The Role of the Teacher
1. Students will be able to discuss how race has been defined historically and in contemporary life in the United States.	Racial Tenet 1	Teach students about "race" and its function in multiple contexts;
2. Students will be able to discuss how ideologies of race influence teacher preparation and teacher practice.	Racial Tenet 3	Encourage student inquiry into how their own racial identities are influenced or impacted by their educational experiences;
3. Students will be able to read and analyze reported data from schools that reflects its level of racial awareness and consciousness as reflected in its curricula and educational programming.	Racial Tenet 2	Use discussions of "race" as a means to interpret and analyze texts, including everyday life;
4. Students will learn the outlining process for organizing research questions related to race and equity.	Racial Tenet 2	Use discussions of "race" as a means to interpret and analyze texts, including everyday life;
5. Students will develop qualitative inquiry tools to raise questions about race driven by their own research interests.	Racial Tenet 4	Promote racially literate thinking as a tool for high academic performance.

The Curriculum: Read, Write, Discuss, Watch, Create, and Question

There are several events that make EDU 331 work. A key component to the course is reading, writing, and discussions, which I view as processing tools for literate thinking. Students keep thematic journals for 12 weeks, and at the end of each journal, they complete an analysis of their thinking. Also, every four weeks, the students complete a "Digital Dump," where they videotape themselves discussing an issue from the literature they found perplexing or interesting that they believe warrants more discussion. These dumps began as five-minute talks and by the end of the semester, they were 15-minute discussions. Students are required to use supportive texts to help their articulations. In some cases, student use the "dumping" as a time to oppose the reading and introduce new insights on a topic that must be research based or vetted through an analytical set of processes.

Students are also introduced to qualitative research processes, where they collect data, learn qualitative coding, work on analysis of data, and present preliminary findings to the class. This portion of the class is critical, for as they begin to deconstruct race in their own lives, they need to see what issues permeated for them, directed by their own needs. Many of my students discover findings that I could not have taught or presented to them in a way that would have gained their further acceptance of depths of racism. The student-directed research often leads them to higher levels of analytic racial thinking because my role is minimized to facilitating their analysis. Aside from all they read about race, equity, and education, they complete the course equipped with the skills to excavate race in more complex ways. Most of my students leave the course invigorated and feeling connected to a community willing to process the complexities of racism and education. However, they complete the course wanting more, and disappointed that the experiences from this course don't carry over to other education courses.

Meet Beth and Darcy

Beth was a cheerful, responsive, and curious student. She grew up in a middle-class family with supportive parents. She pursued scholarships to reduce her family's expenses but understood that no matter the cost, her parents would find a way to pay the college bills. I taught her in EDU 104, where she did exemplary work and led group discussions with respect for the content. While, like most college students, she was certainly concerned about her performance, she pursued her work with an interest for learning that was greater than "getting an A." Beth had strawberry-blond hair and a bold smile. She was never afraid to ask me a question and even more powerfully, she approached her questions as critical rather than matter of fact. I found her presence in 104 necessary to move her peers, but she never imposed her intellect or curiosity upon others. Entering 331 in fall 2009,

Beth was 20 years old and two semesters from completing her degree in Elementary Education with an endorsement in Reading.

Darcy was a curious yet patient student. She grew up in a working-class White family, with a few experiences living in a trailer home community. Despite the sometimes unstable economic situations in her family, she actively discussed her privilege; as a child she was not to interact with, play with, or talk to Black people or "those Mexicans," she reflected. Inasmuch as she knew poverty, the also knew that being White had its own benefits. Darcy completed the EDU 104 course as she entered the Elementary Education program. She used many narratives from her family to help question and challenge ideas presented in class. While she believed equity was necessary for society to advance, she wrestled with reflection; her exposure to racism within her family created tension as she espoused idealistic teacher colloquialisms like "All children can learn." Interestingly, she embraced the tension and worked really hard at naming racism in our class discussions. Part of her abilities rested within her familiarity with racism's everyday discourse among ordinary people.

Beth and Darcy used journaling very differently. Beth used a bulleted form of expression and periodically inserted questions. It was personal, hers. Darcy on the other hand used some traditional writing conventions, recognizing an audience for her journaling process. These varying formats used for thinking were essential. However, all students needed to review their journals and then produce a synthesis of the course based on their personal journeys within it. The synthesis provided another data source to assess my students' engagement with racial literacy.

"Table 2: Journal Analysis of Racial Literacy" aligns excerpts from Beth and Darcy's journals with the tenets for racial literacy. I found the use of language in the written discussions of "race" to reflect the presence of a racial analytic lens and the development of racial literacy.

Table 2: Journal Analysis of Racial Literacy

The Products of Labor: Beth and Darcy Spark

Tenet 1: Teach students about "race" and its function in multiple contexts
Beth: The articles that we read and the discussions that took place truly gave me an understanding of what needs to be changed in our schools. The scary part is that only seven of us learned about these inequities this semester, compared to the large grouping of students who are still blinded from the evident truths that shape our education system.

Darcy: In class, Dr. Brown said something like, ". . . calling yourself white is the same as the white crayon in the crayon box—it doesn't do anything unless the paper is colored." This had to have been one of the best similes (at least I think it's a simile) I have ever heard. It made me think, yeah, us white people feel fine and we think everything is fantastic until someone with darker skin enters the room. Then we start questioning things. We never see ourselves as anything because to us, we are the norm.

Tenet 2: Use discussions of "race" as a means to interpret and analyze texts, including everyday life

Beth: This class was entirely different [than other classes] in that respect. I read texts that were jaw-dropping, participated in conversations that were raw and uncomfortable, and learned that in this day and age, racism is certainly still a part of our nation's culture, whether we want it to be or not.

Darcy: Well, today we had a "real world" type interview with a camera based on our reading of The Heart of Whiteness. It was an interesting experience, one I have never had before, and I found it to be quite helpful. I was able to talk about things and ramble about things I have really never said before. I was comfortable and felt the freedom to say whatever I wanted.

It has become quite obvious how systemic these problems have become, especially when I see them on a weekly basis in the school where I will be student teaching. Teachers scream at some students (typically African-American students), put some on "pedestals" (typically white students), and ignore others (typically Latino-Americans). I've heard teachers talk horribly about certain groups of people (namely Latino-Americans) and have heard other teachers groan when discussing the "racial" demographic of their classroom. It is difficult to know where to begin.

Tenet 3: Encourage student inquiry into how their own racial identities are influenced or impacted by their educational experiences

Beth: After this class, I cannot shake off the inequities I see in today's classrooms. I have to talk, rant, and tell other people about my experiences. Others may not be willing to have discussions about inequities in the classroom, but I certainly will not back down. These issues are way too important to ignore. Racial tensions cannot be turned away for the sheer sake of being awkward and unpleasant. If they are, we will continue on a downward spiral that we tried to erase with the Civil War and then the Civil Rights Movement. Race cannot hide from me any longer and with the help of my peers, I hope to make a change in our schools.

Darcy: All education classes, at least the ones I have taken, weave thin threads of these issues within what is considered more pertinent information. As is quite obvious with the number of students who took EDU 331 this semester, without making these classes requirements, no one would take them. Instead, we have teachers who are teaching in the field without any experience with deconstructing their own beliefs and without any knowledge of why the public schools are the way they are. Coming from where I do and having taken the classes I have, I think it would be quite challenging to find colleagues who would be willing to support me in my ventures.

Tenet 4: Promote racially literate thinking as a tool for high academic performance

Beth: During my time at a local middle school, I had the unfortunate opportunity to see racial tensions and the educational system slam together at full speed. The experience made me feel stressed and outraged, but it did fuel my fire. It ignited a passion within me because I saw exactly what we had been discussing in class. Race, education, inequity: three simple words, three profound meanings, and three reasons why as an educator, I have to be willing to confront uncomfortable issues.

Through my observing experience, I took myself out of the picture and tried to see school through the students' eyes. It was a jail cell, with very little excitement. There was no laughter from the teacher, only loud voices and behavior warnings. There was very little smiling, except by the students, when interacting with one another. The excitement had been burnt out in the classroom, and it was very evident that these types of environments are very much a part of our educational system. It was truly a sad picture, most likely one that educators ignore or have never seen.

Darcy: I have come to realize white teachers can never truly relate to non-white students even without the ideology of racial superiority, let alone with it. In How White Teachers Construct Race, we learn "the teaching population in the US is becoming increasingly white while the student population is becoming increasingly racially diverse." This is particularly worrisome to me as a future white teacher. While I am on the side of not wanting our schools to continually weave the thread of racism through its curriculum, I am unsure where to begin if having a "predominantly white teaching force . . . is not good for anyone."

Every spring semester as students begin registering for their fall courses, I find myself obnoxiously checking our electronic database to see if my EDU 331 has met the minimum enrolled number. This number, eight, determines if my course will happen. Every other day, I am embarrassed either by the fact that the number of students enrolled is still less than eight or overcome with meeting the expectation of transformative teaching when I see that the enrollment number has surpassed the eight. Because the course is now a part of the college's general education curriculum (Elmhurst College Integrated Curriculum), there have been times when the course has "gone through" with as few as six enrolled. What does this suggest? I believe my department administrators know how valuable this course has been, and to pull it for low enrollment has implications. Or at least, I would like to believe this. I also know that I am responsible for promoting the course, because as Beth states, "Others may not be willing to have discussions about inequities in the classroom" (see Tenet 3 Commentary). And as Darcy's extends, "without making these classes requirements, no one would take them" (see Tenet 3 Commentary).

Beth and Darcy's reflections remind me that as with the challenges I offered in my first graduate class, there are those who may want to shut me up. I actively engage the yelling in my ear. *Ayanna, don't teach this content. Shut up. We don't want this content taught—not this way. It is too provocative. It exposes too much.* This noise—this yelling—is my fuel to keep moving. Beth and Darcy's writings are examples of the products of our humility. So today, without fear, shame, regret, or even resentment for the absences of discussions of "race" or the silences among my colleagues when there is a discussion emerging, I check the enrollment. On, July, 16, 2012, at 1:12 p.m., there are ten. Ten women. One freshman. Six sophomores. Two juniors. One senior. Ten. And there is only one me. "The power of one."

References

Bell, D. (1980). Brown v. Board of Education and the interest-convergence dilemma. *Harvard Law Review*, *93*, 518–533.

Bell, D. (1987). *And We Are Not Saved: The Elusive Quest for Racial Justice*. New York: Basic Books.

Bhabha, H. K. (1994). *The Location of Culture*. New York: Routledge.

Bloome, D., & Brown, A. F. (2011). Classroom reading and "All That Jazz." In M. Grenfell (Ed.), *Language, Ethnography, and Education*. New York: Routledge.

Bonilla-Silva, E. (2002). The linguistics of color-blind racism: How to talk nasty about blacks without sounding "racist." *Critical Sociology*, *28*, 41–64.

Brown, A. F. (2008). Constructing "race" through talk: A micro-ethnographic investigation of discussions of "race" among African American secondary students (Doctoral dissertation). http://etd.library.vanderbilt.edu/ETD-db/available/etd-03312008-143259/

Brown, A. F. (2010, April). "Don't make me act my color!" African American literacies as racial literacy. In V. Gadsden (Chair), *African American Literacies*. Symposium conducted at the annual meeting of the American Education Research Association, Denver, CO.

Brown, A. F. (2012). "I once was lost but now I'm found": Teaching against cultural reproduction. In D. Bloome (Chair), *Bridging New Literacy Studies, Classroom Language Ethnography, and Bourdieu's Social Philosophy*. Symposium conducted at the annual meeting of the American Education Research Association, Vancouver, British Columbia.

Brown, A. F., & William-White, L. Y. (2010) "We are not the same minority": The narratives of two sisters navigating discourses and identity at public and private White institutions. In C. Cole

Robinson & P. Clardy (Eds.), *Tedious Journeys: Autoethnography of Women of Color in Academe* (pp. 147–171). New York: Peter Lang.

Carter, S. P. (2001). *The possibilities of silence: African American female cultural identity and secondary English classrooms* (Unpublished doctoral dissertation). Vanderbilt University, Nashville, TN.

Crenshaw, K. (1995). Mapping the margins: Intersectionality, identity politics, and violence against women of color. In K. Crenshaw, N. Gotanda, G. Peller, & K. Thomas (Eds.), *Critical Race Theory: The Key Writings That Formed the Movement* (pp. 357–383). New York: New Press.

Delgado, R. (1995). *The Rodrigo Chronicles: Conversations About America and Race*. New York: New York University Press.

Earick, M . (2009). *Racially Equitable Teaching: Beyond the Whiteness of Professional Development for Early Childhood Educators*. New York: Routledge.

Fordham, S. (1988). Racelessness as a factor in black students' school success: Pragmatic strategy or pyrrhic victory? *Harvard Educational Review, 58*(1), 54–85.

Frabutt, J., Walker, A., & MacKinnon-Lewis, C. (2002). Racial socialization messages and the quality of mother/child interactions in African American families. *Journal of Early Adolescence, 22*, 200–217.

Freire, P. (1970/2000). *Pedagogy of the Oppressed*. New York: Continuum.

Gilborn, D. (2008). *Racism and Education: Coincidence or Conspiracy*. New York: Routledge.

Giroux, H. (1992). Literacy, pedagogy, and the politics of difference. *College Literature, 19*, 1–11.

Giroux, H. (1997). Racial politics and the pedagogy of whiteness. In M. Hill (Ed.), *Whiteness: A Critical Reader* (pp. 294–315). New York: New York University Press.

Goldberg, D. (1993). *Racist Culture: Philosophy and the Politics of Meaning*. Malden, MA: Blackwell.

Howard, T. (2003). Culturally relevant pedagogy: Ingredients for critical teacher reflection. *Theory Into Practice, 42*, 195–202.

Hughes, D., Rodriguez, J., Smith, E., Johnson, D., Stevenson, D., & Spicer, P. (2006). Parents' ethnic-racial socialization practices: A review of research and directions for future study. *Developmental Psychology, 42*(5), 747–770.

King, J. (1991). Dysconscious racism: Ideology, identity, and the miseducation of teachers. *Journal of Negro Education, 60*(2), 133–146.

Ladson-Billings, G. (2009). Just what is critical race theory doing in a *nice* field like education? In E. Taylor, D. Gilborn, & G. Ladson-Billings (Eds.), *Foundations of Critical Race Theory in Education* (pp. 17–36). New York: Taylor & Francis.

Leonardo, Z. (2009). *Race, Whiteness, and Education*. New York: Routledge.

Lorde, A. (1984/2007). *Sister Outsider*. Berkeley, CA: Crossing Press.

Morrison, T. (1992). *Playing in the Dark: Whiteness and the Literary Imagination*. Cambridge, MA: Harvard University Press.

Nasir, N. (2012). *Racialized Identities: Race and Achievement Among African American Youth*. Stanford, CA: Stanford University Press.

Reisigl, M., & Wodak, R. (2001). *Discourse and Discrimination: Rhetorics of Racism and Antisemitism*. New York: Routledge.

Stovall, D. (2006). Forging community in race and class: Critical race theory and the quest for social justice in education. *Race Ethnicity and Education, 9*(3), 243–259.

Twine, F. (2004). A White side of Black Britain: The concept of racial literacy. *Ethnic and Racial Studies, 27*, 878–907.

CHAPTER TEN

At the Helm

The Challenges of Empowering Agriculture Workers to Obtain Their GEDs

MARIA MEJORADO

I was 11 years old when President Lyndon B. Johnson described migrant workers as among the "forgotten Americans" (U.S. Department of Labor News, 1967). My family would have met the 1967 poverty guidelines ($3,850 annual earnings for a family of nine) for the newly approved nationwide GED Program. President Johnson continued, "Their wages are low, their employment uncertain and their housing and working conditions deplorable. Though their needs are great, they often find it impossible to obtain social services available to other poverty-stricken Americans." President Johnson was talking about me and my family.

Although my parents were born in Texas, our family is part of the American immigrant story, as they left their birthplace in search of better employment and educational opportunities for their children. Settling in one of California's richest agricultural valleys ultimately ended our family's migrant lifestyle and ensured that our schooling would not be interrupted. School was highly valued in my family. My mother never wavered in holding us accountable for earning a high school diploma. Thus, a few times each summer, during the hottest and most miserable part of the workday, she would threaten that if we didn't do well in school, we would have to join her to work in the fields every day rather than just during the summer grape harvesting season. It was her way of imparting the importance of education, and despite our poverty we all earned a high school diploma.

César Chávez was an American farmworker, labor leader, and civil rights activist. Along with Dolores Huerta, he established the United Farm Workers Union in

1962. Through the UFW Union they negotiated for better wages and much improved working conditions using nonviolent tactics such as boycotts, pickets, strikes, and later César-led fasts. My parents refused to join the UFW Union for fear the rancheros, for whom we worked for years, would replace us with other workers. It wasn't until middle school that I become aware that portable toilets were made available for our use in the fields through the heroic efforts of the UFW Union. I recall announcing to my parents, that regardless of whether we were replaced by other workers, I supported César Chávez for that one human act, for I no longer had to reduce my water intake in the heat of summer nor hide deep in the grapevines for privacy.

As described by low-income and high-achieving professional Chicanos in Gandara's *Over the Ivy Wall* (1995), stories of past family fortunes and having literature in the home were ways parents demonstrated the importance of education, however this level of home support was often unrecognized by schools. My mother shared stories of her family's past wealth as a way to give us hope and to do well in school. Other examples of Latino parents promoting education included reading the Bible, writing to extended family in Mexico (or in our case, South Texas), having magazines (in our household of 5 older brothers it was *Sports Illustrated*) and having the *Encyclopædia Britannica* in the home. In the 1960s, the encyclopedia was offered in grocery stores redeemable with coupons, the only way my parents were able to purchase a few volumes. Although none of my friends had the complete set of the 26 alphabetic volumes, we often borrowed from one another. If we needed the same volume, we found ways to collaborate, for we knew the importance of supporting each other's academic achievement.

Curriculum Leadership and Purpose

In 2007, I was asked to take the helm of a federally funded General Education Diploma (GED) Program for seasonal agricultural workers by my department's first female chair at a public four-year university. She recognized my administrative experience and my track record for social justice. My agricultural background gave me the edge to tackle some of the unfinished business in the program. I was assigned the role as part of my faculty teaching load. In accepting this role, I felt as if I had come full circle, for I would now be able to help others take the first step toward breaking the cycle of poverty, as I did through education. Thus, this chapter describes the journey of a college professor who heads a program offering the GED, the state certification equivalent to a high school diploma for seasonal agriculture workers, including a focus on how I, as a Xicana, am using personal agency and data to shape the program and curriculum transformation to empower agricultural workers and their families.

Due to the unfinished business I inherited, the first three years as director I simply maintained the structure. However, last year I initiated several pilot projects to address the high attrition rate among our students; unfortunately, the budget could not sustain them. This past spring, I began to focus on instruction to explore ways to keep students engaged and attending class to earn a GED.

Social Context

The U.S. Department of Labor (2005) estimates there are more than three million migrant and seasonal farmworkers in the United States. California has 1,302,797 farm workers (Larson, 2000), the highest farm worker population in the U.S. According to the National Center for Farmworker Health (2012):

- 72 percent of all farmworkers are foreign born with 68% born in Mexico.

- 78 percent are male and 22 percent are female.

- 40 percent of farmworkers have completed grades 1 to 6.

- 28 percent have completed grades 10 to 12.

- Average total family income ranges from $17,500 to $19,999; 23 percent of all farmworkers have a total family income below the U.S. government's poverty guidelines.

- 5 percent of seasonal workers covered by employer-provided health insurance.

Migrant farm workers and students are the most disadvantaged social group in the United States. Migrants change residence and schools two to three times a year, truncating educational progress. Limited English skills block migrants from educational opportunities, and California's bilingual program has been (almost completely) eliminated by Proposition 227, passed in June 1998 and further reduced as a result of No Child Left Behind 2001.

Migrant students are the most educationally at-risk group in the U.S. The National Center Education Statistics (2005) reported that for Hispanics, the dropout rate for 16- to 24-year-olds, including those without a GED, was 27 percent during 2001, and has been nearly four times the rate of Whites and twice the rate of Blacks. Dropout rates in California equal the national rates with the additional challenge of having the largest numbers of limited English or non-English speakers in the U.S., with 1.4 million, 34 percent of the national total of 4.7 million in 2002 (California Department of Education, 2011). Obviously, the need for this GED program remains, four decades since its inception.

Increasingly the GED is a prerequisite for employment in jobs where it was not previously required, while some employers request the GED of their current employees for purposes of job security. Moreover, as migrant youth continue to drop out in large numbers, there is little awareness of the GED as a safety net. Parents are often not aware of the high school's dual requirements (exit exam and credits) to earn a diploma and naively expect their child to graduate by simply attending school. When the GED is not presented as a legitimate and equivalent alternative to the high school diploma, students quietly fade from school almost undetected, and "will likely join their parents in agricultural labor," according to a school administrator in a rural high school (McGrath, 2009).

High Attrition Among Students: Missing the Mark in Annual GED Graduates

Attrition has been a major challenge for the GED program for the last two years. Collecting survey data has helped me begin the "complicated conversation" (Pinar, 2012) with myself, to better understand the issues impacting the program's effectiveness and to expand my thinking about curriculum relevancy. I suspect that the high attrition is a symptom, in part, of what takes place in the classroom. Moreover, the reasons why students do not come to class have been a moving target, in which students give the instructors one explanation, recruiters another, and me a third reason for their poor attendance. If students do not attend class, the likelihood of passing the GED battery decreases significantly. With only two years left in this grant cycle and with less than 50 percent of meeting our annual performance target, it is imperative that students are retained and complete the GED this year or our chances of getting re-funded are significantly reduced, thus ending a much-needed and highly regarded 20 year federal program.

Subjects and Procedures

In order to gain a better understanding of the high attrition rate impacting low GED completion rates, I disseminated a survey to eight part-time instructors and 30 students in four classrooms. I first needed to assess and compare why students drop out of class, and the degree to which instructors know their students' background and motivation for pursuing the GED. I also wanted to see if they had any awareness of their students' current life challenges that could interfere with completing the GED. Second, I wanted to see if recently purchased culturally relevant materials were being used and if it was making a difference in engaging students. Thirty students were present in class two days, during which the surveys were disseminated in four different classroom sites. The survey was composed of 20 questions including a combination of multiple-choice, Likert scale and open-ended questions.

Twenty-four of the 30 students have been in the program for a year or less. Six have been in the program two or more years.

Table 1: Total Participants Surveyed

Total Participants Surveyed	38
Instructors	8
Students	30

Five of the eight instructors have been teaching in the GED program for one year, and one for six months, and two have been with the program for more than two years.

Table 2: Instructor Survey Questions

1.	How many students never show up to class?
2.	How many students show up for fewer than 12 hours (4 classes then drop)?
3.	How many students eventually drop out of the program?
4.	Are there signs that a student is not fully committed to coming to class?
5.	How would you describe your teaching philosophy?
6.	Do you engage students in any strategies to get them to keep coming to class?
7.	Do you use culturally relevant materials such as Raices and Memorias, or others?
8.	Do culturally relevant materials make a difference? How?
9.	How well do you know your students' individual personal stories of their early home experience?
10.	How well do you know your students' individual personal stories about their previous school experience?
11.	How well do you know your individual students' motivation for getting their GED?
12.	How well do you know your individual students' current life challenges which could prevent them from coming to class?
13.	Have you ever incorporated students' personal stories, challenges and/or motivation into the class curriculum?
14.	How do you think the anticipated computer-based GED will impact our students?
15.	What is the most challenging part of teaching students?
16.	What is the most challenging part of teaching in the Program?

The students were asked to consider what could potentially deter them from completing the GED.

Table 3: Student Survey Questions

	Student Survey Questions
1.	When did you start attending class?
2.	How many days on average to do you attend a week?
3.	How many exams have you taken so far?
4.	How many exams have you passed so far?
5.	What could potentially keep you from coming to class?
6.	What keeps you coming to class?

7.	Instead of covering more than one subject in class, would you prefer for the instructors to teach one subject at a time, go test then start another subject?
8.	Would you prefer to cover all other four subjects and leave Math for last?
9.	In September, if class was offered on Saturdays, would you be able to come?
10.	In September, instead of coming to class 3 nights a week, would you be able and willing to come on Saturdays and one night a week?
11.	In September, if classes were held on Saturdays, what time would be best for you?
12.	How well does your instructor know your early life experiences?
13.	How well does your instructor know your previous schooling experience?
14.	How well does your instructor know your reasons for getting your GED?
15.	How well does your instructor know your current life challenges which could keep you from coming to class?
16.	Do you think the new GED test on computers (starting Jan. 2014) will affect you getting your GED?
17.	Does your instructor use strategies to encourage you to continue coming to class?
18.	Does your instructor use culturally relevant materials such as Raices and Memorias, or other books?
19.	Does using materials like Raices and Memorias make a difference in your learning?
20.	Please feel free to write any other comments about your class or the program as a whole

The Program Context

Context for Increased Program Accountability

In 2007, as a result of a transition in new leadership within the national funding organization, there were signs of increasing accountability for all GED programs nationwide. Aware of this trend, the recruiter coordinator and I were in the process of generating a checks-and-balance system when allegations of serving unqualified students were filed with the national funding organization. I received a copy of the allegations submitted by two HEP instructors and a school community liaison, whose sites I closed due to low enrollment. The local Office of the Inspector General (OIG) conducted the audit, which was grueling. In the end, we were commended for the practices and policies we had put into place and were told by the funding agency that this preliminary investigation should not preclude us from being fully considered for another five-year grant. Fortunately, we were awarded another five-year grant for 2009 to 2014.

Data Collection:
Challenges Impeding Program Participation

The lifestyle of seasonal agricultural workers is often in flux with the ebb and flow of harvest seasons and ever-changing work schedules. There are employers who change their employees' work schedules every two weeks. During the harvest season, some individuals work six or seven days a week and some endure 10- to 12-hour work days.

Work-Related Issues

Table 4: Work-Related Issues Impacting Program Participation

Work Related	
Being too tired after work to attend class	9
Work schedules conflicting with class	8
Other responses	5*
Total number of students surveyed	30

*High fuel costs, cherry harvest starting, work out of town, feel stressed after work.

Seventeen of 30 students indicated work schedules and being too tired to come to class negatively impact program participation. Instructors concurred that the primary reason students are not completing the GED is due to changes in work schedules that make it difficult for working adults to consistently attend class. One instructor, a young man just completing a graduate degree, offered: "even though at the time they are registering for the program, they think they can commit coming to class three times a week, their work schedule impedes them from going to class." Another instructor indicated that at least two of his students would be rotating their job schedules for a month and another two students were working late, past the time of the class session.

Family Obligations

Table 5: Family Responsibilities Impacting Program Participation

Family Responsibilities	
Housework as a potential deterrent from attending class	6
Children's needs as a potential deterrent from attending class	4
Spouse and children's needs as a potential deterrent from attending class	1
Other	3*
Total number of students surveyed	30

*Work from July to October; I work and study; I have no time

Thirty-seven percent (n=11) of students indicated that home responsibilities could potentially deter them from attending class. Six of the 11 specified housework as the main reason for missing class, and five indicated having to stay home with their children and/or their spouse. A female instructor offered the following:

"One approved student came to talk to me after a month to let me know that she started the divorce process, right after being approved and would not be attending class." Family obligations such as childcare, lack of spouse support, death in the family, medical needs, and traveling to Mexico were also listed by instructors as other reasons that could negatively impact attendance. Another instructor stated, "their family obligations are conflicting with this new school schedule," referring to leaving home for evening classes two or three nights a week. Historically, the program has been composed primarily of women. This year, 63 percent of our students are women and the gap is closing. I often wondered what students, especially working women with families, endure to commit to three nights a week of classes.

Academic Difficulty

Twenty-six of 30 students or 87 percent indicated some level of academic challenge. Thirty-eight percent of students indicated math was the most challenging of the GED subjects, followed by writing at 31 percent. This concurs with what instructors reported.

Table 6: Academic Difficulty Impacting Program Participation

Academic Challenges	
Language Arts: Writing	8
Language Arts: Reading	3
Social Studies	4
Science	1
Math	10
Total responses	26

Five of the eight instructors confirmed that the difficulty of the curriculum materials was the reason why some students only attend one or two classes, and then drop. One pre-credentialed math instructor stated, "It was too hard" and "students are overwhelmed by the information we cover in three hours the first time they go to class." She added, "Some say that they are not prepared to do this type of math.... Others think it might take them too long to complete the GED, so they drop."

The instructor/trainer who also offers Saturday math workshops stated: "students might be intimidated by the process of testing, feeling nervous about undertaking this endeavor and may feel out of place as they see other students progressing more quickly, while those who just need points to pass get frustrated and quit."

These comments prompted me to ask students if they might prefer focusing on one subject at a time, rather than addressing a several subjects in each class session.

Table 7: Student Preference for Single-Subject Instruction

Student Preference for One Subject at a Time		
	Number	Percentage
Strongly Agree	15	50%
Agree	1	3%
Somewhat Agree	5	17%
Disagree	7	23%
Strongly Disagree	2	7%
Total Responses	30	100%

About half (53 percent) of the students are in favor of focusing on one subject at a time; 17 percent somewhat agree; and 30 percent are not in agreement. Student comments in favor of teaching a single subject include "it would be easier for me to study" and "it will help students get more focused." Others recognize that they or their peers "come more prepared than others," and could go either way.

Table 8: Student Preference for Single-Subject Instruction and Saving Math for Last

Student Preference for One Subject at a Time and Saving Math for Last		
	Number	Percentage
Strongly agree	16	55%
Agree	4	14%
Somewhat agree	2	7%
Disagree	3	10%
Strongly disagree	4	14%
Total responses	29	100%

Sixty-nine percent of students prefer to leave math for last and offered many comments: "I think Math requires more time"; "…is more difficult"; "it's hardest, so better to focus"; "It requires more attention for me"; "it's complicated so it takes more time." Infusing math with the other subjects might hold more promise of succeeding than waiting until the other four subjects have been covered.

Instructors' Knowledge of Students' Backgrounds

In an attempt to ascertain how well instructors know their students, I asked both instructors and students to what degree instructors knew their students' motivation for pursuing the GED; their early home and school experiences; and current life challenges that could get in the way of pursuing the GED.

Table 9: Instructor's Knowledge of Students' Motivation for Pursuing GED

Student Perspective: Instructor's Knowledge of Students' Motivation for Pursuing GED		
	Number	Percentage
Very well	5	17%
Well	11	36%
Somewhat well	9	30%
Not well at all	5	17%
Total responses	30	100%

Fifty-three percent (n=16) of students believed their instructors knew their reasons for pursuing the GED very well or well, and 30 percent somewhat well; 17 percent reported their instructors as not knowing well at all. Fifty-seven percent of instructors (n=4) reported that they knew their students' motivation for the GED well. Forty-three percent of instructors (n=3) reported they only knew the reasons somewhat well. This data points to the need for creating curriculum that incorporates students' motivation for wanting the GED into the curriculum as a way to keep students engaged and coming to class. It is critical for instructors to know what motivates their students to earn the GED certification, because many, as we know from this study, have daily obstacles to overcome such as work, family obligations, and academics.

Knowledge of Students' Backgrounds and Early Life Experiences

I wanted to know to what degree students felt their instructors were knowledgeable about their early life experiences.

Table 10: Instructor's Knowledge of Students' Early Life Experiences

Student Perspective: Instructor's Knowledge of Students' Early Life Experiences		
	Number	Percentage
Very well	1	4%
Well	7	26%
Somewhat well	11	40%
Not well at all	8	30%
No response	3	n.a.
Total responses	27	100%

Only one student felt their teacher knew his or her early life experience well. Twenty-six percent of students felt their instructors knew their background well. Forty percent thought their instructors knew their early life experiences somewhat well; and 30 percent not well at all. Instructors responded similarly: 29 percent reported well, and 71 percent somewhat well.

Table11: Instructor's Knowledge of Students' Previous School Experience

Student Perspective: Instructor's Knowledge of Students' Previous School Experience		
	Number	Percentage
Very well	2	7%
Well	3	11%
Somewhat well	14	50%
Not well at all	9	32%
No response	2	n.a.
Total responses	28	100%

Eighteen percent of students said their instructors knew their previous school experience well, and half indicated somewhat well. Thirty-two percent did not think their instructors knew their previous schooling well at all. Seventy-one percent of instructors (n=5) indicated they knew students' previous schooling background well, and 29 percent (n=2) somewhat well. One instructor shared, "Students tend to tell me their previous [schooling] experience when we do a writing activity where they have to describe their school experience. This helps me understand more in depth their experiences and how I can assist them." At the same site, the math instructor offered that students "also contribute to the class by suggesting different strategies that [they] learned in the past. These strategies are helpful for other students who also learned the concepts in a similar way." While there is a certain level of congruency between the students' and instructors' responses, knowing students' previous schooling experience is an important aspect of teaching that must be at the forefront if curriculum is to be relevant to working adults. Given the goal of completing the GED in one year, knowledge of students' previous schooling is key to helping students overcome challenges they may have previously faced.

Table 12: Instructor's Knowledge of Students' Life Challenges

Student Perspective: Instructor's Knowledge of Student Challenges		
	Number	Percentage
Very well	4	15%
Well	6	22%
Somewhat well	10	37%
Not well at all	7	26%
No response	3	n.a.
Total responses	27	100%

Thirty-seven percent of students felt their instructors were very well aware or well aware of challenges they faced, and 37 percent rated their instructors as knowing somewhat well. Twenty-six percent of students are not confident in their instructors' knowledge at all.

Seventy-one percent of instructors (n=5) felt they had knowledge of challenges students faced that could deter them from attending class, and 29 percent (n=2) knew their students' challenges somewhat well. Instructors appear to be more confident in their knowledge of their students' challenges compared to the students themselves. While this study did not address more personal challenges such as low self-esteem, family, and health issues, these could also impact their chances of earning a GED.

It is concerning that students consistently offer lower rankings of their instructors knowing their background. What would students need to experience in order for them to feel more understood? Five instructors indicated that they incorporated their students' personal stories, challenges, and motivation for obtaining the GED in their classrooms, and some through writing assignments. The three math instructors did not. If handled well, writing and reading assignments, both in and out of class, may be a tool for instructors to get to know each student's background, and a way for students to get to know themselves and their peers and create a community of learners. It can be a very powerful tool, and which we are piloting this year.

Telling Signs of Dropouts

There are definite signs instructors have observed as predictors of student attrition. All instructors have observed behaviors such as leaving class early, missing class altogether without informing the instructor beforehand, or returning without giving a reason for their absence. This is perceived by instructors as students not being committed to the program. Instructors also note that a lack of in-class participation is another sign that a student may drop out. As one instructor put it, "I can tell who does the work and those who do not based on the quality of work assignments they turn in and on the response to participation you get from each student. For example, during writing activities, the committed students want to write more than 5 paragraphs and those who are not, just write a paragraph maximum and say they are done."

Another instructor described the growing number of recent high school dropouts who are the younger class members: "some of these students come as 'extended-immature adolescents,' minds who are still not ready to focus (these students were high school students, but did not graduate)." One of the math instructors complained that the younger students are distracted by texting in class.

Encouraging Student Attendance

Teachers encouraged students to come to class by creating a welcoming environment and motivating them by providing constant positive encouragement. One young instructor tells his students to treat the class like a job. If they arrive late, or miss too many days, their boss will fire them. He claims it has helped attendance. A comprehensive and promising response offered by the instructor/teacher trainer describes various strategies: advocating for parking permits for students; providing his email and phone number for easier access to him; encouraging students to be more cognizant and academically self-directed by reviewing their practice test records sheet frequently; adapting teaching to students' needs; having students share their stories to inspire others; establishing the buddy system for new students; varying his teaching strategies and materials; and offering resources such as GED websites.

New Focus on Instruction

The information obtained in this study is important to consider in analyzing what currently takes place in the classroom and what type of curriculum and pedagogy ought to take place so that students' backgrounds (fears, hopes, and dreams) are known and incorporated into the curriculum. In order to engage students and keep them from dropping out, it is essential to understand their motivation for pursuing the GED, as well as their early life and schooling experiences. Incorporating culturally relevant materials in class and providing ongoing communication and instructor training are other key elements of developing a strong foundation that helps students increase the probability that they will remain engaged in the learning process and obtain their GED certification.

Curriculum: Use of Culturally Relevant Materials

Culturally relevant teaching approaches and materials are well documented as critical to the academic success for students of color (Gay, 2000; Delpit, 1995), for students of color rarely see themselves in literature. Similarly, the GED test preparation materials reflect a Eurocentric perspective. It is currently dominated by the Steck-Vaughn Company (2002). As a standard curriculum, there is little that relates to the life experiences of people of color, much less the experience of our nation's agricultural workers. Thus the teacher, armed with the appropriate materials and orientation, has to bridge the gap between the subject matter, the skill set needed to pass the GED's five-test battery, and their students' experience. The ongoing challenge for most GED programs has been finding Spanish GED materials that reflect the experiences of agricultural workers in the U.S.

Last spring, I learned of a new GED Spanish interdisciplinary text, *Raices: Libro de Preparacion Para el GED y Estudios Secundarios* (*Roots: GED Preparation Book and Secondary Level Studies*) by Muro, Tedeschi, Arnal, Jaurrieta and Laveaga (2011). The unique aspect of this text is that the introduction of each of the 15 chapters begins with a short story or poem referencing the socioeconomic realities of the Latino immigrant. The stories are from an earlier set of volumes entitled

Memorias del Silencio (Silent Memories; see Duarte & Tedeschi, 2009, 2010), written by migrant GED students in El Paso, Texas.[1]

These texts are filled with culturally rich readings and lessons that complement what Hernandez-Zamora (2010) considers essential for the education of students from border communities: personal agency, voice, and student competencies. Validating their experiences and realities is critical for the academic success of immigrant agricultural workers. In Volume 5 of *Memorias del Silencio* (Duarte & Tedeschi, 2009), Andres Muro acknowledges the power of having his students write and publish their stories to be used as legitimate curriculum, which embraces social theorist Maxine Greene's (2007) pedagogical vision of education as "not just a predetermined production or reproduction but is the process of creating ourselves" through art (Duarte & Tedeschi, 2009, pp. 8–9). The opportunity for students "to learn to create art through their stories rather than consuming decontextualized and predigested lessons forces students to engage their own context and reality to create and recreate themselves in the text. In this way, students are actively engaged and able to conceptualize new ideas" (Pinar, 2012). *Raices* serves three purposes: (1) offers GED preparation; (2) gives students and educators an opportunity to learn about the social and economic realities of the Latino immigrant; and (3) validates those experiences and realities that are often ignored in books and preparation materials, thus devaluing the individual (Muro, et al., p. vii). The following poem by Veronica Macias (2005) was first published in the second volume of *Memorias*. It has been reissued as the introduction to Chapter 1 for Language Arts: Writing in *Raices* (Muro et al., 2010).

To My Beloved Farmworker
To my beloved husband Refugio and to my sons Omar and Daniel
In the fields you worked your hands,
hand by hand with the chile,
with the land to harvest,
with your hat a little torn,
and in the handkerchief your sweat.

At dawn
your shadow begins to work.
In your face the fatigue,
but strong, green farmworker you are.

Your youth
was left in the fields of Deming
starting the tractor,

---

1   The first of several volumes was published as an outcome of a joint project between the Community Education Program (CEP) in El Paso Community College and the City of El Paso Arts and Culture Department, which funded the first volume. Since then six other volumes have been published through the publishing company BordersSenses.

harvesting the chile,
preparing the land,
waiting for the onion.

With your strong arms
you gathered the baskets,
smell of wet soil in your clothes.

The harvested land became your brother,
that is how you achieved
your American dream.[2]

Muro (2011) explains how this poem impacts the writer and those who read it.

Because Macias chooses poetry as her medium, history and geography are subtly incorporated into her piece. Since Macias is a GED student, she must acquire reading and writing skills as well as learn American history. Writing about her own experiences allows Macias to acquire writing skills informing the content of her writing with her own knowledge. When she learns American history, she may do this relating other people's experiences to her own. The fact that her experience has been considered valuable should give her confidence and the poem can be a source of inspiration for other students. (p. 7)

In Chapter 1 of *Raices* (Muro et al., 2010), there are 11 different writing assignments related to the poem "To My Beloved Farmworker." Instructors have a wide range from which to select assignments to meet individual student's needs or zones of proximate development.

Table 13: Raices Overview of Chapter 1 Assignments

Chapter 1 Assignments				
Language Arts: Writing	Poem	General questions (13), Correct grammatical errors (10), Rewrite stanzas in own words	Describe self metaphorically, Describe others metaphorically & explain	Write own story in poem, Create drawing related to poem

---

2 Written in Spanish by Veronica Macias; translated by: Minerva Laveaga Duarte. Available at http://borderse.startlogic.com/memorias/volume1/beloved.html

Social Studies	Columbus & Fr. Bartolome's diary entries about ill treatment of the Arawak	Look up 6 key words Write 3-4 sentence paragraph for each	Essay #1: Your perspective on Columbus' diary, #2 on Bartolome's diary, #3 Compare their world with yours	
Science	Earth Science	Description of 4 layers of earth	Questions: Name the layers, Write the most important differences in layers	Look up word and write sentence related to it
Math	Area & Percentages	Find area of farm to raise a fence	Calculations of people who died under Columbus	

My hope in purchasing these materials was for teachers to use them to engage students in meaningful and relevant ways. Throughout the year, instructors commented on their use of these materials; however, I wanted to know to what extent these teaching materials actually were used and whether teachers and students believed that these materials were making a difference. Given that these materials are based on experiences similar to our students', I also wanted to know the extent to which instructors incorporated students' personal stories, challenges, and motivation into the curriculum.

Table 14. Students' Perspective: Instructors Use of Culturally Relevant Materials

Use of Culturally Relevant Materials	Number	Percent
Strongly agree	14	54
Agree	5	19
Somewhat agree	4	15
Disagree	1	4
Strongly disagree	2	8
Total responses	26	100

Seventy-three percent of students agreed that their instructors used culturally relevant materials, 15 percent somewhat agreed, and 12 percent disagreed. Five instructors used *Raices* and/or *Memorias* or other culturally relevant materials.[3] Two did not and one did not respond to the question.

---

3   One instructor used *Sendas Literarias* reading instruments for developing beginning writing skills.

Table 15: Students' Perspective: Culturally Relevant Materials Make a Difference

Use of Culturally Relevant Materials Makes a Difference	Number	Percent
Strongly agree	11	46
Agree	3	12
Somewhat agree	8	33
Disagree	1	4
Strongly disagree	1	4
Total responses	24	100

Fifty-eight percent of students believe it makes a difference, 33 percent somewhat agreed, and 8 percent did not agree culturally relevant materials made a difference for them.

All seven instructors provided reasons why these types of materials are good for students. One instructor did not use *Raices* because it is not yet available in English. I suspect it becomes challenging in a bilingual classroom to not have the same materials available for whole-class instruction. The instructor/teacher trainer shared, that *Raices* "Makes a difference for this student population because it strikes an emotional chord as well as a cultural cord, which in turn makes learning easier." One instructor who uses the activities from the books and who has discussions on the content offered, "It makes a big difference. Students are engaged and enjoy it when they can relate to the reading." Another instructor uses *Raices* often because it is interdisciplinary and each unit in the book is significant and relevant for everyone; this instructor offered that "students feel connected to the content. Also they feel empowered by reading stories that they can relate to." Yet another instructor said "By using *Raices* and *Memorias*, I've [helped in] their improvement in reading skills, not just for Reading, but also in Math, Writing and the other subjects for those students who found the reading portion of the Steck-Vaughn books too difficult."

One pre-credentialed instructor confessed that he used the books when he first started; however, once his students figured out that all the readings had the same message, they got bored. He continued,

> I tried using other cultural readings from my own Spanish classes [in college]. Even though some may be [at a] higher level reading, students tend to like them. These stories are super short but make them relate their lives to the story and have fun while reading.

But he also added, "When I use materials that students can connect to, it makes them more engaged in learning, motivates them because they can connect to the characters in the stories. But the main thing is having more variety of stories that connect to the students besides [the] *Raices* and *Memorias* [books].

I wonder what it was in the "common message" that students found boring? Could students be rejecting these stories due to internalized shame of the ongoing struggles of migrant and agricultural workers? Or did some (younger) students not relate to the experiences depicted in the books? Did this pre-credential instructor need direct instruction in how to effectively present these materials? I agree that having a variety of books is important, for we are attracting more high school dropouts and English speakers.

Reasons given by one of the two math instructors, who do not use culturally relevant materials, were equally compelling and confirmed that it does make a difference "because they [students] put themselves in the situation and [it] is easier for them to understand something they have already lived." The other math instructor offered that "culturally relevant materials make a difference" and "this is especially true for our students because they are able to use their knowledge in [applying] the class concepts. They can relate to the topics and see the real-life application." What kept these two pre-credentialed instructors from using these resources?

This confirms that simply providing materials without direct training is not enough. Signature assignments may need to be incorporated to ensure that there is some uniformity among the classrooms, for it is concerning that only half of instructors indicated using these materials. Yet, almost half of the students agreed that materials like *Raices* and *Memorias* make a difference, for it "makes it easier to learn," "helps me understand the class," and is "something I can identify with." The students' responses build a compelling case that although the GED subject matter may be academically challenging, culturally relevant materials helps to bridge the academic divide and make learning more accessible to them. This I believe is at the core of keeping students engaged and having them return to class night after night.

Next Steps: Changing the Culture of Learning

Writing this chapter created a space to first have a "complicated conversation" with myself; and through surveys, telephone conversations, and a recent in-service training, I've been looking at the past to understand and mobilize (Pinar, 2012) into action this fourth year of the grant. I have been able to reflect, review, and restructure the instruction of our GED program to better serve our students, California's agricultural workers, and their families. The surveys provided insight to make structural, curricular, and pedagogical changes. The students' preference for focusing on one subject at a time gave me the confidence to eliminate the bifurcated structure of separate math instructors and keep the strongest instructors to teach all subjects, including math. Biweekly conference calls and monthly in-service trainings will take place to closely follow, support, and enhance the curricular and pedagogical approaches needed to retain students.

The Role of the Instructors

Inspired by Muro's research (2011) of the multiple benefits his GED students gained in writing and publishing their stories, I propose that our instructors start the year with Language Arts: Writing and Reading in *Raices* (Muro et al., 2011. Muro also reminds us of the role of teachers play as he refers to Freire (1970/2000) who says the teacher must first become familiar with students' social and cultural context (p. 8) and Giroux (1988) who places a great deal of responsibility on teachers to become transformative intellectuals and challenge the status quo (p. 13). These are critical reminders for approaching the effective use of culturally relevant materials as a vehicle for building a community of learners. I envision instructors and students reading and writing as a way to get to know themselves, each other, and their community, and boost their self confidence and self-esteem, especially among women. While only half of instructors reported using students' personal stories as part of the curriculum, this year instructors will be expected to not only prepare students with the knowledge necessary to succeed in the GED, but to engage students about the knowledge they already possess (Muro, 2011 p. 8). Starting with why students want the GED and what it would take to accomplish this goal, they will explore their early schooling experiences and any current struggles that may get in the way of accomplishing their goal These approaches have the potential to transform our teachers and students while creating a community of learners who can take action to support the success of all students.

Muro (2011) also argues the success of adult farmworkers who earn the GED is a result of teachers whom he describes as "transformative intellectuals" who recognize and validate students' background knowledge as valuable and help students engage in border-crossing, and in Giroux's words (1988) who can "create spaces to contest it" (Muro, 2011, p. 13*)*. Changing the current culture to keep students engaged in the learning process outside the classroom could have the greatest impact on students' success and yet presents the greatest challenge. We will grapple with providing practical ways for students to remain engaged between class sessions and hold them accountable, for we know students who study at home are more likely to earn the GED, and earn it sooner. It could be as simple, yet challenging, as using a Freirean approach: having students take a photograph and come to class prepared to discuss and write about it. Changing the student culture will require a commitment to using critical pedagogical approaches and having ongoing dialogue with students and among instructors and staff via conference calls and in-service trainings. Articles related to critical pedagogy and teaching adults will be part of the discussion. Ongoing student data will be collected data to compare these initial findings as the year progresses and help me to maintain the pulse of the classroom.

With the new focus on instruction, and the commitment to the tenets of critical pedagogy and employing students' autobiographies (Pinar, 2012), our

GED program will be in a much stronger position to reach our annual goals as we prepare our students and their families for a brighter future beyond the GED.

References

California Department of Education (CDE). (2011, Spring). *California Language Census*. Sacramento, CA: CalEdFacts.

Delpit, L. (1995). *Other People's Children: Cultural Conflict in the Classroom*. New York: New York Press.

Duarte, M. L. (Ed.). (2006). *Memorias del Silencio: Footprints of the Borderland* (Vol. 2). El Paso, TX: BorderSenses. http://issuu.com/bordersenses/docs/memoriasdelsilenciovol2

Duarte, M. L., & Tedeschi, F. (Eds.) (2009). *Memorias del Silencio: Footprints of the Borderland* (Vol. 5). El Paso, TX: BorderSenses. http://issuu.com/bordersenses/docs/memoriasdelsilenciovol5

Duarte, M. L., & Tedeschi, F. (Eds.) (2010). *Memorias del Silencio: Footprints of the Borderland* (Vol. 6). El Paso, TX: BorderSenses. http://issuu.com/bordersenses/docs/memoriasdelsilenciovol6

Freire P. (1970/2000). *Pedagogy of the Oppressed*. New York: Continuum.

Gandara, P. (1995). *Over the Ivy Wall: The Educational Mobility of Low-Income Chicanos*. Albany: State University of New York Press.

Gay, G. (2000). *Culturally Responsive Teaching: Theory, Research and Practice*. New York: Teachers College Press

Giroux, H. A. (1988). *Teachers as Intellectuals: Towards a Critical Pedagogy of Learning*. Westport, CT: Bergin and Garvey.

Greene, M. (2007). Art and imagination: Overcoming a desperate stasis. In A. C. Ornstein, E. F. Pajak, & S. B. Ornstein (Eds.), *Contemporary Issues in Curriculum*. (pp. 32–38).Boston: Pearson.

Hernandez-Zamora, G. (2010). *Decolonizing Literacy: Mexican Lives in the Era of Global Capitalism*, Buffalo, NY: Multilingual Matters.

Larson, A. C. (2000). Migrant and seasonal farmworker enumeration profiles study: California. Prepared for the Migrant Health Program, Bureau of Primary Health Care Resources and Services Administration. Migrant Health Program.

Macias, V. (2005). To my beloved farm worker. In M. L. Duarte & F. Tedeschi (Eds.), *Memorias del Silencio: Footprints of the Borderland* (Vol. 1, p.83). El Paso, TX: BorderSenses.

McGrath, D. (2009, May 10). Personal communication.

Muro, A. (2011). Pedagogies of change: From theory to practice. *International Journal of Critical Pedagogy, 4* (1), 2–17.

Muro, A., Tedeschi, F., Arnal, P., Juarrieta, L., & Laveaga, M. (2010). *Raices: Libro de Preparación Para el GED and Estudios Secundarios*. El Paso, TX: BorderSenses.

National Center for Farmworker Health. (NCFH). (2012, September). Farmworker Health Factsheet. Buda, TX. NCFH http://www.ncfh.org/docs/fs-Migrant%20Demographics.pdf

National Center for Education Statistics (NCES). (2005). *The Condition of Education 2005* (NCES 82000-031). Washington DC: U.S. Government Printing Office.

Pinar, W. F. (2012). *What Is Curriculum Theory?* New York: Routledge.

Steck Vaughn Company. (2002). *September 11, 2001*. New York: Harcourt Achieve.

U.S. Department of Labor. (2005). *The National Agricultural Workers Survey* 2001–2002. Washington DC: U.S. Department of Labor. http://www.doleta.gov/agworker/naws.cfm

U.S. Department of Labor News. (1967, June 11). *Message on Urban and Rural Poverty*.

U.S. Office of Economic Opportunity. (1968, February).*Technical Assistance Bulletin, 1*(5). Washington DC: U.S. Office of Economic Opportunity.

PART THREE

Third Space

When I heard the learn'd astronomer;
When the proofs, the figures, were ranged in columns before me;
When I was shown the charts and the diagrams, to add, divide, and measure them;
When I, sitting, heard the astronomer, where he lectured with much applause in the lecture-room,
How soon, unaccountable, I became tired and sick;
Till rising and gliding out, I wander'd off by myself,
In the mystical moist night-air, and from time to time,
Look'd up in perfect silence at the stars.[1]

When we sink, submerged in those roles conceived by others, we become aborted possibilities, unable to realize in everyday life, in our relations with others, the politics of our individual and civic identities, the educational dynamics of creation and birth.[2]

We cannot seek achievement for ourselves and forget about progress and prosperity for our community.... Our ambitions must be broad enough to include the aspirations and needs of others, for their sakes and for our own.[3]

Herein lies the tragedy of the age:
Not that men are poor, —all men know something of poverty.
Not that men are wicked,—who is good?
Not that men are ignorant,—what is truth?
Nay, but that men know so little of men.[4]

---

1   Walt Whitman (n.d.). "When I Heard the Learn'd Astronomer." http://www.poetryfoundation.org/poem/174747

2   W. Pinar (2004), *What Is Curriculum Theory?* NJ: Lawrence Erlbaum, p. 31.

3   Cesar Chavez. (n.d.). UFW: The Official Web Page of the United Farm Workers of America. http://www.ufw.org/_page.php?menu=research&inc=history/09.html

4   W. E. B. DuBois (1903/1994). *The Souls of Black Folk*. Chicago: Dover.

CHAPTER ELEVEN

Fighting for a Transnational Third Space in Teacher Education

PETER J. BAIRD & NADEEN T. RUIZ

In general, there are so many stereotypes about Mexico and Mexicans, a lot of which depict Mexico as dangerous, an almost savage place. For me, Oaxaca was one of the most welcoming places. . . . I have my preconceptions/prejudices replaced with actual first-hand experiences. —Bi-TEP candidate, 2010, after completing five months in Mexico

This program should continue in Mexico because it is safe to study and live there, and because our nation desperately needs qualified bilingual teachers who are culturally and linguistically educated to meet the needs of our ethnically diverse learning population. —Bi-TEP candidate, 2011, in a letter to CSU Chancellor Charles Reed

We are breaking the silencing of our voices as transnational teacher educators. In this chapter, we tell the story of the California Bi-National Teacher Education Project (Bi-TEP)—a unique U.S.–Mexico "third space" program for bilingual pre-service elementary teachers that we have directed for the past four years through the California State University (CSU) system and partner institutions in Mexico and Guatemala. Central to this story is how we have had to fight an uphill battle in recent years with CSU to maintain this program, despite the growing need and awareness in the field for globalizing teacher education in general and for bilingual teachers in particular:

The key ingredient is to provide international biliteracy student teaching experiences if we want future teachers to be culturally and globally biliterate in meeting the challenges of this new century. Over 100 universities in the United States participate or provide

some form of student teaching abroad, but only a few are approved to provide bilingual
certification. (Quezada & Alfaro, 2007, p. 111).

With Latino students and families becoming an ever-larger and endangered
portion of the public school population, and with cutbacks in bilingual teacher
education programs throughout California, this project offers a vital opportunity
for U.S bilingual teacher candidates to immerse themselves in the social, cultural,
linguistic, and political environment of neighboring countries such as Mexico and
Guatemala that are deeply interconnected with the U.S. Since the mid-1990s,
Bi-TEP students have lived with host families, taking the same coursework as
their California counterparts from Mexican professors, attending additional semi-
nars offered by Mexican and U.S. experts on the social context of education, and
deepening their Spanish-language skills with daily classes in academic Spanish.
They do student teaching in Mexican public schools that face many of the same
challenges as our own beleaguered educational system, and teach alongside Mexican teachers and student-teachers. In 2010 in Oaxaca, Mexico, they also learned
about the indigenous cultural and linguistic heritage of their students, and were
exposed to the teacher-led social movement that is challenging inequality, neo-
liberalism, and efforts to privatize public education in their country (Denham &
C.A.S.A. Collective, 2008; Kuper, 2009).

The voices of our teacher candidates—who lived, studied, and student-taught
in Oaxaca, Mexico, in 2010 and in Antigua, Guatemala, in 2011—are corner-
stones for our discussion and help explain why we have fought so hard to keep this
international third space open for our students. In addition to these voices, yearly
evaluation reports have provided evidence that we should continue the struggle.
For example, a report by an external evaluator on the five-month Bi-TEP program
in Oaxaca, Mexico, in 2010–2011 analyzed students' perceptions of their experience. That report indicated significant growth on student teachers' pre- and post-
self-assessments along a range of areas including: conversational Spanish (19.4
percent increase); academic Spanish (20.44 percent); general knowledge about
Mexican culture (30.6 percent); knowledge about the Mexican school system
(50.6 percent); and comfort in communicating with Spanish-speaking parents
about school issues (35 percent) (Gold, 2011, p. 7). Significantly, none of these
areas was a strong foci of our stateside bilingual credential program at CSU–Sacramento. It is doubtful that the results described above could have been achieved
without a third-space transnational program such as Bi-TEP.

The voices of our teacher candidates from the past two years tell the story
even more dramatically. Here they link their international experience with their
future profession as bilingual teachers back home in California, including their
role as change agents:

- "I felt that the program gave me a lot of knowledge about the culture of my students, which is something that will be so helpful in the future. I am really excited this semester to take everything I learned in Oaxaca—language, culture, experiences, and tie it to [California] education." (White female candidate, Oaxaca, 2010).

- "Bilingual teachers need to be 'insiders' to a community. This trip has made me realize how deep the understanding of another culture is, and how much first-hand experience with that culture is necessary to be able to understand it adequately."(White male candidate, Guatemala, 2011).

- "It taught me that becoming involved in the community and taking on a social activist role is part of the job." (Latina female candidate, Guatemala, 2011)

A Transnational Third Space

We recently completed a study based on similar responses by our student teachers to open-ended questions about what they learned and valued in the Bi-TEP program (Ruiz & Baird, 2013). There, we argued that the numbers and growth of immigrant and emigrant students and families in both the U.S. and neighboring countries requires a transnational approach to teacher-education (Ruiz & Baird, 2013). Transnational students and their families are those who live and are schooled in two or more countries with close economic, political, and often family ties—countries characterized by unequal size, power, and wealth (Barajas, 2012; Baird & McCaughan, 1979). With over half of California's students and families of Mexican and Central American origin, and nearly one million children in Mexico with U.S. school experience (Zúñiga, Hamann, & Sánchez Garcia, 2008), this reality has long been a part of traditional bilingual teacher education programs with their focus on supporting English language learners and providing dual-language instruction. Obscured or hidden, however, are the structural causes for immigrants to leave their home countries, as well as the class, racial, and legal discrimination they endure within the U.S. as low-paid workers, non-English speakers, and in many cases, undocumented. The families and their children are thus commonly viewed from a deficit perspective (Ruiz, 2011b). Transnational teacher education, on the other hand, offers a third space for U.S. professors and students to replace this deficit approach with a paradigm that (1) sees home languages and cultures as positive funds of knowledge (Moll, Amanti, Neff, & Gonzalez, 2001); and (2) connects U.S. classrooms with the realities of Mexico and other transnational countries of origin (Ruiz & Baird, 2013).

Our study of 34 teacher Bi-TEP candidates gave evidence of perspectives that showed strong connections between them and the people of Mexico and Guatemala (Ruiz & Baird, 2013). In general, the teacher candidates related the new information gained from their international study to the children and families they would be serving in their California classrooms, as illustrated in the quotes above. Specifically, they noted their increased language and cultural proficiency to apply in their future teaching. Bi-TEP participants also spoke of empathy towards immigrants in California struggling with language and cultural differences, citing their own challenges as student teachers in Mexico or Guatemala as a way to help them understand those struggles, at least on a limited level. In addition, Bi-TEP teacher candidates reported their recognition of the role that U.S. historical and current economic policies in Mexico have played in propelling Mexican migration to the U.S. They brought forth counter-evidence to false Mexican and indigenous stereotypes, such as lack of parent involvement in schools. Furthermore, they professed a commitment to social action on behalf of Latino students and families, both in the U.S. and their country of study. In short, this particular study added to a range of other evidence (e.g., program evaluation reports such as the one cited above) that the Bi-TEP curriculum was related to the participants' commitment to transnational solidarity and social justice. The overall result was that Bi-TEP teacher candidates' voices represented features of a paradigm of interconnectedness between the two countries, as shown below in Figure 1 (Ruiz & Baird, 2013).

Figure 1 (Ruiz & Baird, 2013)

Continuum Descriptors

International Tourism	Transnational Teacher Education
(Disconnect)	*(Interconnectedness)*
Individualism	*Comunalidad*/Solidarity
Social Distance	Contact
Essentialized Cultures	Cultural Dynamism/Hybridity
Nation Borders	Transnational "Fabric"
Nation Citizen	Global Citizen
Observation of "Others"	Social Action

Life Histories, Life Paths

Our voices too are part of the story, in particular as organizers of this new international third space that requires so much rethinking about how teacher education can and should be done.

Peter: My life path has taken me from being a monolingual, Euro-American California kid of the rebellious boomer generation to a bilingual and bicultural teacher educator of the still active nearly senior generation. In between the two bookends I became a teenage immigrant to Mexico for part the 1960s and 70s, a social activist in both countries like many of my generation, and a bilingual elementary teacher in midlife as I followed the path of my own children through public schools. Through it all, I have become deeply self-identified and committed to social liberation of people in the transnational world in which I have been raised. I'm told I sound like a Mexican, but still look like the graying *gringo* I am, sometimes confusing but mostly amusing the Spanish speakers I'm around. My father was a mainline Presbyterian pastor who lost his church in the mid-60s for becoming a supporter of the early Civil Rights movement in our hometown of Monterey, California. My mother was a Sunday-school teacher, full-time mother, and leader of literacy classes for immigrants until she died at the age of 90. They raised my siblings and me to love God and serve people; that was it in a nutshell—the social-gospel to be carried out. Their path led them to become teachers and "fraternal workers" at a small Mexico City seminary in 1965. I went to school there, underwent an intercultural transformation in my teens, and eventually went to the turbulent National University of Mexico University before coming back to settle in California and grow my hair and politics. My values and the social movements of the times led me to become a full-time volunteer and journalist for the United Farm Workers union *El Malcriado* newspaper in the early 70s, an anti-imperialist researcher for the leftist North American Congress on Latin America in the late 70s, a union steward and activist during my 15 years as a printer, a protest-singing song leader of the Sacramento Labor Chorus, and eventually a bilingual elementary teacher in urban Sacramento and rural Galt, California. I discovered I love teaching kids and working with their parents, nourishing my desire for teaching and community organizing. Yet the politics in education was irritably consuming and one question loomed for me: "Where was the social justice community in education?"

The answer came in the form of a five-foot-tall bilingual resource teacher who was studying with Dr. Alma Flor Ada at the University of San Francisco. Nancy Jean Smith introduced me to Dr. Ada and the doctoral program of International and Multicultural Education at the University of San Francisco. I qualified for one of the final federal Title VII fellowships for bilingual teachers to earn a doctorate and became surrounded by a community of transformative and inspirational educators. I was delighted to be offered a position in the Bilingual/Multicultural Education Department (BMED) at California State University Sacramento, yet I was in the minority as a white male bilingual/multiculturalist. While some colleagues never seemed to get beyond my "whiteness," regardless of who I am inside, others were able to see and appreciate my particular identity and activism. These multi-ethnic teacher educators became my allies and friends, rooted in our love of teaching and understanding of multiculturalism. One of them saw I was deeply connected to Mexico and had begun a small travel-study program to Oaxaca and Cuernavaca for teachers to learn Spanish and a Mexican social perspective on education—Nadeen, who brought me into Bi-TEP.

Nadeen: All of my adult life, anyone outside of my family has assumed that I am Chicana. My looks, an (almost) accentless Spanish, my choice of profession as a bilingual teacher and bilingual teacher educator, my politics, and my advocacy work—all combine to make that a natural assumption. I have learned through the years that an immediate correction sounds like I am rejecting the label, when instead I actually feel extremely gratified to be thought of as Chicana. So I wait and monitor the conversation, looking for an opening to gently inform that I am the grandchild of Basque (our original last name is Ruiz de Larramendi) and Italian immigrants. I sometimes leave out the Italian side—with many apologies to Noni and Grandpa Dominic—mostly because people are searching for an explanation of my physical features, last name, bilingualism, and work.

Growing up next door to my Basque grandfather, and often out in the orchard with him and my father in our small almond ranch in the California Central Valley, I heard Spanish much more than Italian, especially given that Italian was lost within a generation but Spanish continued with my father on the Basque side. When the opportunity arose in college to study for a year in Spain, I went, knowing that this was my chance to solidify my proficiency in Spanish. I returned from study abroad, considering some sort of international career, or a high school credential to teach Spanish, when I heard of a relatively new profession back in 1975: bilingual education. I was immediately attracted to the idea of functionally using Spanish and English, as opposed to teaching it to high school students solely needing to satisfy the foreign language requirement for university admission.

I accepted my first job as an elementary teacher in the late 1970s. The central California district had a grant to support their new bilingual program that included a component to take my school colleagues and me to Michoacán, Mexico, for a five-week summer program to improve our academic Spanish and Mexican cultural proficiency. For me, it was first and foremost a wonderful opportunity to learn about my students' and their families' historical and sociocultural roots; 30 of my 32 kindergarteners that year were either Mexican or Mexican-American. It was also another chance to study outside of the U.S., the value of which I was convinced during my under-graduate years. But in addition, this program signaled the beginning of a long-time association with Mexican educational institutions.

Since the 1980s, I have worked with the Mexican Ministry of Education, mostly in my predominant area of research, bilingual special education, but also in migrant and deaf education. I continued this relationship during my doctoral program at Stanford University through to my first years as a professor of bilingual multicultural education at Sacramento State University in the early 1990s.

I believe that it was this strong professional connection to Mexican education that propelled my colleague at Sacramento State in the mid-90s, René Merino, to ask if I would assist with an international teacher education program for bilingual elementary candidates taking place in Mexico and California. René and other colleagues from a consortium of campuses in the California State University system had begun what was then informally called the "Mexico BCLAD Program" by partnering with Mexican teacher preparation institutions. After volunteering with the consortium for several years to assist with application and candidate interviews, I went to Mexico in 2001 to teach the language-arts curriculum and instruction course for three weeks to the Mexico BCLAD teacher candidates. By that time, René had retired, and I had become the official representative from Sacramento State to the consortium governing body, the International Teacher Education Council (ITEC). As René had done several years before, I began to search for someone in our department who had both a general passion for both international education and the specific realization that California teacher candidates, teachers, and teacher educators had much to learn from Mexico, its people, educational system, and educational research. There was no question in my mind that Peter was that person.

A Short History of Bi-TEP

We did not invent this unique program, nor are we alone in it today. What was known as the CSU Mexico BCLAD Program was created by René Merino at CSU– Sacramento and other dedicated professors from several CSU campuses in the mid-90s as a unique binational, bilingual teacher education program under the CSU system umbrella for study abroad, "International Programs."

Approximately 150 pre-service teachers studied in Mexico BCLAD between 1997 and 2005, first in Mexico City and later in Querétaro. Unique to Querétaro was the program's relationship with the Escuela Normal de Querétaro, the Mexican public teacher education school that opened its doors to our students, arranged student teaching and supervision, and collaborated on teaching courses that served as equivalents to courses in the CSU bilingual teacher education programs. To this day, bilingual teachers and administrators throughout California who graduated from Mexico BCLAD point to the Mexico immersion experience as being crucial to their development.

Two unfortunate circumstances, however, combined in 2005 and 2006 that proved to be the demise of the CSU Mexico BCLAD Program as it had been originally conceived. The first was the end of a federal grant to support the program. Without extra financial help offered by the grant to offset Mexico and related program costs, student applications to Mexico BCLAD dwindled; the program was cancelled for the 2006–2007 year. The second event was systemic and linked to the ongoing budget crisis felt by every department, college, or division throughout the 23 CSU campuses, under pressure to cut programs in order to reduce spending, including International Programs (IP).

Nadeen: In 2007, we members of the International Teacher Education Council (ITEC) sensed that the program was vulnerable to budget cuts unless we increased our participant numbers. ITEC asked me to submit a federal proposal that would once again provide stipends to Mexico BCLAD students and thereby attract more program applicants.

I wrote the proposal, gathering supporting letters, including one from the CSU International Programs director. Four months later, I received news that the grant proposal would be funded at $1.4 million for five years, 2007–2012. ITEC members were nothing less than ebullient, and made plans to send a cohort of student teachers to Mexico in the 2008–2009 year.

As news of the supporting scholarships began to slowly become known to teacher candidates, 15 qualified students applied to the program in March 2008. In a direct reversal of the letter of support he provided to obtain the grant, the IP director suspended the Mexico BCLAD program due to budgetary concerns in general (he had budgeted a $150,000 subsidiary for the program), and the low number of students, specifically (the program could take up to 25). ITEC sprang into action, first appealing to the IP director on the grounds of the program's effectiveness. When those appeals were not successful, ITEC submitted a description of a revised, low-cost program. The proposed program sent an in-country director for only the fall semester (bringing the faculty cost from $100,000 to $50,000). It also offered approximately $100,000 from the grant to mount the program. Consequently, the budget proposed by the IP director before his decision to suspend the program could have been easily covered by the new plan, with no outlay of funds from IP. ITEC members believed that the budget argument behind the program's closing was thereby refuted. But on May 7, 2008, the IP director reiterated his refusal to reinstate the program. His most frequently cited reason continued to be budget concerns. Verbally, however, he communicated to me that he never felt that Mexico BCLAD was a true "international program."

As ITEC members we were left incredulous. How could this international teacher education program—unique in the U.S. with its certification of fully bilingual/biliterate teachers—be shut down? The answer was that IP had the power to refuse to run the program under their auspices, and that the range of ITEC's efforts to contest the IP refusal came to naught.

Incredulity immediately turned into resolve. After all, we ITEC members were all former bilingual teachers and current bilingual teacher educators. In the face of negative public opinion towards bilingual education, we were used to collective action on behalf of language minority children and families.

Paradigm Matters

Before describing that collective action, we believe that it is important to return to Figure 1 in an attempt to understand the perspective of the IP director that contrasted so starkly with our own: a belief that Bi-TEP was not an international program and did not belong under the same umbrella as traditional, undergraduate study-abroad programs as those CSU IP programs in Italy, Germany, Japan, etc. Figure 1 with its continuum of interconnectedness helps explain that CSU IP was comfortable with programs located on the left side of the continuum, towards intellectual tourism. These programs sent undergraduates for short-term study and immersion abroad to pursue their own academic or personal development. In contrast, the Mexico BDLAD program expected that graduates from its program would emerge from transnational study in solidarity with the people of the target country, both abroad and in the U.S., and engage in social justice work directly related to their learning in the program. Thus, it seems to us, that the Mexico BCLAD program threatened the status quo of IP's traditional study-abroad programs, and was therefore expendable.

A New Way of Organizing Ourselves

The shutting down of the Mexico BCLAD program baffled and disappointed us, yet the immediate tasks before us were to figure out a way to continue without a full-time director, find a program partner in Mexico, recruit students, and not let the program die. We knew that if we were not successful, the $1.4 million from the federal grant would have to be returned to Washington and the program would remain dormant and probably moribund, closing off this third space for our students and downgrading the importance of their skills to work in the neediest communities of California. Thus motivated, we worked with our ITEC colleagues to develop a new way of organizing ourselves: a summer and fall semester program based at CSU East Bay College of Continuing Education, with the federal grant personnel at CSU–Sacramento—director Nadeen, professional development coordinator Peter, and project coordinator Ana María Guillén—taking up the organizational slack left after the withdrawal of CSU IP support. For the academic units, we duplicated the courses offered our first-semester students in the BMED program in Sacramento. Most importantly, we were lucky enough to recruit activist-educator Dr. Lettie Ramírez of Cal State East Bay to become our first part-time in-country director. With the help of other ITEC members, she and Nadeen found a new partner in Mexico to carry out our complicated semester-long program: the Universidad Autónoma de Guadalajara (UAG), a large, well-organized and private/Catholic institution in the central Mexican city of Guadalajara that had a respected teacher education program. Lettie began the first of many trips to work with UAG to set up home-stays for the students, find and develop professors to teach our courses in Spanish, and create student-teaching placements in public schools alongside their Mexican counterparts.

Year three brought more changes to Mexico BCLAD, as Peter was selected by ITEC to become the in-country director and raised the question of moving the program to Oaxaca, Mexico.

Peter: I was delighted to follow Lettie's example in Guadalajara, but Nadeen's and my visit there in year two to see our students showed us that our CSU public education identity and social justice principles were out of place in the private, elite, and very conservative UAG. Consequently, we began to investigate and lay the groundwork for moving our program elsewhere if ITEC agreed. I had been traveling with my wife, Joy, to the state and city of Oaxaca since our two children were young, and had enrolled them in language school during many summers to help them become bilingual and more socially conscious.

In 2006, I was there to witness the birth of the teachers' movement and the allied Asamblea de los Pueblos Populares de Oaxaca (APPO), which led a two-year strike against the corrupt governor of the old ruling PRI party and their own equally corrupt national union, the Sindicato Nacional de Trabajadores de la Educación (SNTE). Their strike had been violently broken and tourism disrupted for several years, but calm had largely returned and I had ventured to bring a small group of teachers and community folks there for two weeks in 2009, administered by CSU–Sacramento's College of Continuing Education. All had gone well and I had made many friends among teachers, residents, and especially with the Instituto Cultural Oaxaca (ICO) where my students studied. Would this be a good place to bring our CSU bilingual candidates? It was, after all, a lovely colonial city that was smaller than Guadalajara; it was the center of Mexico's Teacher and Popular Movement, which shares our commitment to social transformation; and this regional capital presides over one of the poorest and most indigenous populations who have been immigrating to California in record numbers in recent years (Ruiz & Barajas, 2012). Our students could literally get to know the people like those who have immigrated, teach children they might someday encounter in California, and learn the structural reasons behind their migration and educational needs.

The move to Oaxaca all depended upon having a dependable, public Mexican teacher education partner like we had for many years in Queretaro, one in which our students could study under Mexican professors and student teach with Mexican pre-service teachers. I began to follow the teacher contacts I had in Oaxaca and Mexico City, which eventually led to the heads of the Oaxaca teacher's union, Section 22 of the Coordinadora Nacional de Trabajadores de la Educacion (CNTE). After many conversations, they gave their approval and introduced me to the directors of the Centro Regional de Educación Normal de Oaxaca, known by its acronym CRENO. Personnel from CRENO were excited about the possibility of having a relationship with a California university program, even though it wasn't designed as a true exchange program, which they would have preferred. Director Luis Antonio Armenta and associate director Susana Santos Canseco introduced me to a dozen of their best *maestros* who could teach our classes, offered to organize the student teaching experience, and in many other ways demonstrated their total solidarity. At the same time, I met the talented Dr. Pedro Torres

Hernández, a former medical doctor, teacher and tour guide who would become a close friend and our coordinator for Bi-TEP in Oaxaca.

After returning and discussing it over several conference calls, ITEC decided to send a delegation back to Mexico to thoroughly interview all partners in both Guadalajara and Oaxaca and then make a recommendation to ITEC. We made this trip in spring 2010 and wrote a report with our recommendations to pursue the move to Oaxaca and partner with ICO for Spanish-language study and CRENO for classes and student teaching. ITEC agreed with our appraisal and encouraged us to move forward, resulting in our third successful year and first in Oaxaca. The federal grant's external evaluator, Dr. Norm Gold, notes the growth of the teacher candidates' understanding in his executive Report (Gold, 2011). "Two quotes," writes Gold, "capture the candidates' repeated message about the overall uniqueness of Bi-TEP international teacher education program, and its effectiveness in producing strongly committed teachers of English Learners:

"[Studying and student teaching in Mexico]…was significant because we were able to bond with international peers that shared the same passion for teaching. They were incredibly supportive in our quest to learn all about their culture, language and educational system. At the same time, we were able to share about our culture and the United States educational system and philosophies of teaching. It was inspiring to be part of this same generation of future international teachers that understand the importance of education for the future of one's country. "…the highest of this experience was feeling the respect and appreciation that was given to me by my students and colleagues in Oaxaca [Mexico]. It gave me such a sense of pride of profession that I know I will carry with me throughout my career." (Gold, 2011, p. 3).

Closing ceremony at our partner Normal School (CRENO) in Oaxaca, 2010.

Indeed, all of us from Oaxaca or California who watched our 17 candidates walk the stage at CRENO in December 2010 were filled with "pride of profession," and looked forward to the next year of the program when we would make many improvements that had been suggested by a CRENO forum of students and teachers. Students suggested getting to know their *normalista* (Mexican student teacher) counterparts earlier and having even more classes and student teaching with them. The Oaxacan teachers had come to know more about the commonalities and differences between our two educational systems (e.g., we both faced standardized testing imposed from federal mandates), and between students from Oaxaca and California. All were excited about participating the following year.

The Second Blow

Imagine, then our disappointment and incredulity when in early March of the following year we got an email from the provost of our university informing us that Bi-TEP and all CSU programs with travel to Mexico had been shut down. While it was not mentioned in the email, the provost was referring to Executive Order 998 in which Chancellor Charles Reed banned all programs to countries with U.S. State Department Travel Warnings. The basis for that warning was violence along the Mexico–U.S. border, Sinaloa, and some other states that had taken some 22,000 lives, mostly between rival narcotics cartels (*Los Angeles Times*, 2010). The Executive Order was in place in 2010 as we prepared for our first year to Oaxaca, but since there were no patterns of violence there, we requested a waiver for our program through President Alexander Gonzalez of CSU–Sacramento and it was granted by the chancellor's office. In 2011 we repeated our request of President Gonzalez, who agreed to pass our waiver on to the chancellor, but this time, in spite of no changes in Oaxaca, we were denied permission along with all other CSU Mexico programs.

Our response was immediate. We first tried to find out more about the reasons for the change in policy, but could get nothing written from the chancellor's office about the basis for their "risk assessment." We both wrote letters to Chancellor Reed stating (1) the importance of the CSU Mexico BCLAD program in serving underserved populations in California; (2) the $1.4 million federal grant that would be lost; (3) our careful selection of a "location for the program that does not have a record of security problems" and "numerous U.S. university partners" that continue to send students to Oaxaca; and (4) the impact of withdrawing the CSU program on our neighbor and ally, Mexico, in particular what Nadeen called the "important collaborative effort between the two countries to serve the children that we share across borders" (Ruiz, 2011b). Peter sent a detailed letter to Reed with a three-page attachment of our "CSU Bi-TEP Health, Safety and Security Guidelines from 2010" and assurances of our safety consciousness. Yet no answer was ever received to either of our letters or multiple inquiries—only silence.

The Mexican Consul General in Sacramento, Carlos González Gutiérrez, also sent a very strong letter on March 21 to Reed calling for him to grant the waiver in light of the importance of Bi-TEP to Mexico–U.S. relations and to another binational program that Nadeen and Ana María were working on to bring Oaxacan teachers to California:

> The Oaxacan indigenous teacher project arose in direct response to California teachers' calls for assistance in better meeting the academic needs of indigenous students. It's also important to point out that this program works both sides, US teachers also travel to Oaxaca to develop the same abilities and experience as their counterparts from Mexico. (González Gutíerres, 2011).

In a very real sense, we view these two programs, the CSU Mexico Bilingual Teacher Education Program and the program for Oaxacan Indigenous teachers, as an exchange of knowledge and service between our two countries. Furthermore, we see our support of the programs as a shared commitment by our two governments to promote the academic success of students in California from Spanish and indigenous language backgrounds (González Gutiérrez, 2011).

No answer to this letter was ever received by the Mexican Consul General—only silence. Students who had changed their life plans to become bilingual teachers through Bi-TEP and experience Oaxaca also sent many letters to Chancellor Reed, including this one by Joseph Hall of Napa:

> This program should continue in Mexico because it is safe to study and live there, and because our nation desperately needs qualified bi-lingual teachers who are culturally and linguistically educated to meet the needs of our ethnically diverse learning population.... I chose to apply to Sacramento State for a BiTEP credential because of the unique opportunities offered through the Mexico-BiTEP program. No other program in the United States offers the opportunity to study and learn from our neighboring country while earning a bilingual credential. (Hall, 2011)

Joseph's father, Parker Hall, sent his own letter of protest to Reed on April 15, concluding, "I think there is a risk involved but I teach in a public school in Vallejo, and there's risk there. Without risk, there would be no Peace Corps. Please reconsider and allow this program to continue."

Joseph's mother sent the following poignant letter:

> I am an elementary teacher in California. Over the last 25 years I have seen an increase in the need for bilingual teachers. Many recent graduating teachers speak Spanish, but they do not have the cultural understanding and knowledge to teach in heavily bilingual schools....Please reconsider your decision and renew the travel waiver for 2011. It would benefit the participating students in the Bi-TEP program from the five CSU campuses, and it would demonstrate our support for education in Mexico. They are our neighbors and the largest population subgroup in California schools. (Borba, 2011)

This family's pleas were answered with silence, as were most others from students and community supporters.

We were relentless in making phone calls and writing letters to Chancellor Reed's office, but with no or little response from Long Beach. Nevertheless, we still continued our campaign and transnational activities. In early April, Peter and the guests from Oaxaca were able to meet with Tom Torlakson, California superintendent of public instruction, and tell him about the CSU ban on travel to Mexico that was threatening our program and many others. As a member of the CSU Board of Trustees, California's education leader and a former teacher, Superintendent Torlakson was very concerned and offered to make a phone call and write a letter to the Chancellor on our behalf to reconsider the waiver. True to his word and with the help from his staff, the superintendent made a phone call and left a message for Chancellor Reed, then followed up with a formal letter on April 25:

> I am writing this letter to reiterate the concerns I expressed in a message I left for you about the Bi-National Teacher Education Program (BiTEP) being denied a waiver from the travel ban for its session starting in July 2011.
>
> The BiTEP program is of great value to CSU students…. Faculty in California and Mexico have invested enormous time, expertise and effort in developing the program. I believe it is a great example of bi-national collaboration. If the program is unable to proceed this year, I fear it will be difficult to restart in the future. —Sincerely, Tom Torlakson (2011).

Surely, we thought, if anyone could make the case as a member of the CSU Board of Trustees, it would be the superintendent of public instruction. In fact, we were to learn later that neither the phone messages nor the letter from Torlakson warranted a reply from Reed's office. Thus, we were forced to change direction on our plans for Oaxaca, even as we continued to put pressure on the chancellor's office. On April 13 we sent a letter to the ITEC reps stating "We are not giving up hope" and also sent out a general letter to all our students apprising them of the situation and encouraging them to write their own letters to the chancellor.

Bi-TEP 2011 in Guatemala

With Nadeen and Ana Maria in charge of the Oaxaca campaign and communications with students, Peter took charge of investigating a "Plan B" to run a one-month intensive immersion experience in Guatemala. We opted for Guatemala because of the strong indigenous community and bilingual education presence, and leaned toward a month program because our time was running out. So many questions: Would we find an alternative to Oaxaca, or have to stop Bi-TEP for this year, likely losing the funding and everything else along with it? Would the

18 candidates whom we'd prepared for Oaxaca agree to switch gears and come to Guatemala? Was it safe in Guatemala, a country still devastated by a decade of civil war and one of the highest crime rates in Latin America? Could we recreate the powerful learning experiences from the previous years, especially the student teaching? What would be the impact of a shorter program, i.e., one month instead of five months? Who would be our new transnational partners? The only way to find out was to go and see for ourselves.

Peter: Beginning in the first week of May, I relied on the Internet and friends to investigate language schools and education contacts in Guatemala. I was overwhelmed with the generosity and wisdom of the contacts I made among Guatemala educators and indigenous activists—especially with teacher/activist Julio César Ortiz and his wife, Vale. I also got positive responses from half a dozen language schools in Antigua, where I learned it was safe. Thus encouraged, Nadeen and I decided that I would make an investigatory trip to Guatemala and bring back a recommendation for the group's decision.

Four days later, I had found a wonderful school, the Instituto Lingüístico La Union, and had been taken around by its director to visit several families where our students would live, and three needy schools where they could student-teach. I also spoke with his large staff, mostly public school teachers themselves. I discovered that our students would receive one-on-one Spanish-language instruction, transportation to the rural schools that La Union supported, and an extensive guided travel package—all for a price we could afford because of the lower cost of living in Guatemala. The missing piece was arranging with Julio César for a series of Guatemalan experts, bilingual teachers, indigenous activists, and survivors of the Guatemalan civil war to help us learn about the true transnational connections between Guatemala and the United States. This included learning about the tragic role that our own government played in supporting the Guatemalan military and civilian rulers who massacred an estimated 200,000 dissidents and civilians during the 1960–1996 period of *la Violencia*—most of the dead being Mayan men, women, and children (Jonas, 1991).

Our ITEC conference call discussed the recommendation to move Bi-TEP to Antigua, Guatemala, for the month of July 2011. The opinion was unanimous to move the program to Guatemala instead of shutting it down. Peter then wrote a letter to the accepted Bi-TEP students and ITEC representatives on May 6, explaining, "The time has come to thank everyone for our heroic efforts to change the Chancellor's mind about the Oaxaca waiver (MIL GRACIAS), but it has become clear that we must now enact our Plan B in Guatemala" (Baird, 2011). The letter went on to explain the main components of the new program and asked for a yes or no within five days. Nearly everyone said yes!

Student teachers and head teacher (center left) with children at Vuelta Grande rural school outside of Antigua, Guatemala.

There is not space here to tell the entire story of that experience in Guatemala, but it was indeed transformative for the students and for Peter who was the in-country director. The most powerful experiences came from students working in two rural schools outside of Antigua, living with families who were not far above the poverty line themselves, and conducting research on social issues of their own choice with their Guatemalan teachers at La Union. Once again we rely upon three of our teacher candidates to provide the highlights through their written reflections:

- "My perception and understanding changed for the best. The appreciation of different languages and different cultures is deeper. For example, illiteracy is still a big problem. People, especially indigenous people in Guatemala, had land stolen and a *Guerra Civil* started. People were massacred for standing up for themselves. People need to be valued regardless if they speak another language or dress differently. Learning other languages and offering that education to all people of a nation is providing justice." (White male candidate)

- "I am more proud than ever to speak Spanish and be part of the Latino culture in California. I have learned a lot, and will take this love of Guatemala culture home with me." (Latina female candidate)

- "Travel always reminds me of how profoundly lucky I am to be a white person born in a middle-class family in the United States. And how much power and responsibility I hold. Being in Guatemala reminded me that even small actions make a difference, and that I can use my position of privilege to advocate for and with others who lack that privilege." (White female candidate)

Back to Oaxaca in 2012

Once the group returned back to their CSU campuses, we once again took a good look at what our priorities were for Bi-TEP. While Guatemala had shown us that a shorter teacher education experience was possible, and certainly opened our eyes to these brave people as transnational partners, our commitment was to return to the country where most of our immigrant students come from, Mexico. That meant finding a way to get back to Oaxaca. With our own university locked up behind the "risk management" policies of CSU, we made the difficult decision to look for another institution to sponsor the travel portion of Bi-TEP. During our struggle to change the CSU chancellor's mind the previous year, we had learned that the University of California system had a different way of assessing risk for its international programs: regional, not national. With UC–Davis a short distance from Sacramento, Nadeen took the lead in negotiating the delicate change. It was accomplished, but not without warnings from the CSU–Sacramento provost that every connection between Bi-TEP and the CSU must be erased or the program would be "pulled" by the chancellor's office. We were walking a delicate line—wanting to include CSU students in what was now a summer "enrichment" program, while moving the whole travel component to UC– Davis Extension and offering the program to a limited number of UC–Davis bilingual teacher candidates.

With these delicate negotiations behind us, we moved quickly to design a month-long intensive program in Oaxaca for July 2012. Happily, our partners and friends in Oaxaca were glad to have us back and received us warmly when we made a short planning trip there in late February. They told us that their own struggles have taught them to be flexible and that they value their relationship with our faculty and students.

Our curriculum for July 2012 centered on building the candidates' skills and experiences for three weeks in Oaxaca City through language study, family homestay, and a seminar titled "Communication Skills for the Bilingual Teacher," taught by us with help from our Oaxacan counterparts. In the fourth week, Peter, coordinator Pedro, and our dear friend Professor Santiago Gabriel Dolores took the 26 candidates to do student-teaching and live in an *albergue escolar indígena* (indigenous boarding school) in San Martín Peras. This is a town in La Mixteca, a mountainous region of the state that has been the most severely impacted by the collapse in the corn-based subsistence economy, spurring the migration of a large percentage of its male population and many families to the U.S. seventy percent of the children we taught had parents who lived and worked as farmworkers in California. It was truly a transformative, transnational experience and was worth all the trials of bringing it to rebirth.

Conclusions

What are some of the conclusions we can draw about developing and fighting for a transnational third space in teacher education?

We feel that the last two years, during which time we have documented the impact of Bi-TEP in Oaxaca and Guatemala, show that we have been successful in starting to create a transnational and *transformative* third space for deepening the learning of our bilingual teacher education candidates. The candidates became interconnected to the families they lived and worked with, returning to their home country with a level of social justice advocacy and multicultural proficiency that is greater than what we have experienced in our combined 55 years of experience in U.S.-based programs, in particular about the indigenous heritage and languages of many of their future students in California (Ruiz & Baird, 2013). In terms of the interconnectedness paradigm in Figure 1, we are moving and continually pushing towards a transnational teacher education program with graduates who "recognize the unique skills and experiences of K–12 transnational students and their families, and…work across borders in solidarity for the common good" (Ruiz & Baird, 2013, p. 25).

The responses of our students show that what they valued most was the opportunity to become immersed in a transnational community, study and learn about the social context of education in both countries, deepen their biliteracy skills, and do their student teaching alongside teachers from that country. As Figure 1 described, they moved from a paradigm of disconnect to one of profound interconnectedness with the students and families with whom they will work in the United States.

We learned that while deep learning in a transnational third space is best done over a long period of time, it can be achieved in a shorter time if there is sufficient preparation, daily contact with the social reality in a country like Guatemala, and critical reflections guided by the program curriculum.

We know that we benefitted greatly by moving our program to a place like Oaxaca where teachers have a tradition and ongoing practice of leading social movements that reach not only into their own country, but have implications for populations on both sides of the U.S.–Mexican border (Bacon, 2006). Indeed, so many transnational social, artistic, humanitarian and educational endeavors are present in Oaxaca that it has been called "Oaxacalifornia" by more than a few observers.

Our experiences with CSU Chancellor Charles Reed and the officers who carried out his ban on Mexico programs have made us more aware just how undemocratically our public university system is currently operated. We believe that the "risk management" reason we were told was behind their Mexico ban is part of a larger move by this and other U.S. universities toward a "business model" in which students are treated as customers (tuition has doubled in the last four years, tripled in the last decade) and faculty are treated as "education producers" who don't deserve a fair labor contract (Shreck & Sunshine, 2012). We agree with the late Sacramento State's Jeff Lustig's analysis of this problem and its implications for faculty members like ourselves:

> Who will bell the cat? Not the administrators, who nearly all promote the business model. Hopefully the students, while they're here. And the staff. But, I want to suggest, centrally this is a job for the faculty. (Lustig, 2011. p. 19)

As further evidence of the influence of the business model, we recently learned that CSU IP re-opened its Israel program. Israel has a U.S. State Department travel warning, while the Mexican state of Oaxaca—site of our Bi-ETP program—does not. In the following quote from an article reporting the reopening of the Israel program, readers will recognize an earlier, influential character in our narrative, the CSU IP director:

> The travel warning remains in effect, but CSU Director of International Programs Leo Van Cleve announced last calendar year that study abroad to Israel would be reconsidered due to pressure from Jewish organizations, legislators and Israeli diplomats. (Khorasani, 2012, p. 1).

In the meantime, over 400,000 students in the 23 CSU campuses are prohibited from study of any kind in Mexico. Instead, study-abroad students are directed to "safe" countries like China, and thousands of Chinese and other foreign students are admitted to our campuses to balance the budget (Altadena, 2012). Indeed, part of our motivation in writing this chapter has certainly been "belling the cat" in terms of how little the CSU values study in Mexico's safe regions, and reactions from Latino community members such as Sacramento's consul general.

As faculty in charge of Bi-TEP, we believe it is worth fighting for transnational programs that build capacity for our bilingual teacher candidates and ultimately benefit the communities they serve. It has been as rewarding as it has been exhausting these past few years, but we cannot stop our efforts since even the spaces for preparing teachers on our home campuses are under attack. We are seeing that several of the CSU campuses, including CSU–East Bay, are closing down their teacher education programs for bilingual candidates and other programs are being choked by the current budget crisis and lack of faculty hiring. Meanwhile, there is a move to eliminate the foreign language and other requirements for undergraduates of CSU campuses (Lambert, 2012). At CSU–Sacramento, the Bilingual/Multicultural Education Department we have been a part of has championed bilingual education, social justice, and the recruitment of teacher educators of color for the past 15 years, yet now has been downgraded from a department to an "area group" by a budget-driven reorganization of the College of Education (William-White, 2012). It is easy to become discouraged by these losses, but we continue to push back and "fight," following the advice of educator Enid Lee to Nadeen a few years ago to "remain in opposition for a just cause." To this end, Nadeen gave testimony before the California Latino legislative caucus on September 11, 2012, where she told this chapter's story to the legislators in front of both UC and CSU administrators in international education.

There is little doubt that developing international third-space programs such as Bi-TEP are "risky" in terms of external events (tsunamis, wars and other violence, funding) and internal factors (travel bans, institutional desires to minimize risk and reduce budgets, institutional racism and fear of programs that radicalize participants). Yet, citing earlier letters by parents of our teacher candidates, there is risk in teaching in our local schools, and without risk there would be no third-space international programs of any lasting value.

In conceptualizing TTE as a third space that is neither one's home nor "home school," we have placed ourselves within an ideological "third space" that supports our reconstructionist educational agenda (Giroux, 1997). In the introduction to this book, the editors explain that curriculum conceptualization and implementation can be seen in three primary ways: as product, process, and praxis. How do these ways help us understand the curricular dimensions of our experiences in transnational teacher education?

Addressing curriculum as product, the worldview that shapes almost all teacher education is, in our experience, decidedly "unworldly," and certainly not geared to help teacher candidates understand our social placement in the global world context. How did we break the U.S.-centric knowledge base that shapes our curriculum? We left our national first space. Once in Mexico and Guatemala, we then lived with our transnational partners, opened ourselves to their experiences and perspectives of who we are, and partnered with their schools, faculty, students, and communities.

Looking at the process of curriculum, meanwhile, we have found that when students and teachers engage in new and challenging learning in the international or transnational arena, new levels of communication and dialogic learning can take place. On the one hand, the special international knowledge and life experience of the professor can become valued in settings outside the U.S. because it is practical and related to the needs to negotiate in a new culture and language; for example, how to hail a cab, obtain medical help, suggest who is the best person to help answer a question, or set up a visit to a local school. On the other hand, the instructor and pre-service students in an international teacher education program are co-learners because they are both interacting with a new or less familiar environment that they have the opportunity to understand together, such as when the Mexican indigenous healer Doña Queta came and taught our Bi-TEP students and us about healing with herbs within her culturally based view of the world.

In the transnational context, the praxis, reflection and action of curriculum is uniquely capable of allowing students and teachers to break through the barriers of U.S. economic and political interests—something difficult to do when we are surrounded by the pabulums of Fox News and U.S. consumer society. Living in a foreign country intentionally as a non-tourist can force one to throw off the blinders of living in our continental U.S. island. How else can we truly engage students and ourselves in "reading the world" (Freire & Macedo, 1987) from the vantage point of the immigrant workers, the non-Westerner, the outsider, the oppressed, and those who fight actively against this oppression?

Finally, on a personal level, we have been transformed by not only the process of forming this transnational third space for teacher education, but by reflecting upon it in this volume. We have a better sense of how our life-stories impact and are impacted upon by what we teach and where we teach.

2012 Bi-TEP Participants with students in La Mixteca with the banner "Language Brings Us Together."

On March 6, 2013, the new CSU Chancellor responded to pressure and lifted the travel band for all CSU programs to Mexico.

References

Altadena, L. (2012, February 6).Foreign students pay a premium at American colleges. *New York Times*. http://thechoice.blogs.nytimes.com/2012/02/06/international-american-colleges/

Baird, P. (personal communication, May 6, 2011).

Baird, P. & McCaughan, E. (1979). *Beyond the Border: Mexico and the U.S. Today.* New York: North American Congress on Latin America.

Bacon, D. (2006). *Communities Without Borders: Images and Voices from the World of Migration.* Ithaca, NY: Cornell University Press.

Barajas, M. (2012). Mexican-origin indigenous immigration to the United States: A historical and intersectional perspective. In I. Ness (Ed.), *The Encyclopedia of Global Human Migration*. Oxford, U.K.: Blackwell.

Borba, J. (personal communication, April 15, 2011).

Comis, E.(personal communication, April 20, 2011).

Denham. D. & C.A.S.A. Collective (Eds.). (2008). *Teaching Rebellion: Stories from the Grassroots Mobilization in Oaxaca.* Oakland, CA: PM Press.

Freire, P. (1970/2000). *Pedagogy of the Oppressed.* New York: Continuum.

Freire, P., & Macedo, D.P. (1987). *Literacy: Reading the Word and the World.* London, U.K.: Routledge & Kegan Paul Ltd.

Giroux, H. A. (1997). *Pedagogy and the Politics of Hope: Theory, Culture, and Schooling.* Boulder, CO: Westview Press.

Gold, N. (2011). *National Professional Development Program Executive Summary, Bi-TEP 2007–2011.*

Gonzalez Gutíerres, C. (personal communication, March 21, 2011).

Hall, J.B.(personal communication, April 15, 2011).

Jonas, S. (1991). *The Battle for Guatemala: Rebels, Death Squads, and U.S. Power.* Boulder, CO: Westview Press.

Khorasani, K. (2012, January 11). CSU students protest reinstated Israel study abroad program. *Guardian.* http://www.ucsdguardian.org/component/k2/item/25239-csu-students-protest-reinstated-israel-study-abroad-program

Kuper, P. (2009). *Diario de Oaxaca: A Sketchbook Journal of Two Years in Oaxaca.* Oakland, CA: PM Press.

Lambert, D. (2012). Sacramento State evaluates requirements, putting language, history on chopping block. *Sacramento Bee,* April 26, 2012.

Lustig, J. (2011, Fall). The university besieged. *Thought & Action.* NEA. http://www.nea.org/home/50451.htm

Moll, L. C., Amanti, C., Neff, D., & Gonzalez, N. (2001). Funds of knowledge for teaching: Using a qualitative approach to connect homes and classrooms. *Theory into Practice, 31*(2), 132–141.

Pinar, W., Reynolds, W.M., Slattery, P., & Taubman, P. M. (1995). *Understanding Curriculum.* New York: Peter Lang.

Quezada, R. (2005). Beyond educational tourism: Lessons learned while student teaching abroad. *International Education Journal, 5*(4), 458–465.

Quezada, R., & Alfaro, C. (2007, Winter). Biliteracy teachers' self-reflections of their accounts while student teaching abroad. *Teacher Education Quarterly, 34*(1).

Rivera, C, (2011). Security concerns lead Cal State officials to bar students from program in Mexico. *Los Angeles Times,* April 29, 2011.

Rodríguez, E. (2011). Reflections from an international immersion trip: New possibilities to institutionalize curriculum. *Teacher Education Quarterly, 38*(1), 147–160.

Ruiz, N. T. (personal communication, March 21, 2011a).

Ruiz, N. T. (2011b, April). *"Son menos mexicanos" ("They're less Mexican"): U.S. transnational students in Mexican schools.* Paper presented at the annual meeting of the American Education Research Association, New Orleans, LA.

Ruiz, N. T., & Baird, P. (2013). *Transnational Teacher Education: Towards Theory and Practice.* NABE Journal of Research and Practice, Vol 4.

Ruiz, N. T., Barajas, M., McGinty, I. & Romo, D. (In press). *Weaving Learning Communities Across Borders: Mexican Indigenous Students and Families in California.* Sacramento, CA: California Department of Education.

Ruiz, N.T. & Barajas, M. (2012) Multiple perspectives on the schooling of Mexican Indigenous students in the U.S.: Issues for future research. *Bilingual Research Journal, 35*: 125–144.

Shreck, S. & Sunshine, A. (2012). The "For-profitization" of the CSU. *California Faculty,* Spring 2012.

Topete, L. (personal communication, April 20, 2011).

Torlakson, T. (personal communication, April 25, 2011).

William-White, L. (2012, July 1). Advocating for multicultural education and social justice in the age of economic uncertainty. *International Review of Qualitative Research, 5*(2).

Zúñiga, V., Hamann, E. T., & Sánchez Garcia, J. (2008). *Alumnos transnacionales: Escuelas mexicanas frente a la globalizacion.* Mexico: SEP.

CHAPTER TWELVE

All Real Education Is Political

History, Racism, and Progressive Pedagogy

KATHY EMERY

For the things we have to learn before we can do them, we learn by doing them, e.g., men become builders by building and lyre players by playing the lyre; so too we become just by doing just acts, temperate by doing temperate acts, brave by doing brave acts. — Aristotle

Lack of the free and equitable intercourse which springs from a variety of shared interests makes intellectual stimulation unbalanced. Diversity of stimulation means novelty, and novelty means challenge to thought. — John Dewey

In large measure, the race question involves the saving of black America's body and white America's soul. — James Weldon Johnson

History is a choice. —Bayard Rustin

I grew up white and middle class in Concord, New Hampshire. From 1960 to 1973, I attended the public schools in this small-town capital (about 30,000) of a very small state, which was very conservative[1] and 99 percent white.[2] I left Concord to attend a prestigious New England college and taught high school history for 16 years. Today, I teach political science at San Francisco State University and mentor students who are rebuilding SFSU's Experimental College.[3] My 3,000-mile and 57-year journey from small town to big city, from bored student to progressive teacher, from liberal Democrat to radical feminist (among many other transformations) has been motivated by a need to enjoy life. And somehow, I intuitively knew, from the very earliest years, that my happiness, my freedom, or my salvation depended upon everyone being happy, free, or saved. My current pedagogy and curriculum are the result of a long history of experimentation within the nooks and crannies of an educational system that seems determined to discourage analysis while repressing reflection and evaluation in order to preserve an inhumane status quo. My persistence in this search for liberatory education had a great deal to do with needing to reconcile the differences between my identity and my experiences.[4]

An early challenge came from experiencing school as a sorting and socializing process (Arnstine, 1995). Grades 2 through 12 felt like prison to me. I would watch the minute hand take forever to move from one hash mark to the next. Every day was a tortuous countdown to freedom, free to leave school and play on a dead-end street abutting a forest. I loved playing for all the reasons I would read about later in Dewey's *Democracy and Education*. The boys on my street and I invented several variations of baseball and football to deal with exigencies of small rosters and limited space. I made detailed maps of our neighborhood and the forest trails, built submarines out of refrigerator crating, made cities out of Lego blocks and Matchbox cars. This was experiential learning at its best and provided stark contrast to the ritual and sterility of my classroom experience.

My play was not only interesting, complex, and fun, but also fair. My parents modeled a stance towards the world that reinforced my experience that games were more enjoyable when everyone participated in the creation of their aims. My British Canadian Protestant mom grew up in Vancouver (she liked to brag that she used to be a "card-carrying Communist") and my French Canadian Catholic father grew up in Montreal. When very young, I asked my mom why we lived in the United States and rarely visited our cousins. She explained to us that for a French and British Canadian to marry was tantamount to a white and a black marrying in the United States. In what I would eventually learn to be my mother's quintessential hyperbolic style, she often claimed that "no one would marry them, so they fled to the United States while being disowned." In explaining what she meant by "like a black marrying a white," my mother introduced me to the concept of racism. This seed of understanding was planted during my adolescence, took root during my early teaching years, and flowered after a colleague offered me the opportunity to work on publishing the 1964 Mississippi Freedom School Curriculum.

When I was ten (or twelve?), racism took on a very tangible and memorable form for me. A young black man rang our doorbell one day. He was selling subscriptions to *Ebony*. My mother asked him in and offered him a cup of tea. I had never seen a black person. We sat and talked a bit and she bought a subscription. I didn't understand why she invited him in and gave him tea. She explained that, most likely, he was getting a hostile reception from other houses and that it was the least she could do for him. She then proceeded to remind me what "race" meant in the United States. My mother's explanations prepared me to be able to learn something from two books I had to read in high school. Sometime during my high school years (1971–1973), the Civil Rights movement managed to penetrate even the "Live Free or Die" state.[5] I remember reading the *Autobiography of Malcolm X* and Jonathan Kozol's *Death at an Early Age* (the only two books I remember reading in my K–12 schooling.) These powerful stories filled in some of the detail my mother's explanations left out.

These two books, a few French phrases, some science concepts, and a semester-long writing course constituted all that I learned in the classroom. All my real education took place in and around my home. My parents were voracious readers. One entire wall of their bedroom was floor-to-ceiling books. My mother, being an Anglophile, had many books—fact and fiction —about England. By reading everything in their library that was of interest to me, my predilections and ideals were refined and reinforced. I fell in love with Elizabeth I, which put me on the path to majoring in modern European history and becoming a feminist (the latter reinforced by the extreme discrimination I experienced as a female athlete). In trying to read Edmund Wilson's *To the Finland Station,* I was introduced to the concept of historiography—why there are different interpretations of the past. In devouring A. S. Neill's *Summerhill,* I finally realized why I was so alienated by school and what real education looked like. My father ordered the *New York Times* and taught me how to read the paper. I began to look up words in the dictionary upon reading that "McDonalds was ubiquitous" and Spiro Agnew spewed "vituperative billingsgate." During many conversations at home, my parents deeply impressed upon me how vital it was that Johnson defeat Goldwater (1964); that it was a disaster when "tricky Dick" (1968) was elected president (my mother wailed, "doesn't anyone remember what he did to Helen Gahagan Douglas?"); that it was immoral that the U.S. was making war against the Vietnamese (1968–1975); that the government was responsible when the National Guard murdered four Kent State students (1970): and how the Attica Prison riot (1971) summed up what was wrong with America. These positions were in sharp contrast with the ultra-conservative views prevailing in New Hampshire at the time. Reading Dewey (1916) would later explain to me why this contrast had such a profound effect on the way I began to think about myself, and my place in the world.[6]

When it came time to choose a college, I had already decided to major in history and minor in political science. I decided to go to Mt. Holyoke College because it was all women (to be free of sex discrimination) and small (to find what I later learned Vygotsky called "the zone of proximal development" with my professors).[7] During my sophomore year, I discovered that most of my friends were going away for their junior years, so I thought I had better go, too. Of course, I chose England. At the University of Kent at Canterbury, I took a historiography course in which I learned that the truth is on the edge of controversy.[8] This epiphany came during an assignment to read an extended debate between two eminent British historians, R.H. Tawney (1954) and J.H. Hexter (1958, 1961).[9] They had written competing journal articles about whether the English gentry were rising or falling from 1540 to 1640.I read Tawney and was persuaded by his evidence that the gentry were rising in their fortunes and power. Then I read Hexter's response to Tawney's article and was forced, by the evidence, to change my mind. Tawney's riposte brought me back to his point of view. The back-and-forth continued all night. By the time I had read three or four volleys, I had decided that the truth was always temporary, waiting to be updated with the next argument. The more I read, the more interested I became with the complex and detailed picture of 16th-century England, and the less concerned I became with whether the gentry were "rising or falling." I realized that the debate was merely a means to determine a process, which was the end in itself.[10]

My Kent historiography class was also crucial in introducing me to Karl Marx. Although my mother had explained red-baiting and implied that being a communist was a badge of honor, I didn't know what communism was. In reading Marx's *Eighteenth Brumaire of Louis Bonaparte*, I was introduced to the concept of the application of political theory to the interpretation of history. Marx's version of history made so much more sense to me than the "Whig interpretation of history" (Butterfield, 1931) we had read previously. Marx's application of his theory of change (economic base/social and political superstructure) made complete sense to me; whereas, "the history of England is the history of progress" did not (Macaulay, 1852; p. 289). Marx pointed out how I could marry my politics to history. In hindsight, this was the first step towards understanding how teaching (and education) is political.

When I returned to Mt. Holyoke for my senior year, I decided to pursue my interest in political theory and Marxism. In my political theory class, our task was to write our own political theory. As part of the process, we took turns defending our drafts in class. There was one black woman in the class from Harlem. Her theory revolved around her calculation that when the economic condition of the U.S. bottomed out, whites would round up all the blacks and put them in work camps. I watched my fellow white students roll their eyes while she talked, and then I listened while they told her how absurd her theory was. I was not interested in arguing whether or not her theory was true. I was interested in knowing the reality upon which she was constructing her truth. I had learned from my historiography course in England that truth was somewhere beyond the many true versions of it. Every person witnesses an event differently; every person has a different reality based on a unique combination of experiences that they have had. That a working-class black woman's theory would so diverge from the experiences of the highly privileged white women in the class made me realize how narrow my own experiences had been.

I had no idea what to do after I graduated. My advisor and mentor suggested I teach history because I was "so good at it." I balked at the suggestion, remembering how dreadfully bored I was in high school, how little I remembered of what I was taught, and how badly we treated our teachers. As I considered the alternatives to teaching, however, I decided I might give teaching a shot after all, since it would satisfy my desire to be political and study history at the same time. I chose to apply only to private, independent schools for the following reasons: they did not require a teaching credential (friends of mine who had been through credential courses and were teaching told me such courses were a waste of time); I wanted to teach small seminar-like classes; and I wanted to be able to control my curricula. Not only did I want to be able to choose widely diverse and provocative reading material, I also wanted to conduct debates, role-plays, and in-depth discussions of events to fully engaged my students and push them to challenge their preconceived notions of truth. I wanted them to play with the facts so they could achieve ownership over their version of the stories. I was about to discover, however, that private independent schools were not havens of academic freedom.

I applied to 80 private schools and got one job offer. I started teaching at Groton[11] (an elite boarding school in western Massachusetts) in the fall of 1977. I was to teach U.S. history even though I had never taken a U.S. history course in college. I thought I was playing it safe by relying upon the books listed on the syllabus of Mt. Holyoke's U.S. history survey course—a traditional textbook (Blum's *National Experience*), supplemented by:

- Morgan, E. S. (1958). *The Puritan Dilemma: The Story of John Winthrop*. New York: Norton.

- Ryan, Mary (1975), *Womanhood in America*. New York: New Viewpoints.

- Wood, Peter (1975). *Black Majority: Negroes in Colonial South Carolina from 1670 through the Stono Rebellion*. New York: Norton.

I had a miserable year at Groton for a variety of reasons. One reason was the sink-or-swim conditions of the first year of teaching. The second was being an in-the-closet lesbian and radical teacher in an isolated boarding school of the rich and powerful. Once I arrived and started teaching, I think they realized they had made a mistake. Parents began to complain to the administration that I was teaching women's history and black history and not preparing the students for the U.S. history achievement test. When a friend asked me if it was my job at Groton that she was applying for, I realized that I had better tell the school I was leaving before they fired me. I was invited by a friend to share an apartment in New York City, where I would live for the next 15 years while teaching at three different schools.

From 1978 to 1980, I taught ancient, medieval and modern European history at Rye Country Day School, in Rye, New York. At Groton, I was "not preparing my students for the U.S. Achievement test." At Rye, I was "not preparing my students for the Modern European Advanced Placement test." I was mystified at how anyone could actually use these tests as a curriculum guide, never mind spend the entire course forcing students to memorize a huge amount of material while writing essays that were essentially mindless laundry lists. This seemed wrong-headed since: (1) it was very boring; (2) only a few students could succeed, leaving the rest feeling stupid; and (3) it didn't allow students to become critical of the master narrative. I had a miserable second year at Rye for a variety of reasons, not the least of which was that I had naively told my department chair that I was a lesbian. I was not asked back and was on to my next school.

The Calhoun School was an "open classroom" K–12 school on the Upper West Side of New York City. In 1980, Calhoun's Board had just replaced the head of the school, Gene Ruth, with Neen Hunt. From 1970 to 1980, Gene had pioneered a progressive curriculum in a new open-classroom building. From 1980 to 1990, Neen guided the transformation of the school from a progressive "open-space," "learner-centered instruction" school to a traditional college preparatory school (albeit still with an open-space architecture).[12] I was there to witness the wrenching change from 1980 to 1983. These were extremely formative years during which I finally became comfortable in the classroom. My students and the progressive principal who hired me were crucial to this process. The students were products of the progressive years of the school as well as progressive parents of the Upper West Side of Manhattan. We learned together through trial and error. I was looking to achieve behavior and dispositions in my students—I knew I succeeded when I had full and enthusiastic participation in discussions and debates, when the students really listened to each other, and expressed curiosity and wonder in the material being discussed. During my third and final year at Calhoun, I became a lightning rod for a variety of discontent that was brewing; much of it because of the fundamental cultural shift going on, but some of the discontent was based on the usual personality conflicts and power struggles that go on in any tiny, close-knit community. I was fired again. This time, however, the faculty rose up in rebellion and forced Neen to offer me another year's contract. But I knew I was not wanted and started looking for another school.

I managed to learn how not to get fired at my fourth school (in seven years), thus managing to stay for 10 years at the Packer-Collegiate Preparatory School in Brooklyn Heights, New York. Packer had been an all-girls school with an abolitionist past situated in a part of Brooklyn that attracted a critical mass of Caribbean African and African American students.[13] Unlike most high schools, Packer had a two-year art requirement (one year of visual art and one year of performing arts). Many students enjoyed art so much, they signed up for a third or fourth year. With the support of a small band of progressive faculty members, I was able to develop curriculum based upon the ideas I had gained confidence in at

Calhoun: (1) find out where your students are at, and then take them where you want them to go; (2) writing is inextricably connected to critical thinking; (3) to become critical thinkers, students need to be exposed to a variety of well-supported arguments and then taught how to come up with their own thesis; and (4) textbooks and multiple-choice questions are anathema to critical thinking.

And yet, parents still expected me to prepare their students for the U.S. History Achievement and Advanced Placement U.S. History exams. I felt I needed a textbook, but I believed textbooks killed students' interest in history. In trying to marry my ideals with reality, I gave every student in my classes a different textbook—15 different textbooks in three classes of 15 students per class (three copies of 15 different textbooks). I assigned questions to answer, not numbers of pages to read so the students approached their textbook as a reference book, not a secondary source book.[14] As the students discovered the degree to which even standardized textbooks disagreed with each other, most began to have the same epiphany that I had had in England. Most of my students (about four out of five) were able to understand the need to suspend their desire for "an answer" until they learned more detail about the topic. I think they enjoyed the challenge. Some of the students seemed inherently unable to hold two or more competing arguments in their head at the same time. They desperately pleaded with me all year to "just tell them the answer." These students resisted learning how to think for themselves. I offered extra credit assignments (of the student's choosing) to anyone who could not or would not do the assignments I gave.

After several years of vainly trying to affect my students' achievement and Advanced Placement test scores, I abandoned the textbook completely.[15] I developed a thematic approach to my U.S. history course as well as a few units in which my classes explored a part of U.S. history in-depth. For example, one unit explored Colonialism. I wanted to do this after reading Gary Nash's *Red, White and Black* (1999). Nash argued that colonial society and culture was a result of the interaction of Indians, Africans, and European settlers, not just Europeans imposing their culture on the New World. I also began to use selections from Howard Zinn's *A People's History of the United States* (1997b), to help the class explore controversies in labor, women's history, and black history. I began to research Jewish history in the U.S. as well.

After a few years, I thought I was doing a pretty good job in exposing students to a stimulating, multicultural curriculum until a 15-year-old African American student stormed into my office one day. She declared that I wasn't teaching enough black history. So that summer, I put several black history books on my reading list and rewrote my curriculum accordingly. One of the most important books I discovered was E.S. Morgan's *American Slavery, American Freedom* (1975). Morgan ends his almost 400-page examination of the relationship between freedom and slavery in colonial Virginia with a series of questions: "Was the vision of a nation of equals flawed at the source by contempt for both the poor and the black? Is America still colonial Virginia writ large? More than a century after Appomattox the questions linger" (Morgan, 1975, p. 387). My answers to his questions based on the evidence he presented convinced me that slavery and race needed to be fundamental to any U.S. history course.

The more I taught, the more I saw the correlation between my students' contributions to my curriculum and their feelings of agency. I also became convinced that art fundamentally supported the development of thinking, of making connections. The popularity of the art classes led me to interview students about the causes of their enthusiasm. One student insisted I read and work with Betty Edwards's *Drawing the Right Side of the Brain* (2012). After spending six weeks reading and drawing that summer, I was convinced that there was some kind of connection between the aesthetic experience and learning. This connection was made explicit for me by Don Arnstine's brilliant book, *Democracy and the Arts of Schooling* (1995), which he introduced to me as my PhD advisor in 1999.

As I became more ambitious about developing curriculum and pedagogy around empowering students and getting them to think critically, I realized that what I was doing in my classroom was being supported by some teachers but undermined by others. When there was an opportunity to join a committee that would redesign the high school curriculum, I volunteered to become one of its four members. The committee was a response to Heidi Jacobs[16] whom the administration hired to conduct a series of workshops on developing interdisciplinary curricula. Over two years, the four of us essentially reinvented the wheel by designing a progressive high school. We proposed that the transition to our suggested high school curriculum begin with a pilot program—second-semester seniors who wished to participate would drop as many courses as they chose and replace those courses with a self-designed, multicultural, interdisciplinary, experiential and arts-based course of study. I ended up being the program supervisor because no one else wanted to do it. After the first year of this project, the Board of Trustees replaced the head of the school and directed the new headmaster to eliminate the faculty from the decision-making process.[17] Many of my progressive colleagues, as well as I, chose to leave after a few years. We could see that creative, experiential student-centered learning was no longer going to be tolerated in any area outside the art department. I also drew the conclusion that many administrators were attracted to progressive education in theory, but not in practice. It was this experience that led me to write one of my PhD qualification papers on the history of alternative schools in the U.S. (Emery, 2000a).

After ten years at Packer, I decided to move to San Francisco and continue teaching in independent schools there. I did not anticipate that my references would be preventing me from getting a job. I was blacklisted. While trying to figure out what to do with myself, I was able to work on a book project offered to me by a colleague from Packer. Linda Gold was a volunteer on the multicultural committee of The New Press. The editors wanted to publish a teaching edition of Howard Zinn's *A People's History of the United States*. Linda suggested me. The editors (and Zinn) were so pleased with my contributions that they accepted Linda's next proposal—the publication of the complete 1964 Mississippi Freedom School Curriculum. Linda would write the historical context and I would write the teaching materials. The process of getting this book (Emery, Gold, & Braselmann, 2008) published turned out to be an even longer and more arduous process than getting my doctorate. As I worked my way through my coursework, the qualification exams, and my dissertation, I was also working on or thinking about the Mississippi Freedom Schools and the Civil Rights Movement. This connection and my experience with black students in my high school classes led me to one of my dissertation papers explaining why Ebonics speakers lose their voice when learning how to write Standard Classroom English (Emery, 200b).

While I was researching for my dissertation from 1999 to 2000, I was learning about the corporate interest in education reform. I discovered the Business Roundtable and their decision in 1989 to transform public education, replacing the two-tier tracking system of vocational and college preparatory with "high standards for all" (Emery & Ohanian, 2004). This was very depressing, but especially so since I could get very few teachers in the Bay Area to actively oppose the implementation of high-stakes testing in California. As I was also wondering what I was going to do once my PhD was completed, I hoped to solve both problems by volunteering with the San Francisco Organizing Project (SFOP). In 1999, three public high school teachers approached SFOP and asked them to help them organize a community to push the district towards a small school policy. I joined this fight with enthusiasm, ending up on both Boards: SFOP and Small Schools for Equity (SSE, the nonprofit formed to create June Jordan High School in 2003). At the moment that June Jordan was created, SFOP and SSE stopped collaborating. I disagreed strongly with the decision. I was not alone in my disillusionment with both groups.

My experience at Calhoun and Packer, my PhD research, my study of the Civil Rights movement, and my experience with SFOP had taught me that community-initiated (bottom-up) school reform is always opposed by the system in place, regardless of the merits of the reforms. It was the community organizing of SFOP that forced the San Francisco Unified School District to concede to the existence of June Jordan. Without sustained organizing on the part of the community, however, June Jordan would be vulnerable to being closed or, at least, its mission would be thwarted or co-opted, which my research predicted and events proved. SFOP staff and June Jordan's founding teachers did not seem to understand this. In response, I and two other SSE board members decided that San Francisco needed a Freedom School.

Four of us, in the summer of 2005, launched the San Francisco Freedom Summer School. We all came to the SFFS project with different goals, but all agreed that teaching Civil Rights history was fundamental to achieving what each of us hoped for in the SFFS program. I had learned from the failures and limitations of my organizing experiences that the first step in organizing had to be providing people with the experience that every-day, ordinary people like themselves can make change (or as Mike Miller[18] would later explain, "organizers have to be hope peddlers"). We called our program a "freedom school" because we wanted to emulate the goals and methods of the 1964 Mississippi Freedom Schools.

The 1964 Freedom Schools had their genesis at the Highlander Folk School—a program conceived by Myles Horton's own search to replicate what he learned in teaching the residents of the Appalachian hollows how to advocate for the changes they needed in their lives (Horton, Kohl, & Kohl, 1997). Horton established the first Highlander School in 1932 as a training ground for the leaders of the labor movement. Frustrated with the deepening racism of the labor movement, Horton transformed the school into a civil rights academy. Bernice Robinson attended Highlander during the summer of 1955, which led to her becoming the first teacher of the first citizenship school on Johns Island, South Carolina. Robinson explained the role that the citizenship schools played in the movement (taken over by King's Southern Christian Leadership Conference in 1957) in the documentary, *You Got to Move*:

> We would go into communities, set up classes. If there was no community organization in that community, we would organize that first class into an organization so that we would have some influence in the community, some on-going learning process. . . . It's like light coming into the darkness. Once they learned to read and write, they always voted after that. We started with the pilot project of Citizenship Schools and we found that everyone wanted it, and it grew and grew. Really, they were the basis of the entire Civil Rights Movements. . .because people became aware of the power that was in them that they could use to get things done (Phenix & Selver, 1985).

Charlie Cobb proposed Freedom Schools as part of the Mississippi Freedom Summer Project. Those who participated in a three-day conference to write the 1964 Mississippi Freedom School Curriculum were directly informed by the successes of the Citizenship Schools. The Civil Rights movement seemed defeated by the "closed society" of Mississippi in 1962. Mississippi was a special problem for the Civil Rights' strategists as it was a state completely isolated from the rest of the country. In order to break open this "closed-society," SNCC led a coalition of organizations in the implementation of the Mississippi Summer Project, a.k.a., "Freedom Summer." The Project's strategy was to create an alternative state political party to the all-white Mississippi Democratic Party and challenge their legitimacy at the Democratic National Nominating Convention in Atlantic City that August. As part of the process of creating a viable and vital alternative party,

Charles Cobb proposed Freedom Schools to teach Mississippians how to become active agents of social change. These 40 schools became the most successful example of progressive education this country has seen.

Howard Zinn, after being a Freedom School teacher and visiting other Freedom Schools, wrote about how they posed a special challenge to "American education":

> Can we, somehow, bring teachers and students together, not through the artificial sieve of certification and examination but on the basis of their common attraction to an exciting social goal? Can we solve the old educational problem of teaching children crucial values, while avoiding a blanket imposition of the teacher's ideas? Can this be done by honestly accepting as an educational goal that we want better human beings in the rising generation than we had in the last, and that this requires a forthright declaration that the educational process cherishes equality, justice, compassion and world brotherhood? . . . And cannot the schools have a running, no-holds-barred exchange of views about alternative ways to these goals? (Zinn, 1997a, p. 539).

For six summers (2005–2010), the San Francisco Freedom School (SFFS) Summer Program worked to take up this challenge. We offered six consecutive Saturday sessions in July and August (10 A.M. to 4 P.M.) in the parish hall of St. Francis Lutheran Church. It was free; anyone could drop in and no payment was required. Between 12 and 25 people, mostly adults, showed up on any given Saturday. The guest speakers—Civil Rights veterans—were the heart the SFFS Summer Program. Every morning, a different veteran told his or her story. The rest of the day included films, discussions, selected readings, and activities. The veterans were people no one had ever heard of: Jean Wiley, Mike Miller, Bruce Hartford, Don Jelinek, Wazir Peacock, Chude Allen, Cathy Cade, Jimmy Rogers, and Phil Hutchins. In listening to their stories,[19] SFFS participants learned, at the very least, how important everyday people were to successfully transforming a society. I learned from the vets' stories that there are several key components that made the Southern Freedom Movement successful:

- Doing your homework (research)
- Building personal relationships and community
- Building infrastructure
- Developing local leadership
- Creating coalitions
- Using the arts strategically
- Using nonviolent direct resistance strategically[20]
- Learning how to deal with the contradictions within the movement
- Being in the right historical moment

These components are the theoretical framework I teach to my students at San Francisco State University. We study the Civil Rights movement as a case study that illustrates how important the key components are to the success of a social movement. In a research paper, my students apply these concepts to current events. They choose to evaluate an action, put on an event that they then evaluate, or create a course (and defense of course) for SFSU's Experimental College. I am attempting to provide structural, intellectual, and moral support for students so they can, as Bernice Robinson described above in *You Got to Move*, "become aware of the power that [is] in them that they [can] use to get things done" (Phenix & Selver, 1985). I am delighted that two of my former students have used my "key components" (while adding two more of their own) as the basis of a "Student Activism" class. Their course (so far, offered during the last two semesters) has been peopled with a group of Occupy SFSU students who are committed to expanding the scope and membership of the Experimental College as part of a socio-cultural shift they hope to effect within the campus and the wider community.

At San Francisco State University, I am in a place I had envisioned when reading *Summerhill* in high school. It was a vision nurtured by the early Marx's ideals, by the study of history, and by the understanding that African American history is fundamental to understanding U.S. history, an authentic understanding of which is fundamental to successfully building a more just society today. I teach and learn through a curriculum and pedagogy that I developed over time, through trial and error and guided by progressive educational theory, a theory best exemplified by the 1964 Mississippi Freedom Schools and its antecedents, Highlander and Citizenship Schools. I am inspired by the stories of the movement as much as Stokely Carmichael was inspired by Freedom Schools. After attending and teaching in many of the 40 Freedom Schools in Mississippi in 1964, Stokely Carmichael (Kwame Ture) observed:

> I just loved going to talk about the movement or to conduct lessons in those classes. But I also saw something that has stayed with me all my political life. All real education is political. All politics is not necessarily educational, but good politics always is. You can have no serious organizing without serious education. And always, the people will teach you as much as you teach them (Carmichael, 2003, p. 391).

"Real education" is not about sorting, which is what standardized tests are designed to do. Real education is not about socializing, which is what schools are designed to do. Real education is not competitive, but collaborative. It happens when people learn what they want to learn when they need to learn it. Real education is "political" since those who experience it, as Bernice Robinson explained above, "became aware of the power that was in them that they could use to get things done."

Endnotes

1   Meldrim Thomson was the infamous Republican governor of N.H. from 1973 to 1979. From *The Los Angeles Times* obituary: "Thomson drew support from ultraconservatives with positions that included suggesting nuclear weapons for the state National Guard. He once called the Rev. Martin Luther King Jr. 'a man of immoral character whose frequent association with leading agents of communism is well established.' But Thomson also drew votes for his strong anti-tax stance—to this day, New Hampshire has neither an income tax nor a sales tax—and for his philosophy of independence from federal influence" (Associated Press, 2001).

2   The 1970 U.S. Census estimates New Hampshire's total population was 737,681; 733,106 were white and 2,505 were African American (Gibson & Jung, 2001). In my high school yearbook, there are 364 seniors listed, six were African American. The yearbook also notes that 1973 was the year that "A Better Chance Came to Concord." During the 1972–1973 school year, 27 public schools and 133 independent schools hosted 1,371 ABC students of which 71 percent were black recruited from major urban centers. ABC was a program implemented by elite independent school heads, CEOs, and Dartmouth College and funded by major foundations and the U.S. Office of Economic Opportunity (ERIC, 1973). It was the closest I would come to experiencing the effects of the Civil Rights movement during my years in Concord.

3   SF State college students and faculty created the Experimental College in 1968 as part of the school strike that led to the establishment of the first post-secondary ethnic studies department in the nation.

4   My identity is about thinking and reflecting upon who I can become in relationship to my experiences. But if I don't take into consideration the experiences of others, "the influences which educate some into masters, educate others into slaves (Dewey, 1916; p. 84). Alice Miller (1997), among others, argues that children are born with distinct and unique personalities. Dewey (1916, p. 146) argues that "the starting point of any process of thinking is something going on, something which just as it stands is incomplete or unfulfilled." Craft (1984) argues that "there are two different Latin roots of the English word 'education.' They are *educare*, which means to train or to mold, and *educere*, meaning to lead out. While the two meanings are quite different, they are both represented in our word 'education.' Thus, there is an etymological basis for many of the vociferous debates about education today." If we are to become a just society— one in which there are no masters and slaves—it seems to me that we need to create schools that help people become who they (lead out) rather than mold people into who they are not.

5   In sixth grade, we had to write an essay based on New Hampshire American Revolutionary General John Stark's toast, "Live Free or Die." Only later could I appreciated the irony that New Hampshire prisoners make the license plates on which they stamp this state motto.

6   For example: "But intellectual growth means constant expansion of horizons and consequent formation of new purposes and new responses. These are impossible without an active disposition to welcome points of view hitherto alien; an active desire to entertain considerations that modify existing purposes. Retention of capacity to grow is the reward of such intellectual hospitality" (Dewey, 1916, p. 175)

7   Read James Wertsch's excellent and illustrative application of Vygotsky's ZPD theory (Wertsch, 1979).

8   "Truth is on the edge of controversy" was not how I articulated this concept at the time. I developed this particular phrase to explain to my high school students why I confronted them with many different interpretations of the same event. My goal was to force my students to develop their own "truths" through developing their higher-order thinking skills. In Bloom's taxonomical terms, one would call these processes analysis, synthesis, and evaluation (Clark,

1999). In debating the accuracy and meaning of historical events, my students developed "truths" with some foundation in the real world. And those who succeeded did so because it engaged their intellects.

9   See the following syllabus (June 2000) for a complete list of sources contributing to his debate today: http://www.economics.utoronto.ca/munro5/GENTRY2.htm

10   "The only way in which we can define an activity is by putting before ourselves the objects in which it terminates—as one's aim in shooting is the target. But we must remember that the object is only a mark or sign by which the mind specifies the activity one desires to carry out. Strictly speaking, not the target but hitting the target is the end in view; one takes aim by means of the target, but also by the sight on the gun. The different objects which are thought of are means of directing the activity" (Dewey, 1916, Chapter 8).

11   Groton is tied for first place among boarding schools in endowment-per-pupil at over $600,000. It is a feeder for the Ivy-League schools. (You can see how rich and powerful a school like Groton is at the following site: http://www.boardingschoolreview.com/school_ov/school_id/18

12   Interestingly, it takes ten years to change the culture of a school. The most effective way to prevent change is to change the leadership of a district or school every three to four years, which is the average term of urban school superintendents (Eubanks, Parish & Smith, 1997).

13   Critical mass = enough to influence the culture of the school.

14   One of the most provocative questions I discovered was, "What caused Bacon's Rebellion?"

15   Of course, one of the most important questions I had during my PhD studies was "Why are standardized tests impervious to instruction?" James Popham (2001) has one answer to that—one-third of the questions are intentionally correlated to socio-economic status.

16   See http://www.ascd.org/Publications/Authors/Heidi-Hayes-Jacobs.aspx?id=62618361001 http://www.ascd.org/publications/books/104011.aspxfor a current list of Jacobs' work.

17   When I left Packer in 1993, I demanded an exit interview. During this interview, the upper-school principal and dean explained that the Board of Trustees instructed the new Head of School to end faculty input into the decision-making process. I remember that their reasoning had to do with the chaos that such input created.

18   I met Mike Miller for the first time at the 40th reunion of the Mississippi Freedom Schools in 2004 in Oxford, Ohio (where the first batch of summer volunteers was trained). Mike has a long history of organizing: Free Speech movement, SNCC in Mississippi, with Saul Alinsky in Missouri, with Cesar Chavez, as co-founder of the Mission Coalition Organization and co-founder of the San Francisco Organizing Project. He was one of many veterans to speak in the SF Freedom Summer Program.

19   You can read many of these stories at http://www.crmvet.org

20   The strategic use of nonviolent resistance is direct action that dramatizes injustices to the point of creating sympathy from a wider audience and then providing a variety of means by which new people can contribute to growing the movement.

References

Arnstine, D. (1995). *Democracy and the Arts of Schooling*. Albany: State University of New York.

Associated Press. (2001, April 20). Meldrim Thompson; Former N.H. Governor. *Los Angeles Times*. http://articles.latimes.com/2001/apr/20/local/me-53359

Butterfield, H. (1931). *The Whig Interpretation of History*. London: G. Bell and Sons.

Carmichael, S. (2003). *Ready for Revolution: The Life and Struggles of Stokely Carmichael (Kwame Ture)*. New York: Scribner.

Clark, D. (1999, June 5). Bloom's taxonomy of learning domains. http://www.nwlink. com/~donclark/hrd/bloom.html

Craft, M. (1984). Education for Diversity. In *Education and Cultural Pluralism*, ed. M. Craft, 5–26. London and Philadelphia: Falmer Press.

Dewey, J. (1916). *Democracy and Education*. New York: Macmillan. http://www.ilt.columbia.edu/ publications/Projects/digitexts/dewey/d_e/chapter08.html

Educational Resources Information Center (ERIC). (1973). *A Better Chance: Tenth Anniversary Annual Report* (ED102284). Washington DC: U.S. Department of Education.

Edwards, B. (2012). *Drawing on the Right Side of the Brain: A Course in Enhancing Creativity and Artistic Confidence*. New York: Tarcher/Penguin.

Emery, K. (2000a, July). Alternative schools: Diverted but not defeated. Paper submitted to Qualification Committee at UC Davis, California. http://www.educationanddemocracy.org/Emery/ Emery_AltSchoolsPaper.htm

Emery, K. (2000b, July). The politics of ebonics: The intersection of voice, language, culture and identity. Qualification paper. http://educationanddemocracy.org/Emery/Emery_Ebonics.htm

Emery, K., & Ohanian, S. (2004). *Why Is Corporate America Bashing Our Public Schools?* Portsmouth, NH: Heinemann.

Emery, K., Gold, L. R., & Braselmann, S. (2008). *Lessons From Freedom Summer: Ordinary People Building Extraordinary Movements*. Monroe ME: Common Courage Press.

Eubanks, E., Parish, R., & Smith, D. (1997). Changing the discourse in schools. In P. Hall (Ed.), *Race, Ethnicity, and Multiculturalism: Policy and Practice* (pp. 151–168). New York: Garland Publishing.

Gibson, C., & Jung, K. (2001). *Historical Census Statistics on Population Totals by Race, 1790 to 1990, and by Hispanic Origin, 1970 to 1990, for the United States, Regions, Divisions, and States* (Working Paper Series No. 56; Table 6. New England Division). Washington DC: U.S. Census Bureau, Population Division. http://www.census.gov/population/www/documentation/ twps0056/twps0056.html

Haley, A. (1965). *The Autobiography of Malcolm X.: As Told to Alex Haley*. New York: Grove Press.

Hexter, J. H. (1958). Storm over the gentry. *Encounter, 10.*

Hexter, J. H. (1961). *The Myth of the Middle Class in Tudor England*. Evanston, IL: Northwestern University Press.

Holt, L. (1966). *The Summer That Didn't End: The Story of the Mississippi Civil Rights Project 1964, and Its Challenges to America*. London, U.K.: Heinemann.

Horton, M., Kohl, H., & Kohl, J. (1997). *The Long Haul: An Autobiography*. New York: Teachers College Press.

Kozol, J. (1967). *Death at an Early Age: The Destruction of the Hearts and Minds of Negro Children in the Boston Public Schools*. Boston, MA: Houghton Mifflin.

Macaulay, T. B. (1852). Mackintosh's history of the revolution in England, in 1688. In *Essays, Critical and Miscellaneous* (pp. 289–314). https://play.google.com/store/books/ details?id=FtokAAAAMAAJ

Marx, K. (1852). *The Eighteenth Brumaire of Louis Bonaparte*. New York: Die Revolution. http:// www.marxists.org/archive/marx/works/1852/18th-brumaire/

Meier, D. (2000). *Will Standards Save Public Education?* Boston: Beacon Press.

Miller, A. (1997). *The Drama of the Gifted Child: The Search for the True Self*. New York: Basic Books.

Morgan, E. S. (1975). *American Slavery, American Freedom: The Ordeal of Colonial Virginia*. New York: Norton.

Nash. P. H. (1999). *Red, White, and Black: The Peoples of Early North America* (4th ed.). New York: Prentice Hall.

Neill, A. S. (1960). *Summerhill: A Radical Approach to Child Rearing*. New York: Hart Publishing.

Phenix. L. M., & Selver, V. (Directors). (1985). *You Got to Move* [Documentary]. Harrington Park, NJ: Millarium Zero.

Popham, W. J. (2001). *The Truth About Testing: An Educator's Call to Action.* Alexandria, VA: ASCD.

Stack, P. (1992). *The Great Game of Business.* New York: Currency Doubleday.

Tawney, R. H. (1954). The rise of the gentry, 1558–1640. *Essays in Economic History, I,* 173–214.

Wertsch, J. V. (1979). From social interaction to higher psychological processes: A clarification and application of Vygotsky's theory. *Human Development, 22,* 1–22.

Wilson, E. (1940). *To the Finland Station.* New York: Harcourt, Brace &Company.

Zinn, H. (1997a) Freedom Schools, In H. Zinn, *The Zinn Reader: Writings on Disobedience and Democracy* (pp. 529–539). New York: Seven Stories Press.

Zinn, H. (1997b). *A People's History of the United States (Teaching Edition).* New York: The New Press.

CHAPTER THIRTEEN

Mis-education or Malpractice?

A Rallying Cry for an African-Centered Third Space in Curriculum Transformation

LISA WILLIAM-WHITE, JONATHAN LUKE WOOD,
IDARA ESSIEN-WOOD, CACEE BELTON,
GARY MUCCULAR JR., PARRISH GEARY, &
TONI NEWMAN

Historic Context

As United States Secretary of Education Arne Duncan heralds a call for Black males to embrace teaching (Buffenbarger, 2011), he tacitly suggests that racial identity plays an important role in influencing and shaping the educational trajectory of Black children and youth in K–12 public education. Yet, neither the color of the teacher's skin nor the gender of the teacher mitigates the cultural assault that continues to replicate itself in the United States public education—an assault that, in our opinion, must arrest the consciousness and direct the agency of prospective Black teachers (and other allies) who desire to work with Black students, and who desire to counteract the negative effects of racial inequality in students' lives.

To illustrate our point, quality schooling experiences for African American students are continually eroded by No Child Left Behind (NCLB), which privileges narrow curricular goals that emphasize discrete skills (Goodman, Shannon, Goodman, & Rapoport, 2004; Carlson, 2006), while marginalizing cultural engagement practices (Murrell, 2002). And since the inception of NCLB, we have witnessed the intensified and widespread utilization of scripted curriculum based on the false notion of "scientific" teaching methods (Goodman et al., 2004; Carlson, 2006), which is the antithesis of teaching as "artistry" (Ladson-Billings, 1994). Moreover, many Black children are enrolled in inadequately funded schools where the resource gap continues to thwart academic achievement. Leadership practices, in these settings, often focus on technical fixes to close the gap, and strategies for learning circumvent innovative and engaging content knowledge. This "teacher-proof" curriculum and its pedagogical practices continually undermine teacher expertise and culturally relevant practice. And while teachers should be trained as and perceived as competent curriculum developers who base their pedagogical decisions on students' diverse learning needs, this proves illusive. Not all teachers are trained or qualified to develop curricula with intended learning outcomes; many are not exposed to curriculum theory or assessment.

It has been further articulated that within most schools, faculties are often ill-prepared to meet the culture-specific needs of Black children (Ladson-Billings, 2000; Foster & Peele, 1999; Hale, 1994; Brown, 2010; Richards, Brown, & Forde, 2004.). As such, Black learners are most vulnerable in schools where educators lack specific knowledge about their cultural backgrounds (Hale-Benson, 1986; Hale, 2001; Perry et al., 2003). Educators, most of whom are White, typically are unaware of how to draw upon the community integrity practices embedded in African American cultural heritage (Murrell, 2002). For Black children, sound teacher practice includes a focus on positive identity development practices (Murrell, 2002). However, this ideal is far from the reality, as the textbook industry and its materials are typically centralized as the authority on what is taught and how concepts or skills should be taught.

Elucidating the cultural discontinuities that are pervasive for Black learners, it is increasingly the case that the humanistic goals (Nieto et al., 2008) of education are rendered insignificant by bureaucratic attempts to regulate student learning and limit teacher practice. This results in circumstances that continue to pose serious implications for teaching and learning for all children, as the failure of poor and minority students to meet federal and state standards aids the promulgation of the "achievement gap" (Bensimon, 2005; Giroux & Schmidt, 2004; Porter & Soper, 2003). As a consequence, this failure in turn helps to perpetuate the notion of Black learning deficits. And nowhere is this ideological crisis more evident than within the increased discourse on the need for Common Core Standards (Franklin & Johnson, 2008) to raise achievement outcomes. And that the U.S. Department of Education recently endorsed Common Core State Standards, reifying Eurocentric literary traditions and historical events as "official knowledge" that an educated *citizenry* must master, further subjugates Black culture and identity.

As a consequence for progressive teachers, constructivist teaching opportunities and framing social issues from a standpoint of community needs and values are casualties of *doing school*. Hence, teachers are moving further away from opportunities to be caregivers, models, and mentors, as their roles are subsumed by policy and pedagogy, which elevates technical rationalist activity and goals (Craig & Ross, 2008; Noddings, 1995). This morass dictates that teachers behave mechanically, which domesticates their activity and dehumanizes their identities

(Freire, 1970). Thus, we argue that this regimentation perpetuates an ideological crisis and an identity crisis, and a pedagogical mismatch for the recruitment and preparation of conscious Black teachers who question what should be taught in schools and for whose benefit—issues that remain unexamined in the dominant policy narratives on K–12 schooling, achievement, and teacher preparation.

Moreover, the matriculation, retention, and graduation of African American students into university settings continue to be a social asset toward diversifying the academy (JBHE, 2001; Wood, 2008) and providing a potential teaching force to work in K–16 settings. Yet Black students in the academy face many challenges in securing the social, economic, and cultural capital to help them to navigate the predominately White, male, culture of the academy (Anderson et al., 1993; Cornelius, Moore, & Gray, 1997; Fenelon, 2003; Leap, 1995; Moss et al., 1999; McGuire & Regar, 2003). "Entrenched racial and ethnic disparities in college enrollment, graduation, and faculty recruitment" is problematic in solidifying a viable support network for underrepresented students (Toro-Morn, 2010). Yet these issues are often removed from interrogation and critique in discourse about recruiting and supporting a potential teaching force of caregivers, models, and mentors who, in turn, plan to begin careers as K–16 educators.

Additionally, when one is a first-generation African American graduate student, who does one turn to for support, mentoring, and advocacy? The shortage of faculty mentors of color in higher education makes it challenging for many underrepresented students to find support networks who are vested in their professional development (Collins, 2001; Mabokela & Green, 2001). Thus, race is a salient factor in examining how we are situated in our college. For example, African American faculty under-representation is a pervasive and persistent problem in higher education" (Land, 2005), which aligned with a micro-analysis of faculty data. In sum, even on our campus, where Black faculty represented 13 percent of the total faculty, opportunities for engagement with faculty who reflected our backgrounds, community, and curricular interests were generally limited.

This occurs at times because students' desire to engage in scholarly critique around race-based issues may be thwarted in predominantly white institutions (PWIs) where the students' interests are not paramount. In addition, students from underrepresented groups often receive fewer benefits from mentorship relationships than those from dominant groups (McGuire & Regar, 2003). Consequently, these issues helped to forge a greater sense of urgency to develop a learning community to engage more intensively in a curriculum that reflected our community interests and values. These issues are complicated further by the fact that African American scholars are typically not sought after or consulted about the needs of African American students; or, they are rendered invisible in the discourse of educational policy and the need for systemic change (King, 2005).

In sum, these issues threaten American education, democracy, and the notion of quality schooling for Black learners throughout the K–16 educational system. The problems we explicate are exacerbated by the schism that exists between the K–12 educational system and higher education—systems that historically function within silos. Communications between the two systems remain strained and inefficient overall, and discourse about student learning and quality continues to be jeopardized.

Our Concerns for Pedagogical Relevance

We have a crisis of epic proportions in U.S. education, which mandates the intentional recruitment and preparation of radical Black pedagogues who bring a conscious understanding of the historic, social, economic, and political issues impacting Black students' educational access and mobility. Curriculum then must be guided by a focus on African American literacies (Richardson, 2003), which includes a moral imperative to work unrestrained for racial uplift; agency that is analogous to the historic role of Black teachers working within a racialized and segregated educational system (Lynn, 2002; Foster, 1995, 1997).

From this world view, cultural notions of appropriate curriculum, pedagogy, and training are indispensable from community members' perceptions of, and experiences with, education. Yet, until these issues are placed on the table for serious examination and dialogue within educational policymaking, teacher training, and curriculum transformation, recruiting and effectively training Black men and women to teach within the K–16 system will remain problematic. We hold that we have a long way to go in engaging in an open dialogue about curricular relevance for diverse communities of prospective teachers. For instance, Ladson-Billings (2000) echoes Woodson (1933/2008) when she states that African culture is rarely perceived as a "useful rubric" for addressing the academic needs of African American learners. In fact, the gulf in teacher preparation and diasporic frames of reference is evident by homogenous and monocultural approaches to "urban" education preparation (Ladson-Billings, 2000).

Moreover, instructional efforts to make learning more meaningful for diverse students typically consists of fragmented multicultural content due to the lack of multicultural training in teacher preparation programs. Thus teacher quality, as a unit of analysis, must be examined and interrogated from the standpoint of the social and cultural meaning that teaching holds within diverse communities. For us as Black educators, this means that the question of how programs prepare candidates to teach Black children is socially and culturally defined and given meaning through community knowledge and the lived experiences of prospective Black educators.

Thus, conscious that there exists a preparation gap, this study describes how we, as Black prospective K–16 teachers, and a faculty mentor (Lisa) from a PWI created a third space (Moje et al., 2004) for culturally relevant professional development outside the formal strictures of the academy. Our efforts were guided by these foundational principles: (1) that preparation of emergent Black educators (and conscious allies) must be within an African-centered (Asante, 1991; Irvine, 2000; Pollard & Adjirotutu, 2000; Ashanti, 2003) framework if we are to recruit and prepare conscious leaders who are committed to teach and serve Black children and youth; (2) teacher training therefore must cultivate competent Black practitioners who embrace culturally relevant practices that draw upon African-centered intellectual traditions, foregrounding Black students' lived experiences and funds of knowledge. Idara (primary organizer of the group) explains:

> Several of us approached Lisa and asked her if she would serve as a faculty mentor for our ad-hoc professional development group (we called it the Graduate Education Student Association [GESA]). A number of factors led us to ask Lisa to serve: she had conducted research and taught courses on multicultural and urban education. These topics were of primary interest to us, especially her research interests related to African-centered pedagogy. Second, she was a relatively recent graduate from a highly respected research institution. Thus, she possessed energy and passion, along with current knowledge of the skills needed to succeed in graduate education. Third, as a Black woman, Lisa embodied extensive theoretical and experiential knowledge about the impact of racism and sexism in the academy; while enacting her knowledge by serving as a strong advocate of women and students of color. This advocacy held symbolic meaning for us, as it fostered a great affinity towards her on behalf of our mostly Black and majority male student group.

These philosophical, curricular, and pedagogical decisions must guide conscious and informed praxis in order to actualize the ideals of democratic education, which should affirm Black identity development. The methodology of the currere then aims to enable such fusion to occur (Pinar, Reynolds, Slattery, & Taubman, 1995; Pinar, 2012). The currere and situated learning theory (Murrell, 2002) began with *us* and it is our knowledge of ourselves and our lives that serves as the trajectory to deconstruct and reconstruct knowledge. We unequivocally believed that it was critical and necessary to invert deficit models of exploring Black contributions to the field of teaching and curricular by creating participatory structures that drew upon African-centered intellectual traditions and the funds of knowledge. Murrell's (2002) schemata provided a rich model for instituting activity systems that build deeper cultural meaning. Those specific cultural practices include: (1) creating engagement and participation practices; (2) fostering identity development practices; (3) cultivating community integrity practices; (4) modeling practices of inquiry; and (5) organizing meaning-making practices. Thus, we examined and experienced our currere as a living entity—drawing from our lives; immersing in the African-centered intellectual traditions of William Edward Burghardt (W. E. B.) Du Bois and Carter G. Woodson and situated learning theory and practice (Murrell, 2002; Lave, 1991); and from studying insights about cultivating communities of accomplished practice (Ladson-Billings 1995; 2000; Murrell, 2002).

This effort began in tandem with the practical examination and deconstruction of the currere as a vehicle to examine the cultural and material embodiment of our knowledge traditions and values that reflects the proactive integration of curriculum theory and culture-specific instructional development (Castenell & Pinar, 1993; Pinar et al., 1995; Pinar, 2012). The currere is based on four tenets:

- advancing the idea of retelling the story of one's educational experiences;

- imagining future possibilities for self-understanding and educational practice;

- analyzing the relationships between past, present, and future life history and practice;

- and developing new ways of thinking about education as necessary for engaged pedagogical activity.

Furthermore, Murrell (2002) as well as Ladson-Billings (2000) advocate for teacher practice that incorporates culturally established knowledge traditions enshrined in African-centered practices, narrative, and autobiographical traditions, and the utilization of Black rhetorical styles.

Lisa's Perspective on Mentorship in a Third Space

While teaching two courses—Afrocentric Curriculum and Instruction and Discourse on Race and Gender in Educational Settings: African American Emphasis—I listened to the many stories of students of color who have felt marginalized in their professional development and within the curriculum. Black students frequently spoke about the absence of "rigorous" study related to African Americans in their professional programs; and they shared their frustration with inadequate curricular relevance in the college. Several communicated their desire to "organize" to advocate for a college program pathway or department within the college with an explicit emphasis on African American education (Brown & William-White, 2010). At the same time, I yearned to engage these students in an elevated dialogue about hegemonic ideologies within educational programs and policies, opening up new avenues for discourse about culture-specific practices for pedagogical and curricular transformation. My motivation for becoming a teacher *first* and a teacher educator *later* was to work on behalf of my own cultural community, while working as an ally with other culturally diverse communities. And, I had long recognized the absence of African American literacies and pedagogical discussion within my own academic department. This absence reflects the historic absence of a pool of African American candidates in our department and the college as a whole, and the privileging of other communities' cultural knowledge and literacies (immigrant populations and English Language Learners).

The few African American students whom I had the privilege of working with fed my interest in working toward a third space for knowledge construction. In my classes, their stories were powerful and I wanted to be a part of a project to support their personal and professional development and my passions. In addition, the majority of the students had a dual desire to be both practitioners and researchers; and I embodied a dual desire to mentor emergent Black scholars, creating collegial relationships with people who shared my cultural and political interests. And though I was well aware of the statistics that demonstrate how underrepresented faculty may find it challenging to offer the necessary support to emergent teachers while meeting the institutional demands placed upon them, this opportunity fueled me. Thereby my goal was to draw upon African-centered pedagogy (Murrell, 2002; Irvine, 2000; Asante, 1991) and various achievement models that reflects situated pedagogy. Ladson-Billings' (1994, 2000) notion of culturally relevant pedagogy also proved instrumental as it involves three propositions for situating pedagogy for African American students: (1) a focus on academic achievement; (2) building cultural competence, which is knowledge about the uniqueness of the African American experience; and (3) using the former two propositions as a foundation towards sociopolitical critique to help students understand the ways that social structures and practices help reproduce racialized inequities in their lives.

Third Space and the Currere

Through a series of meetings at a local Black bookstore in a working-class, predominately Black community, we gathered to read scholarship on the K–16 achievement gap and explored how African Americans are situated within grades P–16. Disrupting the notion of formal learning needing to take place within the walls of, and regulated by the norms of, the academy, we met outside the campus, reflecting our wish to create a space where we could fellowship and freely dialogue about our lived experiences and about our needs as emergent teachers and scholars. Carter G. Woodson's concept of education for critical consciousness (Gordon, 1993) enabled us to examine the sociopolitical issues, historic knowledge, and race as a unit for analysis and critique.

As a group we decided that dialogue, reading, and writing together would provide a space for our shared pedagogical, community, and professional development/enrichment. Getting started, we utilized five structured writing prompts to reflect on and then write in our journals, with the intention of dialoging in smaller groups before submitting written journal responses to one another:

Table 1: Structured Prompts

1. Why participants decided to pursue graduate study in education at this state university?
    a) Reasons for the choice?
    b) What were you hoping to gain/accomplish?
    c) What were your expectations/ideas about education?
    d) Who or what helped to influence this decision?

2. What issue(s), if any, affecting the Black community is/are important to you (national focus/local focus)?
    a) What spawned your interest in this issue?
    b) Do you have direct personal experiences with this issue?
    c) How has this issue been addressed or not in your graduate education?
    d) What spawned your interest in this issue?
    e) Do you have direct personal experiences with this issue?
    f) What information/ideas have been addressed in your graduate education to help you examine this issue?

3. Reflect on your MA program and the course content that you have taken to date.
    a) What emphasis has been placed on African American issues and content?
    b) What materials have you read that really spoke of or focused on issues of significance for African American communities?

4. Reflect on your collective formal and informal educational experiences to date:
    a) What educators/scholars of African descent have you read in your program that have helped to guide your thinking about issues impacting Black communities?
    b) What educators/scholars have you read outside of your program that have helped to guide your thinking about issues impacting Black communities?
    c) What was the main premise of the arguments raised by these scholars and in what way, if any, have they shaped your thinking about your research interests and/or your personal life?
    d) What work or projects are you currently engaged in, if any, that are explicitly intended to serve African American populations or communities?

5. What do you know about (an) Afrocentric Pedagogy, Culturally Relevant Pedagogy, and/or Critical Race Theory?
    a) To your knowledge, what are some key characteristics of these theories/tenets?
    b) Why do you believe it is purported as a pedagogy for student achievement?
    c) What do you think we can learn from this stated pedagogy for curriculum development at the university level in preparing educators to serve Black communities?

Dialogue and community engagement practices embedded in an African-centered curriculum framework, offers reflexive (Ladson-Billings, 2001) opportunities for professional growth, while enabling us to share and interrogate our own standpoints as individuals and as a group in a historic situation. One of the authors of this chapter, Parrish, spoke about the challenges inherent in the inadequate learning opportunities for Black youth and the need for advocacy informed by knowledge of racialized schooling inequities:

> At-risk and low-income students in general are not what our school systems are designed for. With a system not designed to help students in their primary [years], what system awaits them when they become adults? This is an issue that all ethnic groups, but [particularly] black males specifically face in America…it's as if Jim Crow has worked its way systematically into the educational system. Ethnic students make up a majority of our school systems, but are unable to master education as well as their European counterparts. If we were to research the lower-income [Black] compared to the higher-income students [in relation to similarly situated white students], the educational gap remains the same. Whites and Asian students always outshine the Latino and African American students. Knowing that this gap exists, the educational community has relied upon tests, which clearly show that ethnic students are not able to achieve in our high schools; thus making it easier for colleges and universities to deny them entrance. Now [policymakers] have created the High School Exit Exam [but] what makes the situation worse is that if they [minority youth] are unable to pass this test, they are not given a high school diploma, which is a requirement for college…. For low-income students, they have been systematically exiled from higher education due to poor preparation and lack of resources…. There are only a few ways that I believe African Americans can make it in our educational system and that is with the use of mentors and advocates. The mentors have to be those [who] have succeeded in the system, and the advocates have to be a part of the system to influence change, [while] helping others prepare for whatever obstacles the system creates.

As Parrish suggests, Black students, are products of too little education (Shujaa, 1994) and mis-education (Woodson, 1933/2008), and a lack of academic support networks. Consequently, it is our belief that only through meaningful engagement and participation practices through authentic curriculum can learning foster greater opportunity for collective agency (Murrell, 2002).

Furthermore, as a community, the cultural meaning of pedagogy and curriculum was made manifest as we reflected on the quality of our formal learning with respect to race and representation (Castenell & Pinar, 1993). For example, we wanted to interrogate the dominant narratives about the meaning of culturally relevant pedagogy and culturally competent preparation from the vantage point of our participation in our respective academic departments. Woodson's (1933/2008) views were familiar to us when he asserted that in most colleges and universities, Blacks are only studied as a problem people.

Woodson's (1933/2008) ideas were pivotal to our examination of racial issues. He called for moral purpose and civic duty as an educational imperative to cultivate the needs of Black populations. Sociopolitical consciousness and examination of the Black lived experience within curriculum, in his view, would serve as an essential component of emancipatory learning goals. For Black teachers' training, this meant that the Black teacher needed to subvert the improper education being offered to him by the dominant society in order to develop the skills and agency to work on behalf of Black people. In his book *The Mis-education of the Negro* (1933/2008), Woodson states:

The large majority of the Negroes who have put on the finishing touches of our best colleges are all but worthless in the development of their people. If after leaving school they have the opportunity to give out to Negroes what traducers of the race would like to have it learn such persons may thereby earn a living at teaching…what they have been taught but they never become a constructive force in the development of the race. The so-called school, then, becomes a questionable factor in the life of this despised people. (p. 11)

Woodson spoke of the concept of Black inferiority being "drilled into [Black people] in almost every class he enters and in almost every book he studies," and that the psychic violence needed to be avoided so that Black people could become capable forces who are able to effectively support the development of the race. Woodson's idea resonated deeply for us, but most provocative was his idea that the "bias" perpetuated against Blacks in schools might be the key to forcing Blacks outside of schools.

Du Bois' 1930 address at Howard University is an important text in the discourse focused on cultivating appropriate dispositions in future teachers, particularly in light of the educational policies and practices that are propagated within capitalistic culture (Aptheker, 1973). For example, Du Bois suggested that essential conditions must be internalized by institutions that are committed to democratic education and advancing Black community participation, knowledge development, and economic mobility (Aptheker, 1973). For Du Bois, racial uplift must be the bedrock of American society, particularly embedded within Black teachers' pedagogical efforts and activity. This uplift must be guided by moral purpose, laborious knowledge cultivation, and personal sacrifice.

Du Bois further asserted that a knowledge of African history and our social development is a critical part of the "bone and sinew," of Black liberation struggle; and must be drawn upon as a model to fight against societal forces that thwart Black educational, social, and economic mobility. Thus, the advancement of Black people in life and making a living was just as important to Du Bois in the teaching process as the content of the knowledge. He further believed that teachers of Black people must impart knowledge to human beings whose place in the world is "precarious and critical" (Aptheker, 1973). Luke explains:

African Americans have historically faced educational genocide in the United States. They [Blacks] are critical of education post-segregation due to the fact that education is not culturally relevant and does not speak to the culture of African Americans. Overall, if an education is not culturally appropriate, then it will not truly educate as it cannot speak to the lived, sociocultural realities of Black students.… With this in mind and with the recognition that Blacks in America were brought to the United States against our will through slavery, and have had this country built upon our backs, one must agree that it then becomes the responsibility of the educational system in the United States to make education culturally relevant, to redress the wrongs that have been done to our people. The best part about these pedagogies (Afrocentric and culturally relevant) is that they take the blame off of the students, their families, and their communities, and place the blame of failure in its rightful place, on the educational system. The ideas raised [in these pedago-gies] make me very critical about education in the United States and whether integration worked. For instance, integration assumes that not only the people, but their cultures, values and customs will be integrated. Unfortunately, this never happened in America, and as a result, Blacks in the US are forced to engage in a curriculum that views them as bystanders, not participants.

Luke names a vital component of democratic schooling for pre-service Black teachers (and conscious allies): the necessary and non-negotiable cultivation of sociopolitical awareness that must shape the knowledge, skills, and dispositions of emergent teachers of Black learners.

Toni, who has spent 23 years as an educator, community organizer, and ac-tivist, shared ideas about the precarious nature of education in her personal life:

Our ability to compete academically affects our ability to compete in the world market place. The achievement gap hinders our ability to be competitive and is exacerbated by low expectations, lack of opportunity and being held to a higher standard. Regardless, to restore our people with the understanding of our true greatness academically is impera-tive.... In kindergarten and 1st grade, I went to an all-Black school. It was there that my 1st grade teacher requested that I test for the gifted program. By second grade we moved to an integrated neighborhood (I never had a Black public school teacher again). In our "better" neighborhood, my fourth grade teacher asked me "Why are you in the gifted program?"

My younger sister never had the opportunity to go to the Black school and my parents had to fight to get her tested for the gifted program. The teacher did not believe she was gifted; in fact, since she was shy and didn't speak, they thought she was perhaps "retarded." She tested with a 165 IQ, as a genius, by their standards. Years later, she dropped out of high school with a horrible GPA. Clearly a capable young woman, yet school did not address her needs, nor did it honor her differences. She eventually went to community college, transferred with honors to UC Berkeley and is currently a work-ing professional with graduate and professional degrees. My sister's achievement gap, as expressed by her GPA, didn't tell even a fraction of the story.

Though a Black teacher recognized Toni's talents and ability early on, which led to her participation in gifted programs, Toni recollects that her readiness for this opportunity was questioned later in her primary education by a teacher at the "better" school. Though she never states the ethnic or racial background of the teacher who questions her ability, her narrative reflects that race was a factor as she moved from the support of the all-Black school to the "better" school where she never again had a Black teacher. Toni's narrative also reflects the racial biases embedded in teachers' perceptions about her own, and her sister's, aptitude for gifted and talented education. As she notes, Black mobility is intricately linked to educational opportunity and the power to negatively shape students' lives can be detrimental to achievement. However, her sister's efficacy eventually enabled her to transcend the negative experiences she faced in her education, enabling her to achieve success in obtaining a professional degree. Yet her sister, who did not have Black teachers, floundered in a system that did not recognize or support her academic ability based on inaccurate perceptions.

Discourses about emancipatory learning goals continually reemerge in the texts of contemporary Black scholars (Ladson-Billings, 1992), while calls for reclamation of Black knowledge traditions and creating *communities of care* remain central to informed teaching practice. In addition, what constitutes "optimal learning environments" for Black males (Hopkins, 1997) and females continues to be interrogated from the culture-specific frameworks of Black scholars (Ladson-Billings, 2000; Murrell, 2002). Therefore, African-centered pedagogy remains salient in our thinking about the best practices for training emergent Black educators.

Cultivating Teacher Praxis and the Currere

It was during our Saturday-afternoon writing "boot camps" that most of our efforts to build community, and fellowship and engage with culture-specific pedagogical skills would come to fruition. Creating meaning-making practices is a vital component of African-centered pedagogy, thus literacy for extended conversation and as an elaborated activity provides opportunity for knowledge development, and would serve to provide cultural and pedagogical enrichment opportunities for our group. Thus, the selection of literature that spoke to us and allowed for us to make inter-textual connections is an important component for cultural inquiry. We read each other's responses and wrote "rejoinders" (response papers) based on our reactions to each other's writings and based on salient issues that emerged from our interpretation of and connection with texts. A key feature in our process was the "interspersion of comments" within the rejoinders, which symbolically revealed the level of interest and engagement with each other's experiences, providing a window into examining salient issues or themes (Denzin, 1989, p. 189). This method is recursive, as long as the conversation continued on a topic. The rejoinder responses would then serve as "talking points" for further dialogue and written reflections. As Denzin (1989) notes, the intent of this method is to draw an interpretive circle around our lives to grasp meaning of that life as it has been lived.

The utilization of a guided-writing model helped us to also develop annotated bibliographies of research in order to prepare literature reviews on Black educational issues. We decided that our goal was to prepare manuscripts on Black education to be presented at local, national, and international conferences. McGuire and Regar's (2003) work provided an alternative paradigm that helped us explore our identities as intellectuals in a community, which advances Murrell's idea of creating identity development practices that further oral performance and public talk (2002). Key to this structure is a shared investment in developing scholarly activity, productivity, and opportunities to deal with real-world problems. This approach, embodied within African-centered practices, fosters collective interests (Foster & Peele, 1999) and mutual empowerment that integrates our emotional, physical, and intellectual lives.

We decided to utilize a guided-reading model where we identified an issue of focus; scholarship was located (by Lisa) in the form of articles, studies, and position papers. Each of us maintained responsibility for creating an annotated bibliography for our "assigned" readings to share with the entire group. We held team meetings to read articles and we co-wrote summaries and synopses of position papers on Black education and our experiences. We engaged in a participatory process of reading material to gauge not only our understanding of varied scholarship, but also to foster our ability to effectively speak about the content of the research. Developing orality through public dialogue was a critical component here, notwithstanding the ability to situate our lives and experiences within the larger scholarly tradition.

We examined and reflected on how we understood the method of narrative and autobiography/life stories (Ladson-Billings, 2000; Denzin, 1989) used within the scholarship we read; how these methods aligned with or differed from the currere (Pinar, 2012; Pinar et al., 1995); and how these methods might be used to help tell our stories while reconceptualizing ways to approach curriculum development, particularly related to issues of race. Delgado (1990) reminds us that people of color in our society speak with experiential knowledge that is framed by racism. Cacee's excerpt illustrates this fact:

> We are all familiar with the aphorism knowledge is power, and with the fact African Americans have struggled for both knowledge and power since the inception of this nation. The African American struggle has not been for equality, but for the right to ask for equality; not education, but the right to ask for education. Historically, equality has been nothing more than a fleeting illusion in the minds of African American parents hoping for a better future for their children. In a nation that prides itself in the liberty of individuals to pursue their dreams, freedom of speech, and liberty for all, we find injustice, separate and unequal treatment of [the] impoverished, and people of color….I was one of those impoverished black youth, blessed with the privilege to graduate from a University to enjoy the privileges America has to offer. I correctly use the word blessed; my mother spent years on her knees praying for the Lord's intervention on my behalf, and I owe any success to her belief in the Lord and in me. I did not live the American myth of working hard and pulling myself up by the boot straps. Many people, as with my family, did not always have boots, let alone straps to pull. Treading through the University's curriculum and learning to exist in a dual consciousness of being a black male in a Eurocentric institution did create hardships and often I wished to drop out of school. I learned quickly that all men may be created equal, but we all do not pass through this world with the same cultural, social or net worth.
>
> As a child, I learned early on that education was not for me. I spent the majority of my elementary years in special education programs that did nothing more than confirm and then reconfirm my inability to compete in the academy. By age fourteen, I had completely given up on academics and was on the self-destructive path that I witnessed

many of my "role models" travel. I knew right from wrong and wished to do right. I tried studying, tutoring, reading my textbooks, but always had the same result: academic failure. I developed a self-hatred and believed myself to be inferior to white students. I noticed many of the colored students around me were facing the same obstacles. I now understand race is only involved in academic success to the extent that racism and ethnic bias is allowed; and even though I have proven myself able to endure the rigor of the academy, deep in my soul still exists the little boy petrified of reading aloud or being called to the blackboard to solve a math problem. Never again do I want to feel the sense of powerlessness and worthlessness that I felt in my childhood as a student, nor do I want other children to suffer such defeats. Schools are not safe places for all students and for the unprotected children, who do not know the feeling of academic success—the class clown, the behavioral problem, and special education student, I entered my graduate program as proof that we are capable of success.

Cacee's discourse illuminates his perceptions of African American educational inequality; his perception of his struggles within a system that did not support his needs; his culturally based views of the role that spirituality plays in shaping the Black worldview; and his desire to work toward changing the system to enable other Black children to have positive academic experiences. Sharing his narrative in an honest and transparent way allowed us to encourage each other's voices and experience both through the spoken and written word. Within each of our narratives was the common theme of marginalization, yet resilience kept us steadfast throughout our schooling and outlook as we prepared for and strengthened our praxis.

Through dialogue we were empowered to draw upon the unique sociolinguistic foundations that underlie African-centered pedagogy such as signifyin' and testifyin' (DeCastro-Ambrosetti, 2003). The utilization of our indigenous voices rejected the deficit views that pervade the academy about the formal usage of Black vernacular speech (Woodson, 1933/2008). In the same way, Du Bois states that Black people's education must use the variety of the English idiom that we understand, which should be founded on the knowledge of the history of our people in the United States, and our present condition without whitewashing this history.

Nurturing community integrity practices focused on identity development and a sense of place in an academic community is another specific cultural practice in an African-centered pedagogy. As an illustration, we sought opportunities for democratic access to intellectual resources by forging alliances with community groups. Dismantling academic structures that serve as barriers to the development of Black consciousness, professional development, and community engagement proved pivotal to this effort. Thus, we met with groups of African American faculty and community leaders from the local chapters of the Urban League and the National Association for the Advancement of Colored People (NAACP) to engage in conversation about the greater needs of Black communities locally. As an illustration of how these meeting impacted us, Gary shares his view about community involvement in the preparation of teachers and advocates:

> I had a very strong interest to serve, educate and assist people of color.... In fact, I have always been intrigued with the concept of black identity, black family dynamics, personal and interpersonal relationships, and how they influence each other.... These concepts are a part of me and have always been there. However, I really wasn't sure how to develop strategies or put myself in a position to deal with these things.... What I did know was that throughout my life, I have confronted a lot of spiritual, emotional, and mental brokenness among my peers, classmates and others who look like me. What I also knew was that I wanted to obtain the voice, vocabulary, and skills I needed to be able to discuss this brokenness and dysfunction with confidence [and] wisdom.... The interest was made more prevalent through my belief in God, my upbringing, my education, and my college experience. When I look back and really examine it, my whole life has been dedicated to teaching and counseling people and families through promoting education, spiritual and life counseling, healthy living and healthy lifestyles.... I believe this experience prepared me for attempting the Master's Program. I didn't really plan it that way; it was just relevant when I would talk to different people; the need was so great.

Evident through Gary's words is both spiritual purpose and a sense of agency for Black people's interests. Advocacy as a moral imperative not only compelled his pursuit of graduate school, but also dictates the direction of the work he desires to undertake. This vocation about the purpose of teaching mirrors scholarship where Black male teachers speak about "seein'" themselves in the experiences of their students (Lynn, 2002, p. 119). Fundamentally, the opportunities of urban Black youth are largely shaped by "pervasive, deep racial inequalities," which mandates broader community engagement and activism by those who desire to give back (Lynn, 2002, p. 119).

Our Pedagogical Hopes

The currere as a method proposed by Pinar and others (Castenell & Pinar, 1993; Pinar et al., 1995; Pinar, 2012) advances the idea that retelling the story of one's educational experiences; imagining future possibilities for self-understanding and educational practice; analysis of the relationships between past, present and future life history and practice; and new ways of thinking about education are necessary for engaged curriculum development and pedagogical action. This method is reflected in the culture-specific educational practices espoused within African-centered pedagogy, where narrative inquiry is an essential component of knowledge construction. As a consequence, teacher training efforts and education programs that fail to recognize these essential methods are ill-equipped to develop Black intellectual traditions, while failing to address the needs of the whole learner—the African American teacher whose desire to teach is grounded in emancipatory ideologies.

Our work reveals the intersection between our racial identity; our desire for culturally relevant academic preparation grounded in African-centered intellectual thought; and our embodied beliefs about practices that reflect moral agency. For instance, race held symbolic meaning for members of this group and proved to be a common link across many of our stories; the intersection of race in our "opportunity" narratives combined with a call for culturally relevant professional development for the betterment of the community resonated for us. In addition, a disposition toward establishing communities of care guided our concept of personal agency and was actualized through our professional development activities.

Racialized topics provide rich scholarly perspectives that must not be ignored in the academy or academic research, as these issues reflect a microcosm of community experiences embedded in the larger U.S. sociopolitical context. The data generated from these interactions enabled us to develop greater understanding of our professional identity in relation to African American intellectual traditions, as well as supporting our interpretation of, and engagement with, varied methods that would strengthen our pedagogical and curricular choices. It is from our life stories and funds of knowledge that we have developed our own passionate politics—a desire to work with Black children and youth, and on behalf of Black communities. The anecdotes of people of color obtaining their degrees and returning back to their communities to help those who are less fortunate than themselves resonate for us.

Scholarship that identifies best practices on how to foster culturally relevant teaching and mentorship furthered our individual and shared professional goals. McGuire and Regar (2003) posit that the development of a professional identity and the ability to internalize the occupational norms and values of the academy is furthered by the quality of mentorship that all students can benefit from, particularly those from marginalized groups. Therefore, non-hierarchical, egalitarian relationships were centralized in our efforts; strategies that disrupt the White-male-centric, hierarchical, and competitive mentoring paradigms that are traditionally modeled in the academy (McGuire & Regar, 2003). Dismantling oppressive structures to create a community of learners was preeminent. In that frame, we viewed each other as kin—family members in our endeavors, which meant that hierarchal systems and competitive efforts were rejected. Actualizing this type of community meant that all decisions for the development of scholarly engagement—academic reading and writing related to issues impacting African American communities—were efforts collectively deliberated over.

We chose these methods to honor and acknowledge the knowledge, skills, and dispositions that we cultivated through successfully navigating K–16 education in pursuit of graduate degrees; while at the same time acknowledging that, as Black people, each of us have a racialized story to tell, one that helped to shape our sense of personal and professional agency.

Emergent educators' training must cultivate cultural competence, utilizing culturally relevant practices that draw upon African-centered intellectual traditions, Black students' lived experiences, and funds of knowledge. In fact, we believe that teacher training efforts focused on developing culturally competent educators to teach Black youth, but purely from diversity paradigms, are inept in addressing the needs of those emergent Black teachers whose lived experiences, as part of a racialized group, mandate an elevated discussion of race, the sociopolitical nature of schooling, and its relationship to pedagogy. Yet the notion of curricular and pedagogical relevance often uses ahistorical approaches as it reflects on the historic foundations of American education.

As we reflect on our experimental efforts, we recognize that our work may prove insightful for U.S. Department of Education teacher recruitment efforts, education faculty within teacher education, and curricular scholars who are concerned about and interested in the underrepresentation of African Americans in the teaching pipeline. It is our belief that the establishment of a learning trajectory grounded in emancipatory teaching and curriculum foci will open the door to more African Americans pursuing teaching as a viable career path. Institutional dialogues must examine more effective targeted recruitment of future African American teachers by considering the cultural and curricular landscape that influences their efficacy.

Moreover, as this text shows, teaching holds cultural meaning as it is tied to notions of service, agency, and advocacy grounded in the history of the African American experience in America. For those people who undertake this calling—as caregivers, models, and mentors—there is a profound desire to uplift the race for greater personal, cultural, academic, and economic mobility. Tied to this notion of purpose is a profound understanding that racialized experiences play a significant role in impacting the quality of African American lives. Consequently, teacher education program development and curriculum must examine these issues to effectively integrate culture-specific practices for relevant impact in the training of those who will eventually teach African American children and youth. The failure of African American educators (and allies) to direct their efforts in this manner is part of the miseducation and malpractice that endures in U.S. educational institutions—practices that must be interrogated and disrupted.

References

Anderson, M., Astin A. W., Bell, D. A., Cole, J. B., Etzioni, A., Gellhorn, W., Griffiths, P. A., Hacker, A., Hesburgh, T. M., Massey, W. E., & Wilson, R. (1993). Why the shortage of black professors? *The Journal of Blacks in Higher Education, 1*, 25–34.

Aptheker, H. (1973). The future and the function of the private Negro college. In *The Education of Black People: Ten Critiques 1906–1960 by W.E.B. Du Bois*. Amherst: The University of Massachusetts Press.

Asante, M. K. (1991). The Afrocentric idea in education. *The Journal of Negro Education, 60*(2), 170–180.

Ashanti, K. (2003). Leaders in African-centered education. *The Initiative Anthology.* http://www. units.muohio.edu/eduleadership/anthology/RCI/COM03005.pdf

Bensimon, E. M. (2005). Closing the achievement gap in higher education: An organizational learning perspective. *New Directions for Higher Education, 131*, 99–111.

Brown, A. F. (2010). "Just because I am a Black male doesn't mean I am a rapper!" Sociocultural dilemmas in using "rap" music as an educational tool in classrooms. In D. Alridge (Ed.), *Message in the Music: Hip Hop, History, and Pedagogy.* Wyomissing, PA: Tapestry Press.

Brown, A. F., & William-White, L. (2010). We are not the same minority: The narratives of two sisters navigating identity and discourse at public and private White institutions. In C. C. Robinson & P. Clardy (Eds.), *Tedious Journeys: Autoethnography by Women of Color in Academe* (pp. 149–175). New York: Peter Lang.

Buffenbarger, A. , (2011, February 2). Duncan calls for more Black and Hispanic male Teachers. *Neatoday.* Retrieved July 24, 2011, from http://neatoday.org/2011/02/02/duncan-calls-for-more-black-and-hispanic-male-teachers/

Carlson, D. (2006), Are we making progress?: Ideology and curriculum in the age of No Child Left Behind. In L. Weis, C. McCarthy & G. Dimitriadis, (Eds.) *Ideology, Curriculum and the New Sociology of Education: Revisiting the work of Michael Apple,* (pp. 91–114). New York: Routledge.

Castenell, L. A., & Pinar, W. F. (Eds.). (1993). *Understanding Curriculum as a Racial Text: Representations of Identity and Difference in Education.* Albany: State University of New York Press.

Collins, A. C. (2001). Black women in the academy: An historical overview. In R. O. Mabokela & A. L. Greene (Eds.), *Sisters of the Academy: Emergent Black Women Scholars in Higher Education* (pp. 29–41). Sterling, VA: Stylus.

Cornelius, L. J., Moore, S. E., & Gray, M. (1997). The ABCs of tenure: What all African-American faculty should know. *Western Journal of Black Studies, 21*(3), 150–155.

Craig, C. J. and V. Ross. (2008). Cultivating the image of teachers as curriculum makers. In F. l. Connelly, M. F. He & J. Phillion. *The Sage Handbook of Curriculum and Instruction.* (pp. 282–305). Thousand Oaks, CA: Sage.

DeCastro-Ambrosetti, D. (2003). Sociolinguistic foundations to African centered pedagogy: A literature review. *The High School Journal, 86*(4):31-48.

Delgado, R. (1990). When a story is just a story: Does voice really matter? *Virginia Law Review 76*, 95–111.

Denzin, N. K. (1989). *Interpretive Biography.* Newbury Park, CA: Sage.

Fenelon, J. (2003). Race, research, and tenure: Institutional credibility and the incorporation of African, Latino, and American Indian faculty. *Journal of Black Studies, 34*(1), 87–100.

Foster, M. (1995). African American teachers and culturally relevant pedagogy. In J. A. Banks & C. A. McGee Banks (Eds.), *Handbook of Research on Multicultural Education* (pp. 570–581). New York: Macmillan.

Foster, M. (1997). *Black Teachers on Teaching.* New York: New Press.

Foster, M. and T. B. Peele. (1999). Teaching Black males: Lessons from the experts. In V. C. Polite & J. E. Davis, (Eds.) *African American Males in School and Society: Practices and Policies for Effective Education.* New York: Teachers College Press.

Franklin, B.M. & C.C. Johnson (2008). What the Schools Teach: A Social History of the American Curriculum Since 1950. In M. F. Connelly, M.F. He and J. Phillion (Eds.). *The Sage Handbook of Curriculum and Instruction.* (pp. 460–477). Thousand Oaks, CA: Sage Publications Ltd.

Freire, P. (1970). *Pedagogy of the Oppressed.* New York: Seabury.

Ginwright, S. A. (2004). *Black in School: Afrocentric Reform, Urban Youth, and the Promise of Hip-Hop Culture.* New York: Teachers College Press.

Giroux, H. A., & Schmidt, M. (2004). Closing the achievement gap: A metaphor for children left behind. *Journal of Educational Change, 5*(3), 213–228.

Goodman, K., Shannon, P., Goodman, Y., & Rapoport, R. (2004). *Saving Our Schools: The Case for Public Education Saying No to "No Child Left Behind."* Berkeley, CA: RDR Books.

Gordon, B. M. (1993). Toward Emancipation in Citizenship Education: The Case of African American Cultural Knowledge. In Castenell, L. A. Jr. & W. F. Pinar (Eds.) *Understanding Curriculum as a Racial Text: Representations of Identity and Difference in Education.* (pp. 263–284 New York: State University of New York Press.

Gramsci, A. (1971). *Prison Notebooks.* Albany: Columbia University Press.

Hale, J. (1994). *Unbank the Fire: Visions for the Education of African American Children.* Baltimore, MD: Johns Hopkins University Press.

Hale, J. (2001). *Learning While Black: Creating Educational Excellence for African American Children.* Baltimore, MD: Johns Hopkins University Press.

Hale-Benson, J. (1986). *Black Children: Their Roots, Culture and Learning Styles.* Baltimore, MD: Johns Hopkins University Press.

Hopkins, R. (1997). *Educating Black Males: Critical Lessons in Schooling, Community, and Power.* Albany: State University of New York Press.

Irvine, J. J. (2000). Afrocentric education: Critical questions for further considerations. In D. S. Pollard & C. S. Ajirotutu (Eds.), *African-Centered Schooling in Theory and Practice.* (pp. 199–210). Westport, CT: Bergin & Garvey.

JBHE (2001). No Blacks in the pipeline: The standard explanation for low percentage of Black faculty continues to be much of a red herring. *The Journal of Blacks in Higher Education, 33,* 77–78.

King, J. E. (2005). *Black Education: A Transformative Research and Action Agenda for the New Century.* Mahwah, NJ: Lawrence Erlbaum Associates.

Ladson-Billings, G. (1992). Liberatory Consequences of Literacy: A case for culturally relevant instruction for African American students. *Journal of Negro Education, 61,* 378-391.

Ladson-Billings, G. (1994). *Dreamkeepers: Successful Teachers of African American Children.* San Francisco: Jossey-Bass.

Ladson-Billings, G. (1995). Toward a theory of culturally relevant pedagogy. *American Educational Research Journal, 32*(3), 465–491.

Ladson-Billings, G. (1998). Just what is critical race theory and what is it doing in a "nice" field like education? *International Journal of Qualitative Studies in Education, 11,* 7–24.

Ladson-Billings, G. (2000). Fighting for our lives: Preparing teachers to teach African American students. *Journal of Teacher Education, 51*(3), 206–214.

Ladson-Billings, G. (2001). *Crossing Over to Canaan: The Journey of New Teachers in Diverse Classrooms.* San Francisco: Jossey-Bass.

Ladson-Billings, G., & Tate, W. F. IV (1995). Toward a critical race theory of education. *Teachers College Record, 97*(1), 47–68.

Land, R. R. (2005). Wounded (soul)diers in the classroom: Qualifying the Black teacher's experience. In M. C. Brown II & R. R. Land. (Eds.) *The Politics of Curricular Change: Race, Hegemony, and Power in Education* (pp. 54–75). New York: Peter Lang.

Lave, J. (1991). Situated learning in communities of practice. In L. B. Resnick, J. M. Levine, & S. D. Teasley, *Perspectives on Socially Shared Cognition* (pp. 63–82). Washington, DC: American Psychological Association.

Leap, T. L. (1995). Tenure, discrimination, and African American faculty. *The Journal of Blacks in Higher Education, 7,* 103–105.

Lynn, M. (2002). Critical race theory and the perspectives of Black men teachers in the Los Angeles public schools. *Equity & Excellence, 35*(2), 119–130.

Mabokela, R. O. & A. L. Green, (Eds.) (2001). *Sisters of the Academy: Emergent Black Woman Scholars in Higher Education.* Sterling, VA: Stylus.

McGuire, G. A., & Regar, J. (2003). Feminist co-mentoring: A model for academic professional development. *NWSA Journal,15*(1), 51–72.

Moje, E. B., Ciechanowski, K. M., Kramer, K., Ellis, L., Carrillo, R., & Collazo, T., (2004). Working toward third space in content area literacy: An examination of everyday funds of knowledge and discourse. *Reading Research Quarterly, 39*(1), 38–70.

Moll, L. C., Amanti, C., Neff, D., & Gonzalez, N. (1992). Funds of knowledge for teaching: Using a qualitative approach to connect homes and classrooms. *Theory into Practice, 31*(2), 132–141.

Moss, P., Debres, K. J., Cravey, A., Hyndman, J., Hirschboeck, K. K., & Masucci, M. (1999). Toward mentoring as feminist-praxis: Strategies for ourselves and others. *Journal of Geography in Higher Education, 23*(3), 413–427.

Murrell, P. C. (1999). Chartering the village: The making of an African-centered charter school. *Urban Education, 33*(5), 565–583.

Murrell, P. C. (2002). *African-Centered Pedagogy: Developing Schools of Achievement for African American Children.* Albany: State University of New York Press.

Nieto, S., Bode, P., Kang. E., & Rabile, J. (2008). Identity, community, and diversity: Retheorizing multicultural education for the postmodern era. In M. F. Connelly, M. F. He and J. Phillion (Eds.). *The Sage Handbook of Curriculum and Instruction.* (pp. 176–197). Thousand Oaks, CA: Sage Publications Ltd.

Noddings, N. (1995). Teaching Themes of Care. *Phi Delta Kappa, 76,* 675–679.

Perry, T., Steele, C., & A. G. Hilliard III (2003). *Young, Gifted, and Black: Promoting High Achievement Among African-American Students.* Boston: Beacon Press.

Pinar, W. (2012). *What Is Curriculum Theory?* (2nd ed.). New York: Routledge.

Pinar, W., Reynolds, W. M., Slattery, P., & Taubman, P. M. (1995). *Understanding Curriculum.* New York: Peter Lang.

Pollard, D. S., & Ajirotutu, C. S. (Eds.). (2000). *African-Centered Schooling in Theory and Practice.* Westport, CT: Bergin & Garvey.

Porter, K., & Soper, S. (2003). Closing the achievement gap: Urban schools. *Comprehensive school reform connection.* Washington, DC: National Clearinghouse for Comprehensive School Reform.

Richards, H., Brown, A. F., & Forde, T. (2004). *Addressing Diversity in Schools: Culturally Responsive Pedagogy.* National Center for Culturally Responsive Education Systems. http://www.nccrest.org/Briefs/Diversity_Brief.pdf

Richardson, E. (2003). *African American Literacies.* New York: Routledge.

Robinson, C. C., & Clardy, P. (Eds.) (2010). *Tedious Journeys: Autoethnography by Women of Color in Academe.* New York: Peter Lang.

Shujaa, M. J. (Ed.). (1994). *Too Much Schooling, Too Little Education: A Paradox of Black Life in White Societies.* Trenton, NJ: Africa World Press.

Toro-Morn, M. I. (2010). Migrations through academia: Reflection of a tenured Latina professor. In C. C. Robinson & P. Clardy (Eds.), *Tedious Journeys: Autoethnography by Women of Color in Academe* (pp. 63–96). New York: Peter Lang.

Wood, J. L. (2008). Ethical dilemmas in African American faculty representation. *eJournal of Education Policy.* http://works.bepress.com/jlukewood/1/

Woodson, C. G. (1933/2008). *The Mis-education of the Negro.* Radford, VA: Wilder Publications.

CHAPTER FOURTEEN

Autoethnography of a Mad, Black Student

JAZMIN A. WHITE

Exposition

Writing from *third space* (Bhabha, 1994; Soja, 1996; Moje, et al., 2004), this multi-genre, autoethnographic text reveals my stream of consciousness related to my experiences with curricular content in a department whose foci is critical studies, including how I feel about the absence of culturally relevant curricular content that explores race and representation for me as an African American. I explore how the concepts of "there is no hierarchy of oppression" by Audre Lorde, and "there is no ranking of oppression" by Cherrie Moraga do not adequately address issues related to subjectivity and identity negotiation for me as a Black woman, particularly for a student at a predominantly White institution. Rather, I contend that the emphasis on intersectionality—the interconnectedness of subject positions and oppression, and the symbolic inclusion of all marginalized communities within these homogenous frames—suppress and exclude.

Self-Identification and Experience

I read my "self-identification" paper for class:

My mother has always been big on affirming Black identity, especially after a racialized incident I experienced in my predominately White elementary school, in this predominately White, rural college community where I was born (Arcata,

California, in Humboldt County). Thus, from an early age, I recognized that I was different than my peers. My mother was once a student, then a staff/faculty member on this campus; consequently, I went to school here locally. Thus, it was within the public schools that I began to notice my Black positionality, given that African Americans only represent 1.3 percent of the county, while Whites represent 84.7 percent.

When I was five years of age, my kindergarten instructor, "John," conducted "circle time" so that he could teach a small history lesson. I recall John saying, "Today, class, we are going to talk about Jazmin's people."

My friend Michaela then asked who "my people" were, and at a loss for words, I wanted to know as well. Up until that point, I didn't know that *my people* were different from everyone else's people.

John said: "Good question, Michaela. Once upon a time, 'Jazmin's people' were slaves in this country…" *I guess that was his attempt at culturally relevant pedagogy and inquiry-based learning.*

Some of the children gasped (but I'm pretty sure few, if any children in that class knew the meaning of the word "slave"; we just knew it was bad).

After this kindergarten class that day, I was picked up by my mother who asked me, "How was your day, Jaz?"

"We learned about 'slaves,'" I told her. She looked confused and was probably wondering how and in what context that lesson was delivered.

I continued: "John said that slaves looked like me once upon a time" (as if it was a fairy tale) "and that's why I look different." All my other friends were blonde haired and blue eyed; the class also included brown- and red-headed White children.

I watched my mother stare off in the distance as we drove home in silence. Upon arrival and shortly after entering the door, my mother pulled out a huge continental map, and began to explain the Middle Passage slave trade routes… the slave trade…she spoke of "the door of no return" in the slave house of Senegal and the fortresses in Ghana…and why slavery took place…its consequences… and anything else *she* thought I could grasp at the age of five. And the next day, my mother had a meeting with John about his marginalizing history lesson. And from that point on, my mother became vigilant about dialoguing with me about race; and of course, I took copious mental notes.

Identifying as Black is definitely important to my sense of self. A significant part of my upbringing focused on the effects of being racially different; being Black was one of the reasons my mother chose to leave the Humboldt area to move to Sacramento.

Before that, however, during my second-grade year, I walked home from school one day and asked my mom: "How come I don't have blonde hair, straight hair, or blue eyes?" My mother told me something to the effect of "Black is beautiful; you're unique." I asked other questions, like "how come there aren't other people like me at school?" I told her that I was one of only four Black students in the *whole* school, and we were all in different grades. I also remember asking her: "How come the only Black people that exist are on TV and MTV. Where are the rest of us at?" At that point, and after the barrage of many questions like that, my mother looked at me, and said "We're moving. You need to be connected to other people who look like you; you need to be exposed to diversity." And so we moved at the end of that year because I was convinced that Black people only largely existed in music videos, the only images of Black people I saw outside of my immediate family.

Moving to Sacramento at the age of eight also made me aware of my *whitened* Black identity. All the drill-team-stomping, hand-clapping, double-dutching; Black girls constantly told me and reminded me how *un-black* I was. I didn't fit in for a while, until another Black girl tried to indoctrinate me into *blackness*: "Girl, let me help you; you ain't Black enough," she told me one afternoon on the playground at school.

It was her personal mission to teach me *everything* I needed to know about *blackness*. Looking back, it's actually quite hilarious. What she actually taught me, however, was how to *perform* blackness as an identity. Just as I believe in gender performance (Butler, 1999), I also recognize that a lot of my sense of self has been about performing my race and ethnicity.

During elementary school, my performance of what it means to be Black was probably just compensation for the lack of Black representation in Humboldt County. Somewhere along the lines, *I caught on quickly*.

In high school (due largely to my mother's teaching background and influence), I read scholarship that focused on people of color having multiple consciousness (King, 1988) or what Du Bois calls a "double consciousness" (Du Bois, 1897). These readings deal with how we negotiate the many senses of self we have. From my mother's lectures and teachings, I learned who I am in terms of my multiple selves—school-self, home-self, friends-self, and family-self—all of which served a different purpose.

My mother also taught me the importance of being able to code-switch (depending on the audience) and wearing different masks (depending on what company I was in). Everything was about negotiating my positionality—my blackness, playing it up when I needed to by being strong-minded, loud, direct, assertive, opinionated, outspoken, obnoxiously argumentative, sensational, speaking with a guttural tone to invoke seriousness, posturing, trying to be seen and be heard (Lei, 2003); or playing it down when necessary: being observant, reserved, quiet, looking unengaged and unmoved, a look of a withdrawn/aloof facial expression, a look reflecting the subject matter being unimportant, arrogant in my silence, sitting back listening to White student's opinions and watching people making ignorant comments, trying not to be seen and heard, a more muted, introverted toned-down personality. I caught on quickly and learned that that's how many Blacks maneuver through life, strategically resisting or conforming to systems. Playing the game to beat the system; i.e., being diplomatic, a neutral party, not controversial or overbearing, not ruffling any feathers, not showing your politics and getting along with the status quo to get ahead and advance. *We wear different faces and speak with many tongues* (Anzaldúa, 1995).

After high school, I still wasn't convinced of my blackness, however, so I attended a historically Black college in Alabama. During this time period, I thought maybe I could become *Black* if I was totally surrounded by Blacks. Yet, little did I know that when I went to Tuskegee University, my identity would have little to do with being Black and would be more about my socioeconomic status. Since everyone was Black, I wasn't so *unique* like my mother told me when I was in kindergarten. Apparently, in a room full of Blacks, Africans, and African Americans (yes, they are all different to me now) in Tuskegee, Alabama, race didn't matter in the same way that it did in a room full of Whites. We could generally agree, on some level, upon a shared history, and some of the same racialized experiences; therefore, talking about who we were *as Black people* didn't make much sense. We all knew each other's history and each other's stories. In fact, the *real* story that every Black student and Black professor wanted to know was: "How far has your family come? And how successful is your family now?" That was it!

Bragging about your parents holding MDs, JDs, and PhDs *was Tuskegee University*.... Black elitism through education. Yet, I finally felt like I belonged somewhere. I finally knew it was ok for my mother to have earned a PhD by the age of 33, even though she is only one in the 3 percent of Black PhDs in the nation. *She, however, wasn't really an anomaly in the South.* The other 3 percent existed there, or so it seemed. Based on this exposure, I knew my family existed and I felt affirmed; successful Blacks existed; code-switching Blacks existed; I wasn't so *different* after all. I was/am "theory in the flesh" (Moraga & Anzaldúa, 2002).

After some years at Tuskegee University, I transferred back to Humboldt. It's ironic because they say that life has a way of coming full circle. Maybe I came back to my origins because I now know who I am; and though this area can still be alienating due to the lack of cultural diversity, I am literally and figuratively comfortable in my own skin.

My Black skin has been affirmed time and time again, and so I no longer question why I don't have the long flowing blonde hair. If I want it, I just tack on a blonde weave or rock an Afro. My hair (my physical appearance) has nothing and everything to do with my Black sense of self and I let that be known. Thus, I unapologetically speak up *at all times* because I want everyone to know my presence, my importance. That's what my mother, and Tuskegee taught me.

Examining the Curriculum as Planned: A Journey

I am excited! I am now part of an undergraduate major that truly embodies the type of critical study that I so yearn for—one that melds my home knowledge and experiences combined with my sociopolitical interests. My course schedule reads as follows:

Table 1: Department Course Goals and Key Objectives

Course Title	Goals and Key Objectives
Critical Race, Gender & Sexuality: Theory and Methods	The overall course objective is to provide a foundation in critical social theories and methodologies which inform the fields of Ethnic, Women's and Multicultural Queer Studies.
Ethnic Studies: Multicultural Queer Narratives	We will address the complexity and fluidity of identity, and intersections of race, gender, and sexuality, in diverse works by contemporary U.S. writers and filmmakers.
Critical Race, Gender and Sexuality: Women of Color Feminisms	In order to expose students to the origin of, and debates within, Woman of Color Feminisms, the class will: ▪ Discuss the evolution of feminist analysis in communities of color ▪ Discuss the relationship between Feminisms of Color and the mainstream Women's Movement ▪ Examine the challenges of Woman of Color Feminisms to the notion of the unitary subject ▪ Explore multiple identities as a framework of analysis ▪ Discuss how Women of Color Feminists find ways to articulate their own experience in dialogue with other voices ▪ Study in-depth one community, topic, or issue in Women of Color Feminisms

I enthusiastically look forward to taking courses where I will be able to engage critically about the experiences of Black women in America. I know that racism, sexism, and classism are largely responsible for the way in which Black women are portrayed in, and experience daily the "racialized regime of representation" (Hall, 1997). It is this structure that has contributed to the status and functioning of African American women in institutions (media and schools)—from pejorative representations of personhood (William-White & White, 2011), and discursive discussions of motherhood (William-White, 2012); to reproduction and fertility all encased in negative imagery (Roberts, 1997; Scully, 2002; Silliman, 2004). Additional barriers to equity for Black women also include: overrepresentation in the prison industrial complex and drug addiction (Davis, 2003; Roberts, 1997; Scully, 2002); navigating the negative perceptions associated with the stigma of being welfare and public assistance abusers (Roberts, 1997; Scully, 2002); and the blaming of single mothers for poverty and perceived ills in the Black family and community (Roberts, 1997; William-White, 2012). These archetypes are damaging; these images have been instrumental in depriving the African American woman of opportunities, societal resources, and the recognition of her value as a human being and contributing member of society (Jewell, 1993). I examine my reading list with great anticipation and interest for engaging critically in what is to come…

"Hey, Giddings, 'Where Do I Enter' in My New Department, at My New College?": A Poetic Reflection

Several weeks later, I write:

Did I wholeheartedly believe that the experiences of students
would be brought to the forefront?
Yes, I did think this, *once*
in the classroom
in the learning context.
They'll make room
for active learning
make it interactive
and relevant
ACTIVE ENGAGEMENT
Boy, my excitement!
But this hasn't happened yet
At least, not for this *Subject*!

I also once believed that all subjects would be presented from diverse perspectives
That educational materials would be inclusive
And would transform course objectives.
I thought that critical,
intersectional
inclusive curriculum
would include *us* and all of *them*
But that didn't happen.

Diary Entry: Whose Text Merits Examination and Why?
Dear Diary,
I have been enrolled in my courses for eight weeks and I am *frustrated*. We are half way through the term and my classes have barely attempted to cover Black feminist theories, Black representation, and Black identity formation. Across all of my classes, I was only presented with two or three pages of bell hooks "Feminist

Scholarship: Ethical Issues." Maybe it is about time that I *ask the other question*? (Matsuda, 1991).

I had hoped that we would examine how the intersection of race, gender, class, nation, and sexuality frames the Black female subject, or ways that Black women negotiate and navigate these discursive boundaries! Should I thank Lorde (1984) for empowering every instructor in my department to disregard *my people's* contribution in history by emphasizing intersectionality and the notion that the danger lies in "ranking the oppression" (Moraga, 2002)? Believe me, I get it; our oppression stems from the same roots—colonization and economic exploitation, but I think this is *straight* problematic when we only pay homage *in brevity* to Black struggles. Where is the Black representation?

I do not think that the instructors in my department realize that they have ranked oppression within class discussions and within course required texts. We have read Gloria Anzaldúa "La Conciencia de la Mestiza: Towards a New Consciousness" (half written in Spanish, so I and many others in class cannot fully access the text); Gloria Anzaldúa's, *Making Face, Making Soul*; Gloria Anzaldúa's *Borderlands*; and Cherríe Moraga, *Loving in the War Years*—all of which speak about the phenomenon of having a multiple consciousness and multiple realities as women of color.

Maybe the Black female identity isn't intersectional enough; therefore, we praise Anzaldúa (2007) and Moraga (2002) for being "theory in flesh" because they identify as women of color who also openly identify as *lesbian* women? We have read Moraga and Anzaldúa in *every class!*

I don't want to diminish the work of these authors; but, my gripe is that classes privilege these authors as if they are the *only* significant, foundational, and exceptional women of color in critical studies. I would even argue that solely focusing on these Chicana-lesbian writers achieves the opposite of intersectionality. Magnifying them produces Chicano/a-centered hegemony. When we talk about someone embodying multiple subject positions, is this supposed to mean that the department only takes into account the subject's sexual identity and racial status from *one* ethnic/cultural group's frame? Can my instructors teach beyond the Chicana-lesbian binary?

Intersectionality requires a deep exploration of *difference*. It means understanding invisible and visible forms of difference and the varied histories of diverse peoples. To look at difference means to understand the similar ways that oppression operates through power and hierarchical structures. But I feel that in trying to address all subjectivities and ways that one might be oppressed, the unitary racialized subject unfortunately is neglected.

bell hooks (1994) states that one struggle should not take priority over the other; yet, certain voices have been given priority. Where are Patricia Hill Collins, Barbara Smith, June Jordan, Toni Morrison, Beverly Tatum, Maya Angelou, Alice

Walker, and so on? *Black authors' knowledge is invisible in schools and Chicana literary works are meaningless to my Black identity, consciousness and lived experiences.*
   Whose work is worthy of examination in curriculum?
   Signed, *Mad*

Scribbles During Class: A Note to Self One Afternoon

I recognize the difficulties associated with negotiating and balancing the diverse and complex identities that exist within a classroom context. It must be difficult to decide what communities to focus on, or to decide what texts should be covered within a 16-week semester. Yet, I would think that color-conscious instructors would seek out materials that positively reflect students' identities and they would then initiate discussions about issues, such as race and racism. I raise these issues, but I *perceive* that my inquiry is unwelcomed (by faculty and some of my peers).

I write:

Multiple data points triangulate
to validate my perception
shaping my frustration with the curriculum
and its relationship to Black female representation.

They say:

We are all the same minority—
common bonds,
common histories
that all stem from colonization
and economic exploitation
just different voices.

   Yet, the generic label of *women of color* and *people of color* in describing a curricular focus, or utilized within classroom rhetoric, is a form of color-blind discourse because it allows instructors and students to homogenize *all* marginalized communities across lines of difference. Therefore, instructors may fail to engage students in examining varied communities and *their* differences...
   Color-muted discourse aids the erasure of race. I have come to learn that marginalization is ever present in higher education, *even* within the study of critical social theory in curriculum. Instructors believe that they are being color conscious when making overarching statements about *women of color,* but the labels and *phrases are* generic enough that they *erase* race and minimize the importance of examining the material effects of racism in individual's lives, particularly for those

of us who have historically been labeled as *non-persons or colored* and *subordinated in the United States* based on that status—Black people.

Signed, *Mad*

Oh, By the Way, "We Aren't Covering That…"

Dear Diary,

This is blasphemy! My Theory and Methods instructor stated that the readings that actually address women of color subjectivity and Black positionality *weren't* going to be read in this course. The syllabus states "further readings for *reference only*." REFERENCE ONLY? Not expected for this course: Patricia Hill Collins' *Black Feminist Thought: Knowledge, Consciousness, and the Politics of Empowerment*; bell hooks' *Feminist Theory from Margin to Center*; Kimberle Crenshaw's "Beyond Racism and Misogyny: Black Feminism and 2 Live Crew" in *Words That Wound: Critical Race Theory, Assaultive Speech and the First Amendment*; Beverly Guy-Sheftall, editor of the volume *Words of Fire: An Anthology of African-American Feminist Thought*; and Stanlie James and Abena Busia who are editors of *Theorizing Black Feminisms: The Visionary Pragmatism of Black Women*. There was *also* a note:

> "See also the course: Women of Color Feminisms and: Race, Gender, US Law."

I am pissed. Everything read in Theory and Methods that dealt with persons of color was listed as *optional*. Apparently, these works would take up *valuable* time that is currently being spent discussing dead white theorists: Karl Marx as cited in Kaufman (2003): Antonio Gramsci and Michel Foucault (cited in Stoddart, 2007); Louis Althusser (1971); and Jacques Derrida (1967), to name a few. *Maybe the instructor of this course truly expected that students would receive these readings from the other courses?* The classes that were *believed* to examine people of color's subjectivity and identity politics: "Women of Color Feminisms," "Race, Gender and US Law," "Multicultural Queer Narratives" did not offer any of *those* readings listed on the syllabus; and, to add insult to injury, when issues related to Blacks were raised, the instructors failed to adequately analyze the complexities of the Black positionality—deconstructing Black women's multiple selves or interlocking systems of oppression impacting that group.

If I wanted to investigate *other* theorists (like bell hooks, Audre Lorde, June Jordan, Barbara Smith, Patricia Hill Collins), I, who paid tuition for this course, would have to *take it upon myself*. Perhaps this enables White, *critically-conscious* and *liberal* instructors to relinquish the responsibility and accountability to critically engage in discourse about, or teach Black female authors to classes full of White students? To me, this inaction further displays that people of color (Blacks) truly aren't the political interest of the instructors in this department since the works aren't worth talking about during class time.

As a Black female, I feel as though I have to wear a mask that says: *I believe in being inclusive of other identities, and they should have equal discussion time within the class session.* Yet, I honestly get angry *sometimes* about advocating for "others" needs at the expense of mine! Why must Black women always take a subordinate role in every facet of life? Our needs come secondary to White men, Black men, White women, Chicano/as, and now, lesbians? Indeed, I do believe in the struggles and liberation of *all people,* particularly those of color, yet as a member of a historically oppressed minority group, am I not included in those very same struggles? Black feminist Deborah K. King describes this phenomenon as a "both/ or" orientation; the act of being simultaneously a member of a group, yet standing apart from it.

Audre Lorde even classifies herself as a "Sister Outsider" (1984) in relation to this phenomenon. This state of belonging and yet not belonging is an integral part of Black women's oppositional consciousness. I wouldn't even be able to label my multiple insights about my lived experiences, reality, and consciousness had I not read Black scholarship. I have had to *teach myself* about these authors while in *this* program in order for me to be emotionally, spiritually and educationally fed. I have had to take my learning into my own hands and give it the *possibility of existence*—the foundation of Black women's politics. I must also say that it is because of Black women's politics that all of these *other* women of color politics have derived, which further fuels my anger.

Signed, *Mad*

A Poetic Appeal for Homespace in Curriculum

The Black student has no place,
no homespace
and is displaced.
Instructor, are you aware of my negotiation and navigation?
My identity being divorced from the learning situation?
My internal battle about whether to demand more representation?

If I go along silently with the intersectional curriculum
one inclusive of everyone
does that make me invisible in the curriculum?
I do want liberation for all women:
women of color, working-class women,
poor and disabled women,
lesbians, old women
economically privileged, heterosexual white women
Can we *study* all of them?

Moving Beyond: A Poem

I understand that instructors want to move
Beyond the black and white binary,
call for the need of "intersectionality"
to see the fluidity and hybridity
of identity
but seeing more than the binary
at times allows for the erasure of people, like me
especially when I am the only Black person you see

We need a shift in curriculum
Critical studies that reflect multiculturalism
knowledge, experiences, values,
world views,
traditions
Explore new literature
all of them
that moves beyond ethnocentrism
oh such tensions...

References

Anzaldúa, G. (1995). *Making Face, Making Soul/Haciendo Caras: Creative and Critical Perspectives by Feminists of Color*. San Francisco, CA: Aunt Lute Books.

Anzaldúa, G. (2007). *Borderlands: La Frontera* (3rd ed.). San Francisco, CA: Hubsta Ltd.

Althusser, L. (1971/2001). Ideology and ideological state apparatuses. In L. Althusser, *Lenin and Philosophy and Other Essays* (pp. 121–176). New York: Monthly Review Press.

Bhabha, H. K. (1994). *The Location of Culture*. New York: Routledge.

Butler, J. (1999). *Gender Trouble: Feminism and the Subversion of Identity*. New York: Routledge.

Cliff, M. (1990) Object into subject: Some thoughts on the work of Black women artists. In G. Anzaldúa, (Ed.), *Making Face, Making Soul/Haciendo Caras: Creative and Critical Perspectives by Feminists of Color* (pp. 271–290). San Francisco, CA: Aunt Lute Books.

Collins, P. H. (2009). *Black feminist thought, knowledge, consciousness, and the politics of empowerment*. (2nd ed.). New York: Routledge.

Davis, A. Y. (2003). *Are Prisons Obsolete?* New York: Seven Stories.

Derrida, J. (1967). *Writing and Difference*. Chicago, IL: University of Chicago Press.

Du Bois, W.E.B. (1897, August). Strivings of the Negro people. *Atlantic Monthly*, 80, 194. http://www.theatlantic.com/magazine/archive/1897/08/strivings-of-the-negro-people/305446/

Giddings, P. (1996). *When and Where I Enter: The Impact of Black Women on Race and Sex in America*. New York: William Morrow Paperbacks.

Guy-Sheftall, B. (1995). *Words of fire, an anthology of African-American feminist thought*. New York: New Press, The.

Hall, S. (1997). *Representation: Cultural Representation and Signifying Practices*. London, U.K.: Sage.

hooks, b. (2002). *Feminist Theory from Margin to Center*. (2nd ed.). Brooklyn, NY: South End Press.

hooks, b. (1994). *Teaching to Transgress: Education as the Practice of Freedom*. New York: Routledge.

James, S., & Busia, A. (1993). *Theorizing black feminisms: The visionary pragmatism of black women.* New York: Routledge.

Jewell, K. S. (1993). *From Mammy to Miss America and Beyond: Cultural Images and the Shaping of U.S. Social Policy.* London, U.K.: Routledge.

Kaufman, C. (2003). *Ideas for Action: Relevant Theory for Radical Change.* Cambridge, MA: South End Press.

King, D. (1988). Multiple jeopardy, multiple consciousness: The context of a Black feminist ideology. *Signs, 14*(1), 42–72.

Lei, J. (2003). (Un)necessary toughness? Those "loud Black girls" and those "quiet Asian boys." *Anthropology &Amp; Education Quarterly, 34*(2), 158–181.

Lorde, A. (1984). *Sister Outsider: Essays and Speeches.* Trumansburg, NY: Crossing Press.

Matsuda, M. J. (1991). Beside my sister, facing the enemy: Legal theory out of coalition. *Stanford Law Review, 43*(6), 1183–1196.

Matsuda, M., Lawrence, C., Delgado, R., & Crenshaw, K. (1993). *Words that wound: Critical race theory, assaultive speech, and the First Amendment.* Boulder, CO: Westview Press.

Moje, E. B., Ciechanowski, K. M., Kramer, K., Ellis, L., Carrillo, R., & Collazo, T. (2004). Working toward third space in content area literacy: An examination of everyday funds of knowledge and discourse. *Reading Research Quarterly, 39*(1), 38–70.

Moraga, C. (2002). La Guera. In C. Moraga (Ed.), *Loving in the War Years: Lo Que Nunca Paso por Sus Labios.* Cambridge, MA: South End Press.

Moraga, C., & Anzaldúa, G. (2002). *This Bridge Called My Back: Writings by Radical Women of Color.* Chicago, IL: Third Women Press.

Roberts, D. E. (1997). *Killing the Black Body: Race, Reproduction, and the Meaning of Liberty.* New York: Pantheon.

Scully, J. A. M. (2002). Killing the Black community. In J. Silliman & A. Bhattacharjee (Eds.)., *Policing the National Body: Sex, Race, Gender and Criminalization.* Cambridge, MA: South End Press.

Silliman, J. M. (2004). *Undivided Rights: Women of Color Organize for Reproductive Justice.* Cambridge, MA: South End Press.

Soja, E .W. (1996). *Thirdspace: Journeys to Los Angeles and Other Real-and-Imagined Places.* Malden, MA: Blackwell.

Stoddart, M. C. J. (2007). Ideology, hegemony, discourse: A critical review of theories of knowledge and power. *Social Thought and Research, 28,* 191–225.

William-White, L. (2012). Seeking emancipation from gender regulation: Reflections on home space for a Black woman academic/single mother. *Qualitative Research in Education, 1*(1), 435.

William-White, L., & White, J. (2011). Color marks the site/sight of social difference: Dysconscious racism in the "Age of Obama." *Qualitative Inquiry, 17*(9), 837–853.

CHAPTER FIFTEEN

Thug-Noble/Street-Scholar

Community Activism as Curriculum

MOTECÚZOMA PATRICK SÁNCHEZ

Sociopolitical Context That Shapes Me

This work focuses on the "third space" (Moje et al., 2004) illuminating urban community advocacy and curriculum for social uplift and critical consciousness. This advocacy is an imperative, as I was raised in an environment where too many times I witnessed and experienced the painful realities that poverty and depravation create: a turn towards crime, lack of opportunity, lack of social capital, stress, unemployment or underemployment, poor educational enrichment, transportation issues, teenage pregnancy, violence, drug abuse, poor health care, and limited options.

I was born and raised in Stockton, California. The city is located in California's northern central valley. Forged rapidly during the Gold Rush for which it served as an inland hub with an inland port for those heading to the Foothills from San Francisco to pan for gold, it drew people seeking fortune from all over the world and was faced with challenges since its inception. One of the most ethnically diverse cities in the state and nation, Stockton remains fraught with inequalities and troubles. It ranks as the second-most-violent city in California, behind Oakland, and has a 22 percent unemployment rate (Smith, 2012). Thirty percent of the population lives below the poverty line; it has one of the lowest-ranking school districts in the United States and one of the lowest literacy rates in the nation; at 15 percent, Stockton has one of the lowest rates for degree holders of bachelor's or higher degrees (city-data.com, 2012); and, at 73 years, one of the lowest life-expectancy rates in the state (Daftary, 2011).

As a Chicano who grew up in poverty and who lived a life of struggle, I now use education, art, and advocacy to engage groups in critical discourse related to social and economic inequalities in the community and surrounding area. Moreover, as an Ethnic Studies BA-degree holder who graduated magna cum laude,[1] and as a current graduate student studying to earn a master's in Public Policy Administration in an exclusive Capitol Fellowship Program, I know how to speak the language of academia and the language of the streets; and I use my positionality to serve my community.

Thus, the intersection of the currere (Pinar, 2004, 2012) and spoken-word poetic research methods (William-White, 2011a, 2011b; and William-White & White, 2011) illuminates how I exist as an activist in multiple worlds, within multicultural contexts—within street culture, within mainstream academic institutions, and within city politics—working with and advocating on behalf of those left behind and living in the margins of society.

About Thug-Noble/Street-Scholar

I am an anomaly to the system, while simultaneously being a product of it. The son of a single mother who dropped out of school in the ninth grade, I was raised in poverty with very little social capital. My mother, who is an avid reader, would take my siblings and me to the library at an early age, walking miles to the nearest one, as we had no car. This early exposure to reading and learning instilled the love of knowledge in me.

An honor-roll student, I graduated from the school in my city serving the upper-middle-class population who had ample access to resources. The access to Lincoln High School on the north side of Stockton came as the result of a move. My new address took me from attending a Stockton Unified school, Garfield Elementary on the south side of Stockton, to Lincoln Elementary on the north side. My inclusion in this better district was the legacy of the city's attempt to mitigate the *de facto*[2] and one-time *de jure*[3] segregation prevalent in the city and its educational system. The reality of the city's ethnic segregation was the result of generations of practices and legal ordinances preventing non-Whites from moving beyond certain areas.

As a result of the Civil Rights movement legislation making changes throughout the nation and state, a busing program was instituted in 1979 to attempt integration of students into different schools from different areas. This program

1 With high honors.

2 *De facto*: in reality.

3 *De jure*: by law.

carved out different areas of Stockton, which were impoverished, and predominately of particular ethnic groups, i.e., Mexican, Filipino, Black, and bus them to different areas of the city to attend schools. The idea was to increase access to quality education for those with lesser economic and social opportunities. I happened to live in a "pocket of poverty"[4] on the north side near Holiday Park, Townhomes, and Kentfield, which were concentrated with low-income apartments. Unlike other areas where poverty was more widespread, these areas were within neighborhoods that were more middle class. Needless to say, my reality at home was different from that of my reality at school.

One can also pass judgment about someone for his or her lack of education or knowledge of "professional" language and demeanor, never taking into account the context where one may exist. I've witnessed and experienced this myself, many times. One of the earliest examples is when I was an eighth-grader at Sierra Middle School, the feeder school to Lincoln High. As an honor-roll student, I was eligible to attend a special trip to Great America, an amusement park. I remember being judged and admonished by the vice principal for not going on this trip. He assumed that I wasn't going because I did not want to look smart to my "hoodlum" and "gangster" friends who were my neighbors. In reality, I wasn't going because I did not have the $20 for admission and did not want to burden my family with the cost.

I was too ashamed of being poor to ask for the assistance being offered by the school. I was still traumatized from having to be one of the few kids in class who had to raise a hand in class every day in elementary school for "free lunch."[5] Yet, I did not bother to explain all of that to him, the real reason I would not attend the special field trip. Impressed upon me was how one could jump to negative assumptions based on perceptions without taking the time to understand the circumstances of another. I felt I was written off in his eyes and negatively stereotyped.

I usually did not have what other kids at my school had, not just in terms of material items and wealth, but resources and social capital; yet, academically I never let that hold me back. Although I graduated on the honor roll, I was never invested in by the establishment of the school like other kids who were part of that upper-class network; and I left school without any direction or aspirations for my post-secondary education. I ended up wasting time at the local community college, as I was operating without any clear direction or plan, just a hope for a better life. I had a proverbial destination in mind, but did not know how to navigate my way there.

---

4   "Pockets of poverty" is the term I use to refer to the areas of impoverishment and low-income housing scattered throughout the middle-class neighborhoods of northern and western Stockton where poverty is concentrated in housing projects such as apartment complexes, duplexes, and triplexes.

5   Free lunch programs in public schools gave special tickets for lunch to low-income children, who had to be identified each day in class and line up in their own line to go to lunch.

I had to teach myself how to navigate the educational system by trial and error. I hated growing up in poverty. I hated it with a passion. I hated having to pay with food stamps at the grocery store and I resented not having the opportunities other kids had. I hated feeling less than, and in a society that values material wealth as an indicator of success, this feeling often plays a role in the psyche of those experiencing it. <u>Driven by these emotions, I desired success.</u>

During this time, I became an active advocate and leader among my peers in empowerment philosophies such as those taught in student organizations like Movimiento Estudiantil Chicano de Aztlán (MEChA),[6] which sought to promote Chicano[7] unity and empowerment through political action. I was also inspired by historic figures and individuals such as César Chávez,[8] who led the way for impoverished and exploited farm workers to unionize for more rights, and Malcolm X. After reading the *Autobiography of Malcolm X* (Haley, 1977), I was inspired to not only examine the reality of race and class politics in the U.S., but also to understand the ability of Malcolm X to change his life from that of coming from an disadvantaged background (as I had), to being an intelligent leader on the forefront of the Civil Rights movement in the 1960s. I was inspired by other leaders who fought against oppression and subjugation such as Joaquin Murietta,[9] Juan Cortina,[10] Tiburcio Vásquez,[11] Emiliano Zapata,[12] Francisco "Pancho" Villa,[13] and Crazy Horse,[14] to mention a few.

In going to the community college, San Joaquin Delta College, I witnessed how the students coming from the city's public school district were far behind academically. They were doing remedial work in things I had learned in the ninth

---

6   MEChA is a Mexican American student organization in universities and high schools that promotes student empowerment.

7   Chicano is a slang term used among Mexicans to denote a Mexican who is from *el Norte* or the United States, i.e., Mexican American.

8   Co-founder of the United Farm Workers and civil and labor rights advocate of California.

9   Joaquin Murrieta was a legendary freedom fighter/vigilante of the California Gold Rush to Mexicans of that time period. To Anglos, he was a bandit/outlaw. His story is similar to Robin Hood of Nottingham in English folklore.

10 Juan Cortina was a Mexican general who fought in the Mexican American War and the famous *el Battalla del Puebla* on *el Cinco de Mayo* and fought militarily against oppressive conditions of the Texas Rangers towards Mexicans in Texas.

11 Like Joaquin Murrieta. Vásquez was considered an outlaw bandit in the central valley of California. However his perception of his actions is summed up by his quote, "A spirit of hatred and revenge took possession of me. I had numerous fights in defense of what I believed to be my rights and those of my countrymen. I believed we were unjustly deprived of the social rights that belonged to us."

12 Emiliano Zapata led military forces in the southern states of Mexico during the Mexican Revolution of 1910. His battle cry was *tierra y libertad* (land and liberty).

13 Pancho Villa led military forces in the northern border states of Mexico during the Mexican Revolution of 1910.

14 Crazy Horse was a warrior of the Oglala Lakota who led the successful battle of Little Big Horn against the U.S. cavalry led by Lt. Col. George Custer who was attempting to remove the Lakota from their sacred Black Hills for gold.

grade such as developing a thesis for an essay. The educational disparity was well pronounced. They were being failed by a dysfunctional educational system and were socially culturally disengaged from education. I was thinking that college was supposed to be the next level and there I was in class with students who could not write an essay. My eyes were further opened when I volunteered at Edison High School, a Stockton Unified School District school on the south side. The program was designed to help encourage "at-risk" young men and was called Mexican-American Rites of Passage.

Their realities and challenges were very different from those faced by the average student of Lincoln Unified or the private schools. At Edison and other SUSD schools, the threat of violence was more than a notion; gang culture had a constant presence; students were more likely to talk about who got incarcerated rather than who was going to college; more were likely to have to work after school to help their families make ends meet; more were likely to come from single-parent households; have fewer resources such as new books and quality facilities; and shootings and stabbings were more likely to occur on or near the campus. The students who were facing these challenges were more likely to be primarily Mexican, Black, Filipino, Southeast Asian, and even some poor Whites.

Community Advocacy as Curriculum

My experience coupled with my passion to see *mi gente*[15] and community do better (as well as myself) led me on a path to education and advocacy as a means of fighting inequality and empowering liberation through educational sessions, protests, cultural celebrations, art, and spoken word. While my focus initially was related to the interests of those from my ethnic/cultural background, I include in *mi gente* all those in a similar situation of marginalized oppression and who can relate to struggle, regardless of ethnicity. This also led me to engage in politics, running for mayor as well as engaging in civics as a way of cultivating progress.

A good example of this is when I served as the chair of the Equal Employment Opportunity Advisory Committee for San Joaquin County. Every year, the committee hosts a diversity luncheon to celebrate and promote diversity among the county government employees. In 2011, the day of the luncheon happened to fall on Columbus Day. Traditionally in the United States, this holiday celebrates the explorer and the discovery of a "new world." Knowing the history of colonization of the "New World" and being of Mexican ancestry, I view the legacy of Christopher Columbus in a different way. As such, I proposed asking a Native American speaker to perform a song or "blessing" in honor of Native ancestry on the day as a way of celebrating diversity and recognizing the Miwok natives who were indigenous to the area before it was named San Joaquin County or Stockton.

---

15 My people.

The idea, while welcomed by some, was met with resistance by others. My suggestion offered a different way of viewing Columbus Day by acknowledging that America continues to celebrate a murderer who started the process that would become known as the "American Holocaust"; this exchange was uncomfortable for some of European ancestry who had grown up never questioning the holiday, never knowing the truth. Those who were in opposition to my suggestion were concerned that the diversity luncheon would become "spiritual" or "political." Yet, I devised a way to make everyone happy, while still accomplishing my goal of awareness and celebration. I proposed to make no mention of the genocide, but rather to allude to an alternate view that some indigenous people may have, and to acknowledge the day and legacy of trans-Atlantic contact as "a time of increasing diversity around the world through contact." As the master of ceremony for the luncheon, I introduced the speaker who was also a Vietnam War veteran, and specifically mentioned the existence of natives in the region, with him being a representative who would sing a native song in honor of the day and to honor military veterans. All were happy. And all were made more culturally aware.

Moreover, I have the unique ability to operate in different "worlds" so to speak. The societal barriers that exist to limit access and mobility in a society stratified by wealth and social capital create different realities or worlds in which I can speak both "languages" or code switch. I use this ability to help bridge the gap of inequality, acting as a cultural intermediary. To illustrate my point, I often teach others that youth who drop out of school and may become caught in the prison pipeline are not unintelligent. They learn very well, but many times the knowledge they acquire may lead them towards self-destruction or incarceration, rather than college and career. Many times perception and cultural/social barriers prevent those in power or stakeholders who make up systems from seeing the problems needing to be addressed in this way. Sometimes it is intentional, but other times it is unintentional ignorance.

So I teach. I teach directly to those willing to learn and indirectly to those who are not there yet. Just as I had to learn how to navigate the system of education in order to find success and understand the rules to the game, so to can others like me do the same. I can advocate and lobby as well as admonish the establishment through my work as a legislative aide in the California State Assembly; I can lobby the U.S. Senate to support the DREAM Act[16] in Washington, D.C.; and can criticize and pressure the city government of Stockton to act in regards to crime and problems plaguing the city.

Locally, I have engaged city leaders, such as council members and consultants, in reviewing practices by the police department that are detrimental to the community and certain ethnic communities in particular. Police misconduct, disrespect, agitation, and outright killing of unarmed men by Stockton police of-

---

16 Development, Relief, and Education for Alien Minors. Legislation entered in 2001.

ficers (who are primarily White) occur far too often in the city, especially towards Mexicans and Blacks. The proposed solution was to create a Citizens Oversight Committee, which would operate independently of law enforcement to investigate perceived misconduct, and make recommendations to the council (which ideally would provide oversight for the police department). Yet failing to find common ground with a mostly White, upper-class city government disconnected and uninterested in the needs and concerns of the majority diverse population, I engaged in an alternative strategy related to addressing policy misconduct, which was to take to the streets in protest in order to publicly admonish city leaders who were ineffective and unwilling to demonstrate care about the city's citizens—those who do not control resources, or those who do not reflect their complexion or residential areas.

Advocacy for Those Who Are Neglected and Ignored

"Of course I'm going to say 'I'm a thug' that's because I came from the gutter and I'm still here!" – Tupac Shakur

Having been raised in the impoverished pockets of poverty of Stockton, I also understand the "language" of those at the bottom. The gutter. Society's outcast. Society's thugs. Because I retain so many of the unspoken qualities of my environment, nuances like manner of speech or gate of walk, I am often viewed as that thug.[17] Yet I refuse to accept the paradigm imposed upon me. Instead I take charge and lead by example as a noble (one bearing admirable qualities who carries upon their shoulders the needs and hopes of their people). For many cultures throughout time, nobility was shown by the people who carried the burden of responsibility to do best for the people and provide leadership as well as lead the battles. This paradigm of responsibility rather than privilege is exemplified by Alexander the Great in Macedonia,[18] Shaka Zulu in Africa,[19] Cuauhtémoc in

---

17 While literally defined as a criminal ruffian, by "thug" I mean the sense of one in current-day American society who is cultivated in an environment of hardship and struggle and is criminalized by society both by perception and practice. In my experience, anyone coming from such an environment who is not a punk, and stands up for him- or herself is labeled as such whether he or she is involved in criminal activity or not, especially when he or she is part of an ethnic group that has been historically criminalized. The term also applies to one who reflects his or her environment and is reactive to those conditions rather than proactive in attempting to make change, instead adapting to the dysfunction of the environment.

18 Alexander the Great is regarded by many historians as the most successful military leader in history. He unified the Greek city-states and created one of the largest empires in history after defeating numerically superior forces of the Persian Empire. Educated by Aristotle, he is also responsible for spreading Greek knowledge and culture and founding Alexandria in Egypt, all by the age of 33. He was known to lead his troops from the frontlines during battle.

19 Shaka Zulu was a military leader who united the Zulu people militarily and revolutionized their tactics of warfare and culture in South Africa.

Mexico—Tenochtitlan,[20] Chief Joseph of the Nez Perce,[21] William Wallace of Scotland,[22] and Leonidas of Sparta.[23]

I take responsibility for the community in the community. I understand the desires of those who are marginalized; I understand their needs and can speak to this population in their environment using terms they relate to and understand based on my lived reality. I reach out to areas and people of the city who are neglected and ignored, those whom the establishment would judge as a threat because of appearance (tattoos, haircut, demeanor) and would write off as having nothing to offer. These same people are those whom the establishment would avoid due to fear and prejudice.

Militarily trained in the United States Marine Corps, I understand the importance of strategy and therefore employ many tactics to address people to speak to the disparities so prevalent in my community; those where children are born, live, and die disadvantaged by systems created before their inception:

- Systems of educational disinvestment

- Geographic/social segregation that has children set up for failure

- Systems that trap people in debt and have them bound to economic enslavement

- Systems that foster violence as communities compete among themselves for limited resources

Strategy and tactics are used to enforce these systems of inequity; thus, strategy and tactics must be used to combat them. These tactics can be seen in advocacy, arte,[24] spoken word, hip-hop, writings, speeches, workshops, debates, and media, among others. These vehicles allow me to include academic and sociopolitical concepts as part of an educational discourse of critical thought, exposing my "students" to a curriculum they have never been exposed to, even though they live it on a daily basis.

I learned the tradition of employing concepts and messages through the power of words through hip-hop expression. As an adolescent, I grew up listening to rap

---

20 Cuauhtémoc was the last Tlatoani or Speaker King of the Mexico-Azteca who led his people at the age of 25 to fight against Hernando Cortés and his force of Spaniards and Aztec allies until the fall of their rule.

21 Chief Joseph of the Nez Perce led his people against Gold Rush settler encroachments and held off 2,000 U.S. soldiers while leading his people through many states attempting to escape to Canada during the winter months until he was forced to surrender to save his people from cold and starvation. He was respected by General William Tecumseh Sherman and referred to as the "Red Napoleon."

22 William Wallace was a Scottish knight who led the fight against the English in the Wars of Scottish Independence.

23 Leonidas was a Spartan king who led his personal guard of 300 hoplite soldiers to hold off invading Persian forces numbered in the hundreds of thousands for three days until their weapons failed and they were all killed at the Battle of Thermopylae.

24 Artwork

262 | Critical Consciousness in Curricular Research

music and developed an appreciation and love not only for the music and rhythmic beats, but also the ability of the artists to convey powerful messages. This love of rap music, coupled with my quality education at Lincoln High School, helped foster my growth as a conscious artist and educator. As an honor-roll student, the majority of courses I took in high school were college preparatory and exposed me to great literary works from Shakespeare to Kafka and Homer, among others. I saw similarities in the classic literature I was being exposed to, and the rap music I was listening to from conscience artists like Public Enemy, Common, and Tupac:

To be, or not to be, that is the question:
Whether 'tis nobler in the mind to suffer
The slings and arrows of outrageous fortune,
Or to take arms against a sea of troubles
And by opposing end them. To die—to sleep,
No more; and by a sleep to say we end
The heart-ache and the thousand natural shocks
That flesh is heir to: 'tis a consummation
Devoutly to be wish'd. To die, to sleep;
To sleep, perchance to dream—ay, there's the rub:
For in that sleep of death what dreams may come,
When we have shuffled off this mortal coil,
Must give us pause—there's the respect
That makes calamity of so long life.
For who would bear the whips and scorns of time,
The oppressor's wrong, the proud man's contumely,
The pangs of dispriz'd love, the law's delay,
The insolence of office, and the spurns
That patient merit of th'unworthy takes,
When he himself might his quietus make
With a bare bodkin? Who would fardels bear,
To grunt and sweat under a weary life,
But that the dread of something after death,
The undiscovere'd country, from whose bourn
No traveller returns, puzzles the will,
And makes us rather bear those ills we have
Than fly to others that we know not of?
Thus conscience does make cowards of us all,
And thus the native hue of resolution
Is sicklied o'er with the pale cast of thought,
And enterprises of great pitch and moment

With this regard their currents turn awry
And lose the name of action.
  — Shakespeare, *The Tragedy of Hamlet, Prince of Denmark*, Act 3, scene 1,
    55–87

With all this extra stressin
The question I wonder is after death, after my last breath
When will I finally get to rest? Through this suppression
they punish the people that's askin questions
And those that possess, steal from the ones without possessions
The message I stress: to make it stop study your lessons
Don't settle for less—even the genius asks-es questions
Be grateful for blessings
Don't ever change, keep your essence
The power is in the people and politics we address
Always do your best, don't let the pressure make you panic
And when you get stranded
And things don't go the way you planned it
Dreamin of riches, in a position of makin a difference
Politicians and hypocrites, they don't wanna listen
If I'm insane, it's the fame made a brother change
It wasn't nuttin like the game
It's just me against the world.
  — Tupac Shakur, *Me Against the World*, verse 3

I was exposed to poetry and started writing my own as an outlet to express myself. I discovered that writing about matters on my mind would help me to not only process those issues, but would enable me to release the emotional troubles through expression. This was empowering. And as I began to share my writings, I noticed my poetic expressions would also serve as education and inspiration for others who did not have the same ability to express themselves in a similar way. This showed me how the power of poetry, spoken word, and rap or hip-hop could serve as a tool of empowerment and education. This process, coupled with my academic education and life experience, led to the development my self-concept of the archetype for thug-noble/street-scholar. When I refer to thug-noble, I don't mean to promote irresponsible behavior, but the contrary. The term serves as a juxtaposition of two labels that would not normally be coupled, which represents the juxtaposition of realities among different segments of our society. Thug-noble serves to be a transitional term, promoting that one can advance one's position and conduct oneself with dignity and class despite having humble and disadvantaged beginnings. A thug is defined as a heartless criminal, but in *the hood*, a thug can refer to one who holds his own and does not allow himself to be taken advantage of. I reach out to those forgotten. To save them is to save myself. This is the poetic story of a thug-noble, offered in my spoken-word poetry and lyric:

Spoken word:
There exist in this society
a stratified reality,
one in which the barriers separating the haves
from the have nots
 is thoroughly enforced.

Within the crevices of this chasm,
on the outskirts of stratification
and margins of the proper discourse
lay those such as myself.
Those whose existence is a threat to the established order
reminding them of their vulnerabilities
like a culture that goes viral,
reminding humans as empires,
they can fall with the tidal wave of force
which began in the butterfly wing flap of words.

Awakened from the slumber of self-degradation,
the all too common manifestation
of internal and external colonization.
 I operate in the halls of the empire
with the qualities of the oppressed outside the walls.

Every step taken an indication, it's getting closer to Fall.
For to succeed and escape the trap,
one must adapt,
life is but an act and we all players in it.
But who wrote the roles which would see us lost
with no chance of winning?

Those of us aware enough to understand the game, remain
a surviving enlightened few.
We are as I…

an endangered species
trapped in the concentration camps of conformity

my deformity my pride
to which there are no sides
only great divides
aboard slave ships lost to a turbulent sea
tossed around by violent waves
of mass generality
my mentality
a last defense against
the calamities of failure and bankrupt morality
fallen angels of a paradise lost
with no regard for the cost
to humanity
indecent remains my reality
as it teeters on the hopeless edge of
insanity my plea
the last bastion in the stronghold of an age-old war
for survival
I am in one the end and the revival
my rival epidemic plague
with kill shots so vague
they trickle through cultural IV's[25]
like spray-painted walls and polluted bathroom stalls
existing boldly against
the shadows of illumination
victims of political penetration
my articulation minimal
as my minority dissent becomes trivial even pitiful
my soul as it disintegrates in the crucibles
of melting pots and illiterate assimilation
daily I watch transfixed with assassination
as it lingers
with only so many times I can point the finger
a message addressing the world
on the edge to which I stand
and think
how I
am on the brink
of becoming
extinct.

───────────────

25 intravenous

Lyric:
Trapped in the game on the verge of insane,
daily I try to escape,
and yet still I remain
Training my brain to take the pain,
but it's all in vain,
'cause like a river of flame, it burns deep in my veins,
and like a hot burning coal,
 it burns deep in my soul,
just how long I'll survive—I don't know

Violence is the city
it's a pity I'm from,
where children grow from nursery rhymes
to playing with guns.
In the distance if listen you can hear them drums,
there's a war on the slums,
mental mind state numb,
doped up and dumb
Dum ditty dum as the world turns,
no one gives a fuck that the hood still burns.
No one gives a fuck because no one learns,
instead we're waiting in lines so we can take our turns—
and be the sequel to this evil that got us all unequal.

How many homies look hard,
but their heart is see through
Transparent it's apparent we're falling short of our goals.
How to get to the top—
no one knows 'cause

We ain't got no education
They got careers for us called incarceration
No matter what hood all across the nation
Living is a crime and it's life we're facing

Trapped in the game they got me going to war,
I did my time in the military,
but can't tell you what for.
Trapped in the game I guess because I'm poor,
feeling sorry for the next

not knowing what's in store.

Like fighting the battles for the wicked and rich,
when it's the poor who spill the blood
and the blood runs thick.
Tell me what's a greater crime against mankind—
a ghetto occupation
slanging[26] nickels n dimes[27]?

Or a system of oppression with invisible lines?
Read between the lines and the truth you'll find,
answers to the questions that'll free ur mind.

The game is a set up, and won't shit change until we fed up
 Apathy the poison of dilapidated minds
since you gotta get yours, believe I gotta get mine.
Caesar at the Rubicon[28] crossing the line.

'Cause it's all about money in this land of milk and honey,[29]
 I refuse to go hungry
when your cups running plenty.

Haters on the perch, they don't wanna see me ball,[30]
Hoping I would fall,
with nothing to my name but a mural on the wall

Remembered by the homies with the swig of a 40,[31]
Completin' the process—proving how they showed me

Stay in your place and never speak out of turn.
My words a catalyst to revolution
let it burn, let it burn 'cause

---

26 selling

27 small amounts of illegal drugs

28 Referring to Julius Caeser who crossed the Rubicon upon returning from the conquests of the Celtic peoples
    of Western Europe to proclaim himself "dictator for life." The Rubicon was a shallow river in northeastern
    Italy that served as the boundary outside of the city of Rome that Roman generals were not allowed to cross
    with their armies, lest it be a declaration of aggression.

29 Bible reference indicating the promised land of wealth and abundance.

30 Be successful.

31 40-ounce beer common in poor neighborhood liquor stores.

We ain't got no education
They got careers for us called incarceration
No matter what hood all across the nation
Living is a crime and it's life we're facing

I'm Fatalistically driven, Eastwood—*Unforgiven*,[32]
escaping these prisons that politicians be given
trapped in the game forever
facing hard livin'

In the land of the skantless,[33] ruthless, and bold.
where mama couldn't afford the heat
so my soul grew cold

Surrounded by crime, steady on the grind,
I give a fuck about you
as long as I got mine

I got that shit that you want, homeboy,[34] some shit that you need.
Funny money,[35] hos,[36] clothes,[37] coke,[38] and weed.[39]
The root of all evil ain't money
it's greed.

Trying not to bleed in this life I lead,
trying not to bleed just to feed my seed,[40]
from gauges to Glocks, fat sacks to rocks—put away the *cuete*,[41] *ese*,[42]
here come the cops
'Cause that shit don't stop,

---

32 *Unforgiven* is a Western genre movie directed by and starring Clint Eastwood.

33 Slang for scandalous.

34

35 Slang for Food Stamps that are traded for cash at half the value.

36 Harlots.

37 Referring to selling stolen clothes or "boosting."

38 Cocaine.

39 Cannabis.

40 Child.

41 Mexican slang for pistol.

42 Mexican slang for man.

I doubt it ever will, as street dreams defer[43] to penitentiary steel.[44]

We ain't got no education
They got careers for us called incarceration
No matter what hood all across the nation
Living is a crime and it's life we're facing

Laced within this spoken-word piece and lyrics are multiple concepts: economic disparities, the prison pipeline, politics, violence, crime, impoverishment, ignorance and education, drug and alcohol abuse, war, injustice, hopelessness, culture, independence and dependency, the underground economy, sexism, and community, among others. These pieces become vehicles of outreach and education, provoking thought and contemplation for the reader and listener. These concepts are delivered in rhyme so the audience can better recall, just as Shakespeare[45] and Homer[46] understood with iambic pentameter.[47] Each piece can be a reflective observation of social ills, hoping to elicit awareness to the conditions that should be addressed (a positive proactive direction, or a combination of both). I often use language and lyrics that mix concepts throughout the material rather than solely focus on those concepts (kind of like when I was a child and my mother would smash up my medicine and put it in my Kool-Aid[48]):

I live the life of a hustla, used to be a thugsta.
Haters when I see you better bet I'm gonna mug ya[49]
Hard-headed[50] like a youngsta,
Ladies know I'll love ya, but I'll never trust ya,
playa don't do it or you's a sucka
Prosecute Bush[51] or Obama[52] you's a busta.[53]

---

43 Alluding to the poem *"Dream Deferred"* by Langston Hughes.

44 Prison.

45 William Shakespeare was an English playwright and poet of the 16th century.

46 Homer authored the *Iliad* and the *Odyssey* of ancient Greece.

47 A rhythmic metrical line of verse and poetry since the ancient Greeks.

48 Flavored drink.

49 To look at in a disrespectful way.

50 Stubborn.

51 President George W. Bush.

52 President Barack Obama.

53 A man undeserving of respect.

On that 209[54] grind we ain't hard to find[55]
Exercise your mind or get left behind
Enemy lines in the school of hard knocks
If it ain't the rival gangs, it's the crooked-ass cops
Step the fuck down or fall the fuck back
A soldier on a mission with the 'hood on my back
Stompin' like a King Kong,[56] droppin' my bombs like napalm 'Nam[57]
In the jungles of these streets never trust the police
Refuse to be consumed in the belly of the beast[58]
Singing my song like…
I want my *gente* to be free-e-e, to be free[59]
Build up the schools not the penitentiaries.

Conclusion

I sometimes wonder if I had not grown up facing the challenges I had, or faced the struggles I have, if I would have the perspectives I have; or if I would care about others experiencing similar struggles. While these ideas are conjecture, what I don't question is the fact that I have and I do think about people other than myself. I have come to realize that I am unique (an outlier so to speak). I am actively working to change the conditions of my community and the outcomes of those living in conditions similar to those I experienced, the same conditions I despised as a child. I have learned to use that hatred and passion cultivated in me by my nature, environment, and experience to focus that energy towards positive advancement.

I employ many tools to foster such change, a main strategy being education through spoken word, hip-hop, and ethnic studies. These tools have the power to speak to audiences who have been disadvantaged and disenfranchised; yet I and others who grew up like me receive cultural reinforcement and education through such media. Therefore, I use the communication and academic skills and lessons I have learned to bridge the gap and help others follow the path I am blazing; a path that was blazed for me.

Like me, many have been forgotten and lost in the margins in the society that we live in. I struggled from the bottom, living in poverty to find success in academics and community organizing. Thus, I know that the odds do not favor the marginalized; but that does not mean we are condemned to failure and im-

---

54 Area code for Stockton.

55 Meaning we're not hiding, unafraid.

56 Giant gorilla.

57 Vietnam War.

58 The ghetto, systematic oppression, and struggle.

59 Alluding to the rap song *Umi Says* by Mos def.

poverishment. We can succeed, and in this society education is a great tool to aid in such endeavors.

Education, while not an end-all, can be empowering just as any other tool when used strategically to one's advantage. It has the power to combat the effects of not only economic poverty, but poverty of the mind as well. An educated society is a healthy society. Education should not be mistaken for knowledge, nor an *opportunity* indicator of intelligence, but rather understood as system by which keys can be acquired to open doors or keep them closed. Like a driver's license that allows access to roads, education when coupled with knowledge can cultivate self-actualization, which leads to self-empowerment, which leads to success, which is relative to the individual and or group as defined by their desires and needs, and is something we must actively pursue for it will not be given to us, nor should it be. It is something that must be acquired and achieved through a process of behavior and action.

What should be minimized are the social and economic barriers that oftentimes hold us back or weed us out. Yet the marginalized cannot let that stop us. We must pool resources and knowledge to help others, just as we have been helped either directly or indirectly by those who have struggled for change and advancement before us. We can succeed academically when we realize its power and we strive toward critical consciousness and advocacy.

Even when society deems us thugs to be discarded, we must conduct ourselves as nobles and lead our communities. The challenges are many. The odds are overwhelming. We must therefore be intelligent noble warriors using the best tools of success strategically to escape the jaws of defeat. Mine are empowering education and expression. I lead by example for those who wish to follow. Progress is made, not found.

References

City-data.com. City Profile, Stockton, California. http://www.city-data.com/city/Stockton-California.html

Daftary, A. (2011). Health care in need of a cure. Recordnet.com. http://m.recordnet.com/apps/pbcs.dll/article?AID=/20120701/A_OPINION08/207010304/-1/WAP&template=wapart

Freire, P. (1971). *Pedagogy of the Oppressed.* New York: Seabury.

Haley, A. (1977). *The Autobiography of Malcolm X.* New York: Ballantine.

Macrone, M. (1990). Shakespeare quotes. eNotes.com. http://www.enotes.com/shakespeare-quotes/

Moje, E. B., Ciechanowski, K. M., Kramer, K., Ellis, L., Carrillo, R., & Collazo, T., (2004). Working toward third space in content area literacy: An examination of everyday funds of knowledge and discourse. *Reading Research Quarterly, 39*(1), 38–70.

Pinar, W. (2004). *What Is Curriculum Theory?* Mahwah, NJ: Lawrence Erlbaum.

Pinar, W. (2012). *What Is Curriculum Theory?* (2nd Ed.). New York: Routledge.

Shakespeare, W. (1992). *The Tragedy of Hamlet, Prince of Denmark.* New York: Washington Square Press.

Shakur, T. (1995). Me against the world. (Produced by Soulshock & Karlin). *Me Against the World* (album). Interscope Records.

Smith, S. (2012, July 6). Documents paint a harrowing picture of city's financial ills. *The Record*. http://www.recordnet.com/apps/pbcs.dll/article?AID=/20120706/A_NEWS/207060314

William-White, L. (2011a, May). Dare I write about oppression on *sacred* ground [emphasis mine]. *Cultural Studies <=> Critical Methodologies, 11*(3), 236–242.

William-White, L. (2011b, June). Scholarship revolution. *Qualitative Inquiry, 17*(6), 534–542.

William-White, L., & White, J. (2011, October). Color marks the site/sight of social difference: Dysconscious racism in the "Age of Obama." *Qualitative Inquiry, 17*(9), 837–853.

Diagram of a Process-Based Approach to Inquiry

Each entity shown below works together to engage in deep inquiry related to the storied life of study within the historic moment: (1) the identification, examination, and analysis of the power dynamics that shape the sociopolitical milieu (e.g., race, class, gender, ability, sexual orientation, religion/spirituality, language, nationality and its material effects); (2) the self as a cultural being (shaped by values; world views; socializing agents such as home, school, community, media; subjectivity); and (3) content matter engagement (identification, examination, and analysis of political forces such as national standards or goals, state and district standards, educational codes, national accredition standards, institutional policies and structures, etc.); the philosophical orientations guiding content (e.g., paradigms such as the empirical/analytical, the interpretive, and the critical perspective); and pedagogy (methods and strategies utlized by the teacher).

Figure 1. Recursive Processes of Inquiry

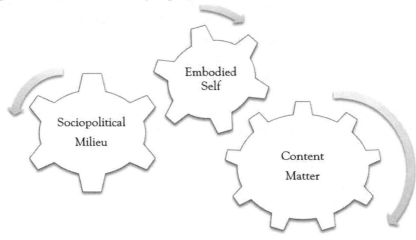

Author Biographies

Peter Baird EdD is Professor of Bilingual Multicultural Education at California State University and In-Country Director of the California Bi-National Teacher Education Project (Bi-TEP). Dr. Baird was raised in Mexico and is a former bilingual elementary school teacher, journalist on Mexico-U.S. issues and co-author of *Beyond the Border, Mexico and the U.S. Today*.

Maggie Beddow earned her PhD at the University of California, Davis, in Education with an emphasis in Language, Literacy, and Culture. She is an Assistant Professor in the Bilingual/Multicultural Education Department at California State University, Sacramento where she primarily teaches multiple- and single-subject social studies methods for English Learners, and a survey course in bilingual education. Maggie is a current board member for the California International Studies Project (CISP) and the Center for African Peace & Conflict Resolution (CAP-CR), and a former board member for the California Council for the Social Studies (CCSS) and California Teachers of English to Speakers of Other Languages (CATESOL). Dr. Beddow was a former elementary and middle school bilingual classroom teacher, and a middle school vice principal and bilingual department chair. Dr. Beddow was recently appointed as director of Sacramento State University's High School Equivalency (HEP) program, one of fifty federally funded educational programs nationwide designed to assist seasonal agricultural workers and their families in obtaining the equivalent of a high school diploma (a GED).

Cacee Belton is currently an administrative analyst/specialist 1 at California State University, Sacramento, working for the University Transportation and Parking Services (UTAPS). During his time as a Sacramento State employee, Mr. Belton has hired, supervised, and mentored numerous undergraduates and one recently graduated master of arts student. The greatest compliment he has received during his time at Sac State came in the form of an email he received from a student who thanked and referred to him as her "dad away from home." Mr. Belton earned a bachelor of science degree in criminal justice, and a master of arts in education (bilingual and multicultural). He plans to apply to an education leadership doctoral program in fall 2013.

Ayanna Brown holds a B.S. from Tuskegee University in secondary education, language arts education. She taught 7th grade language arts while earning her MEd in curriculum and instructional leadership from Vanderbilt University Peabody College. After teaching middle school, Dr. Brown became a scholarships coordinator for Project GRAD and Imagine College, which was a consortium between Metro Nashville Public Schools and Vanderbilt University. Her work centered around planning for high school students, most of whom were first-generation future college students. She completed her PhD at Vanderbilt University in interdisciplinary studies in language, literacy, and sociology, where her research focuses on discussions of "race," contemporary African American studies, and discourse analysis. Her research has been presented nationally and internationally and she has served as a member of the International Reading Association, National Commission on Reading, National Council of Teachers of English, American Education Research Association, and International Federation of Teachers of English.

Ya Po Cha was born in Laos. He came to the United States at the age of 12. He graduated from California State University, Fresno with a BA in biochemistry in 1991. He earned an MA from California State University, Sacramento in 2010. He has taught high school science for over 10 years. For the last 6 years, he has been teaching Hmong as a world language full-time. He is the author of the book *An Introduction to Hmong Culture.*

Kathy Emery taught high school history for 16 years, has a PhD in education and currently teaches political science at San Francisco State University. She co-founded the San Francisco Freedom School in 2005. In 2011, Kathy moved the SF Freedom School to SF State University as a political science course. She is co-author of three books—the teaching edition of Zinn's *People's History of the United States*; *Why is Corporate America Bashing Our Public Schools?* and *Lessons from Freedom Summer.* Her website is educationanddemocracy.org

Parrish Geary is employed in the Matriculation Department at Sacramento City College where he develops, coordinates, and delivers new student orientations and counseling support. He is working on a doctorate in education at the University of the Pacific in Stockton, California. He holds a master of arts in higher education and a bachelor of arts in natural science from California State University, Sacramento

Nicholas Daniel Hartlep (Koh Moil 고모일) is an assistant professor of educational foundations at Illinois State University. Dr. Hartlep's primary research activities have focused on the education and social welfare of Asian Americans, including the model minority stereotype and international and transracial adoption. Dr. Hartlep earned his BS (2006) in elementary education from Winona State University, his MSEd (2008) in K-12 education from Winona State University, and his PhD (2012) in urban education (social foundations) from the University of Wisconsin-Milwaukee's Urban Education Doctoral Program. He is married to Stacey Hartlep. They have three daughters, Chloe Haejin, Avery Hana, and Olivia Eunhae, and live in Bloomington, Illinois. You can follow his writing at www.hartlep.tateauthor.com http://redroom.com/member/nicholas-hartlep and http://ilstu.academia.edu/NicholasHartlep. His forthcoming book titles are *The Model Minority Stereotype: Demystifying Asian American Success* (Information Age Publishing) and *The Model Minority Stereotype Reader: Critical and Challenging Readings For the 21st Century* (Cognella).

Kaying Her immigrated from Thailand to the United States in 1991 with her family. She has lived in Sacramento, California ever since. She graduated from UCLA with a History BA and Sacramento State University with a bilingual multiple subjects teaching credential. Currently she is a substitute teacher and a graduate student in the Language and Literacy Master's Program at Sacramento State University. She enjoys teaching, reading, learning languages, and traveling to new places.

Janice Tuck Lively is an Assistant Professor in the Department of English at Elmhurst College. She teaches courses in beginning and advanced fiction writing, post-colonial and multi-cultural literature, American literature, and issues in race, class and gender. She has published articles and essays in *Perspectives on African American Literature, Journal of Black Studies, Valley Voices: A Literary Review, Encyclopedia of the Harlem Renaissance, Works and Days Journal,* and *Obsidian III: Literature in the African Diaspora.* Her article on the Virtual Harlem Renaissance Project was included as a chapter in the book *Configuring History.* Her areas of scholarship include the Harlem Renaissance and 19th and 20th century African American female writers.

Joanne Larson (Ph.D., University of California, Los Angeles) is the Michael W. Scandling Professor of Education at the University of Rochester's Warner Graduate School of Education and Human Development and Chair of the Teaching and Curriculum Program. Her research examines how language and literacy practices mediate social and power relations in literacy events in schools and communities. She is the editor of *Literacy as Snake Oil: Beyond the Quick Fix* (2nd ed., Lang, 2007), coeditor of the *Handbook of Early Childhood Literacy* (2nd ed., Sage, 2013) and coauthor of *Making Literacy Real: Theories and Practices in Learning and Teaching* (Sage, 2005). Larson's journal publications include research articles in *Anthropology and Education Quarterly, Harvard Education Review, Research in the Teaching of English, Written Communication, Linguistics and Education, Journal of Early Childhood Literacy,* and *Discourse and Society.*

Maria Mejorado is an Associate faculty member in the Bilingual/Multicultural Education Department in the College of Education at California State University Sacramento and Director of the High School Equivalency Program (HEP), a federally GED preparation program for seasonal agricultural workers. A faculty member at CSUS since 2001, she teaches undergraduate and graduate students and those pursuing a teaching credential. Her research interests include community advocacy, mentoring, parent involvement, teaching and learning of seasonal agricultural adults and its impact on their children. Dr. Maria Mejorado was born and raised in Sanger, CA , east of Fresno. Her family migrated from south Texas to the San Joaquin Valley to work in the agricultural fields. She is the last of seven siblings and the only daughter. Her earliest recollection of contributing to the family income was picking cotton and grapes at age four. Dr. Mejorado graduated from Sanger High School, earned a BA from St. Mary's College and an MA from Harvard University. In 2000 she earned a Ph.D. in Education from UC Davis.

Dana Muccular is a behavior consultant for children with Autism Spectrum Disorders, mental, emotional, and mild to severe retardation and physical disabilities, in Sacramento, California. She graduated from California State University of Sacramento with a Bachelor of Arts degree in Family and Consumer Sciences, (concentration in Family Studies, Family Life Education). She graduated with a Master of Arts degree in Bilingual and Multicultural Education. Her research interests include: cultural relevance, critical race theory, qualitative research methodologies, and applied behavior analysis. Her desire is to encourage "minority" students of all ages to learn to advocate for themselves and others within the classroom environment, and to teach parents/guardians to effectively advocate for the children in which they care for.

Gary Muccular Jr. is a social worker for a private foster family agency in Sacramento, California. He graduated from California State University of Sacramento with a Bachelor of Arts degree in Child Development (concentration in Emotional Development) and a Master of Arts degree in Bilingual and Multicultural Education. His central focus of research is multicultural, culturally relevant family education, within the foster care system of Sacramento County. His desire is to not only help successfully transition foster youth out of foster housing but also to create an enriching environment for youth to develop a sense of cultural identity.

Toni Newman earned her MA in special education at California State University (CSU) Sacramento; she earned a teaching credential from CSU, Hayward, and a BA in psychology from University of California, Santa Cruz. Ms. Newman has spent 23 years as an educator, community organizer, and activist. As a researcher and educator, her interest is in the achievement gap, Black American's self-perception, and educational institutions' perception of Black students. Ms. Newman continues to be interested in affecting change through education and cultural awareness. As a community activist, her greatest interest is in Black American culture and how African Americans support and nurture their community. In these efforts, Ms. Newman has founded, sponsored, and collaborated to create educational forums, support groups, and cultural events in Sacramento, Oakland, Santa Cruz, and Los Angeles. She has raised over $100,000 in grant funds for community organizations.

Nadeen Ruiz, PhD, is Professor Emerita of Bilingual Multicultural Education at California State University Sacramento, and Director of the California Bi-National Teacher Education Project (Bi-TEP). Formerly, Dr. Ruiz was Director of Elementary Education at Stanford University and Teacher Preparation at CSU Sacramento. Dr. Ruiz is co-founder of the Optimal Learning Environment (OLE) Project, a research and professional development program that focuses on effective literacy instruction for English Learners in both general and special education classrooms, and for Migrant children. She is the author of numerous articles and books on children's biliteracy development and the preparation of bilingual teachers, regularly presenting on these topics at national and international conferences.

Motecúzoma Sánchez is a poet, hip-hop artist, documentary filmmaker, and educator. He uses his talents as tools to educate and promote empowerment to populations who are underserved educationally and politically. He was a candidate for mayor of Stockton in 2008, and has served on numerous boards and commissions. He currently is a Jesse M.Unruh Assembly Fellow in the prestigious

Capitol Fellows Program, which is ranked one of the top ten fellowships in the nation. He is also a proud father of three children.

Jazmin White recently relocated to the Bay Area after graduating from Humboldt State University with a BA in Critical Race, Gender and Sexuality Studies; and is currently a graduate student studying Counseling and Forensic Psychology at Holy Names University. Prior to becoming a Special Education paraprofessional within a Bay Area Charter School, Jazmin worked in various educational settings: Sylvan Learning Center, CaliforniaState University (CSU) Sacramento's Visions 2000 Math & Reading Academy, and CSU Sacramento's Math, Engineering, Science and Liberal Arts Academy (MESL); collaborating with parents, learners and facilitators to meet the diverse and unique needs of each learner. Throughout her own educational journey and involvement in teaching, advising, and mentoring students, Jazmin remains committed to fully exploring the interplay of race, class and gender within communities of color and its implications.

Lisa William-White has also co-authored/authored chapters focused on Critical Race Theory, Gender Studies and Multicultural Education, Autoethnography and Spoken Word scholarship. Her work appears in *Tedious Journeys: Autoethnographies by Women of Color in Academe* (Peter Lang), *Choosing Democracy: A Practical Guide to Multicultural Education*, 3rd edition, (Merrill/Prentice Hall), *Teacher Education Quarterly, Qualitative Inquiry, International Journal of Qualitative Studies in Education*, and *Cultural Studies < = > Critical Methodologies*. Her latest scholarly endeavors includes the following: a chapter titled, "Becoming a Teacher in an Era of Curricular Standardization and Reductionist Learning Outcomes: A Poetic Interpretation" in *Becoming and Being a Teacher: Confronting Traditional Norms to Create New Democratic Realities* (Peter Lang, forthcoming).

Idara Essien-Wood, PhD, is an associate faculty member in the College of Education at Ashford University. Her research focuses on psychosocial factors impacting the academic success of students of color in postsecondary education. In particular, her research examines student success in natural and physical sciences. This work has informed from her years of experience as a research and quality analyst for biotech and pharmaceutical companies. Idara has presented extensively at national and international conferences on education. She is a graduate of Arizona State University, where she earned her doctorate in educational leadership and policy studies with an emphasis in higher education. She holds a bachelor of science degree in biological sciences from the University of California, Riverside, and a master of arts degree in education (bilingual and multicultural) from California State University, Sacramento.

J. Luke Wood, PhD, is assistant professor of administration, rehabilitation, and postsecondary education at San Diego State University (SDSU). Dr. Wood is co-director of the Minority Male Community College Collaborative (M2C3), a national project of the Interwork Institute at SDSU. He is also co-editor of the Journal of African American Males in Education (JAAME), and chair of the Multicultural & Multiethnic Education (MME) special-interest group of the American Educational Research Association (AERA). Dr. Wood has authored more than 30 publications, including numerous peer-reviewed articles, books, and book chapters. His research focuses on ethical leadership and decision-making in community colleges, as well as Black (and other minority) male success in the community college. In particular, his research of Black males examines factors (e.g., social, psychological, academic, environmental, institutional) that impact their outcomes (e.g., persistence, achievement, attainment, transfer) in community colleges.

Liliya Zhernokleyev currently teaches at an elementary school in California. She received a BA in Liberal Studies and an MA in Bilingual Education from California State University.

Index

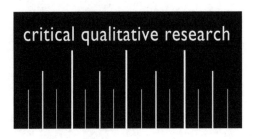

Shirley R. Steinberg & Gaile S. Cannella, *General Editors*

The Critical Qualitative Research series examines societal structures that oppress and exclude so that transformative actions can be generated. This transformed research is activist in orientation. Because the perspective accepts the notion that nothing is apolitical, research projects themselves are critically examined for power orientations, even as they are used to address curricular, educational, or societal issues.

This methodological work challenges modernist orientations and universalist impositions, asking critical questions like: Who/what is heard? Who/what is silenced? Who is privileged? Who is disqualified? How are forms of inclusion and exclusion being created? How are power relations constructed and managed? How do different forms of privilege and oppression intersect to affect educational, societal, and life possibilities for various individuals and groups?

We are particularly interested in manuscripts that offer critical examinations of curriculum, policy, public communities, and the ways in which language, discourse practices, and power relations prevent more just transformations.

For additional information about this series or for the submission of manuscripts, please contact:
Shirley R. Steinberg and Gaile S. Cannella
msgramsci@aol.com | Gaile.Cannella@unt.edu

To order other books in this series, please contact our Customer Service Department:
(800) 770-LANG (within the U.S.)
(212) 647-7706 (outside the U.S.)
(212) 647-7707 FAX

Or browse online by series:
www.peterlang.com